Crime Scene Investigation

D1230926

Crime Scene Investigation offers an innovative approach to learning about crime scene investigation, taking the reader from the first response on the crime scene to documenting crime scene evidence and preparing evidence for courtroom presentation. It includes topics not normally covered in other texts, such as forensic anthropology and pathology, entomology, arson and explosives, and the electronic crime scene. Numerous photographs and illustrations complement text material, and a chapter-by-chapter fictional narrative also provides the reader with a qualitative dimension of the crime scene experience.

Roy Fenoff is an Associate Professor in the Department of Criminal Justice at The Military College of South Carolina (The Citadel). He is also a Forensic Document Examiner and an expert in forgery detection. Dr. Fenoff provides scientific advice, offers training, and conducts forensic examinations for individuals, law enforcement, and law firms throughout the United States and abroad. He earned a B.S. in Entomology and a B.A. in Criminal Justice from the University of Georgia in 2004, an M.S. in Medical/Veterinary Entomology from the University of Wyoming in 2007, and a Ph.D. in Criminal Justice from Michigan State University in 2015. Dr. Fenoff specializes in forgery and document fraud, food protection (food fraud and food defense), and transnational crime. Dr. Fenoff is a published author who has presented his work at a variety of criminal justice, food safety, and forensic science conferences. In addition to his current position at The Citadel, Dr. Fenoff is a voting member of the Forensic Document Examination Consensus Body of the American Academy of Forensic Sciences Standards Board, a member of the Document Security Alliance, the South Carolina Food Safety Task Force, and a research collaborator with the Food Fraud Prevention Academy (formally Michigan State University's Food Fraud Initiative).

Jacqueline T. Fish is the Vice President for Academic Affairs at Charleston Southern University. A former crime scene investigator and Lieutenant in the Knox County, Tennessee, Sherriff's Department, Dr. Fish was also project manager of the National Forensic Academy and worked with the Louisiana State University's National Center for Biomedical Research and Training to develop Advanced Forensics Investigations for Hazardous Environments.

Larry S. Miller is Distinguished Professor and Chair of Criminal Justice and Criminology at East Tennessee State University (ETSU). He received his Bachelor of Science from ETSU, Master of Science from Eastern Kentucky University, and Ph.D. in Health & Safety with collaterals in Forensic Anthropology and Criminology from The University of Tennessee.

Miller, who has worked as a police officer, criminal investigator, and crime laboratory director, teaches in the area of law enforcement and is the author of several books on topics including criminal investigation, criminal justice report writing, police photography, and more.

Edward W. Wallace is the Director of Forensic Training at the New York City Office of Chief Medical Examiner. Wallace is also a Senior Adjunct Instructor and WMD Training Course Developer for Louisiana State University.

Michael C. Braswell is Professor Emeritus of Criminal Justice and Criminology at East Tennessee State University (ETSU). Braswell received his Bachelor of Arts in Psychology from Mercer University in 1969, Master of Arts in Psychology from West Georgia College in 1970, Ed.S. in Rehabilitation/Correctional Counseling from the University of Georgia in 1973, and Doctorate in Counseling Psychology from the University of Southern Mississippi. A former prison psychologist, he taught ethics and human relations courses for more than 30 years at East Tennessee State University. He has published books on ethics, peacemaking, and correctional counseling as well as two novels and a short story collection.

Crime Scene Investigation

Fourth Edition

Roy Fenoff

Jacqueline T. Fish

Larry S. Miller

Edward W. Wallace

Michael C. Braswell

Routledge
Taylor & Francis Group

NEW YORK AND LONDON

Cover image: © Getty Images / ArtistGNDphotography

Fourth edition published 2023
by Routledge
605 Third Avenue, New York, NY 10158

and by Routledge
4 Park Square, Milton Park, Abingdon, Oxon, OX14 4RN

Routledge is an imprint of the Taylor & Francis Group, an informa business

© 2023 Taylor & Francis

First edition published by Routledge 2007
Third edition published by Anderson Publishing 2013

Library of Congress Cataloging-in-Publication Data
Names: Fenoff, Roy, author. | Fish, Jacqueline T., author. | Miller, Larry, 1953 August 26– author. | Wallace, Edward W., Jr., 1963– author. | Braswell, Michael, author.
Title: Crime scene investigation / Roy Fenoff, Jacqueline T. Fish, Larry S. Miller, Edward W. Wallace, Michael C. Braswell.
Description: Fourth edition. | New York, NY: Routledge, 2023. | Revised edition of Crime scene investigation, [2014] | Includes bibliographical references and index.
Identifiers: LCCN 2022024043 (print) | LCCN 2022024044 (ebook) | ISBN 9780367204662 (hardback) | ISBN 9780367204679 (paperback) | ISBN 9780429261657 (ebook)
Subjects: LCSH: Criminal investigation. | Crime scene searches. | Evidence, Criminal. | Forensic sciences.
Classification: LCC HV8073 .F485 2023 (print) | LCC HV8073 (ebook) | DDC 363.25/2—dc23/eng/20220523
LC record available at https://lccn.loc.gov/2022024043
LC ebook record available at https://lccn.loc.gov/2022024044

ISBN: 978-0-367-20466-2 (hbk)
ISBN: 978-0-367-20467-9 (pbk)
ISBN: 978-0-429-26165-7 (ebk)

DOI: 10.4324/9780429261657

Typeset in Giovanni
by codeMantra

Access the Support Material: www.routledge.com/9780367204679

Dedication

To all the CSIs, evidence techs, investigators, and students who are committed to crime scene investigation and processing, we owe you a debt of gratitude. You are indeed preserving the scenes where victims can no longer provide testimony; you are the voice of the victims, the experts who identify, collect, and preserve physical evidence and present it to our courts in order for justice to prevail. Thank you for your service and your commitment to life-long learning as technologies advance. This fourth edition is dedicated to your service. Thank you for your perseverance.

Roy Fenoff

Jacqueline T. Fish

Larry S. Miller

Edward W. Wallace Jr

Michael C. Braswell

Contents

ACKNOWLEDGMENTS xv
CONTRIBUTORS xvii
DIGITAL ASSETS xxv

CHAPTER 1 Introduction: The CSI and Forensic Investigation 1
Introduction 1
The Role of the Crime Scene Investigator in
Forensic Science 3
Jobs and Descriptions 4
    CSI 4
    Forensic Scientist 6
    Forensic Anthropologist 6
    Forensic Nurse 7
    Certification and Professional Development 7
    Expert Witnesses 10
    Ethics and Professionalism 12
    Challenges to Forensic Science 13
Forensic Evidence and the Crime Scene 15
    Class versus Individual Characteristics 17
    Direct Evidence 18
    Circumstantial Evidence 18
    Natural Variation 19
Legal Issues and the Crime Scene 19
    Search Warrants 19
    Admissibility of Evidence 21
    Frye v. United States 22
    Federal Rules of Evidence 22
    Daubert v. Merrell Dow Pharmaceuticals, Inc. 23
    Chain of Custody 23
    Documentation 24
Scientific Issues in Crime Scene Investigation 27
    Controls 27
    Standards 27
    Overlapping Roles 28
References 29

CHAPTER 2   The First Response and Scene Search 31
             Introduction..34
             The FBI'S 12-Step Process.....................................36
             Determining the Scope of the Crime Scene.............37
                 Boundaries 37
                 Multiple Scenes...38
                 CSI Personal Safety Concerns 38
                 Restricting Access...46
             Interacting with Detectives....................................47
             Performing Initial Walkthrough/Preliminary
             Assessment of the Crime Scene.............................48
             Identifying Other Resources 49
                 What's There and What's Not There 51
                 Family Members 51
                 Witnesses 52
                 Suspects at the Scene......................................53
             Taking the Final Steps...53
             Searching the Scene..53
                 Search Patterns...56
                 Vehicle Searches...57
             Reconstructing the Crime 58

CHAPTER 3   Documenting the Crime Scene:
             Photography, Videography, and Sketching..........59
             Introduction..60
             Photography...62
                 Cameras...63
                 Video Cameras..65
                 External Flash..66
                 Lenses and Filters 66
                 Post-Processing of Evidence Photographs...........67
             Crime Scene Sketches...70
                 Floor Plans..72
                 Elevation Plans..73
                 Site Plans 74
                 Cross-Sectional Plans......................................75
             Bloodstain Patterns, Body Positions,
             Clothing, and Wound Diagrams/Sketches.................77
             Title Blocks and Legends.......................................77
             Measurements 78
                 Technological Advances in Measurement...........80

CHAPTER 4   Fingerprints and Palmprints 85
             Introduction..86
             Principles of Fingerprints and Palmprints.................87
             Fingerprints as Physical Evidence...........................89
             Inked Impressions 89

Elimination Prints 91

Suspect Prints 92

Fingerprinting the Deceased 92

Establishing Identity 94

Latent Fingerprints 95

Latent Fingerprints in Children 95

Deciding Which Method to Use 97

Locating and Documenting 99

Methods and Techniques of Developing
and Collecting Latent Prints 100

Lifting Latent Fingerprints 103

Other Lifting Methods 104

IAFIS and Latent Print Examinations 109

Reference 110

CHAPTER 5 Trace and Impression Evidence 111

Introduction 112

Trace Evidence 114

Hairs and Fibers 114

Glass, Soil, Paint, and Other Materials 119

Gunshot Residue 122

Trace Evidence Summary 123

Impression Evidence 124

Forensic Podiatry 126

Footwear Impressions 127

Tire Impressions 128

Bitemark Impressions 129

Photographic Techniques 131

Inked Impressions 132

Casting and Lifting Techniques for
Impression Evidence 133

Impressions in Snow 134

CHAPTER 6 Bodily Fluid Evidence 137

Introduction 139

Toxicology 140

DNA Techniques and the Impact of
Technological Advances 141

DNA and Crime Scene Investigation 142

DNA Probative Value 143

Touch DNA 144

Blood 145

Seminal Fluid 147

Saliva 149

Other Bodily Fluids 149

Urine 149

Vaginal Secretions 150

Sexual Assault: Special Considerations...................150
Locating, Collecting, and Preserving Bodily
Fluid Evidence 151
    At the Crime Scene..151
    From a Victim or a Suspect....................................152
    Condom Trace Evidence 158
Use of DNA to Identify Victims 159
References 160

CHAPTER 7   Blood Spatter Evidence 161
Introduction..162
The Nature of Blood Spatter Evidence 163
Documenting Bloodstain Pattern Evidence.............169
Detecting Invisible Bloodstains...............................171
Photographing the Scene...171
Interpreting Evidence 172
References 174

CHAPTER 8   Firearms and Toolmark Evidence...................... 175
Introduction..176
Bullets and Cartridge Casings..................................179
Class Versus Individual Characteristics 182
Locating, Collecting, Packaging, and
Submitting Evidence..184
Trajectories and Measurements 190
    Laser Protractor Kit 196
    Laser Trajectory Rod Kit 197
Distance Determination...199
National Integrated Ballistics Information
Network (NIBIN)..202
Gunshot Residue Testing 203
Serial Number Restoration 204
Toolmarks... 205
    Testing and Comparison Techniques.................. 206

CHAPTER 9   Arson and Explosives 209
Introduction..210
Crime Scene Processing...212
    Area of Origin 213
    Burn Patterns 214
    Impact of Fire Suppression on the Crime Scene.215
Why Investigate Fire Scenes? 216
    Covering Up Another Crime 217
Product Reliability...218
    Code Violations 219
Motor Vehicle Fire Investigation.............................219
Collection and Preservation of Arson Evidence 221
    Accelerant-Detection K-9 222

Electronic Detectors and Instruments.................223
Forensic Light Source/Alternate Light Source....226
Preservation of Evidence 226
Recovery of Burned Bodies..228
Identification Techniques 229
Bomb Scene Investigations 230
Locating and Collecting Evidence of
Explosive Devices...232
Post-Blast Investigation Techniques 232
References 235

CHAPTER 10 The Electronic Crime Scene 237
Introduction..239
Cybercrime: The Internet Age................................. 240
Prevalence of Cybercrime 243
Identity Theft... 243
Spyware...245
Internet Crimes Against Children 245
Pornography 246
Predators 246
Cyberstalking, Cyberbullying, and Other
Harassment...247
Social Networking Sites and "Sexting"..............249
Computer Intrusions: Hackers 250
Scams...252
Processing the Electronic Crime Scene...................253
Computer Hardware...257
Individual Computers...257
Network Computers..258
Peripheral Equipment..259
Virtual Evidence 259
Cellphones and Smartphones.............................260
Tablets and Other Mobile Devices......................261
Fax and Digital Answering Machines
and Caller-ID Devices...262
Biometric Technology...262
Digital Crime Scene Analysis...................................262

CHAPTER 11 Documentary Evidence...265
Introduction..267
Procedures for Handling and Recording
Evidentiary Documents 268
Investigative Techniques for Examination of
Documents 270
Machine-Produced Documents 274
Handwriting Identification 275
Court Acceptance of Document Examination 281

Scientific Validity and Reliability.......................281
Handwriting and Forensic Psychology
Applications 282
Physical Profiling...283
Age..283
Gender 284
Handedness...285
Literacy and Occupation..............................285
Physical and Mental Health.........................286
Behavioral Profiling..287
Forensic Linguistics, Statement Analysis,
and Handwriting 291
Questioned Document Case Study 293
References 296

CHAPTER 12 Motor Vehicles as Crime Scenes.........................301
Introduction...302
Photography..302
Hit-and-Run Cases 305
Trace Evidence 307
Types of Physical Evidence.................................307
Collection Techniques 309
Stolen Vehicles...310
Chop Shops...310
VIN Locations 311
Electronic Vehicle Tracking and Recovery.........313
Odometer Tampering 314
Processing Exterior Surfaces of Vehicles...............314
Latent Fingerprints 316
Trace Evidence 316
Stolen Property...318
Contraband Search 319
Motor Vehicles as Weapons................................319
Documenting Injuries..................................320
Accidental Death—Suicide—Homicide...................321
References 322

CHAPTER 13 Death Investigation 323
Introduction...324
Medicolegal Death Investigation 326
Structure and Bias 329
Authorization 330
The Death/Injury Scene 332
Preparation 332
The Autopsy..334
The Report..337
Death Certification 338

Cause of Death 338

Manner of Death 340

Postmortem Interval 342

Pattern Recognition 349

Natural Deaths 349

Trauma 350

Role of the CSI at Autopsy 364

Identifying Remains 369

References 372

CHAPTER 14 Forensic Anthropology, Odontology, and

Entomology 373

Introduction 374

Anthropology 374

The Determination of a Skeleton's Age at Death 376

Maturation 376

Changes in the Pubic Symphysis 378

Osteon Counting 378

Osteoarthritic Lipping 379

The Determination of a Skeleton's Sex 380

The Pelvis 380

Septal Apertures of the Humerus 383

The Determination of Race (Ancestry) and

Stature from the Skeleton 383

Anthropometric Measurements 383

Stature: The Estimation of Stature from

the Long Bones 384

Odontology 385

Human Dentition 386

The Anatomy of a Tooth 388

NamUs 391

Entomology 392

The Determination of Time Since Death 392

Stages of Decomposition 393

Fresh Stage 393

Bloated Stage 394

Decay Stage 394

Dry Stage 394

Collection and Handling of Insects at the

Crime Scene 395

Assessment of the Crime Scene 396

Collecting and Preserving Adult Insects 396

Collecting and Preserving Immature Insects 396

Collecting Climatic Data 397

References 399

CHAPTER 15 Documenting the Actions of the CSI and
Presenting Facts in Court 401
Introduction 402
Case Files 403
Crime Scene Protocols 405
Releasing the Scene 407
Cross-Contamination 409
The FBI Crime Laboratory 410
Communicating with a Crime Lab 411
Evidence Submittal to a Crime Lab 412
Case File Preparation 413
Working with the Prosecutor's Office 413
Pretrial Preparation 414
Professional Credentials 414
Courtroom Testimony 415
Demonstrative Exhibits 417
The Importance of Physical Evidence 417
Ethical Considerations 418
Emerging Trends 418
References 420

CRIME SCENE SUPPLY CHECKLIST 421
GLOSSARY 423
INDEX 433

Acknowledgments

We owe so much appreciation to the many contributors to this book; they have worked decades upon decades to discover the techniques that are contained in this volume. It is a massive task to bring all that expertise from across the nation into one textbook that is used by many universities and organizations to educate the CSIs, evidence techs, and investigators of the future. We would be remiss if we did not mention the undying support each of us has received from our families as we worked to complete this fourth edition of Crime Scene Investigation. So, to all our family members, we love you and will never forget those endless hours spent away from you while we compiled this book!

Roy

Jackie

Larry

Ed

Mickey

Contributors

William M. Bass, Ph.D.

Forensic Anthropologist, The University of Tennessee (Emeritus)

is a world-renowned forensic anthropologist and founder of the Outdoor Anthropological Research Facility (more commonly known as the "Body Farm") at the University of Tennessee (UT) in Knoxville. For more than 40 years, Bass taught anthropology to students and law enforcement officers across the nation and around the world. Every state in the union employs forensic anthropologists who studied under the tutelage of Bass. As a Professor Emeritus, Bass resides in Knoxville, and has coauthored the Jefferson Bass series of books. He also teaches a Time Since Death seminar for the National Forensic Academy in Knoxville and was one of the first individuals honored as a Diplomat by the American Board of Forensic Anthropologists. His impact on the discipline of forensic anthropology is immense, as evidenced by the existence of one of the largest modern skeletal collections in the world, which is housed in UT's William Bass Skeletal Collection. Bass has played a prominent role in hundreds of death investigations including the Noble Georgia Crematory remains investigation. In 2011, the William M. Bass Forensic Anthropology Building was opened at the University of Tennessee as the result of the many years of work and fundraising by Dr. Bass to provide students with state-of-the-art facilities. He is a contributor to Chapter 14.

Diane Bodie

Crime Scene Investigator, South Carolina Law Enforcement Division (retired)

is retired as a senior agent with the South Carolina Law Enforcement Division (SLED), where she was assigned as a crime scene investigator. Her career spans more than 35 years, including 6 years at the

FBI and 26 years with SLED. She now works as an investigator for the Richland County Sheriff's Office and serves as a national consultant and facilitator in the area of impression evidence and fingerprint classification. She collaborated with the National Center for Biomedical Research and Training on forensic course development and teaches for the Amber Alert program. Diane served as a member of the Disaster Mortuary Operational Response Team (DMORT) for several years. She is a contributor to Chapters 4 and 5.

Arthur Bohanan

Police Specialist, Knoxville Police Department (retired)

has spent more than 45 years of his life dedicated to the study of impression evidence. His research and work focus on the physical characteristics of children's fingerprints and how they differ from adult fingerprints and on the invention of a machine that aids in the development of fingerprints on the bodies of deceased victims. Bohanan began his career in the fingerprint unit at the FBI; then he became a police officer for 25 years at the Knoxville Police Department in Tennessee. He holds a patent to the CBC fingerprint device, and he currently teaches Amber Alert and criminal investigative techniques to law enforcement officers nationwide. Bohanan is certified by the International Association of Identification as a latent print examiner and senior crime scene analyst, and he devoted hundreds of hours working at Ground Zero while he was a member of the Disaster Mortuary Operational Response Team (DMORT) after the September 2001 attacks. He was also deployed to work in Louisiana after Hurricane Katrina devastated the area in 2005. Bohanan is currently working with Carson Newman College to establish another research facility to study the effects dead bodies have on the environment. He is a contributor to Chapter 4.

Karen Berka Bruewer

M.S. Forensic Scientist and Consultant, KMB Forensics

is a forensic scientist specializing in the examination of physical evidence and testing evidence for the presence of bodily fluids that can yield DNA samples for analysis. She worked for a number of years at the Indiana State Police Crime Laboratory and provided training to law enforcement officers across the country on DNA analysis. Bruewer was also a consultant for the University of Tennessee and assisted in the development of curricula that is being taught nationwide. Currently, she is the owner of KMB Forensics, a consulting firm, and teaches forensics at a local college in Van Wert, Ohio. She is a contributor to Chapter 6.

Chris Rush Burkey

is an Associate Professor in the Department of Criminal Justice and Criminology at East Tennessee State University where her primary research focus is sex crimes and forensic document analysis. She has worked with several state and local agencies regarding various criminal justice matters such as program evaluation, forensic training, and investigative policies and regulations. She has published several articles in peer-reviewed journals including *Deviant Behavior* and the *Journal of Interpersonal Violence*. She is also the author of *Forensic Investigation of Sex Crimes and Sexual Offenders* and *Sexual Abuse within the Church: Assessment, Intervention, and Prevention*. She is a contributor to Chapter 9.

James Claude Upshaw ("Jamie") Downs, M.D.

Forensic Pathologist

is coastal Georgia's first regional medical examiner. He has been continuously employed as a medical examiner and consultant in forensic pathology since 1989 and was Alabama's state forensics director and chief medical examiner from 1998 to 2002. Downs graduated from the University of Georgia in 1983. He completed Peace Officers Standards and Training at the Southwest Alabama Police Academy. He received his medical degree and residency training in anatomic and clinical pathology and his fellowship in forensic pathology from the Medical University of South Carolina. The latter included a rotation through the Metropolitan Dade County Florida (Miami) Medical Examiner Department and internship at the FBI's Behavioral Sciences Unit in Quantico, Virginia. He is board certified in anatomic, clinical, and forensic pathology. Downs has lectured extensively in the field of forensic pathology and has presented at numerous national and international meetings in the fields of anatomic and forensic pathology. He is a consultant to the FBI Behavioral Science Unit in Quantico, Virginia, having authored four chapters in their manual on Managing Death Investigation, and was the primary author of the FBI's acclaimed Forensic Investigator's Trauma Atlas. He has authored several books and chapters in the fields of forensic pathology and child abuse, and contributed to Chapter 13 of this book. His areas of special interest include child abuse and police use of force. He serves on the Forensic Committee of the International

Association of Chiefs of Police, as well as the boards of the American Board of Medicolegal Death Investigators and Medical/Investigational Advisory Board of the Sudden Unexplained Death in Childhood Program.

Jeff Fuller

Bomb Technician (retired)

is a graduate of the University of South Carolina who retired after 35 years of law enforcement service. Fuller received advanced bomb training with the FBI, ATF, Israel National Police, and British Ministry of Defense. For 20 years, he worked as a Bomb Technician at the South Carolina Law Enforcement Division (SLED) and retired at the rank of Lieutenant while serving as commander of SLED's nationally recognized bomb squad. As Chairman of the National Bomb Squad Commanders Advisory Board, Fuller worked closely with the FBI and the FBI Bomb Data Center in certifying bomb technicians, accrediting bomb squads, and setting standards for all the bomb squads in the United States. Fuller is now a consultant, specializing in IEDs, Civil War Ordnance, and corporate security issues. He is a contributor to Chapter 9.

Heidi H. Harralson, M.A., BCDE

Forensic Document Examiner

is a court-qualified and board-certified forensic document examiner. She has lectured extensively to professional organizations and universities on the handwriting sciences internationally. She has published original research in peer-reviewed journals on forensic handwriting and document examination topics. She has authored three books, namely, *Developments in Handwriting and Signature Identification in the Digital Age*, *Forensic Handwriting Examination of Motor Disorders & Forgery*, and *Huber & Headrick's Handwriting Identification: Facts & Fundamentals*, 2nd ed. She has been consulted by attorneys, and public and private clients internationally. She is a board-certified diplomate through the National Association of Document Examiners. She holds a Bachelor of Science in the behavioral sciences, a Master of Arts in handwriting science and forensic document examination, and a forensic crime scene technician certificate. She is an affiliate professor at East Tennessee State University where she teaches courses in forensic document examination and forensic communications. She is a contributor to Chapter 11.

Jimmie Hester

Tennessee Highway Patrol (retired)

was the special agent in charge of the Criminal Investigation Division of the Tennessee Highway Patrol. He retired from his 33-year law enforcement career in August 2005, and is currently working as the law enforcement liaison for Tennessee LoJack Corporation. Hester led the development of the Auto Theft Division for the Tennessee Highway Patrol and over the years has investigated thousands of criminal cases involving vehicles, heavy equipment, chop shops, interstate property thefts, and other related crimes. He has lectured and taught for numerous national and regional training academies as well as state and federal agencies and authored the Trailer Identification Manual distributed nationwide to law enforcement agencies. Together with Patricia Hester, he presents training seminars to agencies and professional organizations nationwide. Hester and Hester are adjunct instructors for the National Forensic Academy at the University of Tennessee and have trained hundreds of criminal investigators on crime scene investigation, interview and interrogation, and crime related to vehicles and cargo trailers. He is a contributor to Chapter 12.

Patricia Hester

Tennessee Highway Patrol (retired)

has been instrumental in developing and delivering training across the United States for motor vehicle law enforcement officers. She specializes in vehicle identification and recovery, odometer fraud, title and driver's license fraud, and vehicle homicide. She has 27 years of experience in the Criminal Investigations Division and is past president of the International Association of Auto Theft Investigators. Together with Jimmie Hester, she presents training seminars to agencies and professional organizations nationwide. Hester and Hester are adjunct instructors for the National Forensic Academy at the University of Tennessee and have trained hundreds of criminal investigators on crime scene investigation, interview and interrogation, and crime related to vehicles and cargo trailers. She is a contributor to Chapter 12.

Rusty Horton

South Carolina Farm Bureau Insurance Company's Special Investigations Unit

is the field supervisor for the South Carolina Farm Bureau Insurance Company's Special Investigations Unit (SIU). During his tenure with the Farm Bureau, Horton has specialized in the area of fire origin and cause investigations. Horton has 25 years of experience in the fire investigation field, conducting both public and private sector fire investigations. He holds designations as an IAAI-Certified Fire Investigator and a NAFI-Certified Fire and Explosions Investigator. Rusty served as a principal to the NFPA Technical Committee on Fire Investigations in 2009 and has been actively involved in the development of new and revised text published in the NFPA 921 – Guide for Fire and Explosion Investigations. He is a contributor to Chapter 9.

Michelle Hudson

Former Agent with the South Carolina Law Enforcement Division

has worked in fire investigations including response to the scene of arson fires and fires where fatalities have occurred. Hudson completed advanced and specialized training in fire and arson investigations including courses through the Bureau of Alcohol, Tobacco, Firearms and Explosives (ATF) and the South Carolina Fire Academy. Hudson received her undergraduate degree in Criminal Justice and Sociology from Charleston Southern University. She is also a graduate of the South Carolina Criminal Justice Academy. She is a member of the South Carolina International Association of Arson Investigators (SCIAAI). She is a contributor to Chapter 9.

Blake Lawrence

is a graduate of Marshall University in Digital Forensics and Information Assurance. He also holds degrees in chemistry and criminology from East Tennessee State University in addition to completing a graduate certificate in Forensic Document Examination. He has presented his work at the NADE (National Association of Document Examiners) conference, the 4th annual Kentucky Intelligence Colloquium, has received recognition for his work with OSIX (Open Source Intelligence Exchange) through Marshall University. He currently lives in the DC Metro area with his wife and works in Digital Forensics with Moss Cape LLC while pursuing his master's degree in Cybersecurity with Liberty University. He is a contributor to Chapter 10.

T. Paulette Sutton

University of Tennessee Medical Center (retired)

was the assistant director of Forensic Services at the Regional Forensic Center in Memphis, Tennessee. Her academic appointments at the University of Tennessee (UT) Memphis include associate professor of Clinical Laboratory Sciences and instructor in the Colleges of Medicine and Nursing. She has been a practicing forensic scientist for the Division of Forensic Pathology at UT Memphis since 1977 and specializes in bloodstain pattern analysis and crime scene reconstruction. Sutton also serves on the faculty of the National College of District Attorneys, National Science Foundation, University of Arkansas Criminal Justice Institute, National Forensic Academy, Northwestern University School of Law, and the University of North Texas. She is a member of the FBI Laboratory's Scientific Working Group on Bloodstain Pattern Analysis, the Forensic Science Editorial Review Board for CRC Press, and the International Association of Bloodstain Pattern Analysts. Her honors include the Lecturer of Merit Award and Distinguished Faculty Award from the National College of District Attorneys and the Outstanding Service Award from the FBI. She is a contributor to Chapter 7.

PHOTO CONTRIBUTORS TO THE FOURTH EDITION

Officer Randy Unterbrink, Charleston Police Department
CSI Ashleigh Dockery, Charleston Police Department

Digital Assets

Thank you for selecting *Crime Scene Investigation*, fourth edition. To complement the learning experience, we have provided a number of online tools to accompany this edition. Two distinct packages of interactive digital assets are available: one for instructors and one for students.

FOR THE INSTRUCTOR

- Test Banks compose, customize, and deliver exams using an online assessment package in a free Windows-based authoring tool that makes it easy to build tests using the unique multiple choice and true or false questions created for Profiling and Serial Crime. What's more, this authoring tool allows you to export customized exams directly to Blackboard, WebCT, eCollege, Angel, and other leading systems. All test bank files are also conveniently offered in Word format.
- PowerPoint Lecture Slides reinforce key topics with focused PowerPoints, which provide a perfect visual outline with which to augment your lecture. Each individual book chapter has its own dedicated slideshow.
- Lesson Plans design your course around customized lesson plans. Each individual lesson plan acts as separate syllabi containing content synopses, key terms, directions to supplementary websites, and more open-ended critical thinking questions designed to spur class discussion. These lesson plans also delineate and connect chapter-based learning objectives to specific teaching resources, making it easy to catalog the resources at your disposal.

FOR THE STUDENT

- Self-Assessment Question Banks enhance review and study sessions with the help of this online self-quizzing asset. Each question is presented in an interactive format that allows for immediate feedback.

- Case Studies apply what is on the page to the world beyond with the help of topic-specific case studies, each designed to turn theory into practice, and followed by three interactive scenario-based questions that allow for immediate feedback.

ADDITIONAL RESOURCES

For a more in-depth course experience, we suggest the following supplemental books:

Crime Scene Investigation Case Studies, by Jacqueline T. Fish and Jonathon Fish (ISBN: 9781455731237)

- Learn crime scene investigation through original case studies that show you how to process and document a criminal investigation from first response through to sending a report to the prosecutor's office.
- Get up to speed on the state-of-the-art investigative techniques employed in the cases.
- Practice your investigative and report writing skills with the "Your Turn" chapter.
- Develop your critical thinking skills with questions that explore the nature of the case, the conclusions drawn, and alternative outcomes.

Criminalistics Laboratory Manual, by Elizabeth Erickson (ISBN: 9781455731404)

- Original crime scene scenarios engage students, drawing them into the forensic scientific process.
- Practical, hands-on crime scene processing activities with clear, detailed instructions for how to perform each laboratory exercise.
- Laboratory objectives, key terms, review questions, and a glossary of terms keep the student focused on what's important.
- Laboratory activities can be completed without access to a fully equipped forensic science lab.

CHAPTER 1

Introduction: The CSI and Forensic Investigation

KEY TERMS

Biological evidence

Chain of custody

Circumstantial evidence

Corpus delicti

Crime scene investigator (CSI)

Direct evidence

Forensic anthropologist

Forensic evidence

Forensic nurse

Forensic scientist

Modus operandi (MO)

Physical evidence

Transient evidence

What You Will Learn

This chapter sets the stage for the aspiring CSI as well as offers an opportunity for seasoned professionals to update their knowledge on various facets of the CSI profession. An introduction to various subspecialty areas related to forensics is included to validate the many scientific and practical aspects physical evidence adds to criminal investigations.

INTRODUCTION

You only get one chance to do it right the first time, so you'd better do it right. In short, if you think of it—do it—or have a good reason why you didn't. Because if you don't, someone—who gets paid considerably more than you and by the hour—will ask why you didn't. And a jury will be watching.

—James C. Upshaw Downs

Reconstruction of a crime scene is essential in determining the events that took place prior to, during, and after a criminal act has occurred. Physical and biological evidence will play a crucial role in linking the suspect to the victim and the location of the crime as well

DOI: 10.4324/9780429261657-1

as providing support or contradictions of witness/victim/suspect recollections of the incident. An accurate and objective crime scene search yields the "story" told by the evidence so that it is reasonable and convincing to a jury. **Forensic evidence** is used to provide impartial facts and is often referred to as the "silent witness."

The **crime scene investigator (CSI)** plays an important role on the collaborative team that includes the lead detective, the medical examiner, the prosecutor's office, and the forensic scientists at the crime laboratory. Depending on the type of physical or biological evidence and the examinations that are performed, a number of scientists and technicians may be involved in the analysis of the evidence. It is highly recommended that CSIs contact and meet crime lab personnel so that they establish a professional relationship and feel comfortable in calling the lab when seeking expert advice for dealing with the unusual situations that will be encountered at crime scenes. This is a two-way street, because oftentimes the forensic scientist will have questions that can best be answered by the CSI who collected and submitted the forensic evidence being examined.

America's criminal justice system continues to evolve as new technologies and advanced forensics analyses become accepted in the courtroom. The veracity of the technology and subsequent examination results all hinge on the procedures that are practiced at the crime scene—where the chain of custody begins.

Every crime scene is different, and although a standardized set of procedures must be followed at every location by the CSI, experience and observation will assist in developing a strategic and operational plan for processing the area. Proper scene security will ensure integrity and reduce the possibility that evidence will be altered, destroyed, or go undetected by the CSI during the crime scene search (see Figure 1.1).

FIGURE 1.1

A crime scene investigator with the Denver Police Department places evidence markers next to the Hummer limousine in which Denver Broncos cornerback Darrent Williams was shot and killed while riding inside. Bullet holes can be seen in the door and to the left of the door, and the rear passenger window is shot out. *AP Photo/Ed Andrieski.*

The actions of the first officer on the scene and subsequent emergency responders prior to the arrival of the CSI must be documented and communicated to the detectives and other investigators as work on the scene progresses. The identification, collection, and preservation of physical and biological evidence must be completed in an unbiased and objective manner so as to ensure that in the final analysis (which occurs in the courtroom), the jury receives untainted and unquestionable forensic evidence as the jurors seek to find the truth and render a fair verdict.

Items that may or may not have evidentiary value must be identified, collected, preserved, and examined under the strict guidelines of the criminal rules of evidence. Proper evidence collection is one of the most important components of a criminal investigation and prosecution. Physical and biological evidence may link a suspect to a crime or prove someone's innocence. The job of a CSI is to process the crime scene without bias, letting the evidence speak for itself.

MAJOR GOALS OF A CRIME SCENE SEARCH

- Recognition and identification of forensic evidence
- Collection and proper preservation of the evidence
- Reconstruction of the crime
- Assisting detectives in forming a theory about the crime

THE ROLE OF THE CRIME SCENE INVESTIGATOR IN FORENSIC SCIENCE

"Forensic science" begins with the effective identification, documentation, collection, and preservation of physical and biological evidence at the crime scene (see Figure 1.2). The evidence is then subjected to scientific analysis in the crime laboratory, and the results of the examinations yield forensic evidence for consideration by the court. Ultimately, the evidence will be presented as proof that a past event occurred (a crime was committed) and will prove the identification of the perpetrator. There will be two versions of the event: the prosecution's allegations and the defendant's story. A trial is conducted to allow the jury to determine which version is a correct depiction of the events leading up to the incident and the identity of the participants. The job of the CSI is to properly recognize, identify, collect, and preserve those pieces of evidence that begin the process known as justice. The CSI must present a true and accurate representation of the crime scene to the court, remaining objective and unbiased throughout the proceedings. The court will weigh the value of the evidence and determine guilt or innocence.

CSIs are responsible for two of the four steps in the admissibility of physical and biological evidence for consideration by the court (recognition and collection; see Box 1.1). The knowledge, skills, and abilities of CSIs are

FIGURE 1.2
A grid excavation of a clandestine grave.

BOX 1.1 FOUR MAJOR FACTORS THAT DETERMINE THE VALUE OF FORENSIC EVIDENCE

1. **Recognition**—The CSI must have the knowledge and understanding to recognize potential items of physical and biological evidence located at the crime scene.
2. **Collection**—Utilizing the appropriate skills and following accepted protocols to gather and preserve the physical and biological evidence.
3. **Testing Procedures**—The application of acceptable scientific procedures to analyze the physical and biological evidence.
4. **Courtroom Presentation**—Qualifications of the witnesses to provide objective reports on the forensic analysis of the evidence.

invaluable to the final determination of the facts. CSIs must be highly trained and able to conduct objective and unbiased crime scene searches if the vital information available at a crime scene is to be accepted by the trial judges and juries. Forensic evidence leads to the development of the linkages among the victim, perpetrator, and the scene of the crime.

JOBS AND DESCRIPTIONS

CSI

Everyone you ask knows what the most popular meaning of the three letters *CSI* are—crime scene investigator. Thanks to the public's appetite for crime-related television shows, a mythical creature capable of gathering evidence, performing amazing scientific analysis at lightning speeds, and arresting perpetrators all in 47 minutes of primetime television has emerged and holds today's young people transfixed. This seemingly glamorous occupation only minimally represents the true job responsibilities of the CSI in today's law enforcement agencies.

There are as many varying titles as there are job descriptions, depending on the jurisdiction. CSIs can also be referred to as evidence technicians, crime scene technicians, criminalistics officers, forensic investigators, or crime scene analysts. No matter what they are called, these highly trained multidisciplinary professionals have a primary duty to complete the investigation of a crime scene by identifying and locating forensic evidence, documenting the location and condition of that evidence, collecting and preserving the evidence for transport to the crime laboratory, and maintaining the chain of custody (i.e., the documentation of the location) of the physical and biological evidence at the scene in order to preserve the integrity of the investigation.

CSIs do process items of evidence—such as conducting examination for latent fingerprints or performing presumptive tests for the presence of blood—at crime scenes (see Figure 1.3). However, the majority of scientific analysis occurs at the crime laboratory, and the personnel who generally complete such examinations are forensic scientists who specialize in the specific techniques utilized to analyze and interpret forensic evidence. CSIs can be sworn police officers or civilian personnel. Local law enforcement agencies determine these classifications, and there are no national standards of training or education for becoming a CSI. Many agencies require an applicant to become a police officer and then move into the investigative division after completing several years in the patrol division. Others hire civilian personnel and then train them as CSIs. However, these positions are not paid on the same scale as certified police officers, and they do not have arrest powers. Whether certified or civilian, the qualified CSI must successfully complete many specialized courses in order to develop the knowledge, skills, and abilities required to process the scene of a crime effectively.

FIGURE 1.3
CSIs do not wear glamorous clothing or white lab coats when they are processing crime scenes. This investigator is working a hazardous crime scene and is wearing Level B protective gear.

Although the increased public awareness of crime scene investigation has brought recognition to the importance of the tasks these highly skilled individuals perform on a daily basis, there has been no appreciable increase in the number of positions within police agencies. Larger agencies usually require a two- or four-year college degree for applicants, whereas small and rural agencies generally do not require a college degree for employment.

The successful CSI must master technical skills including taking photographs, sketching and documenting scenes, processing items of evidence for fingerprints or other impression evidence, utilizing advanced software and technology-based equipment, and communicating well with prosecutors and other members of the investigation team. It is also imperative the CSI be proficient in critical thinking and problem-solving skills. There may be physical challenges at every crime scene, so he or she must be agile as well as capable of working in environments that may be hazardous or unpalatable to the average person. CSIs must be able to analyze the situation, determine what steps have to be taken to identify, document, collect, and preserve forensic evidence—whether the crime scene is inside an abandoned warehouse, on a bridge spanning a waterway, or at a clandestine gravesite 20 miles from the nearest highway.

Hazardous materials (Hazmat) and Hazardous Work Operations and Emergency Response (Hazwopper) training is becoming more common for CSIs, so you should be able to work in personal protective equipment. This involves the ability to wear a self-contained breathing apparatus, which may weigh 30 to 40 pounds, a Level A or B protective suit, face mask, gloves, and boots for extended periods of time. Hazmat and Hazwopper courses are available through community and technical colleges.

Forensic Scientist

The **forensic scientist** works in the crime laboratory performing scientific analyses on physical and biological evidence submitted by the CSI. A forensic scientist will have a four-year degree in chemistry, biology, or another applied science and must complete one to two years of bench training before achieving adequate expertise to perform examinations without the direct supervision of another scientist.

Depending on their area of expertise, forensic scientists perform analytic tests for DNA, toxicology, serology, trace evidence such as hairs and fibers, and arson debris, as well as other tests that require scientific instruments and strict adherence to established protocols that ensure the objective analysis of evidence. Most forensic scientists are employed by state crime laboratories or at the FBI Forensic Laboratory if they are participating in the analysis of forensic evidence. However, some forensic scientists are privately employed and work as independent consultants for defense attorneys. The number of private DNA laboratories is increasing across the United States. These labs are also seeking scientifically qualified laboratory analysts to fill a growing need as private citizens recognize the value of DNA in determining paternity and resolving other civil matters.

Forensic Anthropologist

The **forensic anthropologist** can be a vital member of the crime scene investigation team by providing assistance in a variety of ways. If human remains are located, law enforcement personnel may seek a forensic anthropologist to help ensure that all the remains are identified and collected from the scene after photographs and a detailed sketch of the location and position of the remains have been documented. The forensic anthropologist will be able to verify whether the remains are human or animal, identify the number of victims, and possibly establish a sequence of events that may indicate the approximate time that has passed since death occurred.

Back in the lab, the forensic anthropologist will assist in cleaning up skeletal material so that it can be examined for evidence of trauma that may be visible from the bones. Gunshots and knife wounds often leave marks or fracture patterns that can be interpreted by a skilled forensic anthropologist and will contribute valuable information to the case detectives.

When a forensic anthropologist studies the remains of an unidentified victim, a profile of the victim is developed. The examination yields data that contributes to this profile and includes gender, approximate age, body stature, ethnicity, handedness, and some generalized information about the overall health of the subject.

Forensic Nurse

The forensic nursing specialty is a growing field in which registered nurses are trained in the scientific aspects of identifying and collecting physical and biological evidence from living patients. The professional **forensic nurse** provides an additional investigative function, because he or she works directly to treat the injuries of victims of violence, criminal activities, and motor vehicle crashes. Healthcare providers trained in the importance of evidentiary materials and legal issues can present credible and objective testimony and protect the chain of custody when the crime involves either a living victim or a deceased individual who is transported to a medical facility.

Victims of crimes arrive in hospital emergency departments (EDs) and may not be able to communicate with the healthcare providers due to physical injuries or language barriers. One of the most valuable team members in the ED is a registered nurse who has also been trained in recognizing potential victims of elder abuse, sexual assault, psychological or child abuse, and more frequently, individuals who are under the control of human traffickers and domestic violence. Forensic nurses are also called on to document medical observations of subjects who may be victims of suspicious deaths, suicide/attempted suicide, or other such traumatic occurrences. Many victims are not willing to cooperate with police officers but will confide in nurses—and the professionally trained forensics nurse may be the key to gathering physical and biological evidence that leads to the arrest and conviction of someone who is preying on adult or child victims (see also Box 1.2).

Certification and Professional Development

CSIs can pursue a number of professional accreditations in order to meet basic and advanced standards. The competent CSI will seek continuing education opportunities through attendance at conferences

BOX 1.2 OTHER FORENSIC SPECIALTY AREAS

- **Forensic Archeologist**—A scientist who utilizes archaeological recovery techniques at scenes of mass graves or exhumations.
- **Forensic Botanist**—A specialist who can aid in determining time since death or assist in placing a suspect or victim at a location by studying the anatomy of plant evidence.
- **Forensic Entomologist**—A scientist who can evaluate the life cycle of insects found at the scene or on the body of a victim to assist in establishing investigative leads such as the movement of a body after death, manner of death, and the postmortem interval (PMI).
- **Forensic Odontologist**—A dentist with special training in the evaluation and handling of dental evidence, including bitemark comparison and the identification of victims/suspects.
- **Forensic Pathologist**—A medical doctor with additional specialty training in the determination of injuries and disease that cause death.
- **Medical Examiner**—A medical doctor with five or more years of specialized training in recognition of the cause and manner of death.
- **Coroner**—An elected or appointed official who conducts death investigations. The coroner is not required to have a medical background, and his or her duties are dictated by jurisdiction.

and training seminars, as well as advanced educational programs. The International Association for Identification (IAI) offers numerous recognition programs that require the applicant to successfully complete a number of proficiency tests and includes tenprint and latent-print, bloodstain pattern, footwear, forensic art analysis, forensic photography, forensic video, and four levels of crime scene investigation (http://theiai.org/certifications/). The standards for certification are high—and achievement of this certification will underscore competence to perform the job duties when qualifications are under scrutiny by a judge or jury.

Certifications are often designed in a two- or three-tier format to encourage continuous professional development and build subject-matter expertise. Written proficiency examinations are essential to ensure the credibility of the certification programs. Often an applicant must complete additional years of service within a specific tier in order to apply for consideration and testing for the next echelon of certification. Accomplishments such as achieving recognition among one's peers in the discipline demonstrate technical competency and enhance the veracity of an investigator's testimony.

The largest professional organization of practitioners, researchers, and scientists is the American Academy of Forensic Sciences (AAFS), which has about 6,200 members in the United States and 67 foreign countries. The application of science to the law spans the spectrum of forensic disciplines and includes 11 sections (see Box 1.3). The

AAFS publishes the *Journal of Forensic Science* and conducts annual meetings at which members from every profession—including engineers, dentists, educators, psychiatrists, lawyers, physicians, and many other fields of expertise—present research findings that enhance the practice of forensics from the crime scene to the courtroom (www.aafs.org).

BOX 1.3 SPECIALTY SECTIONS OF THE AMERICAN ACADEMY OF FORENSIC SCIENCES

- Criminalistics
- Digital & Multimedia Sciences
- Engineering Sciences
- General
- Jurisprudence
- Odontology

- Pathology/Biology
- Physical Anthropology
- Psychiatry/Behavioral Science
- Questioned Documents
- Toxicology

BOX 1.4 LIST OF PROFESSIONAL ORGANIZATIONS OFFERING CERTIFICATIONS AND CREDENTIALING BASED ON AREAS OF PROFESSIONAL EXPERTISE AND EDUCATION

- American Academy of Forensic Sciences
- American Board of Criminalistics
- American Board of Forensic Anthropology
- American Board of Forensic Document Examiners
- American Board of Forensic Odontology
- American Board of Medicolegal Death Investigators
- American College of Forensic Examiners
- Association for Crime Scene Reconstruction
- Association of Firearm and Tool Mark Examiners
- Board of Forensic Document Examiners
- Evidence Photographers International Council
- High Technology Crime Investigation Association

- International Association of Arson Investigators
- International Association of Bloodstain Pattern Analysts
- International Association of Computer Investigative Specialists
- International Association of Forensic Nurses
- International Association of Identification
- International Crime Scene Investigators Association
- International Forensic Imaging Enhancement Society
- International Institute of Forensic Engineering Services
- National Association of Document Examiners

Many of the professional organizations offering certifications and credentialing have specific interests and restrict membership to credentialed professionals (see Box 1.4). There are also several state groups affiliated with the national or international parent organizations that provide continuing educational training seminars and maintain local associations for law enforcement and other first responders who are interested in promoting professionalism within their disciplines. The Internet provides a wealth of information, including membership requirements for each organization. In the year 2000, the Forensic Specialties Accreditation Board (FSAB) was formed to objectively assess, recognize, and monitor the various forensic specialty boards that certify individual forensic scientists and specialists. The FSAB provides accreditation to those certifying bodies that meet stringent requirements for training, education, experience, and testing of individual forensic scientists and specialists (www.thefsab.org).

Expert Witnesses

It is the duty of the expert witness to educate the jury and provide testimony using terminology that is easily explainable and not misunderstood. Clarity, simplicity, and honesty are essential elements of expert witness testimony. Reports should be written in nontechnical terms that allow the scientific protocols utilized in the forensic examination of physical and biological evidence to be adequately explained. Questions can arise during the translation of technical terminology into lay terms, because not everyone agrees about the intended meaning of some terms and phrases. Clarity is essential, and terminology that may be misconstrued by defense attorneys must not be used in final reports. Supervisors must also review reports and conclusions with an unbiased attention to detail to ensure that the paperwork submitted is clear and concise. This final work product will follow the case throughout the entire criminal justice process (see Figure 1.4).

The testimony of an expert witness may be challenged in the following ways:

- The case may not require the expertise.
- Basic qualifications and ability to give an opinion in the field may be at issue.
- The examiner may have insufficient education or experience to have anything of value to offer (no value added).
- The methodology utilized to support the opinion may not be scientifically sound or capable of supporting the proffered opinion.
- The methodology may be scientifically sound, but the opinion based on the method is not sufficiently derived from that scientific methodology.

The *quality* of the exam and examiner are important, however, because testimony must be objective and free of bias. Witnesses cannot deliberately omit relevant facts or encourage incorrect conclusions; these are distortions of the facts. Overstatement of the facts or a suggestion of guilt will cost an expert witness his or her integrity.

Each time a potential expert witness is presented to the court, credentials must be scrutinized in order to assess the merit of any opinions offered by the witness during testimony. The court considers that knowledge gained through education, training, and experience is sufficient grounds for qualification as an expert witness. The ability and competency of the witness must be demonstrated by the presentation of credentials, college degrees, continuing education, attendance at conferences, and information about publications and ongoing research projects. The number of years the witness has been employed in the profession also plays a key role in establishing credibility before the court.

FIGURE 1.4

State Bureau of Investigation agent Duane Deaver explains how his tests of blood spatters found inside Michael Peterson's home strengthened his opinion that the writer's wife, Kathleen Peterson, was beaten to death. A Durham County jury eventually found Michael Peterson guilty of the murder of his wife. He was sentenced to life in prison without the possibility of parole. AP Photo/Sara Davis, Pool. *AP Photo/Sara Davis, Pool.*

The judge presiding over the hearing will render a decision on the "expert" status of witnesses. Once credentials have been established, the expert witness can provide opinions based on the outcomes of examinations and the significance of the findings. Although it is not possible for any expert to render an opinion with absolute certainty, as an advocate of truth, the expert must base opinions on a reasonable scientific certainty.

Every witness is a building block in the case being presented by the prosecution, and it is up to that office to determine the strategy for the presentation of evidence to the court. Generally, the case begins chronologically, with the arrival of the first officer/responder on the scene. The CSI will present testimony beginning with arrival and proceeding through the entire crime scene process. In some instances, this may require several hours on the witness stand, and the CSI must be prepared to explain every processing step as well as the photographs and documentation that were created throughout the investigation. The witness will be "painting the picture" of the crime scene for the judge and jury, and every decision that was made is subject to further inquiry by both the prosecution and defense teams.

Preparation for courtroom testimony is a skill that the CSI will gain over time. He or she must work with the lead investigator, the prosecutor, and all forensic scientists who completed examinations of forensic evidence related to the case. The testimony is choreographed by the prosecutor to present an orderly progression from time of arrival of officers on the scene, through the chain of custody of the forensic evidence, to the final analysis and conclusions of the scientists working on the case. Every facet of the investigation is subject to scrutiny, and the witness should refresh his or her memory of the investigation with notes prior to meeting with the prosecutor so that he or she can assist with case preparation.

If you are an expert witness, remember that once you are sworn in and are on the witness stand, your integrity and professional expertise are open for inspection, and you must be prepared to answer all questions posed by the attorneys as they present your credentials to the court. You must be familiar with the scope of your testimony and where your expertise ends. Make sure the prosecutor is familiar with all the actions you took, the examinations you performed, and that the chain of custody of the physical and biological evidence is clearly presented to preserve the integrity of your work and the evidence. It may be necessary for you to provide a list of questions to the prosecutor so that the important facts are conveyed in the courtroom. If the defense attorney begins to attack you or the protocols you followed at the scene, it is the prosecutor's responsibility to provide assistance through the legal process. Remember to discuss these possibilities prior to the start of any criminal proceeding.

Ethics and Professionalism

The mission statement of the Tennessee Bureau of Investigation (TBI) is "That guilt shall not escape nor innocence suffer." This statement covers ethics and professionalism in law enforcement in one sentence (www.tbi.tn.gov). Many state and local organizations such as TBI offer Citizens' Academy applications, which provide opportunities for future CSIs to learn more about the profession while still in school.

The CSI must be professionally neutral to be an effective and professional investigator. You must remain objective, and all your actions must be unimpeachable as you follow the prescribed protocol at every crime scene. Acts of commission (intentional) and omission (unintentional) are not permitted and may be criminal in themselves. For example, an act of commission would include failure to collect a blood sample at the crime scene. An unintentional act, one of omission, would be failing to refill a container of fingerprint powder after processing a scene before responding to the next burglary call.

Integrity, honor, and duty are synonymous with the oath taken to uphold the law. If a defense attorney can attack the procedures followed at the crime scene, none of the forensic evidence will be allowed in court. Discrediting the chain of evidence, the scientists, or the science is known as the *O.J. effect*, named from the murder trial of O.J. Simpson in 1995, and has become a key defense technique.

Advances in forensic science have met the standards for court acceptance, and defense attorneys are now focusing their strategies on the actions (or inactions) of the investigators at the crime scene. By following the established protocols of the agency, an investigator will reduce or eliminate the possibility of crucial evidence being excluded due to oversight or human error.

The expert witness does not want to live with the possibility that a guilty person escapes prosecution or that an innocent person is punished based on the actions of the investigator. You should preserve the chain of custody, take all necessary precautions to prevent cross-contamination or deterioration of physical or biological evidence, and leave the analysis up to the scientists and the prosecutor. There may be other reasons that justice is not served, but integrity and honesty on the part of the CSI will place the burden on the court system. It is up to the judicial system, not the CSI or the case detective, to weigh the evidence and come to a determination of guilt or innocence.

CSIs, detectives, forensic scientists, prosecutors, defense attorneys, and the judiciary all have professional and moral obligations to work ethically and professionally. Legal, scientific, and ethical values can become entangled in the courtroom, but the most critical aspect of the trial is that the guilty are convicted and the innocent are exonerated.

Challenges to Forensic Science

In 2005, Congress commissioned the National Academy of Sciences (NAS) to examine critical forensic science issues including challenges facing the various forensic specialties, disparities and fragmentation in the forensic science community, lack of mandatory standardization, certification, accreditation, interpretation of forensic evidence, need for research, and legal admission of forensic science. The National Research Council of the NAS publicized its report titled "Strengthening Forensic Science in the United States: A Path Forward" to Congress in early 2009 (www.ncjrs.gov/pdffiles1/nij/grants/228091.pdf). This report has received widespread media attention, and several conferences and meetings at law schools have been conducted throughout the United States to publicize the report's recommendations to the legal community.

The overriding message of the NAS report is that forensic science has failed to meet the demands of science. Essentially, the committee calls for an overhaul of the practice and procedures of many forensic science disciplines, including fingerprint analysis, toolmark and firearms identification, questioned document examination, hair and fiber evidence, and identification of shoe prints and tire tracks. Some of the recommendations are not surprising in light of the negative media attention that crime labs have received over the years with respect to errors and procedural problems with forensic evidence. The NAS committee proposes 13 recommendations:

1. Have Congress establish an independent federal entity, the National Institute of Forensic Sciences (NIFS), to oversee and establish standards, research, forensic practices, education, certification, accreditation, and development of technology.
2. Establish standard terminology and reporting procedures.
3. Conduct research to address issues of accuracy, reliability, and validity.
4. Remove public forensic laboratories from the administrative control of law enforcement agencies or prosecutors' offices.
5. Conduct research on human observer bias and sources of human error.
6. Develop tools for measurement, validation, reliability, information sharing, and proficiency to ensure quality control and best practices.
7. Make forensic scientist certification and laboratory accreditation mandatory.
8. Establish quality assurance and quality control procedures.
9. Make mandatory the enforcement of a national code of ethics.
10. Develop academic-level education and training programs.
11. Improve medicolegal death investigation by removing and replacing current coroner systems with research-based methods and board-certified forensic pathologists.
12. Create nationwide fingerprint data interoperability.
13. Prepare and train forensic scientists to work with homeland security issues.

These recommendations are provided within the context that Congress establishes the NIFS so that there is an existing entity that can oversee and enforce the recommendations offered by the committee. Although it may be years before an entity such as the NIFS is created, if in fact it becomes a reality, the NAS report has been widely distributed and publicized, educating judges and lawyers as to the challenges and limitations of the forensic science disciplines. Now, more than ever, forensic practitioners are facing ever-increasing demands in the courtroom.

The NAS committee and critics of forensic science have made valuable recommendations that require the attention of forensic scientists. However, although improvements in procedures and research are absolutely essential, it seems that the establishment of certifying bodies and methodologies as well as some of the research that has been conducted may have been overlooked by the committee. Forensic scientists have already addressed or are currently addressing many of the problematic areas addressed by the NAS report. The groundwork has been laid for establishing board certification, publishing scientific reliability and validity studies, improving education and training, conducting proficiency testing, and developing methodological procedures. Forensic scientists in the public and private sectors need to take personal responsibility in meeting the challenges proposed by the NAS committee by being tested in recognized certification programs, participating in proficiency testing, maintaining scientific methodology and training standards that exceed the minimum standards, and participating in and promoting research in validity and reliability studies. The important work that has been accomplished during the past several years has propelled the field toward scientific acceptance, but more work is needed to standardize the field, and further research is required to quantify, especially, the limitations of forensic science.

Since the issuance of the report and subsequent studies, the National Institute of Justice (NIJ) has compiled a comprehensive website promoting forensic science and providing information (www.nij.gov/topics/forensics/welcome.htm).

CSI students should visit this site to learn more about the types of training and funding that are available for developing expertise in specific forensic areas.

FORENSIC EVIDENCE AND THE CRIME SCENE

Forensic evidence, when properly identified, collected, and preserved, can link the suspect to a victim, to the crime scene, to a weapon, or to other physical or biological evidence (see Box 1.5). These linkages are especially significant in crimes of violence, and the more linkages that are established, the higher the probability that the suspect committed the offense. Forensic evidence is subdivided into two basic categories: physical evidence and biological evidence. **Physical evidence** covers items of nonliving origin, such as fingerprints, footprints, fibers, paint, tire or shoe impressions, weapons, ammunition, and building materials. Physical evidence may be used as corroborative evidence, which tends to confirm or support the theory of the crime. This type could also be considered as circumstantial evidence, which indirectly infers a particular conclusion regarding the crime (www.nij.gov).

BOX 1.5 FORENSIC AND BIOLOGICAL EVIDENCE

Forensic Evidence: Two Types
Physical Evidence (Nonliving Origin)

- Fingerprints
- Footprints
- Fibers
- Paint
- Tire marks
- Building materials
- Glass
- Firearms and ammunition
- Questioned documents

- Computers and mobile devices

Biological Evidence (Originates from Living Sources)

- Human bodily fluids
- DNA
- Hair
- Bone
- Pollen
- Plant material
- Animal hair or bodily fluids

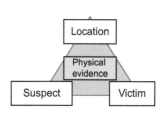

Linkages to establish associations between the suspect, victim, and crime scene. What does the physical evidence reveal?

FIGURE 1.5
Linkages.

Biological evidence originates from a living source and includes DNA, blood, other bodily fluids, hair, skin, bone, animals, or plants. The examination and analysis of biological evidence may identify the donor. Analyses conducted by scientists on biological evidence can provide compelling evidence if the CSI has taken the proper steps to prevent degradation or contamination of the evidentiary material. Biological evidence must be dried and protected from sunlight and moisture when it is collected and preserved by the CSI.

Exchanged physical or biological evidence can be overlooked or contaminated if it is microscopic or trace evidence (hairs or fibers). Linking a suspect to a victim is the most important and common type of linkage that can be established by physical or biological evidence (see Figure 1.5). However, it is also important to link a person (suspect, victim, or witness) to a location through physical evidence. The scientific analysis of the evidence will provide essential information and investigative tools and will enable detectives to validate or repudiate the credibility of witness statements.

Physical and biological evidence is valuable in many aspects, and proper recognition, documentation, collection, and preservation can reveal data that will aid the investigation by

- Providing essential information on the facts of the case—the *corpus delicti*
- Revealing the *modus operandi* (MO)—the preferred method of operation
- Demonstrating linkages among the victim, suspects, locations, and objects

BOX 1.6 ASSOCIATIVE EVIDENCE

Items of physical evidence located during a crime scene search can be used to demonstrate linkages or to "associate" the victim to the suspect or to a particular location. For example, pieces of a torn movie ticket could be located at the scene of a burglary, and the other half of the movie ticket found in the suspect's pocket on arrest. These two pieces of evidence would be considered associative evidence linking the suspect to the scene of the crime. Another common use of associative evidence is during the investigation of hit-and-run accidents in which fragments of headlight glass or paint chips from the suspect vehicle are matched to trace evidence that is recovered from the clothes or body of a victim or other vehicle. Associative evidence can be valuable to the detective when there is very little testimonial evidence and the case must be built around circumstantial and physical evidence.

- Proving or disproving witness statements
- Identifying a suspect through DNA or other individualization
- Classifying unknown substances
- Reconstructing the crime scene—how a crime was committed
- Developing investigative leads

See Box 1.6.

Class versus Individual Characteristics

The CSI must be aware of the differences between the individual and class characteristics of physical evidence. Most items of physical evidence located at a crime scene cannot definitively be linked to a single person or object. It is the responsibility of the CSI to locate all possible physical evidence at a scene and discuss the outcomes of the forensic analysis with the crime laboratory scientist, the lead detective, and the prosecutor in order to provide a cohesive and objective presentation of the evidence. In most courtroom proceedings, it is a preponderance of the evidence that the jury will consider. It can be physical or biological evidence that consists of class or individual characteristics and may often exclude people from the investigative process.

Class Characteristics

Physical evidence cannot always be related to a common origin with a high degree of certainty; therefore, when it can be associated only with a group and never a single source, it is placed into a class. It is not usually possible for the examiner to assign exact or even approximate probability values when comparing class evidence. Polyester fibers are a good example of class evidence. Examination will yield information regarding the makeup of the fibers, but it is not possible to state affirmatively that the fibers came from a specific rug. Significance may be attached to the location and number of the polyester fibers in relation to the victim, suspect, and/or crime scene; however, the forensic scientist cannot objectively state that a specific rug was the source of the fibers.

Individual Characteristics

Individual characteristics are distinct differences in the physical or biological evidence that allow it to be associated with a single source with a high degree of certainty. This permits the forensic examiner to determine the uniqueness of any single object or piece of evidence. The mathematical probability that there are two identical sources of the unique individual evidence is astronomical or beyond human comprehension. The scientist can state in court the scientific conclusion that excludes the possibility of identical sources of the physical or biological evidence or, more simply stated, beyond a reasonable degree of scientific certainty.

Items of physical evidence that can be individualized and associated with a single originating source when the quality of the evidence is high are impressions of fingerprint ridges, toolmarks, bullet and casing comparisons, footwear and tire impressions, and handwriting. For example, DNA testing can exclude people from further consideration based on the highly discriminatory analyses that are now available and are accepted routinely in courtroom proceedings. The scientist will be able to state his or her conclusions to the court to a reasonable degree of scientific certainty based on the validity of accepted laboratory analyses.

Direct Evidence

Establishing a fact without the need for further analysis is known as "**direct evidence.**" An example of direct evidence is a video of a store robbery where the perpetrator's face is clearly identifiable on the recording or the statement of an eyewitness who was in the store at the time the suspect entered the store. This type of evidence does not require inference or assumption. It is based on personal knowledge or observation and directly proves or disproves an allegation or disputed fact.

Circumstantial Evidence

Most of the evidence examined in the forensic lab is **circumstantial evidence**, and it is up to the forensic scientist to provide an explanation through his or her analysis. This type of evidence is more objective than direct evidence. The CSI must guard against contamination of the evidence at the crime scene or throughout the transport process to the evidence/property section. Circumstantial evidence is based on reasoning and not direct observation of a fact. If knowledge can be inferred from testimony provided at trial, it is circumstantial evidence.

Natural Variation

Repeated specimens will display normal variations—whether one is studying pattern formations in rock or handwriting samples. It is not possible to observe exactly the same characteristic of any object without obtaining intrinsic differences; the result will vary from instance to instance. Part of the variation detected will result from actual differences among the instances being compared, and part of it comes from variation in the measurement process. The process of observation or measurement involves human intervention—another natural system that is just as subject to intrinsic variation as any other system.

LEGAL ISSUES AND THE CRIME SCENE

Court rulings, interpretations of court rulings, new legislation, and policies and procedures impact the operations of law enforcement agencies on a regular basis. There is no single authority to provide the information on a timely basis, so the investigator must remain attentive to specific agency procedures to remain in compliance. State laws and criminal codes are the basis for standard operational procedures, and jurisdictions employ attorneys working as prosecutors or solicitors who are responsible for ensuring that agency employees are properly advised when new court rulings affect day-to-day operations. Professional organizations publish journals and newsletters to keep members apprised of changes, and it is incumbent on the investigator to stay abreast of current events and emerging trends and the potential impact on agency protocols.

The US Constitution and the Bill of Rights provide constitutional guarantees to all citizens, and all law enforcement representatives accept an oath to uphold those rights and privileges.

Search Warrants

The Fourth Amendment protects against unreasonable search and seizure, and every time evidence is removed from a scene, it must

STATE OF _____)
)   **SEARCH WARRANT**
COUNTY OF _____)   _____

TO THE SHERIFF OR BONDED LAW ENFORCEMENT OFFICE OF THIS STATE OR COUNTY OR THE COUNTY OF _____ OR MUNICIPALITY OF _____

It appearing from the attached affidavit that there are reasonable grounds to believe that certain property subject to seizure under provisions of (Statute) of the _____, as amended, is located on the following Premises:

**DESCRIPTION OF PREMISES (PERSON OR THING)
TO BE SEARCHED**

Dwelling or Business Address: _____
 City, State, Zip _____
Location Description: _____
Now, therefore, you are hereby authorized to search the subject premises for the property listed below and to seize such property if found:

DESCRIPTION OF PROPERTY

Item #1 _____
Item #2 _____
Item #3 _____

This Search Warrant shall not be valid for more than ten days from the date of issuance.

A written inventory of all property seized pursuant to this Search Warrant to

_____ Department Property Control & Disposition Officer in Charge

Within ten days from the date of this warrant, such inventory to be signed by the officer executing this warrant, and a copy of such inventory shall be furnished to the person whose premises are searched if demand for such copy is made.

A copy of this Search Warrant shall be delivered to the person in charge of the premises searched at the time of such search if practicable, and, if not, to such person as soon thereafter as is practicable; in the event the identity of the person in charge is not known or if such person cannot be found after reasonable diligence in attempting to locate the person; a copy shall be attached to a prominent place on such premises.

City, State _____   _____
Date _____   Signature of Judge

FIGURE 1.6
A typical search warrant.

conform to both the Fourth Amendment constraints and relevant court rulings. Jurisdictional requirements vary, and investigators should obtain search warrants if consent to search cannot be obtained from someone who is legally authorized to permit the search (see Figure 1.6). Local prosecutors must be consulted in regard to the affidavit and application for a search warrant.

To ensure the integrity of the evidence, first responders must protect and secure the crime scene until the appropriate search and seizure documents are acquired. These steps will establish a chain of custody that cannot be impeached during subsequent court proceedings.

Mincey v. Arizona (1978) dictated what actions law enforcement personnel are authorized to take without first obtaining a warrant. First, officers can enter a scene to search for victims and render aid in areas in which a victim could reasonably be found. Second, responding officers may enter the scene to search for a perpetrator(s)—again only in areas where a suspect could be located. Third, while officers are legally in a location performing either of the two aforementioned actions, they may seize items of evidentiary nature that are in plain view; however, this should occur only in exigent circumstances, such as an unsecured weapon.

Seizing evidence in plain view circumvents the documentation aspects of the crime scene search and should not be utilized unless the evidence is transient or presents a danger to those present. Outside of these conditions, a search warrant must be obtained in order for the forensic evidence to be admissible in court. **Transient evidence** is defined as physical or biological evidence that may be lost forever if not immediately preserved. For example, a shoe impression found in a melting bank of snow would be considered transient in that it must be photographed, measured, and cast with dental stone before it melts away.

Just as forensic evidence that was obtained illegally cannot be admitted into court, any subsequent information that was derived from the excluded evidence is referred to as "fruit of the poisonous tree" and cannot be brought before the court for consideration. The analogy of this legal doctrine arises from the thought that if the tree (the physical or biological evidence) is tainted, then any fruit (subsequent information) derived from that evidence would also be tainted.

Admissibility of Evidence

CSIs must be knowledgeable about the guidelines the court system must follow when ruling on the admissibility of evidence and testimony. The availability of advanced analysis procedures and new technology does not automatically provide for the results of those findings to be accepted by the court. Scientific validity of the process and the results must be established by the attorney seeking to introduce the evidence to the legal proceedings. The actions taken by a CSI at the scene will be scrutinized by all parties engaged in the criminal or civil process, so all investigators must be cognizant of the legal requirements imposed by previous court decisions and established standards. The prosecutor's office will be responsible for ensuring that the legal standards are met and that the appropriate forensic scientists or discipline experts are available to provide testimony regarding the scientific basis for the analysis. However, the CSI must possess an understanding of the theory and practices that validate the evidence collection and examination processes.

Frye v. United States

In 1923, the Circuit Court of the District of Columbia rejected the admission of a polygraph (lie detector) test on the basis that the reliability of the instrument had not been proven (*Frye v. United States*, 1923). The validity of the claim that the polygraph instrument could detect deception had not been established. According to the court, the physical and mental conditions of the subject being questioned as well as the skill and knowledge of the polygraph examiner provided too many variables that could not be controlled, so the court would not admit the findings as "scientifically valid." Without this designation, the use of the polygraph was not allowed. The result was the *Frye* test, which established the criteria that define judicial acceptance of scientific advances. Basically, the ruling requires expert testimony to be based on scientific principles or procedures that have already been generally accepted within the scientific community. Courts will hear testimony from experts in the field and will consider scientific papers before determining the acceptability of the technique.

Federal Rules of Evidence

The US Congress creates legislation including the Federal Rules of Evidence, and the most current revisions were enacted in December 1, 2011. They may be viewed on the US Court web page (www.us-courts.gov/uscourts/rules/rulesevidence.pdf). The use of these rules is mandatory for all federal courts. Many states have also adopted them in an effort to establish consistency among the various levels of criminal proceedings. Specific rules that are of interest to CSIs include Rule 402, concerning relevancy, and Rules 701 and 702, regarding testimony by lay and expert witnesses. The trial judge is responsible for determining the qualifications of an expert witness and whether the witness will be allowed to offer an opinion based on knowledge, skill, training or education, and experience.

Daubert v. Merrell Dow Pharmaceuticals, Inc.

In jurisdictions where Federal Rule 702 is not utilized, legal practitioners have adopted the guidelines established by the *Daubert* case for allowing testimony relating to forensic evidence. The court will require proof that the scientific basis underlying the opinion is generally accepted in the scientific community and is relevant and reliable. The US Supreme Court ruling in *Daubert v. Merrell Dow Pharmaceuticals, Inc.* (1993) tasks trial judges with judging the admissibility and reliability of scientific evidence presented in their courts. Judges must assume the responsibility of becoming the gatekeeper in determining the admissibility of scientific evidence. They must consider whether the scientific technique or theory can be and has been tested and subjected to peer review and publication, the potential rate of error for the technique, the existence and maintenance of standards, and whether the theory or method has attracted widespread acceptance within the scientific community.

Prior to accepting expert scientific testimony, the judge must determine if the reasoning or methodology underlying the testimony is scientifically valid and can be applied to the facts at issue. This is known as the "relevant and reliable" standard of *Daubert*. Generally speaking, the *Daubert* relevancy standard means the information to be presented to the court has the capability to make some fact that is of consequence to the action more or less probable than it would be without it.

Chain of Custody

From the moment someone alerts the police or emergency 911 center that a crime has occurred, the clock is ticking. Documentation of every person, action, statement, and observation forms an essential link in the chain of custody. Beginning with the arrival of the first emergency responder on the scene of the crime, activities will be scrutinized by dozens of people—all in various roles working to ensure that justice is served and that communities remain safe.

Preventive measures to protect and preserve the crime scene must begin immediately. As soon as life safety issues have been resolved (Is the environment safe for officers/firefighters/medical personnel to enter? Is the victim alive or deceased? Is the perpetrator still on the premises?), access should be restricted and the process of documentation begun.

The **chain of custody** refers to the documentation of the location of all forensic evidence at all times. It is important for the CSI to stress the importance of the chain of custody *of the entire crime scene*. From the time the first officer or emergency responder arrives on the scene

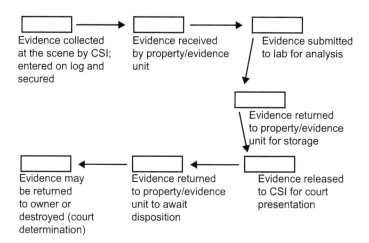

FIGURE 1.7
Chain-of-custody flowchart.

until the detective releases the location at the conclusion of the crime scene search, the integrity of the entire area must be maintained and documented as each individual item of evidence is logged on the evidence sheet, photography log, and crime scene sketch. The "who-what-when-where-why" questions must be addressed in the investigator's notes and communicated to the detectives so that valuable time will not be wasted tracking down first responders to determine their actions prior to the arrival of the CSI.

The chain of custody will provide a chronological timeline that accurately depicts the journey of the evidence during the life of the case (see Figure 1.7). It portrays the actions that were taken to identify, collect, and preserve the integrity of the forensic evidence and plays an essential role in the admissibility of evidence into courtroom proceedings. A break in the chain of custody will weaken or may even disqualify the evidence and remove it from the consideration of the court. Even a gap or oversight in the documentation process can be costly and lead to the exclusion of critical information necessary to convict or exonerate the suspect.

Documentation

Every action must be documented extensively in notes, photographs, sketches, and reports. The purpose of documentation is to create a permanent record of the condition of the crime scene and the forensic evidence. It is critical for all documentation to demonstrate a logical and systematic plan for processing the crime scene. The four stages that must be completed during documentation include (1) taking notes, (2) taking photographs, (3) sketching, and (4) making video. No shortcuts are to be taken; for example, videography does not replace photography.

Scene documentation allows the CSI to make detailed notes, videotape the crime scene to provide a three-dimensional view of the area and the location of forensic evidence, take photographs, and diagram the scene to include measurements and other notations.

Videos and photographs of the initial scene will provide records that can be studied in depth by detectives and prosecutors as cases are prepared for courtroom presentation. The final step—sketching—generally requires a rough sketch completed during the initial walk-through and final sketches that are made at the conclusion of the scene investigation (see Figure 1.8).

Advances in digital technology have modified some agency protocols regarding the use of photo logs. Most high-end digital SLR cameras now create the documentation of time, date, and camera settings through an electronic timestamp on the photo. Agencies that are still utilizing film cameras should maintain a hand-generated photo log that includes all pertinent information including roll number, time and date, camera settings, distance to subject, and a brief description of the photo.

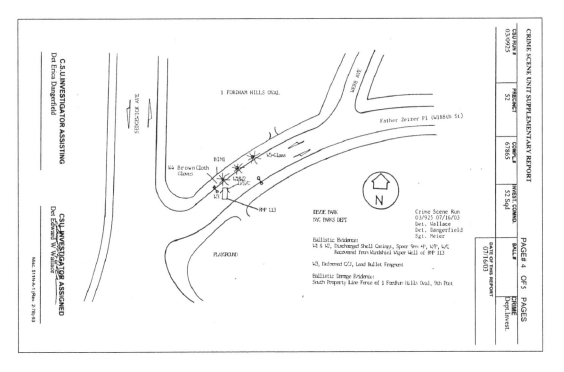

FIGURE 1.8
Outdoor crime scene sketch.

Many times the actions of a CSI come under attack by the defense attorney—not because of procedure, expertise, or abilities but because the documentation lacks accuracy. All notes must be reviewed as reports and sketches are finalized (see Figures 1.9 and 1.10). If a savvy defense attorney cannot attack a CSI's skills on the scene, he or she will look for anything amiss in the extensive paperwork in an attempt to discredit the investigator, the forensic evidence, the protocols followed, and/or the chain of custody.

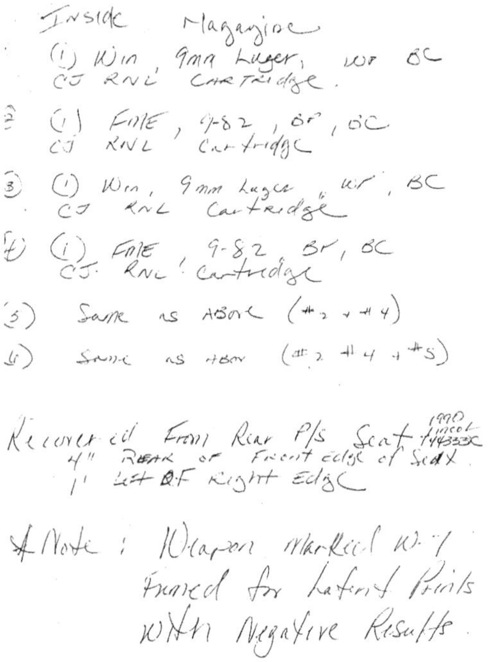

FIGURE 1.9
Investigator notes made at a crime scene.

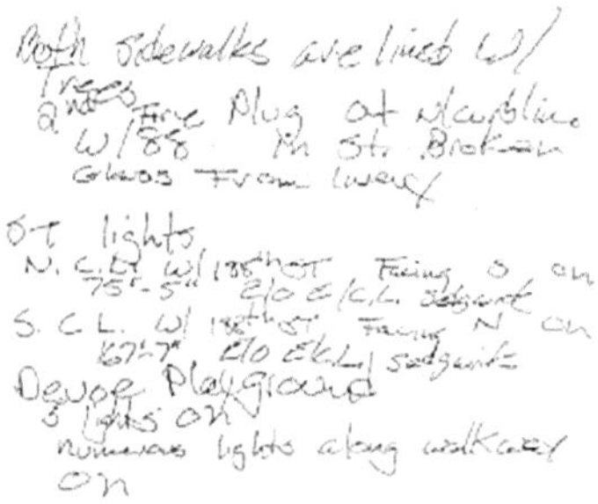

FIGURE 1.10
Investigator notes listing forensic evidence at a crime scene.

SCIENTIFIC ISSUES IN CRIME SCENE INVESTIGATION

Crime laboratories must operate under established protocols and written guidelines to ensure the integrity of the scientific analyses conducted in the facility. Many laboratories seek certification from the American Society of Crime Laboratory Directors (ASCLD) in order to demonstrate a commitment to perform objective examinations of forensic evidence. The ASCLD standards require ongoing professional development for scientists as well as performance reviews that document that state-of-the-art technologies are being utilized to complete the evidentiary examinations. The organization seeks to improve the quality of laboratory services that are provided to the criminal justice system, and ASCLD certification is a voluntary action intended to demonstrate to the public that the laboratory maintains an independent, impartial, and objective system for assessment by other scientific colleagues.

Controls

Quality control practices are essential for maintaining the integrity of testing and test results in a scientific environment. When analysis of evidentiary materials is conducted, another test, a control, is performed in parallel that is designed to yield predictable results. These results will confirm the reliability of the experimental results on the physical or biological evidence that is being tested. The control will be documented and included in final laboratory results that are available to the court for scrutiny should a defense counsel contest the legitimacy of the scientific analysis.

Standards

Scientific comparisons occur when an item of physical or biological evidence with an unknown origin is evaluated against a known standard. A known standard is one whose origin can be verified. For example, many times a CSI will collect known standards such as buccal swabs or body hair from a suspect in order to provide the forensic scientist with a reference. After completion of the analysis of the known and unknown evidence, the examiner will be able to determine if both items originated from the same source. It is important to obtain standards for comparison, and the CSI must observe the same rules of evidence collection, preservation, and chain of custody as is followed for every type of forensic evidence—whether at the crime scene or from a suspect.

Overlapping Roles

In this introductory chapter, you have been introduced to the world of crime scene investigation, the many aspects and expectations of this profession, and other specialized fields that overlap and contribute to a successful investigation. It is important for the aspiring investigator to realize that the CSI holds a crucial position within the criminal justice system but seldom has access to the state-of-the-art facilities and equipment that are featured on today's television shows. Crime scene investigation remains the primary means of establishing linkages between a victim and a suspect or the suspect and the crime scene. The opportunities for success are increasing as scientific discoveries advance the application of technology to an ever-widening cross-disciplinary approach to solving crimes. Criminal justice programs across the nation are reporting larger numbers of students enrolling in undergraduate and graduate programs, which ensures a constant influx of new thought that leads to new discoveries.

As you continue through this textbook, you will be introduced to many new concepts and practices that will require you to develop insight into the processes that make crime scene investigation a valuable component of the criminal justice system. In order for you to apply the new knowledge you have gained from the textbook chapters and classroom lectures, you will be introduced to a fictional crime scene investigation titled "Murder in the New Year." At the end of each chapter, you will gain more information on the ongoing investigation that will assist you in linking the practices and procedures taught in the textbook to the homicide investigation.

Discussion Questions

1. Discuss the basic principles for the first law enforcement officer on the scene. Specifically, what are the do's and don'ts?
2. Discuss the general procedure of the crime scene investigator. What steps should be followed?
3. Discuss the importance of collecting evidence legally. Who determines the legality of the evidence? In the final analysis, who must be convinced of the importance of the evidence collected?
4. What is the difference between direct and circumstantial evidence?
5. What is the importance of the *Daubert* rulings as related to forensic evidence?

REFERENCES

Daubert v. Merrell Dow Pharmaceuticals, Inc. (1993). *509 U.S. 579.*

Frye v. United States. (1923). *293 F. 1013.*

Mincey v. Arizona. (1978). *437 U.S. 385.*

National Research Council of the National Academies. (2009). *Strengthening Forensic Science in the United States: A Path Forward.* Washington, DC: National Academies Press.

The First Response and Scene Search

What You Will Learn

From the initial call through the conclusion of the investigation, CSIs can face many challenges and potentially dangerous situations. Information concerning personal protective equipment, other safety concerns, the initial walkthrough, and a search of the scene are covered in this chapter.

MURDER IN THE NEW YEAR

The First Response

Tom Smith threw a cedar log onto the crackling fire in the massive stone fireplace. Living in a cabin on seven acres bordering a national forest had its rewards, peace and quiet being numbers one and two. Tom looked out the window at the swirling snow. He had put the finishing touches on a pot of his world-famous flame-thrower chili and brewed a pot of strong, deep-South sweet tea. The pre-game show was in full swing, and kick-off was a half hour away. Chili, sweet tea, satellite TV, and the recliner—all the necessities for Super Bowl Sunday. What held the promise of a perfect evening was shattered with a single phone call from none other than his old friend, Detective Mavis Fletcher.

DOI: 10.4324/9780429261657-2

"Hi, Tom. It's Mavis."

"Detective Fletcher, please tell me you are calling to wish me a belated Happy New Year."

Mavis Fletcher smiled to herself and sighed. "I do wish that were the case. And I mean that from the bottom of my Super Bowl Sunday heart. I know how much you look forward to the big game."

"That can mean only one thing—you plan to join me for the festivities."

"Afraid not, Tom. Put the chili in the fridge and DVR the game. I'm going to need your attention more than the Super Bowl needs it."

Tom turned off the television. "What's the deal, Mavis?"

> The bodies of James Morton and his wife, Margie, were discovered by their daughter and her husband when they came over to watch the game with them. On the face of it, it looks like it could be a murder-suicide, but as you and I both know, looks can be deceiving.

"True enough," Tom replied. "True enough."

***

Detective Mavis Fletcher handed Tom Smith a steaming cup of Starbucks coffee.

"Starbucks, Detective," Tom said as he warmed his hands on the cup. "I'm impressed. Have we made a New Year's resolution to go first-class in the coming year?"

"Nope," Mavis replied. "Since you're giving up the Super Bowl to lend a hand, I figured you deserved a venti Starbucks."

Tom raised his cup of coffee in acknowledgment before taking a sip. He watched as an assistant handed Detective Fletcher a set of level C personal protective equipment (PPE) including coveralls with shoe covers, a mask, and gloves.

"Standard procedures when bodily fluids are present in a crime scene. We don't need to take in any physical evidence that would contaminate the area, and we sure don't want to take any out on our clothing," said Mavis.

Tom hesitated midway through his cup of coffee, poured the rest out on the ground next to his truck, and accepted the set of PPE from the CSI van. After donning the suit, gloves, and mask, he and Mavis crossed the outer perimeter of the crime scene and together they made their way into the Morton's residence. Mavis Fletcher surveyed the crime scene in the kitchen. Madge Johnson, the victim's daughter, and her husband, Bob, were seated in the nearby living room awaiting a ride to the police station. With the snow quickly piling up outside, they were reluctant to drive their own car downtown, so Mavis had arranged for one of the agency's four-wheel-drive vehicles to transport them to the Detective Division where their formal statements would be taken.

After an initial crime scene walkthrough with the responding officer, Mavis asked, "What's your initial impression, Tom?"

"Hmmmm … initial impression. Well, let's see. Officer Scott—you remember Officer Scott from the 'Holiday Homicide Case'?"

Mavis raised her eyebrow. "The one you chewed out for not protecting our last crime scene from contamination?"

"That's right," Tom continued. "And it seems that Officer Scott also remembers that encounter. That said, I want you to know that I have made every effort not to—as you put it—'freak him out' like I did last time."

> Actually, Officer Scott did an excellent job isolating Mr. and Mrs. Johnson away from the primary crime scene by moving them into the living room and away from the kitchen. It just wasn't feasible to put them out in the snow while he waited for us to arrive.

"Good for him," Mavis replied. "Now back to your initial impression."

Tom Smith looked toward the sofa where the daughter and son-in-law were seated.

> My initial impression is that it looks like a murder-suicide, including a typed suicide note compliments of Mr. Morton, but as you and I both have learned, initial impressions often prove to be unreliable. The daughter and her husband did contaminate the crime scene a bit … tracked some blood around … used the bathroom … that sort of thing. According to Officer Scott, Mrs. Johnson said her mother and father were having some marital difficulties.

"What kinds of difficulties?" Detective Fletcher queried.

Tom shrugged, "She was screwing the Dean."

"Tom!" Mavis whispered, nodding toward the daughter and son-in-law. "Show a little decorum."

> Sorry, Detective. Margie Morton was having an affair with Dean Michael Sellers for whom she worked as his executive assistant. Apparently, her husband, James Morton, who is also chair of the art department in the college where Sellers was dean, found out about the affair. The two were, according to the daughter, trying to work things out although they were having a difficult time. At one point, Margie thought about leaving James, and he was none too happy with that option.

Mavis Fletcher wrote on her notepad as Tom spoke. "Where's Sellers in all this?"

"The daughter says her father told her he confronted the erstwhile Dean in Sellers's office and verbally threatened him."

Mavis kept writing. "Any chance they were seeing a marriage counselor or pastor?"

"Not that the daughter knew of," Tom replied.

"What about the crime scene itself?"

Tom motioned for Officer Scott to join him and Detective Fletcher.

> Officer Scott was first to arrive. Apparently, the daughter found the door locked and the television on. Snacks were sitting on the coffee table although a bowl and chips were scattered in the kitchen where the wife fell after being shot in the back of the head. It looks like the husband then shot himself in the heart. It appears that Margie died instantly. Given the amount and trail of blood, the husband may have lingered a bit before succumbing to his wound. He may have tried to move … a bit strange, but not outside the boundaries of what we have seen at other crime scenes.

Tom Smith looked at the young officer next to him. "Anything else you want to add, Officer Scott?"

"Not really, sir … just that it seems a little strange, more of a gut feeling."

Mavis Fletcher put her pen and notebook in her coat pocket. "What does your gut say, Officer Scott?"

"It's just that given what her daughter says about the two of them trying to work things out, it seems odd that Mr. Morton would shoot his wife execution style."

"Odd, indeed," Mavis replied. "Still, she had threatened to leave him."

She looked out the window. It was beginning to snow harder. "What a way to start a new year," she said as they exited the residence.

INTRODUCTION

Too often law enforcement officers and other first responders fail to thoroughly assess the value of the crime scene and overlook items of potential evidentiary value to the investigation. The problem of "swoop and scoop"—that is, moving in quickly to recover evidence and then proceeding to the next call for service—can preclude the identification and collection of all the evidence.

Patrol officers, firefighters, and emergency medical personnel are usually first to arrive on the scene, and generally all safety concerns will have been identified and, where possible, addressed before CSIs enter the area. Always be aware of your surroundings. Perpetrators may be hiding in the immediate area, and there is always the potential for booby traps and other hazardous conditions.

Assess the physical conditions of the location to identify other hazards that could prevent you from working safely at the crime scene (see Figure 2.1). Weather conditions, electrical hazards, the potential for toxic fumes (such as natural gas), and the stability of the structure all should be evaluated prior to entering the scene. Do not overlook the potential danger from animals, such as the victim's dog, which may be overprotective of its owner and react violently when approached by a stranger.

FIGURE 2.1
Bone scatter with flag markers.

Always ensure the stability of the situation when developing the action plan. If hazardous conditions exist, report them to the officer in charge of the investigation so that an efficient and effective crime scene investigation can be, upon correction of the hazardous conditions, conducted. In some instances, the level of **personal protective equipment (PPE)** that must be worn inside the crime scene may impact the amount of physical evidence that can be gathered as well as the amount of time a CSI can work within the secure perimeter.

If the environment is toxic or potentially contaminated with chemical, biological, or radiological/nuclear hazards, it will be designated as an exclusion zone, and a Hazmat team will assume responsibility for developing the safety plan.

Under these circumstances, only essential CSI personnel who are certified as Hazardous Material Technicians or CSIs who have been made aware of the risks/hazards, have completed just-in-time training on associated hazardous material issues, and passed baseline medical monitoring are allowed to process these types of scenes. They will enter the hazardous environment under the watchful eye of a Certified Hazardous Material Technician to complete the assignment. This requires expertise that is typically beyond the scope of the regular CSI, but is a potential option for future training. Although many large law enforcement agencies now require CSIs to complete Hazmat training, this higher level of preparation is not standard for smaller local departments.

Distraught family members or anxious witnesses may also present risks to the investigating officers and must be removed from the primary area quickly and safely. Additional safety issues may arise if a crowd gathers; the commanding officer on duty should be notified if this potential exists. Not only does an uninformed crowd present safety issues, it can hamper or delay the arrival of additional resources or equipment by blocking paths or street entrances. Always ensure officer safety before proceeding.

Before you enter a crime scene, be sure the location is within the legal boundaries of your jurisdiction and all search and seizure issues have been properly addressed. Although this may seem trivial—after all, why would you be dispatched to a crime scene if it is not within your jurisdiction?—this problem does occur. City limits, county lines, or nautical boundaries are invisible lines, so they do not impede your ability to carry out your responsibilities, but their significance may surface in a courtroom. Your narrative statement and crime scene sketch should contain a venue statement that verifies that the actions occurred within the legal jurisdiction of your agency.

Oftentimes the physical evidence and crime scene processing are textbook perfect, and the defense attorney will focus on other aspects of the investigation in an attempt to keep his or her client from being convicted. There are many documented cases in which jurisdictional issues and conflicts over which agency should conduct an investigation have led to numerous delays and the dismissal of charges because of technicalities not associated with the investigation itself. These situations can be avoided by double-checking with the dispatcher to ensure that you are within your jurisdictional domain and that all appropriate agencies have been notified before you begin a detailed crime scene investigation.

Do not overlook the need for a representative of the prosecutor's office to be notified of the situation. It is possible that search warrants must be secured before you can legally conduct a crime scene search. Whether the prosecutor or solicitor must be present at the crime scene is a matter of jurisdictional procedure. It is mentioned here to ensure that physical evidence recovered from a crime scene investigation is admissible in the courtroom and will not be excluded because of the lack of a search warrant.

THE FBI'S 12-STEP PROCESS

Every crime scene is different; however, fundamental steps must be followed to ensure that the integrity of the physical evidence is not compromised. Many law enforcement agencies have adopted the Federal Bureau of Investigation's 12-step process to gather and protect evidence at the crime scene. By following the standardized process at every type of crime scene, the CSI may be assured that every step is performed methodically, which simplifies court testimony.

The 12-step process is as follows:

1. Prepare
2. Approach scene
3. Secure and protect scene
4. Initiate preliminary survey
5. Evaluate physical evidence possibilities
6. Prepare narrative descriptions
7. Depict scene photographically
8. Prepare diagrams and sketches of scene
9. Conduct a detailed search
10. Record and collect physical evidence
11. Conduct a final survey
12. Release scene

These steps are all common-sense actions that document the crime scene and the procedures followed by the CSI to identify, collect, and preserve the physical evidence at the crime scene. The steps are intuitive, logical, and applicable to every type of investigation.

DETERMINING THE SCOPE OF THE CRIME SCENE

You should point out potential physical evidence to medical personnel or firefighters who may still be inside the scene. Be sure to document emergency responders (names, badge numbers, station assignment) who are inside the crime scene. Instruct them not to clean up the scene. Determine everything that has been altered, touched, or moved by emergency responders and document these facts in your notes. Immediately exclude unauthorized and nonessential personnel from the area and report this on the exit log being maintained at the access point.

Create a pathway that will minimize contamination and alteration of the crime scene. If it is possible to determine the path of the perpetrator and another way into or out of the area exists, isolate the perpetrator's path so that you protect any potential physical evidence that may be located in that area. Identify the focal point(s) of the scene and extend outward. Set up physical barriers and ensure a log of all personnel who enter or exit the scene once the perimeter has been established and is being maintained by the assigned safeguarding officer. This log should correlate with the notes you have made regarding what personnel were at the scene when you arrived. With these actions, you have begun to establish the timeline for the scene, which will not conclude until the scene is released to the case detective or the officer in charge.

Boundaries

Secure areas where the crime occurred, where potential evidence is located, or that are potential entry/exit paths of suspects and witnesses. When establishing boundaries, you need to always secure a larger area and then reduce the area as additional information is determined that will decrease the perimeter of the scene. It is always possible to make the area of the crime scene smaller, but it is usually difficult to increase the perimeter because you cannot ensure the integrity of the area outside the original perimeter. Do not develop tunnel vision; keep an open mind and be sure that all boundaries can be controlled/secured.

Establish physical barriers using crime scene tape, rope, cones, barricades, vehicles, and personnel. Existing structures, such as walls, gates, and rooms, can also be utilized as barriers. In outdoor situations, utilize trees, telephone poles, or other existing physical barriers to establish a perimeter. Always remain cognizant of the need to block the view of the crime scene from the public (and the media). This is essential in order to maintain the integrity of the scene investigation as well as to provide some privacy to the victim(s) of the crime.

There are no definite rules for establishing boundaries of conventional crime scenes, unlike hazardous material crime scenes; they may change if additional scenes are identified during the course of the investigation. A final reminder is to always be aware of the potential of impression evidence (footprints and tire marks) when establishing the perimeters. Isolation and protection are crucial to preserving this transient type of evidence. Be alert for any discarded items that may be found on the entry/exit path(s) used by the perpetrator. For example, cigarette butts, beverage cans or bottles, or other articles that may not be considered out of place could contain important DNA or other trace evidence that will link the suspect to the scene.

Multiple Scenes

Crime scenes are not limited to a single location. Generally, the primary scene is the location where a victim is found; however, additional (secondary) scenes may be identified and must be linked to the primary scene. Examples include the victim's car or other mode of transportation, place of employment, or another public area such as a park or a gym. As suspects are identified, additional secondary crime scenes, such as residences or vehicles, may become part of the total crime scene investigation. Multiple scenes may also mean multiple jurisdictions are involved in the investigation. Most agencies will have multijurisdictional agreements that predetermine areas of responsibility in the event a crime expands into more than one jurisdiction. Joint investigations may be necessary, particularly when there are multiple incidents; for example, a serial arsonist does not respect the city limits signs. It is important that all agencies work together rather than independently to eliminate duplication of work and share information as it is developed.

CSI Personal Safety Concerns

The primary reason the CSI is dispatched to a crime scene is to conduct a forensic investigation. It is up to every individual to be cognizant of the safety issues and hazardous conditions that may present dangers to emergency responders and investigators. This section is included so that you will develop personal security measures that become routine and lessen the possibility of exposure to situations that can be potentially hazardous to your health. Departmental guidelines are designed to protect employees and must be followed; however, additional information has been provided that may enhance the safety of the CSI and other coworkers at the crime scene as well as prevent **cross-contamination** of physical evidence (i.e., the transfer of material between two or more sources of physical evidence) (see Box 2.1).

BOX 2.1 SAFETY MEASURES

- Do not eat, drink, smoke, or use cellphones in the crime scene.
- Be alert for biological, chemical, radiological/nuclear, environmental, or mechanical hazards.
- Watch for sharp objects such as hypodermic needles, knives, razors, broken glass, nails, exposed metal, or other objects.
- Do not use the bathrooms at the crime scene.
- Never pick up broken glass with your hands. Use clean or sterile, single-use, disposable, brushes and dust pans, tongs, forceps, or tweezers, and place the pieces in clean or sterile secure containers.
- Place all syringes, needles, and other sharp objects in a puncture-resistant container with a biohazard warning label. Never recap or place covers such as erasers over hypodermic needles.
- When searching confined spaces, ensure you are trained and certified to enter these locations with the proper PPE and environmental safety monitoring equipment.
- When searching and probing restrictive or obstructed locations, such as under a bed or behind large immovable objects, use mirrors, flashlights, fiber-optic cameras, and other tools before placing your hands in these spaces. Do not overlook the potential for poisonous spiders and/or snakes in narrow or confined dark areas.
- Always use caution in unknown environments. Exotic pets may pose a hazard; poisonous snakes, scorpions, and spiders can startle the unsuspecting CSI.
- Always wash your hands or other skin surfaces thoroughly and immediately if you come into contact with any bodily fluid. The universal decontamination solution is a diluted solution of bleach, soap, and water 1:10, or 70 percent isopropyl alcohol.

Personal Protective Equipment

First responders and CSIs should never enter the crime scene without the appropriate PPE. Gloves, Tyvekt suits, shoe covers, and eye and respiratory protection are essential for ensuring personal safety and for protecting the crime scene from accidental contamination or cross-contamination (see Figure 2.2). Remember Locard's exchange principle. There are many hazards, both obvious and hidden, that demand the CSI be vigilant to maintain a safe working environment for all personnel involved in the investigation. The crime scene must be viewed as a source of contamination; human blood and other **biological fluids** (wet or dry) may be present.

Of utmost importance is the personal safety of the CSI and other first responders. Aside from the obvious safe arrival at the scene and initial survey to determine that there are no immediate threats to the safety of those first responders, precautions must be followed to minimize the risk of personnel coming into contact with potentially infectious materials. The Occupational Safety and Health Administration (OSHA) requires employers to train employees and supply them with appropriate PPE for the job functions they perform.

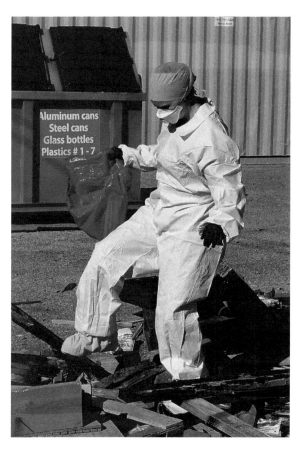

FIGURE 2.2

CSI in personal protective equipment (PPE) Level C.

Bloodborne Pathogens

Bloodborne pathogens are infectious disease-causing microorganisms that may be found or transported in biological fluids. Be sure to treat all human blood and bodily fluids as though they are infectious. Fluids other than blood that may contain pathogens include urine, feces, tears, sweat, nasal secretions, saliva, semen, vaginal secretions, breast milk, and vomitus. The human body contains cerebrospinal fluid as well as synovial (joints), pleural (chest), peritoneal (abdomen), amniotic, and pericardial (heart) fluids that can carry bloodborne pathogens.

The most common bloodborne pathogens are human immunodeficiency virus (HIV/AIDS), hepatitis, rabies, and sexually transmitted diseases (STDs). Barrier protection should be used at all times to prevent skin and mucous membrane contamination with blood or bodily fluids. Barrier protections include disposable gloves, lab coats or coveralls, and eye and face protection. These types of protection are necessary to minimize exposure to occupational hazards. Remember that the use of PPE does not reduce the hazard or guarantee total protection; it is used to minimize the exposure or contact with potentially hazardous materials.

Gloves

You should never wear leather or fabric gloves. Instead, use chemical-resistant (nitrile) gloves (see Figure 2.3). Latex is the next most common type of disposable glove, but many people have (or develop) an allergic reaction to latex products. When gloves are not used, direct contact or absorption can result in the possibility of contamination through the skin of the CSI.

Always wear two pairs of gloves (double-glove technique) to prevent cross-contamination and prevent exposure that could occur from a tear in a single glove. Remove all jewelry prior to putting on gloves. Always wash your hands immediately after removing gloves. Change gloves often to reduce the possibility of cross-contamination. Change them immediately if they become punctured or torn.

Face Protection

Safety goggles or glasses should be used at all times. Consider the use of a face shield during activities that are likely to produce droplets of fluid. A face mask must be used with goggles or safety glasses, as it does not provide adequate protection if used alone.

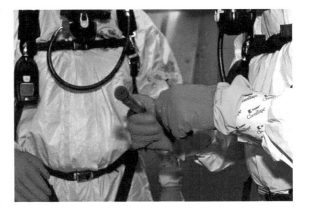

FIGURE 2.3
Gloves are available in various sizes for all types of uses and materials. Make sure the gloves you are wearing are the type you need for maximum protection.

Inhalation is the most common route of exposure for most materials that are health hazards. Airborne contaminants may be dust, aerosol, smoke, vapor, gas, particulates, or fumes. A disposable dust/surgical mask will filter out large particulate matter but does not provide respiratory protection from chemical vapors or biological contaminants. An air-purifying respirator (APR) or self-contained breathing apparatus (SCBA) is required if the CSI is going to work in a potentially contaminated environment. A high-efficiency particulate air (HEPA) filter, combined with activated charcoal, attached to the APR provides additional protection as air is drawn through the filter by the wearer.

Be alert to the possibility of indirect contamination if you touch or rub your face with contaminated gloves.

Protective Clothing

Disposable lab coats or Tyvek coveralls provide important barrier protection for duty uniforms. Most are waterproof, providing protection against biological contamination and limited chemical splash protection. Shoe and hair covers must always be used by the evidence technician at the scene to eliminate the possibility of cross-contamination among various locations.

Remember that if you are wearing contaminated gloves, everything you touch will also become contaminated—cellphones, cameras, pencils, notepads, eyeglasses, and so on. You need to change gloves after removing other items of protective clothing. Plan a system of control, containment, collection, and disposal of all contaminated clothing and/or equipment. Utilize a plan for access and exit control that minimizes contamination of equipment and personnel.

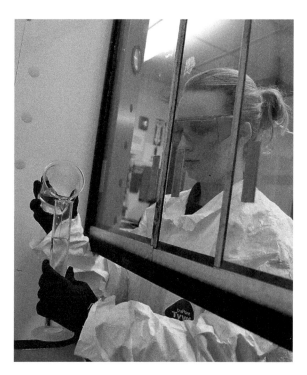

Decontaminate equipment after use with a daily prepared solution of household bleach, soap, and water diluted 1:10, or 70 percent isopropyl alcohol or other appropriate disinfectant.

Light Source Safety

CSIs often utilize state-of-the-art technology, including alternative light sources, and must be aware that it is essential to protect the eyes from direct and indirect exposure. Irreversible eye damage can result from exposure to direct or indirect light, and all personnel in the vicinity of the light source must wear protective eyewear appropriate for the light source (see Figure 2.4). Goggles and laser-protective eyewear must guard against the maximum operating wavelength of the laser source.

FIGURE 2.4
Protective goggles are designed for various tasks. Consider whether you need to protect your eyes from splashes or UV light when selecting PPE equipment.

Toxic Industrial Chemical and Biological Scenes

Investigating a scene contaminated with or involving toxic industrial chemicals (TICs) or biological threat agents (BTAs) is very dangerous (see Figure 2.5). The CSI must exercise caution, good judgment, common sense, and attention to detail. Any mistake may be the last mistake the investigator ever makes. Never taste anything, and never smell anything.

At the scene of a murder or suicide, do not collect pills, powder, or medicine bottles until you are wearing gloves; some substances can be absorbed through the skin. Collect the items, place them in an evidence bag or other suitable container, seal everything to prevent loss or contamination, and transport the package to the laboratory. Be sure to wash your hands after removing your gloves.

If hypodermic syringes are present at a crime scene, do not handle them without gloves. Do not put syringes with exposed needles into any kind of package where the needle could potentially stick through the package (see Figure 2.6). This includes envelopes, plastic bags, and cardboard boxes in particular. Use specially designed sharps containers or puncture-resistant containers to secure needles and other sharp objects.

Check trash and garbage containers, commodes, medicine and other cabinets, and anywhere else a concerned friend or family member might have secreted empty pill bottles, spraycans, or other drug paraphernalia— but, of course, do so only after obtaining a search warrant or valid consent to search. An empty aerosol container in the trash can could be a clue to an accidental or volitional inhalant death.

A victim may choose to or accidentally succumb to pesticides or other readily available (and low-cost) poisons or TICs (hydrogen sulfide). In the form available to the general public, most of these poisons or TICs can be safely handled, provided the required precautions are followed (see Figure 2.7). It is worth saying again, however: Don't taste or smell anything! If you are not sure what chemical is being dealt with, assume the worst. You don't have to eat or inhale these poisons for them to kill you. Some of them can be absorbed directly

through the skin. Wear PPE, obtain assistance from your jurisdiction's hazardous material team, and/or call the local poison control office for proper handling instructions.

FIGURE 2.5
CSIs using Level B PPE to process a crime scene in a potentially toxic environment.

Multiple bodies, including those of pets, squirrels, birds, rats, and so on, indicate a serious and immediate concern. If there is no obvious reason for the deaths (from wounds), there might be a toxic industrial chemical or a BTA present. Natural gas (methane) and carbon monoxide are common problems associated with some suicides. There is also the possibility a terrorist may have released a poison, TIC, or chemical warfare agent (CWA) into the environment. Notify the fire department and the utility company as well as the Hazmat Response Team (HRT). These agencies have proper detection equipment and can mitigate hazards or render the scene safe.

Industrial scenes can be particularly dangerous to the CSI. Tanks, sumps, sewers, and the holds of ships can store or build up lethal quantities of gases, some of which are toxic in their own right and some of which merely displace the oxygen necessary for life. Only trained responders should enter these types of environments wearing the proper safety equipment, which may include a self-contained breathing apparatus (SCBA). If an almond odor is detected, cyanide is a possible TIC that has been released. The odor of rotten eggs (a very good possibility in empty petroleum storage tanks and holds

FIGURE 2.7
Common products can contain caustic materials or poison. Always use the proper PPE.

FIGURE 2.6
Syringes improperly disposed of create hazards for CSIs and others. This recyclable bottle contains several used syringes.

of ships) may indicate hydrogen sulfide. Hydrogen sulfide is more toxic than hydrogen cyanide. Do not enter the area until it has been rendered safe by the HRT.

Every day, law enforcement officers locate clandestine methamphetamine labs, which are extremely hazardous environments. Only specially trained and certified personnel should be involved in such investigations until the harmful chemicals have been removed from the location.

Chemical spills are complicated and dangerous. HRTs have been trained to render these scenes safe and to conduct follow-up investigations. The scene should be secured, and personnel should remain outside the perimeter until the Hazmat team leader authorizes entry.

HazCom: Right to Know

OSHA requires employers to provide hazard communication (HazCom) training and safety information to all workers (OSHA 29 CFR 1910.1200) (see Figure 2.8). Because there are many chemicals involved in processing items of evidence, it is important that CSIs know how to use chemicals properly without creating working conditions that may be hazardous to their health or otherwise create a harmful work environment. Material Safety Data Sheets (MSDSs) must be readily available (either on paper or electronically) in the primary work location for every chemical that presents a physical or health hazard, and proper storage precautions must be followed (see Figure 2.9).

Your employer must (1) develop, implement, and maintain at each workplace a written HazCom program; (2) compile a list of every chemical that is in use with MSDSs on each; and (3) list the methods or procedures the employee will perform that involve the use of the chemicals. Precautionary measures must be included in the HazCom program. Written protocols must be established that ensure that appropriate emergency procedures are in place in the event of an accident.

All chemicals must be properly labeled (in English) with the appropriate hazard warnings affixed to the containers. These labels are known as the Hazardous Materials Identification System (HMIS), and adhere to the following color standards: Blue indicates a health hazard, red indicates flammability, yellow indicates reactivity, and special information (such as what PPE to wear) is provided in the white section. HMIS labels also use a numerical system from 0 (no hazard) to 4 (severe hazard) to indicate the severity of the hazard (see Figure 2.10). These labels must appear on every container of hazardous materials, and if a product or chemical is removed from its original container, the second container must also be labeled with the appropriate information. Always regard any unlabeled container as dangerous.

Approved OSHA threshold limits, including signs and symptoms of exposure and any medical conditions that may be aggravated by use of the chemical, must also be on the containers. If the chemical is listed as a potential carcinogen by either the National Toxicology Program or the Agency for Research on Cancer, this information must be included on the label as well.

Proper emergency and first-aid procedures and the name and contact information of the chemical manufacturer must appear on the container. Chemicals used for processing evidence can create a physical hazard. Examples include combustible liquids, compressed gases, explosives, flammables, unstable mixtures, or water-reactive agents.

There are many routes of exposure, including inhalation, ingestion, skin contact/absorption, and injection. Acute effects occur rapidly as a result of short-term exposure and are of short duration, whereas chronic effects occur from exposure over time and/or of long-term duration. Every employer is required to conduct training for employees with regard to safety and hazardous situations. Every CSI must become familiar with the OSHA guidelines and stay abreast of the annual updates because new chemicals and processes are constantly being added to the list of acceptable practices.

FIGURE 2.8
HazCom placards must be placed in areas where chemicals are used.

FIGURE 2.9
Material Safety Data Sheets (MSDSs) are required to be readily available for every chemical that presents a physical or health hazard.

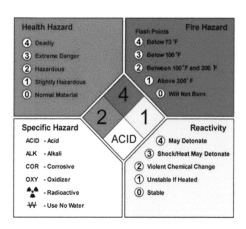

Warning labels affixed to the chemicals, the HazCom procedures provided by your employer, and sufficient information are all available on the Internet, but it is the responsibility of the CSI to take appropriate measures to safeguard individual health and ensure a safe working environment.

Determine what is needed for PPE and ensure that authorized personnel are utilizing PPE before they enter the crime scene. **Biohazard bags** must be available for proper disposal of the PPE after it has been doffed by the exiting scene personnel.

FIGURE 2.10
Numbers are used to convey the physical properties of the chemical. The higher the number, the more serious the threat.

Restricting Access

Immediately restrict all movement of persons at a crime scene to prevent them from altering or destroying physical evidence (see Figure 2.11). Move everyone outside the immediate area and instruct other officers to obtain identification of all suspects, witnesses, bystanders, victims, family members, and friends. Oftentimes the first responders will have established a preliminary perimeter; it is your responsibility to determine whether this perimeter is sufficient or should be adjusted to ensure proper evidence identification and collection.

Ingress

Maintain the integrity of the scene by restricting entry to the primary CSI, the lead detective, and in the case of a death, the medicolegal death investigator, working for the medical examiner or coroner. The preservation and protection of the crime scene are paramount so that

FIGURE 2.11
Always establish barriers to keep the crime scene contained.

physical evidence will not be altered, destroyed, lost, or contaminated. All personnel entering the crime scene must sign in on the log and be instructed they will be required to provide DNA and/or fingerprints as a standard practice.

Egress

Utilize the established entry/exit route to minimize alteration to the crime scene. When footprints are present, it is important to identify prints made by first responders to minimize the need for matching/eliminating known samples later. Every person who exits the crime scene must sign out on the official log maintained by the perimeter security officer.

Unauthorized Personnel

Law enforcement officials and other nonessential personnel should immediately be excluded from the scene. Some agencies require written reports and the issuance of subpoenas to all personnel who enter the crime scene. These policies generally discourage nonessential personnel from seeking to enter the perimeter by ensuring a court appearance to explain why the person crossed the boundary established by the CSI. The most challenging aspect is restricting access to high-ranking police officials who arrive on the scene to "provide assistance and show support for the officers." Remember that rank does not stop scene contamination from occurring. Divert all nonessential personnel to the command post located outside the secure perimeter.

Media representatives will usually be present, and they should be referred to the agency's public information officer or the ranking official present outside the perimeter. CSIs should not be engaged in making public comments because they will be providing testimony in future legal proceedings.

INTERACTING WITH DETECTIVES

Interacting with detectives is an integral part of the CSI's job. Individual agency policies will dictate the chain of command and delineation of duties among the investigation teams. Follow all departmental guidelines for notification of supervisors and call for assistance as appropriate.

Begin a list of all first responders on the scene so that information about scene alteration can be clarified (see Box 2.2). It may also become necessary to obtain elimination and/or standard/reference samples (DNA, fingerprints, footwear, etc.). Proper identification and contact information are essential to the investigator.

BOX 2.2 WHAT SHOULD BE IN A CSI'S NOTES?

- Time and date of notification, type of crime, how notified, by whom
- Time of arrival on the scene, weather conditions, climate, lighting, safeguards, outdoor and indoor temperature
- Fixtures, doors, windows, gates, and their condition (open/shut, locked/unlocked, forced entry, tool marks, etc.)
- Odors and other changing or deteriorating items (wet footprints, melting ice cream)
- Identification and appearance of persons in the crime scene and purpose
- Location and condition of items within the scene (evidence, victims, etc.)
- Items that were moved or changed, by whom, and for what purpose

- Appliances (off–on, hot–cold)
- Personal items—either missing or in place (wallet, keys, shoe)
- Vehicles (engine hot–cold/doors locked–unlocked, ownership, damage, etc.)
- What tasks were performed and who completed those tasks

PERFORMING INITIAL WALKTHROUGH/ PRELIMINARY ASSESSMENT OF THE CRIME SCENE

The general rule of the **initial walkthrough/preliminary assessment** is "Look—but don't touch." The initial walkthrough is the opportunity to determine the nature and extent of the crime scene. The lead detective will utilize the preliminary survey to develop a general theory of the crime and prepare a narrative description of the scene. The perimeter of the crime scene and the entry/exit route used by responders should be discussed with the lead detective. This is also the time for the CSI to create the rough sketch that can be utilized to establish the location of evidence and the order of collection. Photographic and video plans can be established and initiated during the walkthrough, which will assist the detectives and additional crime scene personnel when assignments are made.

A minimal number of personnel should participate in this important stage to prevent activity that could destroy evidence before it is identified. The initial walkthrough is designed to provide an overview of the situation and allow the lead detective, the medicolegal death investigator (MLI), and the CSI to develop a strategic plan for examination and documentation of the entire scene. Under ideal circumstances, the first emergency responder on the scene should accompany the lead detective and CSI on the walkthrough to document any changes that have occurred (e.g., fire suppression or lifesaving efforts of medical personnel).

Note the location of all possible evidence and devise a plan that works from general to specific. The exception to this rule is the identification of transient evidence that must be documented and collected before it disappears or is permanently altered. Environmental factors can adversely affect evidence. In many instances, the degradation or loss of evidence must be prioritized when developing the crime scene evidence collection and processing plan of action. Fragile or perishable evidence must be documented, photographed, and collected immediately.

Crime scene searches must be conducted in an objective, systematic, and methodical manner. Because no two scenes are alike, it is impossible to provide a single checklist to cover all potential scenarios, but the CSI must establish protocols and follow them each and every time a crime scene is processed. Specific agency policies will dictate actual procedures; however, certain fundamental guidelines exist that must be followed to ensure integrity of the evidence.

If adverse weather conditions are imminent, more manpower than would normally be assigned may be required in order to process the scene before weather destroys the evidence. Keep in mind that when dealing with an outdoor scene, the weather can, and frequently does, change during the midst of an investigation. Adequate planning will offset challenges created by conditions that are out of the control of the crime scene team.

Communication among detectives and other crime scene personnel is essential. An organized and systematic plan will eliminate duplication of effort, establish specific duties for each team member, and maximize the results of the crime scene search. It is essential that all information be shared among the team members so that vital physical evidence is not overlooked.

Outside scene searches should always be conducted during daylight if possible to avoid the loss of any physical evidence that might not be seen under adverse lighting conditions. This will not always be possible, however, and your agency must have provisions for acquiring generators and lights that will sufficiently illuminate the crime scene areas. Oftentimes these resources are available through the fire and emergency services units. The CSI should be familiar with the services provided by other emergency responders and how to obtain permission for the use of those resources when necessary. Always identify and establish a secure area that will be used to document, package, and store evidence until it is moved to the CSI office or laboratory. Maintaining the chain of custody and the integrity of the crime scene is of utmost importance. If additional equipment will be needed, designate a separate staging area for the delivery and use of equipment.

IDENTIFYING OTHER RESOURCES

Many types of crime scenes require a team effort to ensure accurate identification, collection, and preservation of all physical evidence. The lead investigator and the CSI should assess the scene and identify additional personnel and forensic needs (see Box 2.3). The perceptions of others will aid in the analysis and planning stages prior to the initiation of the crime scene search.

Specialists, such as bloodstain pattern analysts, entomologists, or engineers, may be needed to provide technical services that are outside the skills of a law enforcement agency. Utilize sources such as local

BOX 2.3 POTENTIAL TEAM MEMBERS

1. **Medical Examiner/Coroner's Medicolegal Death Investigators—** Depending on local and state regulations, these individuals may be required to report to death scenes.
2. **Forensic Anthropologist—**This person can be a valuable resource for identification of skeletal material.
3. **Hazmat Response Team—**Organized teams, usually based within local fire departments, will assume control of situations in which chemical or other containments have been detected.
4. **Cadaver-/Bomb-/Drug-Sniffing Dogs—**Specially trained canines can greatly enhance the crime scene investigation in locating clandestine graves, explosive materials, or caches of drugs.
5. **Additional Evidence Technicians/Equipment—**This includes specialty teams, such as clandestine laboratory investigators, or equipment that is not usually dispatched to crime scenes such as a generator, tents, fans, etc.
6. **Prosecutorial/Legal Resources—**Some jurisdictions require the prosecutor's office to send a representative to specific crime scenes to facilitate processes such as securing additional search warrants.
7. **Dive/Underwater Search Teams—**These teams are particularly useful when searching for missing persons, recovering bodies from vehicles that have sunk to the bottom of bodies of water, or searching for weapons that have been discarded in water.
8. **Aerial Search Team—**In addition to assisting in searches, this crew of specialists is equipped with photographic equipment and video cameras to preserve the crime scene from a wider perspective.
9. **Other Agencies—**Other team members may include local, state, regional, or federal multijurisdictional task forces. Team members have been predetermined as to the types of calls or locations where they will respond. Memos of understanding should be in place among agencies that establish protocols and areas of responsibility prior to incidents occurring. Additional specialized equipment may also be available through agreements with other agencies.

universities, the state crime laboratory, state investigative agencies, or federal agencies to maximize the identification and collection of all physical evidence. Never attempt to gather evidence that you have not been trained to collect; rely on the experts because they are the ones who will be required to testify in future court proceedings.

Prior to beginning the crime scene search, ensure that adequate supplies for evidence collection and packaging are available on site. Protective clothing, lighting, shelter, transportation, equipment, adequate communications, food, water, medical assistance, and security are all considerations that must be addressed to avoid problems after scene processing has begun.

Once the needed resources have been identified, convey this information to the appropriate supervisors and dispatch centers responsible for contacting the team members. In addition, remember to advise the personnel who are securing the entry to the crime scene so they will be expecting additional authorized personnel.

Upon arrival of the additional personnel, assign and record task priorities to the team members. Use copies of your original rough sketch to explain the crime scene processing plan and to brief arriving personnel before they enter the perimeter of the site.

What's There and What's Not There

Crime scene investigation can be straightforward, or it can present challenges that require a multidisciplinary approach to resolve. First responders can be misled, and the scene that appears to be an accidental fire may have, in fact, been staged to cover up additional offenses. Remember that physical evidence does not lie, but hasty conclusions can cause the investigator to miss valuable clues. No item is too insignificant to record. If it catches your attention, document it. Particularly in the instance of arson investigations, additional crimes may be uncovered, ranging from insurance fraud to homicide. The CSI must be diligent and observant and follow standard protocols for every type of scene response.

If a death has occurred, it may be homicide, suicide, natural, accidental, or undetermined. The medical examiner/coroner's office will issue the findings and confirm the cause and manner of death. If the death is suspicious or questionable, it may resemble an accident or natural death and have been staged to mislead the detectives and misdirect the investigation. Does the scene or the evidence appear to be fabricated? Are there items that appear to be purposely hidden? What is missing from the scene that should have been there? Are there unusual items or circumstances out of the ordinary?

When the scene includes the death of a person, it must be processed as if a homicide has occurred. It is up to the medical examiner and the detectives to arrive at the final conclusions. Conduct an objective search for physical evidence and provide all documentation to the detectives. In reality, you may be processing a scene that is an insurance fraud or an attempt to cover up other crimes that have been committed. The case detectives will be able to utilize the information from the crime scene search to assist with the determination of the final classification of the crime.

Family Members

Crime scenes are potential hazardous situations in many aspects. The CSI should always remember that family members, suspects, witnesses, and bystanders may be experiencing tremendous personal anxiety—and reactions are not always predictable. It is important for your safety (as well as that of others on the scene) to be cognizant of potential conflicts and aware that your actions can contribute to the escalation or de-escalation of the situation. Your communication skills may defuse potential conflicts and reduce the need for you to utilize your defensive tactics skills. Again, to ensure safety, the commanding officer should make certain that an appropriate number of officers are on the scene to keep it safe for everyone.

Family members have also tried to prevent the detection of a suicide or embarrassing accidental death by destroying or hiding evidence, such as a note, medicine bottles, a gun, or other physical evidence. It is impossible to predict how the sudden or unexpected death of a loved one may impact family members. They may simply be distraught and attempt to clean up the scene prior to the arrival of the CSI. Family members must be moved to another location outside the primary crime scene as soon as emergency responders arrive on the scene.

Witnesses

Keep witnesses separate and away from others and each other. Obtain valid identification from every witness, and document that identification in your notes. Witnesses should not be allowed to talk to each other because their conversations may lead to distortion of their original observations.

Suspects at the Scene

Suspects may attempt to destroy or remove incriminating evidence at the scene and should never be allowed to return to the crime scene. This may contaminate the scene and will destroy the value of any trace evidence that might be used to link the suspect to the victim and/or the scene.

TAKING THE FINAL STEPS

Brief the detective taking charge of the investigation on completion of your responsibilities as a CSI. Relay all information and observations you have included in your notes. The CSI must always document factual information—not opinions. See if there is any newly developed information that would require additional CSI or investigative services related to the investigation. If so, document and perform the required work. If not, inquire into closing the crime scene.

SEARCHING THE SCENE

Prior to beginning a crime scene search, it is imperative that the detective leading the investigation make the appropriate determination regarding the need to secure a search warrant. Law enforcement officers must have obtained permission from the owner of the property or secured a search warrant to conduct a search for physical evidence that could later be used in criminal proceedings.

The Fourth Amendment of the US Constitution protects against unreasonable searches of homes and seizures of property. To legally search another person's property in the United States, an officer must demonstrate probable cause and provide an accurate description of the place to be searched and the persons or things to be seized. *Probable cause* refers to having a good reason why you believe the evidence is present. It is always best to secure a search warrant. However, there are four exceptions that allow a warrantless search:

1. **Emergency**—The police have reason to believe an emergency exists.
2. **To prevent destruction of evidence**—Evidentiary material may dissipate or be removed before a warrant can be obtained.
3. **Consent**—The suspect, family member, or owner of the property may consent to the search. This consent must be documented.
4. **Pursuant to a lawful arrest**—When an arrest is made, a police officer is allowed to search the person and his or her immediate surroundings.

In 2004, the US Supreme Court expanded the search limits to include the search of a car after a suspect has left it and the search of passengers and the passenger compartment.

Crime scene searches must be conducted in an objective, systematic, and methodical manner. It is impossible to provide a single checklist to cover all potential scenarios because no two scenes are alike. The CSI must follow established protocols each and every time a crime scene is processed. Specific agency policies may dictate actual procedures. However, certain fundamental guidelines exist that must be followed to ensure the integrity of the evidence.

As indicated earlier, if adverse weather conditions are imminent, the investigation may require more manpower than would normally be assigned so that the scene can be processed before weather destroys the evidence. Because the weather can and frequently does change during the midst of the investigation of an outdoor scene, adequate planning can minimize the challenges created by conditions that are out of the investigator's control. A good example is a footprint that needs to be preserved with a cast. The footprint should first be photographed and then covered if it is raining or about to rain. After the rain has stopped, the cast can be made. Casts of footprints and tire prints should be moved to the top of the priority list when determining the order of processing the scene.

Communication among detectives and other crime scene personnel is essential. An organized and systematic plan eliminates duplication of effort, establishes specific duties for each team member, and maximizes the results of the crime scene search. It is essential that all information be shared among the team members so that vital physical evidence is not overlooked. CSIs should be assigned to specific areas for processing, but prior to releasing the scene, they should exchange notes and review the areas that others have searched to ensure that all physical evidence has been located, documented, collected, and preserved.

Outside scene searches should always be conducted during daylight if possible to avoid the loss of any physical evidence that might not be seen under adverse lighting conditions. This will not always be possible, however, and your agency must have provisions for acquiring generators and lights that will sufficiently illuminate the crime scene area. Another important item to carry in your vehicle is a small tent canopy that can provide shade on sunny days and serve as a shelter from inclement weather.

Identify and establish a secure area that will be used to document, package, and store evidence until it is moved to the CSI office. Chain of custody and integrity of the crime scene are of utmost importance. If additional equipment will be needed, designate a separate staging area for the delivery and use of equipment. Avoid contamination of the scene by using only one entry/exit path. One way to clearly mark this path is to place a strip of crime scene tape down to indicate the path for everyone and eliminate the possibility of confusion. Establish an area for personnel to don and doff PPE, equipment, and make sure biohazard bags are available for disposal of these items.

Prior to beginning the crime scene search, assess the need for additional personnel, including forensic specialists. If the investigation team decides to seek other expertise, have the communications center begin the notification process.

It is necessary to prioritize evidence collection by conducting a careful and methodical evaluation of all physical evidence. The proper order for collection and preservation of evidence is as follows:

1. Transient
2. Biological
3. Latent

Focus on easily accessible areas and then proceed to out-of-view areas. Use a systematic search pattern and focus on the most to the least transient. Move from the least to the most intrusive processing methods and continually assess environmental factors. Don't forget to look up. Searchers sometimes fall into the habit of always searching on the ground or down low, and many miss physical evidence that is above eye level. In addition, the investigator should remember that there may be multiple crime scenes, but they will be processed one at a time in a systematic and orderly manner.

Develop an air of curiosity about everything—even the smallest items. A seemingly innocuous item may become the decisive piece of evidence later in the investigation. In addition, don't forget to develop a healthy skepticism. Things often are not what they seem to be. Never accept conditions or appearances without questioning them. Crime scenes are often staged to cover up criminal activities.

You might need to organize groups of searchers depending on the type and location of the crime scene you must search. If so, document each searcher and make assignments to specific teams. If circumstances dictate a variance from standard procedures, document this in your scene notes.

Search Patterns

The crime scene should be searched with a systematic, methodical process to avoid missing any physical evidence or destroying evidence. Generally, search patterns are categorized into the following six types (see Figure 2.12):

FIGURE 2.12

Five of the six types of crime scene search patterns. (The link search technique is not a geometric pattern.)

- **Strip Search**: A good example of this pattern would be mowing a lawn. The lawn mower usually overlaps each strip as it cuts the lawn. The strip search pattern uses straight strips, and the searchers overlap each strip. The strip should be manageable, generally two to four feet in width.

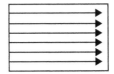
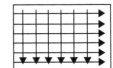

- **Grid Search**: This has also been called the "double-strip method." A grid search is made in one direction, and then it changes to a 90-degree angle and is searched again. This generally uses two searchers, one following one direction and the second following the perpendicular direction. Although time consuming, this type of search allows the same area to be searched twice at different perspectives and with different lighting angles.

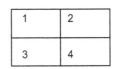

- **Link Search**: This is one of the most common and most productive search patterns. It

is based on the four-way linkage theory and seeks to find associations among the scene, victim, suspect, and physical evidence. Although it is not a geometric pattern, it is not random. Each step is based on findings and observations and by applying logic and the reasonable probability that, based on that particular crime, evidence will likely be located in a particular location.

- **Zone Search:** Better used for indoor searches, such as one room at a time, this method can also be used outdoors if the area to be searched is "zoned off." Zone searches can be prioritized, with each zone being searched twice by different searchers to ensure that no physical evidence is overlooked.
- **Wheel Search:** Also known as the "ray" or "pie" search pattern, using this pattern, crime scene searchers start from a critical point, such as the body, and travel outward along straight lines or rays. This method is usually used only for special situations. It is difficult to use in large searches and has limited application.
- **Spiral Search**: This is an inward or contracting spiral search pattern. Searchers start at the outer boundary and circle the crime scene toward the critical point. The outward method involves starting at the critical point and circling outward. Physical barriers at the scene may present problems. This method is more commonly used for outdoor scenes.

The method of searching the scene will be dictated by the environment, size of the scene, and availability of manpower and resources. Do not forget to examine every aspect of the scene, including ceilings and walls. Physical evidence has been found in unlikely or unusual places. Look inside shoes, under rugs, behind furniture and pictures, on top of curtains, in ceiling tiles, and such for evidence. Look for signs of an attempt to clean the scene by using spackling, fresh paint, or cleaning solutions. For safety's sake, do not search with your hands in areas you cannot see.

Throughout the crime scene search, it is essential to maintain security, both for the safety of those conducting the search and for the integrity of all physical evidence that is located. The lead CSI must ensure that all evidence is properly documented prior to collection in order to verify location, description, and collection techniques. Each piece of evidence must be collected and packaged separately to prevent cross-contamination. Ideally, there will be at least two CSIs assigned to these tasks.

Vehicle Searches

Vehicle searches present their own set of problems, including restricted space, interior, exterior, undercarriage, and location where the vehicle was found (see Figure 2.13). Vehicles should be towed to a secure location for processing. However, you should conduct preliminary searches for evidence (e.g., paint, soil, or other debris such as hair or fibers) that might be dislodged during the trip to the impound area. Do not forget to check for broken headlights or taillights, windows, or mirrors, or other fabric and paint impressions on the exterior of the car. Take samples before you allow the car to be moved from the scene. Process both the interior and exterior for latent fingerprints. The most likely areas are door handles, outside and interior mirrors, windows, and around the trunk lock area. If a car is located outside in cold or wet weather, it should be towed to a secure indoor facility and allowed to warm up or dry before being processed for latent fingerprints. Use tape lifts and fingerprint tape to collect trace evidence such as hairs and fibers from carpeting and seats.

FIGURE 2.13
This vehicle has been involved in a recent impact and also has damage from a previous collision.

RECONSTRUCTING THE CRIME

The primary goal of a crime scene investigation is to reconstruct what happened and identify the perpetrators of the crime. To this end, the CSI should conduct an investigation that will help determine the sequence of events, the identity and movements of victims and perpetrators, and the location of evidence (see Figure 2.14).

Each item of evidence must be identified, documented, collected, and preserved. Remember that as these steps take place, it is possible to uncover additional evidence. Follow the same procedure to first document and then collect the new evidence. Each item must be closed, sealed, marked, and identified on the evidence log and in notes when collected.

FIGURE 2.14
Investigation tools.

Establish and maintain the chain of custody. When the evidence sample is collected, it must be sealed and marked by the CSI. Time, date, location, and the CSI's name or initials must be on the outside of each seal. Individual department policies may dictate additional information, such as an incident or case number.

Obtain control or standard samples in addition to the evidentiary physical evidence. It is important for the CSI to recognize that the crime laboratory will need standard samples for comparison purposes. Soil, vegetation, and insects may be vital for comparison standards to establish the location and age of evidence. If the evidence is not identifiable, it will be analyzed and compared to reference libraries containing reference samples in an effort to determine the origin of the evidence. Consider the need to obtain elimination samples from others who have access to the crime scene. It may be necessary to obtain search warrants prior to obtaining these samples, and this determination should be made by the detective working the case.

Crime scene notes, photographs, and the sketch will provide the best documentation of the crime scene investigation, but none of these techniques is sufficient alone. Everything that has been done in an investigation should be recorded. Scene notes are cumbersome when describing complex spatial relationships such as floor plans; a photograph cannot convey sound, temperature, or smells; and a sketch cannot capture the level of detail of a photograph.

Remember the basics: You have only one chance to process the original crime scene. Do not give up control of the scene until you are certain you have conducted a complete and thorough search. In the case of a homicide investigation or suspicious death, you might need to retain control of the scene until after the autopsy or preliminary forensic testing is complete. Maintain police control over the scene to ensure integrity and prevent the loss of additional evidence that may be needed based on the medical examiner's or pathologist's findings. The chain of custody of evidence and the crime scene must remain intact and unassailable in the courtroom.

Discussion Questions

1. Discuss the big picture that a first responder should keep in mind when arriving on scene.
2. Who should and shouldn't be allowed to enter a crime scene, and what procedures should be used for authorized responders?
3. Although no two crime scenes are exactly alike, discuss the general procedures for the initial assessment of a crime scene.
4. What steps are taken when the CSI and a case detective do the crime scene walkthrough?
5. When prioritizing the search procedures of a crime scene, what is the usual order for collection and preservation of evidence, and what is the importance of each?

CHAPTER 3

Documenting the Crime Scene: Photography, Videography, and Sketching

What You Will Learn

Accurate documentation is critical to preserving the condition of the crime scene. Photographs, sketching, videography, and the CSI's notes are essential tools for the prosecutor who is preparing a case for trial. This chapter uses various types of sketches to demonstrate how physical evidence is graphically depicted, incorporating accurate measurements and digital photography with existing documents for case investigation purposes.

MURDER IN THE NEW YEAR

Documenting the Crime Scene

Ed Ellwenger, the crime scene technician, had already dusted for prints, shot a high-definition video of the crime scene, and took good-quality digital photographs of specific points of interest before Mavis and Tom had arrived. When they arrived, Ed filled them in:

> The new high-intensity flash attachment made all the difference in catching the details, especially outside. There seem to be three different sets of tire tracks. Mrs. Morton's SUV is parked in the garage. One set matches Mr.

DOI: 10.4324/9780429261657-3

Morton's car. The daughter and her husband's car is parked behind his vehicle. There also seems to be another fresh set of tracks although the daughter's vehicle has compromised the image to some extent. We'll also need to check the GPS systems on both their cars.

Mavis, Ed, and Tom quickly devised their crime scene processing plan.

Ed has already photographed the tire tracks and is getting ready to cast an impression with dental stone in the tracks before they are obliterated by the falling snow. Since the tracks are going to soon disappear under the fresh snow, he will process that transient evidence now and then come back inside to complete his work after the cast is made,

Tom explained to Mavis.

"Good thing the snow has just started. A couple of hours of 'White Christmas' and there would be little, if anything, left to cast."

Mavis nodded her head in agreement. "How's your sketch coming along?"

Without taking his eyes off his work, Tom replied, "Just about finished." Meanwhile, a patrol vehicle arrived to take the Johnsons to the police station so that they could give a formal statement and the crime scene could be processed without further contamination.

Ten minutes later, Mavis sat across the kitchen table from Tom, poring over his sketch. "So your measurements and the wound's angle and point of entry indicate to you that the wife was shot at close range."

Tom rubbed the stubble on his chin.

That's right. The husband's demise is somewhat less clear. Although he could have shot his wife and then shot himself, the position of his body and blood trail suggest at least the possibility that he was trying to move … or maybe when he fell, he just rolled into an odd position.

Mavis continued studying the sketch. "Or maybe he was trying to get the phone, which is located on an end table five feet away?"

"Second thoughts, perhaps," Tom replied. "Second thoughts, seconds too late."

Tom stretched. "Of course, there's always another possibility."

Detective Fletcher looked up. "What's that?"

Tom rose from his chair. "Maybe a third person was present."

Mavis looked at her watch. "Perhaps. Once we analyze the third set of tire tracks, we should have a better idea of who that visitor might be."

INTRODUCTION

The first step in the investigation of any alleged criminal activity begins with the crime scene. It is the beginning point for determining what actions have taken place, and yields proof that a crime has been committed. The main purpose of documentation is to record and preserve the location and relationship of physical evidence at all crime scenes. Your efforts will "set the stage" for the prosecutors, defense attorneys, the judge, and the jury when the case enters the courtroom.

The main objectives of a crime scene investigation are to:

1. Reconstruct the incident.
2. Ascertain the sequence of events.
3. Determine the method of operation (*modus operandi*).
4. Disclose the motive.
5. Uncover what property was stolen and from where.
6. Determine what the perpetrator may have done before, during, and after the event.
7. Identify, document, collect, and preserve physical evidence of the crime.

The process of documentation should follow these objectives and help to substantiate them. Documentation will also validate the condition of the crime scene upon your arrival, confirm that proper scene security was established, and ensure the integrity of the physical evidence. While time consuming, this step is critical in your work. It is essential that the identification, collection, and preservation of physical evidence be completed in an unbiased and objective manner. Through the use of photography, **videography**, notes, and sketches, the CSI is able to convey this information to the court and jury in an untainted and unprejudiced manner.

The tools required to properly document the crime scene include:

■ Notepad
■ Clipboard and/or digital tablet device
■ Graph paper
■ Writing instruments (pens, pencils, markers)
■ Still camera with external flash and extra batteries
■ Video camera
■ Tripod
■ Measurement instruments (tape measures, rulers, electronic measuring devices, perspective grids, etc.)
■ Evidence identification and position markers or placards
■ Photographic log
■ Compass

The location of all physical evidence should have been noted during the initial walkthrough (preliminary survey) of the crime scene and a plan formulated to process the area working from general to specific. Detailed notes and descriptions must accompany every item of evidence you identify and collect. Many CSIs and detectives use digital audio recorders to supplement their written notes. These digital files can then be downloaded and transcribed for inclusion in the case files.

As mentioned in Chapter 2, an exception to the general-to-specific rule would be in the case of the identification and preservation of transient evidence. You must document, collect, and preserve evidence that is extremely fragile or subject to be lost or damaged if it is not immediately safeguarded. Examples of transient evidence are hairs and fibers that may blow away, wet shoe prints that may dry and become invisible, chemicals that may evaporate, charred documents, and other perishable materials.

Remember, as a CSI, you are seeking to build a true and accurate representation of the crime scene. Scene notes, photographs, and sketches are crucial to every criminal investigation. Accurately documenting the crime scene means recording the physical characteristics of the scene and the evidence located there and creating a record that provides a truthful and correct depiction for others—whether they are investigators, lawyers, or members of the jury. The first rule in collecting physical evidence is to document the evidence through notes, photographs, measurements, and sketches before the evidence is collected or touched.

PHOTOGRAPHY

Systematic and detailed photographs are essential to ensure that the crime scene is depicted accurately. Moreover, they provide additional details beyond what information is provided in your scene notes. You must maintain a photo log of every shot taken, and if possible, you should have a partner making these log entries while you are photographing the scene. Most high-end DSLR cameras record the camera information (date, time, camera settings, etc.), but you will need to document what each shot depicts on the photo log. Begin taking photographs from the general to the specific in a progressive and orderly manner. You must provide an orientation to the scene and also depict the relationship of the evidence in the crime scene.

Begin taking photographs down the street from the scene, and as you approach the location, continue to take exterior shots including driveways and/or entrances. Nearby buildings should also be photographed to indicate relationships to the primary crime scene. Always take pictures of entries and exits, house numbers, mailboxes with names, balconies or stairwells, and other architectural features. Show all possible approaches to the crime scene, entrance to the scene, all perspectives of the scene, and finally the exit from the crime scene.

Remember to photograph vehicles the same way; show their relationship to other cars, surrounding areas, and structures. Take ground-level photographs—all sides, license plate, VIN, decals/bumper stickers, and other unique identifiers. If photographing vehicles at night, be sure to hold the flash away from the camera and at an angle when photographing license plates to prevent reflective glare from obliterating the plate numbers on the recorded image.

Take overlapping photographs of the overall crime scene. These will provide a 360-degree view of the area. Remember the four compass points: north, south, east, and west. If you take photos from each of these angles, you will be able to provide a full and accurate overview of the scene. For major investigations, aerial photographs should be taken as soon as possible so as to depict a crime scene that has not been altered by weather, time, or other environmental factors. When the crime scene investigation is concluded, it is a good practice to walk back through and take a final photograph of each area to document the condition of the location when you left the scene.

If possible, take photographs in natural light and then add additional oblique lighting or external lighting to highlight pattern or impression evidence. Practice these techniques before you need to use them on the job. After taking several photographs of the evidence undisturbed, add a scale and take more photos. Low-light situations will also require you to use a flash and a tripod to produce photos with enough contrast. You may be required to use the "**painting with light**" technique in dark outdoor scenes (see Box 3.1).

Cameras

There are two basic types of cameras: still cameras and video cameras. The selection of cameras for **crime scene photography** should be made with care. Disposable cameras, cellphone cameras, and

BOX 3.1 HOW TO PAINT WITH LIGHT

1. Two people are generally required for painting with light; one walks around with a flash or strobe unit while the other remains at the camera. The camera is placed on a tripod.
2. With the shutter of the camera set and locked open (T or B setting), the photographer holds his or her hand over the camera lens to keep out stray light. The photographer should be sure not to touch the lens so as to blur the image.
3. The person with the flash or strobe in hand walks to the first position from which a flash would be fired, instructs the photographer to remove his or her hand from the camera lens, and then fires the flash. The person firing the flash should stand as far back behind the flash as his or her arms can stretch to avoid being illuminated in the photograph. The photographer then replaces his or her hand over the lens, being careful not to touch the camera or lens itself.
4. The person with the strobe walks to a new position and repeats the process again and again until the entire area to be photographed has been illuminated. It is best to take numerous photos in this manner to be sure a good photograph is produced. It may take as many as 20 or 30 flashes to capture a large area.
5. When all the flashes have been completed, the photographer releases the shutter lock to close the shutter. One photograph will now have an image with multiple flashes that illuminates the scene (see Figures 3.1 and 3.2).

FIGURE 3.1
A night photograph using a single flash.

FIGURE 3.2
The same scene portrayed in Figure 3.1, but the photograph was taken by using the "painting with light" technique.

consumer-type point-and-shoot cameras should be avoided because they do not have the versatility that professional-grade cameras have. Generally, still cameras should be 35 mm and/or single-lens reflex (SLR) cameras with removable lenses and the ability to make manual adjustments to focus as well as other settings. Still cameras should have the ability to use a flash "off-camera" and have "bulb" or "time" settings for prolonged exposures. This is important for photographing blood treated with luminol and latent fingerprints treated with fluorescent powder, as well as for painting with light techniques. Most DSLR cameras have built-in flashes and "hot shoes" for mounting external flashes. Video cameras should have a zoom lens and the ability to turn off the audio (microphone) manually.

The SLR camera has long been the standard for professionals and for police photography. The camera is lightweight, versatile, and relatively inexpensive. A wide variety of cameras, interchangeable lenses, and accessories are available. DSLR cameras have almost completely replaced the traditional 35-mm film SLR as the camera of choice for police photography. However, due to the ease at which digital images may be manipulated and altered, police agencies should adopt a **standard operating procedure** (SOP) when using digital photography. The SOP should state how original digital images are to be archived and what changes in the image are acceptable (i.e., contrast enhancements, color shifts, filtration, etc.). An SOP will help ensure that the original untouched image that was taken at the crime scene is archived in case any question as to manipulation of the image is raised. Controls should be in place to treat digital images the same way as any other piece of physical evidence.

DSLR cameras are available in varying resolution capabilities measured in megapixels. Most current DSLR cameras are available with 10 to 14 or higher megapixel resolution. If enlargements of greater than 11 × 14 inches are to be made from digital images, the higher the megapixel capability of the camera, the better the enlarged image will appear. Digital images enlarged excessively may result in a **pixilated image**, which looks like blocky squares in the enlarged image.

Most DSLR cameras may be set to record images in JPEG (Joint Photographic Experts Group) or TIFF (Tagged Image File Format). Many DSLR cameras also allow the camera to be set to RAW, where the photographic image has not been compressed, encrypted, or processed in any way. It is generally best to use TIFF or RAW when recording images for police use because these two formats do not compress the original image, thereby preventing the loss of image data. Also, most DSLR cameras will record the date, time, camera settings, and, in many cameras, the GPS location of each image. Using TIFF and RAW settings on the camera will greatly increase the memory requirement for recording images. Also, digital cameras are notorious for using up battery power quickly. The CSI should always carry extra batteries and memory cards to the crime scene.

Video Cameras

Video cameras or camcorders are especially useful in reconstructing events and in placing the scene in perspective. However, certain rules should be followed when using a video camera to record the scene. Camcorders record sound as well as video, and the microphone should be turned off during the recording of a crime scene. It can be disconcerting for a jury to view and hear a video with excessive background noise or police officers behaving inappropriately at the scene. Instead, the photographer should narrate what the jury is seeing while on the witness stand. We have all seen videos that shake and move too quickly from scene to scene. This can also be distracting to a jury. To avoid shaky videos, use a tripod. Use pan motions slowly and begin scenes using a wide-angle perspective. Slowly zoom into specific areas of interest; then slowly zoom back to a wide angle before changing the scene or panning. Some camera tripods have accessory dolly wheels that may be useful for reducing the shaking of the camera when moving from room to room. The choice of a camcorder for crime scene investigations is basically a matter of use and budget. Nearly all digital camcorders are infrared sensitive and can be used with infrared filters. This makes digital camcorders very useful where infrared images may need to be photographed.

External Flash

Most DSLR cameras allow the use of an external flash to be mounted on the camera. External flashes are generally more powerful than the built-in or pop-up flash on DSLR cameras. An external flash also allows the photographer to direct the flash in a particular area in the scene or bounce the flash off a light-colored surface. External flashes may be dedicated to a particular make or model of camera. A dedicated flash allows the flash to "talk" to the camera and provide proper automatic exposure settings.

External flashes are useful in many crime scene photography situations. The flash may be held off-camera at an oblique angle to footprints and tire prints to create shadow to bring out details of the sole prints or treads. An external flash may also be used to illuminate areas in shadow such as a piece of evidence under a car or under a bed. External flashes are also good for close-up photography to illuminate small items of evidence and injuries. Some external flashes, called "ringlights," are circular and fit around the lens of the camera. Ringlights are useful for close-up photography and reduce the amount of shadow that might be created by using a flash.

Lenses and Filters

Lenses for DSLR cameras are interchangeable with the same make of camera so that several lenses may be used on one camera body. Some lenses are wide angle (40 mm or less), and some are telephoto, which may go as high as 1,000 mm or more. Most lenses are of the zoom type, which range from 18 mm to 55 mm, 25 mm to 70 mm, 35 mm to 70 mm, 80 mm to 200 mm, and so on. Normal lenses are in the 50 mm range (48 mm to 52 mm). A normal lens is one that duplicates what the human eye perceives. Lenses selected for crime scene photography should be macro-capable. A macro lens is one that can take a very close photo of an object and remain in focus. This feature is especially desirable in close-up photographs of trace evidence and latent prints. When using the macro mode, the photographer should turn off the automatic focus on the camera and focus the lens manually.

Most DSLR lenses have filter threads on the front of the lens that allow for filters to be screwed in front of the lens. Most photographers place an ultraviolet (UV) or skylight filter on the lens to protect the lens surface from scratches and dirt. However, if you are using an alternate light source or ultraviolet viewer, you should remove the UV or skylight filter before taking photographs with ultraviolet light. These filters are designed to reduce or eliminate UV light from the photographic image. Instead, barrier filters should be used with UV light and alternate light sources. Barrier filters allow the fluorescence to be recorded without the violet color. Camera barrier filters used with alternate light sources are either orange or red and are the same as the goggles worn to observe fluorescence.

A polarizing filter is a useful filter, especially for photographing on shiny surfaces, mirrors, or through glass. Polarizing filters bend the light to reduce glare or "hot spots" on the photograph. Color filters are useful when using black-and-white film or when the digital camera is set on black-and-white mode. Red filters will remove red color and enhance blue color in black-and-white images. Blue or green filters will remove blue or green and enhance red in black-and-white images. Remember, these techniques will work only with black-and-white film or imaging. Shooting in color with a red filter will result in a completely red photograph. Infrared filters may be also useful, especially on DSLR and camcorders because they are infrared sensitive. **Infrared** is generally used to differentiate among dissimilarities in pigments (such as ink) and in recording gunshot residues on clothing.

Post-Processing of Evidence Photographs

It is critical for crime scene photography to be accurate. The photographer should always strive to ensure that aperture, shutter speed, and film speed are in balance to provide a proper exposure. Proper setting of white balance will ensure that the color is correct. A photographer can account for all settings, however, and still come out with photographs that are not as true and accurate a representation of the scene as he or she might like. **Post-processing** is what a photographer does to a photo after it has been taken in order to correct such errors. When properly performed and documented, the post-processing of crime scene photographs is a powerful tool that greatly improves the amount of information a photograph conveys.

Why Post-Process?

Oftentimes, a photographer will take a number of photos that look good when viewed on the digital camera screen but when viewed on larger monitors and prints do not accurately represent how the scene looked. Photographers will post-process to provide the most accurate image possible of what the photographer saw at the scene.

Imagine a well-equipped crime scene photographer taking a picture of a scene under sodium lights. Even an expensive high-end camera may have trouble white-balancing this scene to give true and accurate colors. The photographer could simply take a reading from a color meter (which determines the temperature of the light) and then later adjust the color temperature to this reading in post-processing. This would obviously be a great improvement over the photograph as shot.

Post-Processes

The simplest and most common form of post-processing is orientation. Many photographers do not even recognize changing orientation as a form of post-processing. Changing the orientation does, however, change how the photograph is viewed and how the photograph is interpreted. Close behind orientation is brightness. This simple adjustment allows a photographer to correct for poor lighting (too dim/too bright). The third simple correction is contrast. Contrast affects color saturation and can bring back color to a washed-out, overexposed photograph. These are all gross adjustments equally affecting the entire photograph. Such gross adjustments are often referred to as **global adjustments** because they affect the entire world within the image.

Other more advanced post-processes available include color conversions for contrasting, enlargements/cropping, sharpening/blur reduction, and noise reduction. These processes can be applications of simple digital filters or more advanced processes such as high dynamic range techniques or photo stacking. No legitimate forensic processing technique alters the subject matter of a photograph by addition or removal. Image processing can be thought of as writing a sentence and underlining the important part. While the meaning of the sentence is the same with or without the underlining, it makes the important part easier for the reader to see.

Post-Processing Methodology

When post-processing, as with any other crime scene investigation process, you should follow certain rules:

1. No subject matter should be added to or removed from a photograph. This is an absolute rule, with *no exceptions*.
2. When post-processing, always work on a copy, and protect the original.
3. Always document every step in the post-process. Photoshop has a log that writes directly to the image file any process performed to that file. This feature must always be turned on. Many departments also require written records of any post-processes performed.
4. Always be able to explain the purpose for the post-process. Why did you do it?
5. Be able to explain the process and the effect it has on the photograph (*Frye* hearings).
6. Be able to explain how you learned the process and how much experience you have with it (*Daubert* hearings).

Example: The Photoshop Infrared Filter

In cases of physical injury from an assault, the actual injury may be quite difficult to see. The use of filters can provide much-needed contrast, allowing officers, attorneys, judges, and juries a clearer understanding of the photographed injury. Through a complex algorithm, the visible-light color photograph is converted to a black-and-white near-infrared image. It is important to note that this is not a true infrared photograph, which requires a specially modified camera and will record reflected light from blood beneath the skin, which is not visible at all under normal light. The algorithm used in the near-infrared digital process is absolutely consistent, repeatable, and based in sound scientific theory. This filter will often allow for a better visualization of injuries involving blood in and on the skin (bruising, lacerations, and gunshot residues). Anything visible in the processed image is visible (however faintly) in the original color photograph.

When the digital IR filter is applied, everything red turns dark (see Box 3.2). This allows for areas of redness or bruising to show up in contrast to the surrounding skin. Skin pigmentation (with the exception of very dark pigments) has a limited effect on the contrast effect. The yellow slider can be used to improve contrast in darkly pigmented skin by increasing the percentage of yellow. Contrast can be even further improved by using the red slider to reduce the percentage of red. Photoshop stores slider settings in the history log. Slider settings should always be recorded in any written photographic logs. Side-by-side comparison of original color images and converted near-infrared images will often greatly aid in visualizing the extent of injuries.

BOX 3.2 STEPS TO USING THE IR FILTER IN PHOTOSHOP

1. Open an image. Copy the image and close the original.
2. Click on the "Image" pull-down menu.
3. Go to "Adjustments" and then click on "Black & White."
4. At the top of the Black & White panel, click the down arrow at "Preset."
5. Click on "Infrared." If contrast needs improvement, utilize the yellow and red sliders.
6. Save the new file.

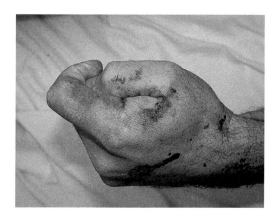

FIGURE 3.3
Photograph of bruising and gunshot residue on hand.

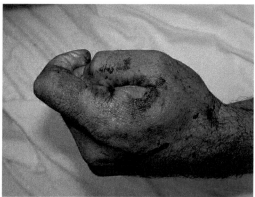

FIGURE 3.4
Photograph after post-processing with an infrared filter in Photoshop.

As shown in the sample images (see Figures 3.3 and 3.4), this technique allows for easier detection and viewing of injuries and gunshot residues. When viewed side by side, the darkened areas in the post-processed photo (Figure 3.4) are visible (albeit faintly) in the color photograph (Figure 3.3). Again, subject matter has not been changed—only ease of viewing that subject matter.

CRIME SCENE SKETCHES

While photographs provide a two-dimensional (2D) image of the crime scene, sketches can be used to compile a three-dimensional (3D) image of the scene. Using sketches not only enhances the investigation but can provide additional perspectives to jurors in the courtroom.

The crime scene sketch is the permanent record of the actual size and distance relationships of the scene and physical evidence. The sketch must correspond and link the photographs and video recordings and provide a graphic depiction of the scene. During the initial crime scene walkthrough, you created a rough sketch that was used to note all evidence as the strategic plan for processing was developed. Now this sketch should be used to record all measurements and accurately show angles and distances between items in the sketch. A sketch is the simplest and most effective way to present distance measurements. The camera position used for crime scene photographs may also be noted on the sketch.

A final sketch is normally prepared for courtroom presentation and may not show all measurements. You need only show what is significant. It should be uncluttered and accurately represent the location of all physical evidence by using a legend as a reference. A **legend** is an explanatory note that shows specific information of interest and/or the definition of symbols used on the sketch or map. Title all sketches using case identifiers and a directional orientation (usually north). If the finished sketch is not drawn to scale, a notation should indicate this information on the sketch. If a sketch is drawn to scale, care must be taken to ensure that all items are in proper perspective. For scale drawings, computer software programs such as SmartDraw or 3D EyeWitness are very useful.

Once it is established that a rough field diagram or sketch needs to be prepared for a crime scene investigation, the CSI selects one of the following four basic types of rough field diagrams to prepare:

- Floor plans
- Elevation plans
- Site plans
- Cross-sectional plans

Every death scene is unique. The issues of each death scene dictate the type of diagram or sketch needed and what methodologies and equipment are needed. These issues include:

- The type of death scene (e.g., a "conventional" or High Consequence Event [HCE])
- The location of the death scene (e.g., inside or outside)
- The scale of the death scene (e.g., small or large)
- The number of fatalities
- And, most important, the capability of the jurisdiction (e.g., availability of trained personnel, equipment, databases, software, and logistics)

Once any of the basic drawings (floor plans, elevation plans, site plans, or cross-sectional plans) are made, multiple copies can be produced and used for a variety of purposes. For example, different types of evidence can be placed on separate copies of the sketch.

Floor Plans

Rough field diagrams or sketches of indoor death scenes are usually referred to as **floor plans**. Floor plans are 2D, bird's-eye views of a room or a series of rooms that make up a floor of a structure or building (see Figure 3.5). These 2D drawings typically depict the walls, doors, windows, furniture, kitchen, bathroom, and HVAC fixtures, as well as decedents and all physical evidence located at the death scene (see Figure 3.6).

Floor plans should not be cluttered with extensive measurements; a separate sketch should be prepared with all the dimensions and measurements of the walls, doors, windows, and fixtures placed on the outside of the walls. Furniture and fixtures should be represented by their geometric shapes, and evidence should be represented by unique evidence numbers. The corresponding measurements for the

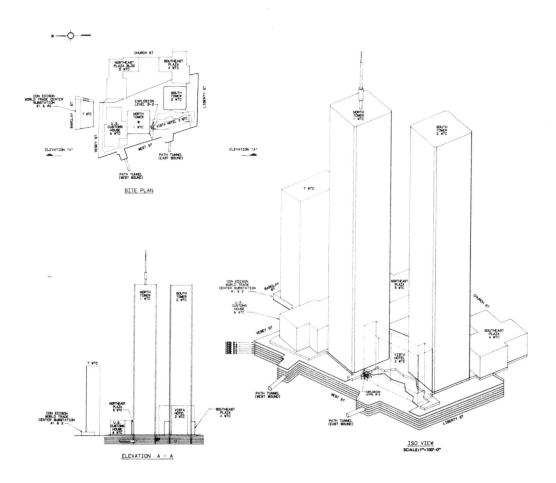

FIGURE 3.5

Types of sketches with the World Trade Center as example. SmartDraw legal software.

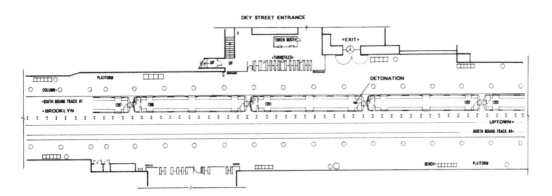

FIGURE 3.6
A floor plan of a subway station.

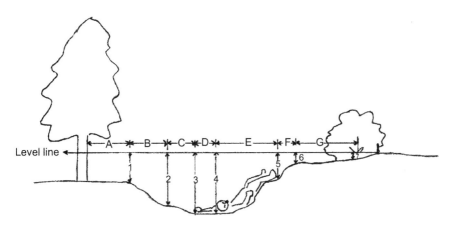

FIGURE 3.7
An elevation sketch.

locations of these items should be included in the written documentation notes and/or an evidence log.

Elevation Plans

Rough field diagrams or sketches called elevation plans can be used for both indoor and outdoor death scenes (see Figure 3.7). **Elevation plans** are 2D, side-view representations of the walls, sides of furniture, cabinetry, and fixtures of an interior scene. For an outdoor scene, elevation plans represent the exterior facades of buildings, the sides of vehicles, and miscellaneous outdoor objects such as mailboxes (see Figure 3.8). Elevation plans can be extremely helpful when you are documenting ballistic damage evidence, ballistic

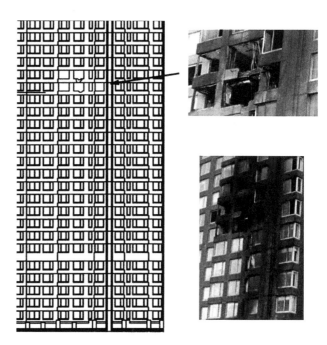

FIGURE 3.8
Elevation plan and photos of plane crash into the side of a skyscraper used for a court presentation.

trajectories, post-blast damage, and blood-spatter evidence. As with floor plans, elevation plans should not be cluttered with measurements. All necessary measurements should be placed to the outside of the sketch, and all items of interest should be illustrated on the sketch, with measurements for their locations on the elevation plan included in the written documentation notes and/or the evidence log (see Figure 3.9).

Site Plans

Rough field diagrams or sketches known as site plans are used for outdoor scenes. **Site plans** are 2D, overhead views of exterior locations (see Figure 3.10). These plans typically illustrate building lines, property lines, curb lines, fence lines, tree lines, public utilities, lighting, streets, roads, highways, bridges, tunnels, rail lines, bodies of water, and, in special cases, topography (or the elevation height contours of the land). Depending on the scope of the crime scene, an outdoor scene can easily overwhelm the CSI. It may be necessary to break large outdoor scenes into sections, making the scenes more manageable for both the CSI and the case detectives. Remember, site plans of most locations can be obtained from many

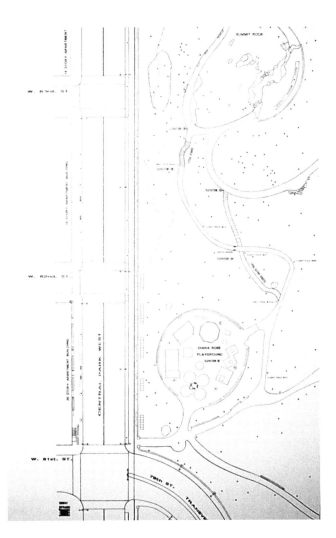

FIGURE 3.9
Example of an overall site plan.

different sources, including the Internet and computer software database packages such as GIS systems. The measurements and dimensions for site plans should follow the guidelines as outlined for floor plans and elevation plans.

Cross-Sectional Plans

The last rough field diagrams or sketches of interest to the CSI are the cross-sectional plans (see Figure 3.11). **Cross-sectional plans** are 2D drawings most easily described as cutaways of the exteriors of elevations.

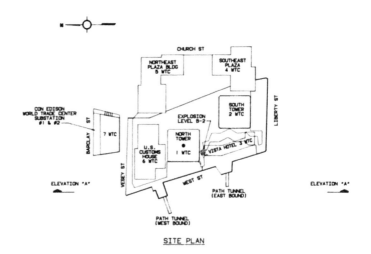

FIGURE 3.10
Site plan for the World Trade Center complex prior to September 11, 2001.

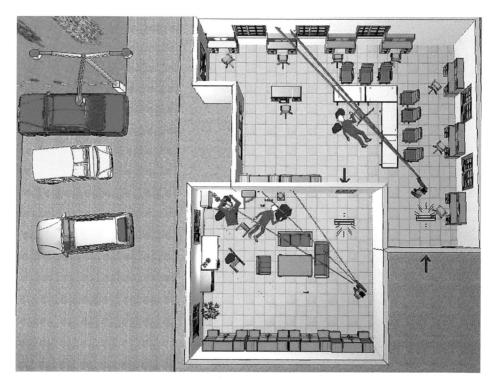

FIGURE 3.11
A 3D sketch of a crime scene created with *3D EyeWitness software*.

These cutaways reveal the interior, floors, and subterranean levels of buildings or structures. Cross-sectional plans are very useful for documenting clandestine burial graves, anthropological digs, post-blast craters, and post-blast damage. Again, the measurements and dimensions for cross-sectional plans should follow the guidelines as previously outlined for the other types of plans.

BLOODSTAIN PATTERNS, BODY POSITIONS, CLOTHING, AND WOUND DIAGRAMS/ SKETCHES

Besides sketches of the scene, the CSI must be able to produce rudimentary diagrams of the following:

- The bloodstain patterns associated with the incident
- The decedent's position or pose
- The decedent's clothing and the location of such items
- Defects to the clothes associated with the decedent's attack, struggle, injuries, or death
- Any other type of forensic evidence
- The location of the decedent's injuries, wounds, and any other forensic evidence associated with them
- The morphology of the decedent's injuries and wounds
- Any other unique identifying features, such as
  - Tattoos
  - Surgical scars
  - Old injuries or wounds
  - Piercings
  - Birthmarks
  - Birth defects

TITLE BLOCKS AND LEGENDS

All diagrams and sketches, regardless of the type of plan, require that some basic information be included on the sketch. This information is usually recorded in the **title block** or legend. The following are some examples of this information:

- The type of plan and the drawing's location (e.g., "Floor Plan of 410 Williams Ave., Apartment 3C")
- The date the sketch was prepared
- The CSI's name and identification information
- The scale used (e.g., 1/5 1'-0"), or an indicator that the sketch is not drawn to scale

- Indicator arrow to show northerly direction
- The evidence legend, if applicable

MEASUREMENTS

Four methods are used to take measurements and locate evidence at the crime scene:

- Triangulation
- Baseline measures
- Polar coordinates
- Perspective grid measurements (photogrammetry)

Triangulation involves measuring the distance from two fixed points to the location of the evidence (the third point). Triangulation measures are recorded on a log and transferred to a sketch upon completion of the measurement process. Triangulation measures are generally made for outdoor scenes where there are no right angles from which to base measurements. For example, if a body is found lying in a field, the investigator should locate two fixed points, such as large trees, fence lines, barns, or outbuildings, to be utilized as the two points and then measure from them to the body (the third point). Generally, at least two triangular measurements should be made to the body, one from the head and one from the feet.

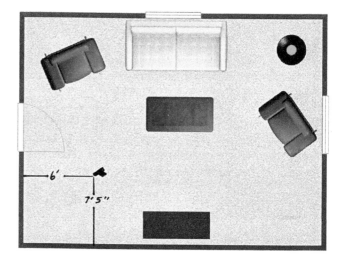

FIGURE 3.12
An illustration of baseline or coordinate measurement.

Baseline measures are the most common form of crime scene measurement and are generally used for indoor crime scenes (see Figure 3.12). Baseline measures require right angles (90 degrees) so that one measurement is made from a fixed point, such as a door or wall to the evidence, and the second measurement is taken from a wall 90 degrees from the first measure to the same point on the evidence.

Using **polar coordinates** is the third method of taking measurements to document the location of evidence at a crime scene. This 2D coordinate system indicates the location of an item by providing the angle and distance from a known point. A transit or compass is necessary to measure the angles. The only practical application of this method is outdoors in large areas, such as for a plane crash or bomb site scene.

The fourth method of measurement is called the **perspective grid** method or photogrammetry. This method involves the use of a 1- to 2-foot square placed in the scene and photographed (see Box 3.3). This allows every item in the photograph to be measured. While not as accurate as tape measurements, by placing the square in the photograph of the scene, rough measurements can be made at a later time if it becomes necessary. Perspective grid measurements do not require 90-degree angles and can be used for outdoor crime scenes or traffic accident scenes as well as indoor scenes. The scene needs to be relatively flat in order for accurate measurements to be made using this method.

BOX 3.3 HOW TO TAKE PERSPECTIVE GRID PHOTOGRAPHS

1. A one- or two-foot square sheet of heavy cardboard or photo mat board is prepared in advance. It should be positioned so that the bottom edge of the grid is along the lower edge of the photographic field of view. The camera may be elevated somewhat to improve the accuracy of the grid measurements.
2. Several photographs may need to be made, overlapping each other, if the entire scene cannot be seen in one photograph.
3. Print the photograph in as large a format as possible—8 3 10 or 11 3 14—to aid in drawing lines. Extend the rear and far edges of the grid to rise beyond the left, right, and top edges of the photograph. Continue drawing lines to these "vanishing points" until the rows of "squares" cover the photograph area to be mapped.
4. Prepare an orthogonal grid map from the photograph. Angular lines represent the camera's angle of view. The sample figures illustrate a one-foot grid (see Figures 3.13–3.15).

FIGURE 3.13
A photograph of a victim with the perspective grid in the photograph.

FIGURE 3.14
A photograph of a crime scene with lines drawn to "vanishing points."

Technological Advances in Measurement

Larger police departments may utilize modern technology, including computer-aided drafting and design (CADD) software, global positioning system (GPS) units, geographic information systems (GIS), total station surveying system (TSSS) units, and laser scanner units. These advanced tools are available to provide precise electronic distance measurements and are useful when it becomes necessary to map a large-scale event.

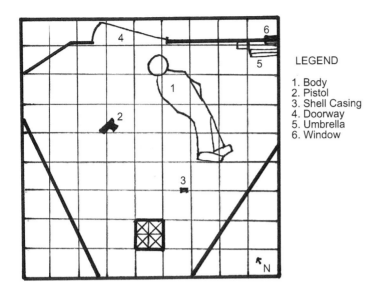

FIGURE 3.15
An orthogonal grid map made from the photograph used in Figures 3.13 and 3.14. Each grid measures one square foot.

CADD Software

CADD software, which was designed for engineers and architects, produces mechanical drawings of products as well as engineering and architectural plans. CADD software has been adapted for crime scene/death scene investigations to produce "to scale" plans of crime scenes and create three-dimensional models of these scenes. A skilled prosecutor will request an integrated presentation containing photographs and videos using available CADD software. These advances in technology can provide jurors with a total multimedia presentation of a death scene and its reconstruction. These 3D models can be animated for crime scene reconstruction purposes, allowing investigators, medical examiners, prosecutors, and juries to view the virtual crime scene from many different perspectives.

GPS Units and Software

GPS units and software utilize the various navigational satellite systems in orbit around the planet to provide locations and directional and tracking information. This technology is usually suitable only for outdoor use, since it requires antenna lines of sight for the satellites to fix the location. By combining the GPS system with the appropriate CADD or mapping software, you can easily produce various types of plans and maps. The systems can plot 3D (latitude, longitude, and elevations of sea level) positions of evidence and

FIGURE 3.16

A TSSS instrument.

other items as well, and this information can then be transferred to sketches, site plans, and maps for preservation of the scene.

GIS Software and Databases

GIS software and databases utilize various technologies to collect, build, and create inventory plans and maps. GIS software can assimilate and analyze plans, maps, and other informational databases, such as crime scene evidence. The data can then be shared with multiple responder agencies to aid in sharing geographic knowledge and managing an incident.

TSSS Units

TSSS units are fully automated surveying systems (see Figure 3.16). TSSS units combine the power of a computer with automated transit/laser surveying information and allow other data, such as GPS information and documentation notes, to be entered into the unit. The system integrates with CADD software and is capable of producing highly accurate and sophisticated crime scene/death scene plans. The TSSS requires that a datum point be located and fixed. It develops highly accurate surveys based on its ability to measure horizontal angles, vertical angles, and slope distances.

The TSSS is similar to an automated version of the manual polar-coordinate plotting system. However, unlike the polar-coordinate system, some available TSSS units require only one person to operate them, whereas others require two. There are also TSSS units that can function in either the one-person or two-person mode. Another benefit of the TSSS over the manual polar-coordinate system is that TSSS does not need to be set up on high ground to obtain elevation information accurately. The accuracy of these units is within millimeters for distances and within 1/1,000 of a degree for angles. Significant drawbacks of the TSSS are the associated high costs of purchase, maintenance, and training required to integrate this technology into a crime scene unit, medical examiner's office, or coroner's office.

Scan Station Laser Scanner Units

A scan station laser scanner unit is a computer-controlled digital camera combined with a 3D laser scanner that can photograph and measure anything in its field of view—360 degrees around the unit, 45 degrees below the unit, 90 degrees above the unit, and out to a distance of 134–150 meters. It uses many of the same technologies utilized in the TSSS, so it is engineering-survey accurate, but it's also fully automated. While the TSSS can measure only one point at a time and requires one to two persons to set up and operate it, a datum point to fix the unit's position in the scene, and extensive training, the scan station laser scanner can be set up by one person can be remotely operated by means of a laptop computer, takes 50,000 3D measurement points a second, doesn't require a datum point to fix its position, and, comparatively speaking, is user friendly.

The scan station laser scanner system integrates with CADD software and is capable of producing highly accurate and detailed 2D and 3D crime scene plans, as well as sophisticated 3D animations (see Figure 3.17). However, a drawback of the scan station laser scanner systems is its initial cost to purchase the units. The CSI should know if a nearby agency has this equipment and whether a trained operator is available through a mutual aid agreement.

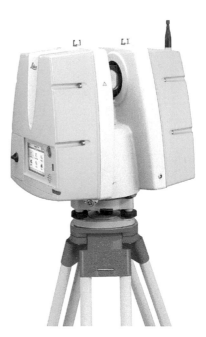

FIGURE 3.17
A scan station 3 laser scanner.

Discussion Questions

1. Discuss the importance of documenting a crime scene. What are the objectives, and what is the importance of each?
2. Discuss the tools needed to document a crime scene properly. What is the importance of each?
3. What are the four basic types of rough field diagrams, and when should each be used?
4. When you are prioritizing the search procedures of a crime scene, what is the usual order for collection and preservation of evidence, and what is the importance of each?

Fingerprints and Palmprints

What You Will Learn

Fingerprints are the world's oldest means of individual identification, and most of the work completed by CSIs hinge on latent fingerprinting and impression evidence. Many processes are available to reveal hidden physical evidence, and this chapter provides a look at those procedures that have been scientifically proven and accepted in court.

MURDER IN THE NEW YEAR

Fingerprints and Latent Prints

Tom Smith looked at his watch and then at his longtime friend and crime scene technician. "Ed, you want me to call out for a pizza? It's almost 9 p.m." Tom knew, like all CSIs, that a good crime scene technician could make you, and an incompetent one could break you.

Ed looked up from the back door entrance. "Yeah, make mine a double pepperoni."

DOI: 10.4324/9780429261657-4

Tom made the call and put his cellphone back into his shirt pocket. "I'll stop and pick them up on the way to the police station."

Ed stood up and rubbed the back of his neck.

> I've bagged Mr. and Mrs. Morton's personal effects; checked out the front, back, and garage door with the ALS, and fingerprinted the victims. I thought for a minute that I had left the postmortem spoon in my other kit, but I found it stashed under the Porelon ink pad.

"Did you check the outside doors for latent prints?" Tom replied.

Ed pulled off his nitrile gloves. "Sure did—about an hour ago. They'll check out the bodies for latent prints at the morgue."

The morgue transportation unit arrived to pick up the bodies of the deceased victims and deliver them to the autopsy suite at the medical examiner's office. When Ed had completed processing the crime scene and retrieved all his equipment, the house was secured, and he left to join the investigators at the police station. Fresh pizza awaited him once he arrived in the detective division.

INTRODUCTION

Fingerprints are an infallible means of establishing identity. Historical research has revealed the use of fingerprints on clay tablets in ancient Babylon. In the 1890s, Sir Francis Galton calculated the possibility of there being more than 64 billion different fingerprints, and yet after millions of individuals have been fingerprinted, no two identical fingerprints have been found.

Friction ridge patterns begin to form during the third month of fetal development and never change until the final disintegration of the body after death except to enlarge during growth or if subjected to disease or mutilation. Identical twins come from the same fertilized egg and have the same genetic makeup and can even have the same type of pattern on corresponding fingers, but they have different fingerprints. While other personal characteristics will change throughout the lifetime, fingerprints never change.

In addition to fingerprints, palmprints, footprints, lip prints, and ear prints are unique to individuals, but fingerprints have been accepted universally as a positive method of identifying individuals. Recent court challenges have sustained the uniqueness of fingerprints as the most infallible source of personal identification. Fingerprint identification is known as **dactyloscopy** and involves comparison of impressions made by friction ridges.

All fingerprints are divided into three classes of general patterns: **loops, whorls**, and **arches.** Sixty to 65 percent of the population sport loops. Only about five percent have arches, and the remaining 30–35 percent have whorls. Within each of these, three general classifications are additional categories (see Figure 4.1). Loops can be

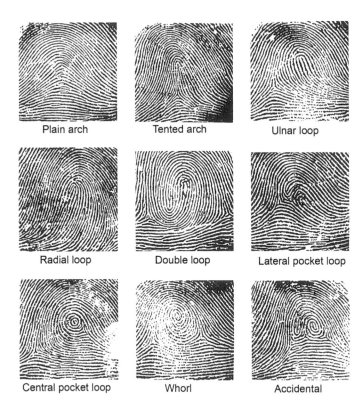

Plain arch   Tented arch   Ulnar loop

Radial loop   Double loop   Lateral pocket loop

Central pocket loop   Whorl   Accidental

FIGURE 4.1

Fingerprint pattern types.

ulna (flowing toward the little finger) or radial (flowing toward the thumb). The forearm has two bones, the ulna and the radial, and the flow of the friction ridges coincides with the location of those bones. The four major whorl classes are plain, central pocket loop, double loop, and accidental. Both loops and whorls have identifying characteristics known as the core and delta. Arches can be plain (a smooth flow of friction ridges) or tented (a spike in the central pattern area).

Once the pattern type and classification have been determined, the friction ridges are examined for **minutiae**—smaller features such as short ridges, splitting ridges (bifurcations), dots, and ending ridges (see Figure 4.2). The uniqueness and arrangement of the minutiae are what fingerprint examiners compare to positively link an individual to fingerprint impressions.

PRINCIPLES OF FINGERPRINTS AND PALMPRINTS

Fingerprints are a reproduction of friction skin ridges found on the palm side of the fingers and thumbs. Similar friction skin is also

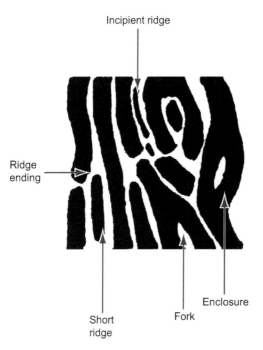

Incipient ridge

Ridge ending

Short ridge

Fork

Enclosure

FIGURE 4.2
Sample minutiae characteristics on a typical fingerprint.

found on the palms and soles of the feet. The epidermis (outer layer of the skin) and the friction skin are composed of hills (ridges) and valleys (grooves). Skin ridges contain pores that are the openings for ducts from the sweat glands (called eccrines), and perspiration is deposited on the surface of the skin. As the finger touches a surface, perspiration and oils are transferred onto that surface, leaving the finger's ridge pattern (fingerprint).

Fingerprint residue includes a composition of both inorganic and organic substances secreted from the eccrine (sweat) glands. Amino acids, proteins, and glucose are present in the fingerprint residue, but it is composed of approximately 99 percent water. Processes for developing latent fingerprints are based on using a chemical compound or applying powders known to react with the various substances in the fingerprint residue.

Many infamous criminals have tried to obliterate all the ridge characteristics on the hands. Undergoing various forms of self-imposed torture, including dipping the fingers into acid and surgically removing the skin from the tips of fingers, failed to permanently remove all the friction ridges from the skin, and identifications by a skilled fingerprint examiner were still possible.

Palmprints are often used to verify identification; however, there is no extensive database for the maintenance of palmprint files. They are not typically gathered when processing individuals arrested for routine criminal charges, and are generally obtained only when major case print files are built on suspects. Major case fingerprint files are extensive files that contain complete **inked impressions** of each finger, the palms, sides of each hand, and completely rolled handprints. An expert fingerprint examiner can complete a "match" based on the same scientific premise of fingerprint classification: that minutiae are uniquely placed and are not duplicated on another individual.

We are most familiar with footprints being taken of newborn babies at hospitals to preserve proper identification; however, because DNA has become such a widely accepted routine practice, infant footprinting is becoming less common. As with palmprints, there is only a small database of footprints on file—usually belonging to arrested individuals who do not have fingerprints (i.e., have no hands).

Ear prints and lip prints are relatively new studies and have not been accepted by the scientific community. Both methodologies follow similar classification techniques using minutiae as print classification. Ongoing studies and attempts to create databases are under way, and although these two biometric measures are not widely used, scientists and researchers in Europe are actively pursuing the potential for future use of these types of impression evidence.

FINGERPRINTS AS PHYSICAL EVIDENCE

There are four common types of fingerprints:

- **Visible**—These prints are usually made when the friction ridges are coated with a substance that is transferred to another surface—such as fingerprint powder.
- **Plastic**—These prints are impressions left in a soft material, such as soap or wax.
- **Latent**—These prints are hidden or invisible to the naked eye.
- **Wet**—These prints are made in liquids, such as blood.

Visible prints generally need no additional processing and are clearly recognizable. Plastic or indentation prints display distinct 3D characteristics and do not require enhancement for visual identification. Both latent and wet prints pose challenges to the CSI, and various techniques must be utilized to ensure proper preservation and collection of the prints. Once fingerprints are located on an item of evidence, they must be photographed without a scale and by placing a scale in subsequent pictures before any other steps are taken to either preserve or process the prints. A scale is necessary for examiners to ensure a 1:1 ratio when comparing photographs to other impressions (see Box 4.1).

INKED IMPRESSIONS

A standard Henry 10-print fingerprint card is used for collecting inked impressions of a subject's fingerprints. Before fingerprinting, a subject must wash and dry the hands completely to remove any contaminants or foreign particles that might prevent accurate ridge

BOX 4.1 *DAUBERT* RULINGS

In 1999, defense attorneys for Byron C. Mitchell challenged the admissibility of fingerprint evidence in *United States v. Byron C. Mitchell*. According to the defendant's attorneys, fingerprints could not be proven to be unique under the *Daubert* guidelines. The judge heard arguments for one-and-a-half days and then issued two rulings: first, that human friction ridges are unique and permanent throughout the area of ridge skin; and second, that human friction ridge skin arrangements are unique and permanent (*United States v. Byron C. Mitchell*, Criminal action no. 96–407, US District Court for the Eastern District of Pennsylvania).

detail from being recorded. Both the officer obtaining the prints and the subject being printed should sign the fingerprint cards.

The top of the card contains 10 squares, and each fingertip is rolled nail to nail in printer's ink or on a Porelon pad and then placed in the proper location on the fingerprint card (see Figure 4.3). The right hand is always fingers 1 and 5, and the left hand is always fingers 6 and 10. To make sure you have obtained all the classifiable friction ridges, the print should extend below the first joint of the fingerprint. Prints must be obtained using properly spread ink, and using a single, smooth rolling action to prevent smudges, shadows, or other inconsistencies that might prevent accurate classification. The delta and core (if present) should be clearly visible in every print. The number one reason for fingerprint card rejection by the **Integrated Automated Fingerprint Identification System** (IAFIS) is the failure of the fingerprint technician to fully roll the bulb of each finger from nail to nail and tip to the first joint. Many people are familiar with placing a finger on an inkless pad and placing it on a check at the bank. This is not a rolled impression, and while an examiner can use it for comparison purposes, it is not the proper procedure when taking fingerprints to be used for submission to a local or state IAFIS.

If the fingerprints are being obtained using a digital-based biometric system, no ink or fingerprint cards are used, but the same techniques must be mastered and used whether using old-fashioned ink

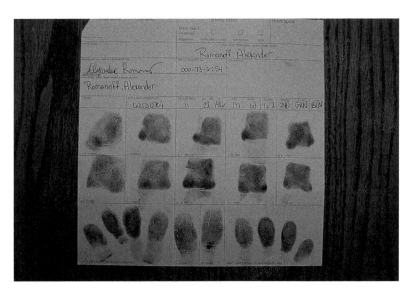

FIGURE 4.3
A standard 10-print fingerprint card.

or the latest technology. Digital processing allows the fingerprint images to be transmitted immediately to the state agency and from there to the FBI for classification and matching. Inked impressions must first be converted to digital images at a local IAFIS workstation prior to being transmitted for matching or classification through IAFIS.

After all 10 fingers are printed individually plain or flat impressions are taken. This involves placing all four fingers of each hand down simultaneously on the bottom of the card and then placing each of the thumb prints in the adjacent blocks (see the bottom of Figure 4.3). **Plain impressions** are used to verify that each individual rolled print has been placed in the proper sequence at the top of the card.

Elimination Prints

A latent finger or palmprint identification is the determination that two corresponding areas of friction skin impressions were made by the same person to the exclusion of all others. Elimination prints are inked fingerprints taken from persons with legitimate access to the crime scene (homeowners, family members, etc.). A fingerprint technician will take fully rolled fingerprints on standard cards that will then be used to eliminate latent prints from case investigation (see Figures 4.4 and 4.5). These fingerprint cards will remain in the case file and are not entered into the database.

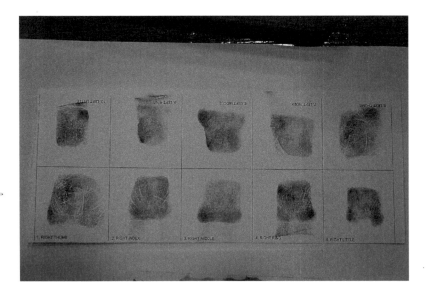

FIGURE 4.4
Elimination fingerprint pad.

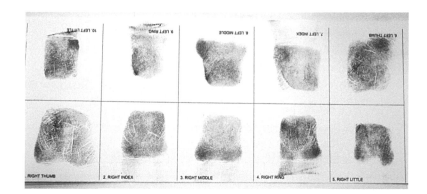

FIGURE 4.5
Rolled fingerprints on elimination card.

Suspect Prints

Fully inked and rolled fingerprint impressions are taken of each suspect for two reasons: first, as a comparison set that will be looked at against any latent fingerprints that were retrieved at the crime scene; and second, if the suspect is charged with a crime, the fingerprint cards are submitted to the state identification agency to establish a criminal history. The state agency will then supply the digital images and the arrest information to the FBI for inclusion on the criminal identification database. Major case prints include taking full palmprint impressions and the sides of each finger and hand and ensuring that all palm surfaces with friction ridges are entered into the subject's criminal history files.

FINGERPRINTING THE DECEASED

Inked fingerprint impressions of the deceased should always be taken and placed in the investigation files. Even if a positive identification of the victim has been obtained, the case file should always contain inked fingerprints that can be used for later confirmation if necessary. In many investigations, these inked impressions will be used to eliminate any prints the victim may have left and reduce the number of latents that must be compared by an examiner.

Deceased victims present unique challenges for the CSI (see the postmortem finger extenders in Figure 4.6). Taking inked fingerprints involves the use of a curved fingerprint card strip holder, often referred to as a "dead man's spoon," to obtain rolled impressions of each finger (see Figure 4.7). The fingerprint card is cut into two strips (one for each hand), and the strip fits into the slots on the spoon. A specially designed spatula fitted with an ink pad (see Figure 4.8) is

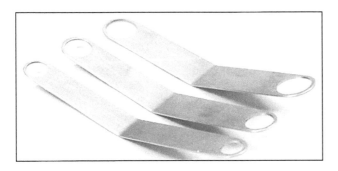

FIGURE 4.6
Postmortem finger extenders.

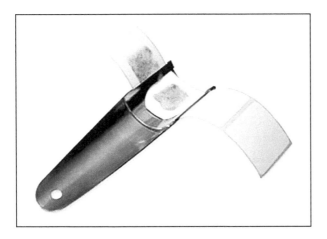

FIGURE 4.7
Postmortem spoon with card inserted.

used to place ink on each digit, and then the finger is pressed into the curved spoon to obtain the impression. The strips are then taped onto a standard fingerprint card that will be scanned and electronically transmitted through IAFIS.

Varying circumstances of death may prevent the CSI from following the standard procedure outlined here. Depending on the condition and location of the body, extra steps may be necessary to obtain fingerprints. For instance, victims who have been submerged in water may have lost their outer skin, and exposure to extreme heat conditions will mummify a body.

Fingertips with badly distorted ridges may need to be injected with tissue builder to obtain classifiable fingerprints. To do this, tie off the digit below the first joint using string or twine and inject fluid with a hypodermic needle under the skin to plump up the flesh. This step

FIGURE 4.8
Postmortem inking pad.

makes it possible to then apply ink and the strip holder to record the fingerprints of the deceased individual. Another method of obtaining classifiable fingerprints is to use boiling water. The method requires that the body, or just the hand, be placed on an examination table capable of evacuating liquids. Next, one of the hands is placed on top of a sponge, palm up, and boiling water is carefully poured onto the friction ridges of the palms and the fingers. This technique has been shown to plump up the flesh and, more important, the friction ridges to allow the fingers and palms to be processed by any number of methodologies (e.g., inked, greased/oiled, transferred to process paper, or dusted directly and lifted).

Frequently the fingers must be removed from the victim and processed at a crime lab to acquire classifiable impressions that can be used to verify identification of the person. In some jurisdictions, the fingers and/or hands must be removed by the medical examiner; however, in many locations, the CSI will collect the fingers, individually label and secure them, and submit them to the FBI or state crime laboratory for processing. As with any other type of body part, the fingers/hands must be packed in ice, and the appropriate labels indicating biological samples must be affixed to the exterior of the packaging. The CSI should arrange for immediate transportation and submission of the fingers/hands to the appropriate crime laboratory.

When human remains are putrefied, the CSI will need to secure the peeled skin or fingertips from the victim. Often it is possible for the CSI to don gloves and then slide the peeled fingertip skin over his or her own gloved finger and ink and roll a classifiable fingerprint.

ESTABLISHING IDENTITY

It is important that individuals have their fingerprints recorded and stored in a safe location. Although the military and many employers retain civilian fingerprint records as a means of identification, millions of people have never created a fingerprint record. Many parents take the precaution of having their young children fingerprinted and then retain these cards in family records in the unlikely event of a catastrophic incident or victimization that would require law enforcement authorities to need fingerprint information.

FIGURE 4.9
Using fingerprint powder to dust for latent prints.

LATENT FINGERPRINTS

Latent fingerprints are created by the deposit of oils and/or perspiration on a surface, and the resulting impressions are generally invisible to the naked eye. CSIs must be trained to make an accurate determination of the proper methodology to process an item for latent prints (see Figures 4.9–4.11). The determination should be based on a number of factors, including the location of the print, type of surface on which the print is found, environmental conditions, portability of the evidence, and availability of equipment. The CSI must also consider whether the type of process selected will interfere with additional forensic analyses that may be necessary. For example, would the investigation be better served by a DNA analysis instead of a fingerprint analysis? Or are both examinations useful and available?

LATENT FINGERPRINTS IN CHILDREN

Children leave very fragile latent fingerprints that will completely dissipate within a very short period of time. This occurs because the residue from a child's fingerprints consists of free fatty acids and is highly volatile. Research has shown that latent fingerprints left by an

FIGURE 4.10
Latent fingerprints developed with magnetic fingerprint powder.

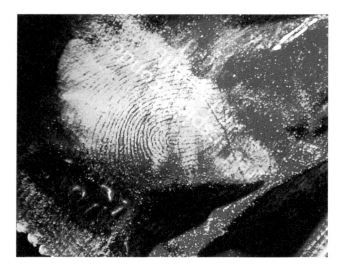

FIGURE 4.11
Latent fingerprint developed with fluorescent powder and photographed using a long-wave ultraviolet lamp.

adult may survive for days and even weeks, whereas fingerprints left by a child under the same conditions may disappear within four to six hours. This is very significant when investigating crimes involving young or prepubescent victims. For example, child kidnappers usually transport their victims in a car or other vehicle. However, when processing a recovered vehicle, the CSI may not find any latent fingerprints indicating the child was ever in the vehicle. The fragile latent fingerprints will vanish if the vehicle is not immediately moved to a cool, shady location for processing. In such cases, it is also extremely important to use minimal fingerprint powder on the suspect vehicle. Because the fingertips of children are so small, it is easy to overprocess a latent print, causing the ridge detail to clog with powder and yield unidentifiable prints. In this instance, the vehicle should be processed for DNA as well as trace evidence including hair and fibers.

DECIDING WHICH METHOD TO USE

The method of processing an item for latent prints and the order of process depends on several variables: the type of surface that is being examined, the location of the surface, and the physical conditions of the crime scene. Enhancement and visualization techniques can be utilized after the prints have been photographed and documented. The experienced CSI will be able to determine the most effective means for seeking additional prints, which ranges from applying fingerprint powder with a brush to a synchronized process of various chemical treatments. Always begin with the least destructive method and follow proper protocols until the best possible image enhancement is achieved. Never attempt to "lift" or preserve a latent fingerprint until it has been photographed.

The development and enhancement of latent fingerprints is accomplished by physical, chemical, and instrumental techniques. Nonporous surfaces (e.g., glass) must be processed differently from porous surfaces (e.g., paper or wood) because of the absorption of various components of the fingerprint residue by porous materials.

Chemicals are used for processing latent prints on porous surfaces because the friction ridge secretions are dissolved into the surfaces, and the chemicals must react with the secretions and not with the surface. Silver nitrate, iodine fuming, and **ninhydrin** are some of the more common chemical processes utilized for enhancing latent fingerprints (see Figures 4.12 and 4.13).

Many of the chemical techniques must be applied in a properly equipped laboratory setting, and most local agencies do not have these facilities. Do not attempt any process unless you have been properly trained and are experienced with the procedure. When requested by the investigating agency, the crime lab will perform all processing and examination techniques that are appropriate.

Any number of minutiae may be present in a single latent print, depending on the quality and size of the print. Fingerprint examiners look for the relationship of the minutiae when comparing latent fingerprints—and only one dissimilarity can exclude a print from

FIGURE 4.12
A partial palmprint developed using the iodine-fuming process.

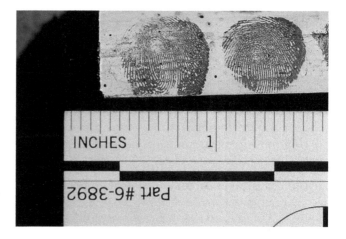

FIGURE 4.13
Latent fingerprints developed using magnetic powder with ABFO scale in photo.

further consideration. The International Association for Identification (IAI) concluded that "no valid basis exists for requiring a predetermined minimum number of friction ridge characters which must be present in two impressions in order to establish positive identification" (IAI Standardization Committee Report 1, 1973).

Locating and Documenting

The most common method of locating latent fingerprints at a crime scene is the use of a high-power light source and oblique illumination of the surfaces being examined.

The **alternate light source (ALS)** is a high-intensity light focused on a crime scene through a fiber optic cable using various filters. The ALS is portable and can be taken to any crime scene (see Figures 4.14 and 4.15). There are various types of forensic light sources, but they all operate on the same principle: organic materials can be made to fluoresce and will be visible through the proper use of filters and safety goggles. Latent fingerprints and bodily fluids are much easier to locate when the scene is searched utilizing one of the various ALS systems available to law enforcement agencies.

It is common today to find a portable ALS unit in the toolkit of most CSIs. These devices work by focusing a specific wavelength of light over an area where latent evidence may be located. Bodily fluids, including saliva, semen, and urine, will fluoresce. More powerful ALS units are employed in the crime laboratory. Using higher watt bulbs and a range of filters, lab analysts can search for evidence through the UV and infrared spectrum.

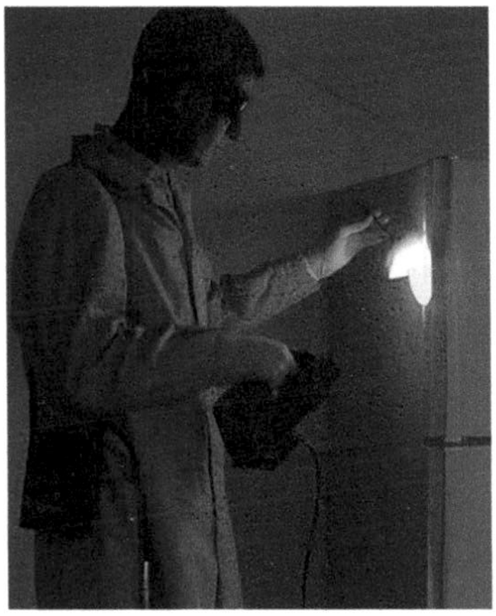

SAFETY TIP

An ALS or forensic light source emits visible and invisible light beams that can cause irreversible eye damage and sometimes skin damage if not properly used. All personnel must wear protective eyewear in the vicinity of the light source.

FIGURE 4.14
Searching the crime scene with a portable alternate light source (ALS).

FIGURE 4.15
Portable ALS units are available in various sizes.

Fingerprint and bodily fluid evidence can be located within the blue/green spectrum. The CSI must always wear protective goggles when searching a crime scene with an ALS. In addition to eye protection, the goggles (usually orange or red) filter out all other colors to aid in detection of physical evidence not visible to the naked eye. To photograph the evidence identified with an ALS, you must place a photographic camera barrier filter on the lens. Use the same color of filter as the color of goggles you are wearing.

The CSI can use intense white light to locate shoeprints, hairs, fibers, or impressions left in dust. Once the latent forensic evidence has been located, the white light can be used to provide the oblique lighting necessary for proper photography of the evidence.

Blood does not fluoresce unless a reagent is applied. When you are searching a crime scene using an ALS, you can detect blood because it appears black under the UV light. This preliminary indication is often used as a presumptive test and indicates the need to apply a reagent for confirmatory purposes. There are several reagents that have been specifically formulated for the detection of blood at a crime scene.

Methods and Techniques of Developing and Collecting Latent Prints

Many chemical processes, dusting powders, and portable, high-intensity light sources are available today to assist CSIs in locating and preserving latent fingerprint evidence. The CSI must consider many variables, however, before processing latent fingerprints at a scene because some of the available processes will not be successful in every venue.

Fingerprint powder is applied with a camel-hair, feather, or fiberglass brush or with magnetic wands. Aerosol fingerprint powders are also now available and can be used effectively with a cardboard containment kit to direct the aerosolized powder to the area where latent prints may be located.

After the application of the powder, the prints are photographed. The now-visible prints are preserved by applying fingerprint tape or a hinge lift over the impression, smoothing out air bubbles, and then lifting the tape with the fingerprint impression adhering to it. The entire piece of tape should be placed onto a blank card for preservation. If a hinge lift is being used, replace the backing on the tape to preserve the latent print. Disposable brushes may be used to eliminate the possibility of cross-contamination of items being processed at the crime scene.

Gray powders are usually used on dark surfaces and black powders on light surfaces to provide the most contrast for examining and photographing prior to prints being lifted and placed on the evidence card. Bichromatic powders are a combination of gray and black powders that can be used on either a light or dark surface to further enhance the contrast between the latent print and the surface on which it is found.

A magnetic-sensitive powder and magnet brush offer an alternative method of processing when the surface would potentially hold traditional fingerprint powder (e.g., when dealing with prints on leather seats or rough plastics). When you use the magnetic wand and powder method, only the powder touches the print, and there is less chance of damaging the latent print.

Fluorescent powders can also be used to develop latent prints when the color of the surface obscures the print. These powders fluoresce under ultraviolet light, which increases the contrast and enhances the ridges of the latent print. Fluorescent powders are generally used on surfaces that do not reveal prints using conventional powders. After processing, the latents are photographed before being lifted and preserved on evidence cards.

Many of the chemical processes used to develop latent fingerprints involve fuming techniques utilizing various chemicals. Again, these are dependent on the type of surface, condition, presence of contaminants, and likely age of the evidence being processed. If an item has been wet, the water-soluble component of the latent print will be missing, and another process must be utilized to detect the presence of latent fingerprints.

Ninhydrin (Ruhemann's purple) is a chemical that is sprayed onto the surface of an item of evidence, causing prints to begin to appear within an hour. However, it can take from a few hours to up to 10 days for weaker prints to emerge. The ninhydrin reacts with amino acids to form a purple-blue–colored print (see Figure 4.16). Ninhydrin's ease of use makes it a popular substance for processing evidence, but other techniques yield much better results. Ninhydrin

FIGURE 4.16
Envelope treated with ninhydrin spray.

is most effective when processing paper items for latent prints. Controlling the temperature and humidity of the processing chamber can speed up print development. It is important to remember that if you are using a series of chemical processes (such as iodine and DFO), you should use ninhydrin last. It is not useful on items that have been (or may have been) wet.

DFO (1,8-diazafluoren-9-one) is a chemical that makes visible latent prints on porous materials by reacting to amino acids. After treatment, the item must be air-dried and then baked. An ALS must then be used to view latent prints. DFO has proven to yield two-and-a-half to three times more latent prints on paper than was previously possible using ninhydrin. The DFO process can be applied before but not after ninhydrin processing. DFO requires the use of a light source, but the resultant prints are much more luminescent at room temperature than those developed with ninhydrin. DFO-treated items will retain a yellow-stained background.

More recent studies have identified **IND** (1,2-indanedione) as a new chemical process that reacts to the amino acids in fingerprint residue and develops more fluorescent images when viewed with an alternate light source. Research indicates that IND develops better and more complete latent prints than ninhydrin, and is much easier and more economical to use. The type of evidence being processed must be considered, however, before selecting IND as the chemical process of choice. It does not work well on recycled products, cardboard, or newspaper.

FIGURE 4.17
Cyanoacrylate portable fuming tent.

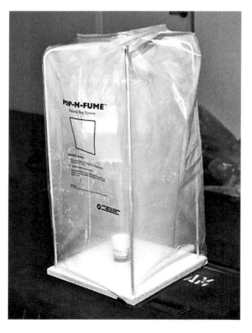

Physical developer is a chemical process that can be used on evidence after iodine or ninhydrin processing has failed to yield latent prints. It is a silver nitrate–based liquid reagent and is very effective for processing items of evidence that may have been wet at one time. The advantage to using physical developer is that it has a tendency to develop older prints and is an excellent reagent for paper bags and currency. Other items that can be processed with physical developer include porous items such as concrete statuary, clay-fired bricks, rubber or latex gloves, both sides of adhesive tape, and unfinished wood. Physical developer is very versatile, but prints that are developed must be preserved through photography.

Processing items of evidence for latent fingerprints using Superglue (cyanoacrylate) can take place at the crime scene or in a controlled laboratory environment (see Figure 4.17). Fumes are a problem, however, and you must allow for adequate ventilation when the chamber is unsealed and fumes are released.

Portable fuming wands are available—or a Superglue fuming tank can be created by using an airtight container (such as an aquarium with a lid), a coffee cup warmer, a piece of aluminum foil, a few drops of Superglue, and a source of humidity. As the fumes from the heated Superglue surround the piece of evidence, they react with amino acids and glucose (components of the fingerprint) and will make the friction ridges appear because a sticky white material forms along them. It may be necessary to enhance these now-visible prints with fingerprint powder or dye stains for photographing and lifting to preserve the evidence.

Iodine crystals placed in a fuming cabinet with the evidence and then heated will reveal latent prints that must be photographed immediately. The prints begin to disappear when the iodine-fuming process ends. There are methods of "fixing" the prints that can cause them to remain visible for several months, but photographs should always be taken immediately to document the original latent prints. Iodine fuming should be used for processing items with a porous surface, but this technique has been found to be insensitive to latent fingerprints that are more than a few days old. Because other chemical processes have emerged since iodine fuming was discovered, its use has diminished during the past few years. Iodine fuming interferes with the ability to subject evidence to other forms of chemical processing and should not be used initially to locate latent fingerprints.

Crime laboratories have established protocols that include the selection and sequencing of chemical processes for latent fingerprints. This list should be included in every local agency's standard operating procedures (SOPs). A good reference is maintained by the Chesapeake Bay Division of the International Association of Identification. This information is available on the association's website under "Chemical Reagents-Selection & Sequencing of Latent Fingerprint Processing Techniques" (www.cbdiai.org/Reagents). It is important to consider the type of material on which suspected latent prints may be found because chemical processes are sometimes more or less effective on specific materials. Also, remember the environment as well as your level of training and experience when it comes to chemical processing of forensic evidence.

Lifting Latent Fingerprints

Once the latent fingerprints have been located, developed, and photographed, it is necessary to collect and preserve them as evidence

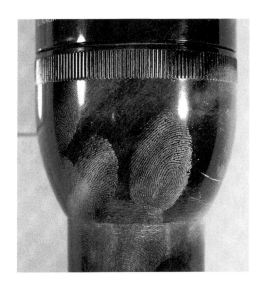

FIGURE 4.18
Latent prints on black
surface developed with
white powder.

(see Figure 4.18). The standard technique involves placing clear adhesive fingerprint tape over the latent print, being cautious not to allow air bubbles to form under the tape as it is applied (see Figure 4.19). The tape lift is then placed on a 3 × 5-inch card with a background that contrasts with the color of the print (e.g., black powder/white card). After you have placed the latent print on the backing card, enter the identifying information on the reverse side of the card answering the who, what, when, and where questions to maintain the chain of custody. Enter the latent prints on the evidence log, and carefully package the cards to prevent damage being done during transport from the crime scene to the evidence storage area. Many agencies now use hinge lifters, which consist of plastic material coated with adhesive similar to tape, and backing material to preserve the latent print.

Other Lifting Methods

Gelatin or rubber lifters are flexible methods of lifting and preserving latent fingerprints, shoe prints, trace evidence, and footwear impressions in dust. Gel lifters are composed of a backing layer, a rubber layer, and a clear cover. They come in various sizes and colors to accommodate the many circumstances you will encounter at the crime scene. Always photograph the print after it has been lifted and

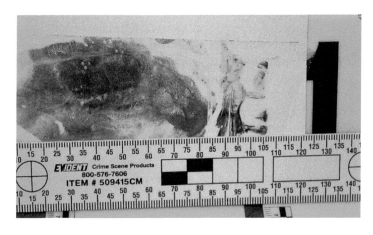

FIGURE 4.19
Latent fingerprint placed on white card using tape lift method. ABFO scale placed in the photograph for reference purposes.

before you place the clear cover over the print. A putty-like casting material is often the best method for lifting and preserving latent finger-prints from curved surfaces such as doorknobs. The putty is mixed with a catalyst that promotes hardening of the material. Latent prints are located and dusted using powders and brushes (see Figure 4.20). After the print has been photographed, the casting material is spread over the latent print and allowed to air dry. When the cast has set, it can be peeled off the object and placed face up on a latent print card. It is then covered with either clear acetate or fingerprint tape to preserve the ridge detail. It can also be scanned into the IAFIS database for comparison.

FIGURE 4.20
Latent prints developed with magnetic powder and lifted with a silicone casting agent. Place clear tape over the prints to preserve the ridge patterns.

Locating latent prints on adhesive tape is possible by using adhesive-side (or sticky-side) powder that is painted on the sticky side of the tape with a brush. The tape is then rinsed with clear water, and the sticky-side powder adheres to the fingerprint residue. This procedure works particularly well on duct tape (see Figure 4.21) and can be repeated until the maximum contrast has been achieved. This type of powder is not recommended for use on dried-out paper tapes or labels, but it can be used after cyanoacrylate (Superglue) fuming has been attempted.

Another substance, **gentian violet**, can also be used to process adhesive tape. However, it is more hazardous to use than other substances because it contains phenol. It is a staining solution that contains

FIGURE 4.21
Latent print developed on sticky side of duct tape using adhesive-side fingerprint powder.

crystal violet dye and produces a purple latent print. Gentian violet is included in this discussion because some tests show latent prints that were not developed with sticky powder may appear with the subsequent application of gentian violet. The reverse has also been found to occur when the first application of gentian violet has failed to reveal latent prints; using sticky-side powder has resulted in revealing fingerprint residue on the tape. Gentian violet is extremely messy and quite toxic but is very effective on fresh latent prints left on adhesive tape. This process is best left to experienced crime laboratory personnel.

Processing Wet or Bloody Fingerprints

It is possible to process wet or greasy items for latent fingerprints using **small particle reagent (SPR)**, which works like a liquid fingerprint powder. SPR contains a powder that is suspended in water and detergent and is sprayed directly on the item to reveal latent fingerprints. An alternate means of processing items is to immerse them in a tray (if you are in a lab environment). The powder adheres to the lipids (fatty substances) in the fingerprint residue, and a gray print will develop. Once the friction ridges are revealed, clear water should be applied on the now-visible print, and then it should be photographed. Gel lifters or tape can be used to lift and preserve the fingerprint after it has dried. SPR is particularly useful for processing vehicles that have been submerged or items that are wet and too large to transport back to the evidence processing area. SPR is especially useful on items that have been soaked in accelerants. It is not very effective on items that have been wet and then allowed to dry.

The preservation of bloody fingerprints usually requires special techniques to enhance and protect this fragile evidence. By definition, these types of prints are not latent because they are visible, but they must be preserved through photography and collection to be used for comparison purposes. Amido black, Coomassie blue, leucocrystal violet (LCV), Crowle's double stain, diaminobenzidine (DAB), luminol, and tetramethylbenzidine (TMB) are the most common enhancement reagents utilized by CSIs for bloody prints. The scientific community has concluded that the use of these products does not interfere with DNA profiling that may be conducted on the evidence at a later date. While these substances are very valuable tools, the user must be trained and experienced in their application. Chemical enhancement requires extensive training in both the mixing and utilization of the products.

Greasy or waxy surfaces present the CSI with the need to enhance friction ridge impressions so that the latent print can be photographed. It is often not possible to lift prints that are found on surfaces that are contaminated with greasy or waxy substances. Sudan black is a dye that stains the lipids (fatty substances) in fingerprint residue. The most effective method for using Sudan black is to dip the evidence into a tray of the chemical and then rinse with clear water. Photograph the latent prints after they have dried. Latex gloves can be processed using Sudan black, but it is not for use on porous or absorbent items. Evidence that has been processed with Superglue fuming can also be treated with Sudan black to enhance the friction ridges for documentation purposes.

Lifting Latent Prints from Skin

FBI research led to the conclusion that the bodies of homicide victims should be examined for latent fingerprints. Ideally, this examination will take place at the morgue prior to any refrigeration of the body in order to locate prints that might be destroyed through the cooling of the skin temperature or by the moisture that naturally occurs through the cooling process. However, latent prints are very fragile and easily lost or damaged by friction, moisture, or cross-contamination by liquids (water, urine, blood, or other bodily fluids). Any of these problems can occur to a body placed in a body bag for transport to a morgue. In some instances, the examination should take place in the field to prevent the potential loss of critical physical evidence.

The body should be at room temperature for maximum success, but it is possible to locate latent prints after refrigeration. To do so, allow all condensation that has occurred on the body to evaporate before attempting the fuming process. Frost-free refrigeration is best for preserving latent fingerprints on skin because it keeps the sebaceous oils of the latents from melting on the victim's skin.

For deceased bodies suspected of having latent fingerprints on the skin, first examine the suspected area with white light at various oblique angles and document in written notes and with photographs. Follow with an ALS examination, using various wavelengths. Contusions (bruising) under the skin, perhaps caused by an attacker grabbing a limb or choking a victim, may not be visible on the skin until sometime later, but may be made visible under ALS.

The results of the examination will be documented in the same manner as the white light examination, but the photography will require filters for the lens.

Superglue fuming has been found to be the most effective means of processing a body for latent fingerprints, followed by the application of fingerprint powders to enhance the ridge detail. As noted earlier, portable Superglue fuming devices are available that can be taken to the morgue to process the body of the victim. Several devices are available for application of this technology, including the **CBC (cyanoacrylate**

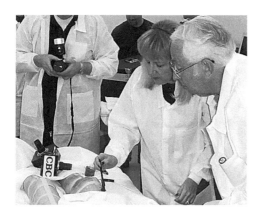

FIGURE 4.22
Latent fingerprints being lifted from a dead body using the cyanoacrylate blowing contraption (CBC), as Arthur Bohanan (right), inventor of the CBC, looks on.

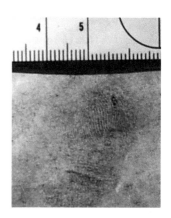

FIGURE 4.23
Latent prints from a living person developed by cyanoacrylate.

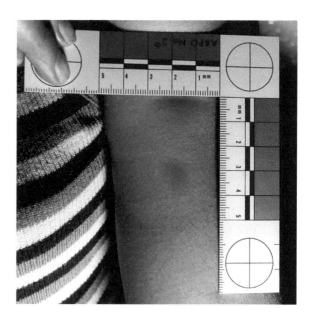

FIGURE 4.24
Latent fingerprint developed on victim's forearm using fingerprint powder and cash register tape method described in the text.

blowing contraption), the first patented Superglue fuming applicator that is portable and generates sufficient fumes to reveal latent fingerprints on a deceased individual (see Figures 4.22 and 4.23).

An alternative way to process skin for latent prints is using cash register paper tape, a standard pencil, and black magna powder (see Figure 4.24). Do not use glossy, heat transfer, or recycled paper tape for this method. Wearing clean latex or nitrile gloves, remove the paper tape from its packing, unwinding several rotations of the paper. Tear off and discard this paper so that you will be working with uncontaminated paper tape. Place a pencil through the center core of the cash register tape. Holding the pencil on both sides, gently push the roll onto the skin of the victim, several inches away from the suspected latent fingerprint. Have a gloved assistant hold down the loose end of the cash register tape; then, while applying even pressure to the tape, roll the tape over the suspected fingerprint and a few inches past. Tear the tape off at the roll. Turn over the tape to expose the side of the tape that was in contact with the victim's skin. Place the tape down on a clean, dry, flat work surface and process the paper with the black magna powder.

If a latent fingerprint is developed, take photographs and document; then package it in a manner that will safeguard the latent. For example, you could tape it to the inside of a cardboard box for transport to the lab.

Remember the print is a negative image and must be photographed and corrected before it is entered in the IAFIS. This method works well for live victims of sex crimes, assaults, and other crimes in which the victim's skin was touched or grabbed by an ungloved assailant. Hospital or other personnel who are working with the victim should be reminded not to touch or wash the areas the suspect may have touched. It is important to process the skin of these victims as soon as possible because a live victim's core body temperature remains at about 98.6°F, which may cause the sebaceous oils of the suspect's fingerprint to melt so the latent print would be lost.

IAFIS and Latent Print Examinations

For more than 100 years, the Henry 10-print classification system was the sole means for classifying and filing fingerprint cards. Early in the 1970s, computer technology advanced to the point that it became possible to scan fingerprint cards and then allow computers to do the searching and develop a list of potential hits. Human intervention is still required to verify the match, but this computerized function has greatly improved the usefulness of fingerprint searches.

The IAFIS converts the images of a fingerprint into digital minutiae and records the relative position and orientation of the minutiae. The search algorithm is so advanced that it is possible to make thousands of fingerprint comparisons in a second. A list of prints with the closest correlations to the scanned image is presented to the fingerprint expert, who makes the final verification of the match. Although television shows regularly display automated searches with confirmed hits being produced by a computer with no human intervention, this is simply Hollywood at its finest.

IAFIS databases are utilized to classify and store the 10-print card images and also for searching unidentified latent fingerprints against the known database. For an identification to occur, the 10-print card has to be present in the database. There is a lack of consistency among the states as to types of crimes that get entered into the IAFIS records; however, more than 18,000 agencies voluntarily contribute fingerprints to the IAFIS database.

The IAFIS is maintained by the FBI. It allows a latent print examiner to search unknown latent impressions and can provide valuable investigative leads to detectives in adjoining states or across the nation. More than 73 million sets of fingerprints are maintained in the system's criminal file, which is the largest database in the world. Responses can be generated within 27 minutes if the fingerprints are submitted electronically to the system, which has been operational since 1999. Again, while the search and comparison can be automated, a human must still verify the match between the two prints and be qualified to testify in court as to the veracity of the identification.

There are also more than 34 million sets of civilian fingerprints in the IAFIS. Mainly these prints are provided by the military and government agencies of their employees. The FBI has also entered information on 73,000 known and suspected terrorists. Not only fingerprints are stored in the IAFIS, but also criminal history files; mug shots; photos of scars or tattoos; and physical characteristics including height, weight, aliases, and eye and hair color information are available from the database.

Annually, more than 50 million submissions are received by the IAFIS, with an average volume of 159,000 per day.

Discussion Questions

1. Discuss the classes of general patterns of fingerprints. What are their differences, and how do they relate to the general population?
2. Discuss the different types of fingerprints. What are the challenges of each? What are the different procedures used for each, especially if they are to be used in a court of law?
3. Discuss the method(s) used to locate fingerprints. What are the different procedures used for each method? If more than one method can be used, which method should be tried first? Why?
4. Why is it important to learn techniques for lifting latent fingerprints from the skin of live or deceased victims?

REFERENCE

United States v. Byron C. Mitchell, Criminal action no. 96–407, U.S. District Court for the Eastern District of Pennsylvania.

Trace and Impression Evidence

What You Will Learn

Impression evidence includes shoes, bites, tools, and any other instrument that leaves a depression or mark in a softer surface. Many times, you need to utilize a casting agent to preserve impression evidence, and these techniques are included in this chapter.

MURDER IN THE NEW YEAR

Trace and Impression Evidence

Ed Ellwenger was in the CSI Unit unpacking the physical evidence secured from the Morton's house. He was replacing filters in the evidence vacuum for his next assignment. "Tom, I can't believe you found a federal grant that paid for the new evidence vacuum. We haven't had a single problem with cross-contamination since we got it."

Tom poured a cup of freshly brewed coffee and smiled.

> Wish I could take credit, but the truth is Professor Edwards over at the college did us the favor. He had enough left in his forensics budget to buy the vacuum and loan it to us on more or less a permanent basis.

DOI: 10.4324/9780429261657-5

Detective Mavis Fletcher shut the front door behind her and pointed at a table outside the offices. There was a box of fresh donuts with steam still rising from them and a container of coffee awaiting the team once the physical evidence was turned over to the property unit.

"Detective, donuts in the morning is one thing, but donuts at night is quite another. What's the occasion?"

Mavis Fletcher looked at the empty pizza boxes still sitting on the counter outside the door as she took off her coat. "Gentlemen, it's almost 11 p.m. There's no better dessert for a late-night pizza than a chocolate-covered donut from Mel's Donut Shop. Consider the donuts your reward for working overtime. Any new developments?" The trio exited the CSI office area and sat down in the hallway.

Ed took a donut from the box. "We had enough dental stone to get a pretty good impression of the partial tire track from what looks to be a possible third vehicle."

Tom popped the rest of his donut into his mouth.

> We also noticed two broken fingernails on Mr. Morton's right hand, so we scraped under the fingernails and swabbed the hands for a DNA sample— just in case there was a third party involved who may have struggled with Mr. Morton.

Mavis looked at Tom with something between a grimace and a grin. "Tom Smith, didn't your mother teach you not to talk with food in your mouth?"

Tom licked a sliver of chocolate icing off his forefinger. "She did her best, but as you can see, that particular lesson didn't take."

INTRODUCTION

Edmond Locard is credited with recognizing the theory of exchange. He stated very accurately that every contact leaves a trace. Also referred to as **Locard's theory of exchange**, the concept supports the following three statements:

1. Traces of the victim and the scene will be carried away by the perpetrator.
2. Traces of the perpetrator will remain on the victim, and the victim may leave traces of himself or herself on the perpetrator.
3. Traces of the perpetrator will be left at the scene.

Any item *can* and *may* be physical evidence that a crime has occurred. **Trace evidence** can provide valuable leads for investigators, but first it must be recognized as evidence by the CSI. Even if the trace evidence cannot be positively identified as having originated from a sole source to the exclusion of all others, it can still corroborate other types of evidence and create linkages between the suspect to the crime or to the victim, to a specific item, or link the victim to the scene.

It is essential for the CSI to realize the significance of trace evidence even though it may not be linked to the crime until late in the investigation. Any item with a unique surface can be examined and compared for individual characteristics. Impressions left in or on a surface can be used to corroborate or disprove statements, including actions, inactions, and movements of the victim and/or the suspect. In some instances, trace evidence may establish time frames and the sequence of events that took place in the crime scene.

Scientists and lab analysts are always working to develop new tools and techniques that will enhance the visualization of trace evidence; however, the skill and observation practices of the CSI lead to the location of trace evidence. For an informative PowerPoint slide presentation on trace evidence (hairs and fibers), visit the following link to view a workshop presented by Kornelia Nehse, Forensic Science Institute, LKA Berlin, Germany at the 2011 Trace Evidence Symposium in Kansas City: http://projects.nfstc.org/trace/2011/presentations/Nehse-Fibre-Transfer1.pdf.

Always document the location of any trace or impression evidence as it is identified during the crime scene search. Photographs are permanent and admissible in the courtroom if you have correctly identified every picture on the photo log. Be sure to take photographs both with and without ABFO scales to present an accurate depiction of the condition or position of the evidence when identified at the crime scene. An **ABFO scale** is a photographic scale designed by the American Board of Forensic Odontology that is used to ensure accurate depiction of injuries and other items of physical evidence (see Figure 5.1).

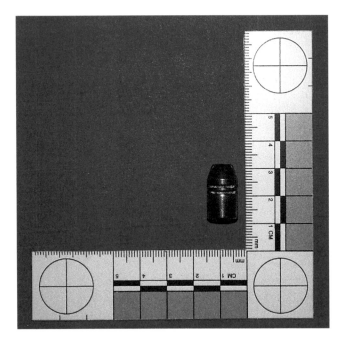

FIGURE 5.1
An ABFO scale next to a bullet cartridge.

Complete your documentation of the location of the evidence on the sketch and in your written notes.

The chain of custody must be maintained throughout every step of the crime scene and evidence processing work. The presence or absence of evidence may be crucial in proving the sequence of events or in creating the linkage among the suspect, victim, and the crime scene.

The CSI should collect **control or blank samples** (also referred to as *comparison samples*) of all physical materials gathered as potential forensic evidence. A **standard or reference sample** is retrieved from a verifiable source or location and must be submitted for comparison against unknown or suspect materials. For example, when processing an outdoor crime scene where soil samples are being collected, you should also collect enough samples to allow for comparison of evidence that may be identified later in the investigation.

Often it is advisable to take **elimination samples** from individuals who have had legal access to a crime scene to be used as a comparison with evidence collected from the scene.

TRACE EVIDENCE

Hairs and Fibers

Scientific advances in crime laboratory analysis techniques have greatly increased the value of hairs and fibers to the crime scene investigation (see Figure 5.2). Microscopic examinations, coupled

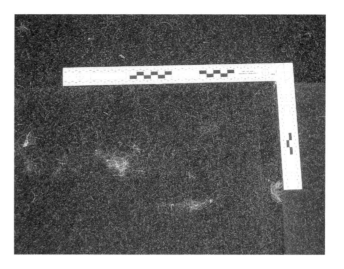

FIGURE 5.2
Trace evidence hairs.

with DNA analysis, can positively link human hairs to the originating individual (see Figure 5.3). Human head hair and pubic hair have unique properties that allow for comparison even if there is not enough skin cell material attached for standard DNA analysis. Mitochondrial DNA (mtDNA) analysis is advancing the capabilities of the crime laboratory, however, and some DNA profiles have been generated from hair samples that did not contain root material. Even if DNA analysis is not possible, human hairs can reveal race, portion of the body from which the hair originated, and color of the hair. The age of the donor cannot be determined using currently available technology. Some analysis can reveal whether drugs have been used and over what time span, which can become important factors in an investigation. Other analyses may be able to determine whether the hair was forcibly removed.

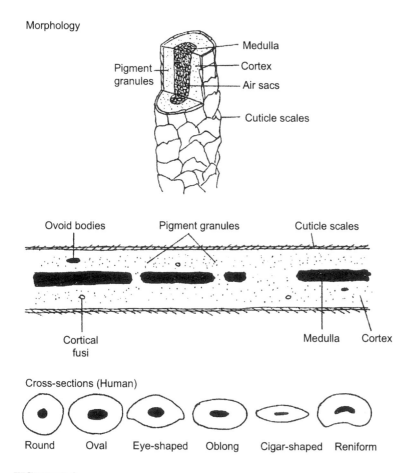

FIGURE 5.3
Diagram of human hair morphology.

Arm and leg hairs and hairs from other parts of the body do not exhibit enough characteristics for comparison purposes (see Figures 5.4 and 5.5). When gathering control samples for the laboratory, you should collect 50 full-length hairs from various locations on the head, and two dozen pubic hairs to ensure that the analyst has adequate samples for comparison. Head hairs should not be cut; they should be pulled. The pubic area must be combed first to gather any loose or transient evidence before samples are pulled for comparison.

It is not difficult for a scientist to differentiate between human and animal hairs (see Figure 5.6). Analysis of animal hairs will identify the species of the animal (see Figure 5.7), but again these results provide information that could be useful in developing linkages among the suspect, crime scene, and victim or in corroborating or refuting a victim or suspect's statements to investigators.

Cross-transference of fibers can occur in virtually every crime scene, from a hit-and-run to a burglary attempt. The transfer of fibers occurs every time a person sits on a couch or a car seat. Direct contacts between two surfaces create fiber transfer. Consider where a perpetrator came into contact with a victim and search for fibers. Use an alternate light source (ALS) to assist in locating trace evidence, and photograph in place before collecting the hairs or fibers.

There are two broad groups of fibers: man-made and natural. Natural fibers are derived from animals. They include wool (from sheep), mohair and cashmere (from goats), and fur (from rabbits, mink,

FIGURE 5.4
Close-up of an arm hair. The fragmented medulla is visible in the shaft of the hair.

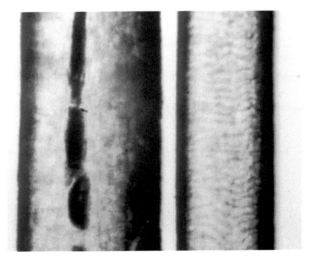

FIGURE 5.5
Close-up of a human head hair and arm hair from one individual.

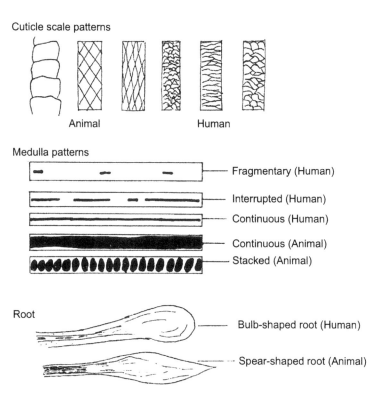

Cuticle scale patterns

Animal   Human

Medulla patterns

—— Fragmentary (Human)

—— Interrupted (Human)

—— Continuous (Human)

—— Continuous (Animal)

—— Stacked (Animal)

Root

—— Bulb-shaped root (Human)

—— Spear-shaped root (Animal)

FIGURE 5.6
Differences between human hair and animal hair.

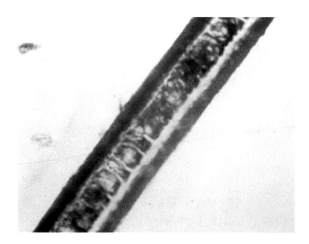

FIGURE 5.7
Close-up of a cat hair.

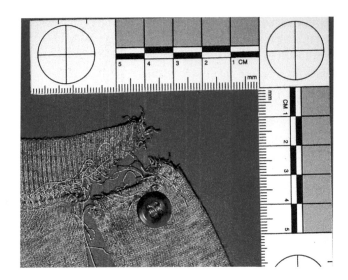

FIGURE 5.8
Torn piece of shirt fabric matched against the shirt.

beaver, etc.). The most prevalent plant fiber is cotton. The wide use of undyed white cotton fibers in clothing has made its evidentiary value almost meaningless, but because the CSI has no way of measuring the value of individual evidence, he or she should collect all fibers found at a crime scene. Currently, there is no scientifically accepted analysis that can definitively match a fiber strand to a garment unless torn edges can be matched, but researchers are working to develop these individualizations.

Man-made fibers include rayon and nylon; they are more often referred to as synthetics. The evidentiary value of fibers is related to the laboratory's ability to trace the origin of the fibers. The best possible circumstance is to match the torn edges of cloth together (see Figure 5.8). The evidence then becomes individual evidence instead of class evidence, the latter being all that most fiber comparisons can provide. Fiber evidence may not be visible to the naked eye, and alternate light sources should be used at the scene to identify potential locations of this type of trace evidence (see Figure 5.9).

FIGURE 5.9
Comparison microscope photos of fiber found at the scene (left) and fiber from suspect's clothing (right).

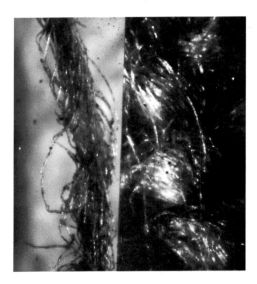

Preserve fiber evidence by inserting sheets of paper between the layers and on top of clothing to avoid cross-contamination. Loosely fold or roll the suspected surfaces where the fibers are located inward; then secure and seal in paper bags. Do not combine pieces of evidence. If you are submitting a rug or piece of carpet, use large sheets of paper on the surface to protect it before carefully folding or rolling the item. If you think a body may have been wrapped in a blanket or carpet, use adhesive lifts on exposed areas of the body to try to locate fibers (or hairs). If you have a single fiber that you are afraid may be lost in transit (see Figure 5.10), carefully remove it with tape and place it in a piece of paper that is then folded using a "druggist fold" (see Table 5.1), secured and sealed inside another container.

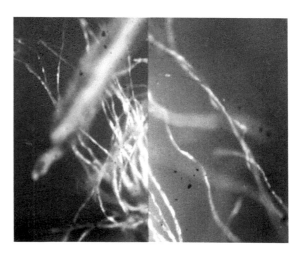

FIGURE 5.10
Comparison microscope photos of nylon fibers.

Glass, Soil, Paint, and Other Materials
Glass

Most of the time, glass gathered as evidence at the crime scene is too fragmented to provide positive identification. However, the presence of glass within the crime scene may later tie the suspect to the scene if the same fragments are found, for example, in the vehicle of the suspect or embedded in his or her clothing or body (see Figure 5.11). Glass fragment examination generally yields only class characteristics—not individual characteristics. Fracture patterns may be reproduced if sufficient glass is recovered to allow the analyst to reconstruct a section of glass (e.g., a headlight) from a hit-and-run suspect vehicle. Many times the imprint of a headlight can be found on the body of a pedestrian struck and killed by an unidentified vehicle. Glass fragments are usually embedded in the body of these victims and must be recovered by the medical examiner during the autopsy. While you may not have a suspect vehicle identified, these pieces of trace evidence may later provide the missing link between the victim and the vehicle.

It is not always possible to collect enough glass to enable a reconstruction of broken fragments. However, adequate sample collection may provide the possibility for the forensic scientist to individualize the fragments to a common source. This is important in hit-and-run cases or burglary investigations. It is important to place the suspect at the scene of a crime—whether he or she is a small-time burglar or a hit-and-run assailant. Control samples are also important because the investigator is trying to establish linkages among the vehicle, crime scene, and victim.

Table 5.1 The Steps to Complete a Druggist Fold

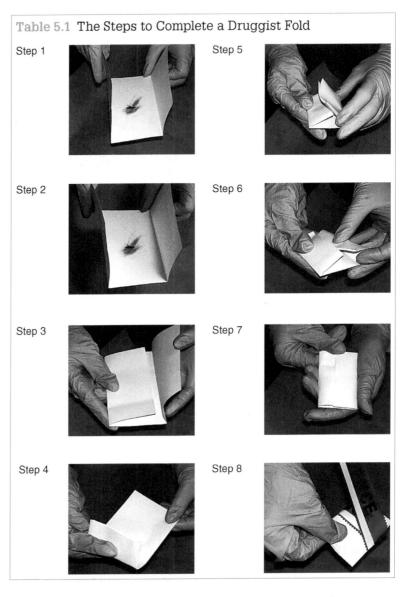

Step 1

Step 2

Step 3

Step 4

Step 5

Step 6

Step 7

Step 8

Determining the direction and force of an impact on window glass can be accomplished by examining the fracture patterns surrounding the hole (see Figure 5.12). Radial fractures spread out like spokes from the center of a wheel. Concentric fractures encircle the hole or point of impact (see Figure 5.13). When a high-speed projectile—a rock or a bullet—penetrates glass, it will create a crater at the point of impact. Just like a bullet wound, the entry side is smaller than the exit side of the impact site. It is not possible to accurately determine the size or circumference of the projectile because the angle of impact can distort the size and create an elongated hole rather than a spherical entry point.

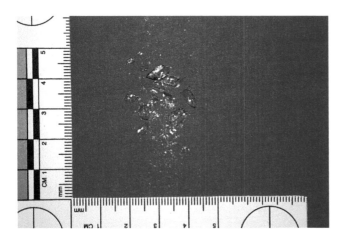

FIGURE 5.11
Small particles of glass can be valuable in establishing linkages.

You should always accurately document the glass as it appeared on arrival on the scene. Photographs, sketches, and written notes are especially important because this type of evidence is fragile and likely to be destroyed—particularly if you are dealing with the glass of a vehicle window. Glass fragments must be packaged in solid containers to avoid further breakage. If you have a suspect's clothing to submit for examination, package each piece separately in paper and sealed bags to secure against loss. Examinations to determine the direction of impact or force require the CSI to gather all remaining glass in the headlight or reflector—and, if possible, indicate interior and exterior surfaces. The presence of dirt, paint, grease, or putty may indicate the exterior surface of the headlight.

FIGURE 5.12
Radial fracture pattern in glass.

FIGURE 5.13
Concentric fracture pattern in glass.

The FBI maintains a database that contains density and refractive indices and elemental analyses. For cases in which positive identifications cannot be made, examiners provide a probability statement that the fragments were at one time from the same source. While not conclusive on its own, this type of corroborative evidence can be admissible in court.

Soil

Transferability between the suspect, a suspect vehicle, and the scene makes soil samples valuable associative evidence and can provide a linkage in the investigation. Even if you have not identified a crime scene, gather soil evidence; it can be compared whenever a crime scene is located. Remember not to be misled by the color of soil. It is always darker when wet. Samples must be examined under identical laboratory conditions to yield accurate results. Scientists estimate that there are more than 1,100 different soil colors, so this determination should be left to the experts at the crime laboratory. Remember, the CSI's job is to gather evidence and known samples and submit them to the crime laboratory for analysis.

It is important to gather control samples when you are collecting soil samples. In most cases, only the top-surface layer of soil will be picked up during the commission of a crime, so that is all you need to gather when you are collecting physical evidence. Usually, about a tablespoon is all that the lab requires for a comparative analysis. Samples should be packaged and clearly labeled in individual containers. Always collect soil samples from alibi locations to substantiate or disprove the suspect's statements. EPA-certified clean/sterile containers should be used to gather soil samples because soil may contain pollen and other microorganisms that may allow for more individualization of the soil when analyzed by the crime laboratory.

Do not make any effort to dislodge soil from garments or shoes. Submit the entire item to the crime lab wrapped in paper and secured inside a paper bag. The analysts at the laboratory are skilled in identifying and removing this type of trace evidence to ensure that the full sample is obtained.

Gunshot Residue

Gases and powder create blowback on the rear of a gun, which deposits primer, lead, barium, and antimony that can be detected by swabbing the suspect's hands (see Figure 5.14). Use a cotton swab moistened with nitric acid to swab the surfaces of the suspect's hands. Gunshot residue may remain on the hands for up to six hours

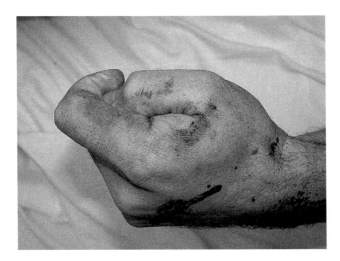

FIGURE 5.14
Gunshot residue on index finger and thumb web on hand of victim.

after a weapon has been fired. Although gunshot residue tests are controversial—that is, there are as many negative results as inconclusive reports—the CSI should always take the time to swab the hands of suspects and victims. Even if the case you are investigating appears to be suicide, by taking the precaution of swabbing the hands, you are protecting any potential trace evidence that may exist on the hands of the victim. Always bag the hands of a deceased victim before sending the body away from the crime scene to protect all potential trace evidence until it can be retrieved at the morgue. Fingernail scrapings may yield suspect DNA or other trace materials that might be lost during transport from the crime scene to the morgue.

Trace Evidence Summary

Some agencies and crime labs advocate the use of evidence vacuums for collecting debris and dirt. However, because of the various hoses and filters involved in vacuuming, there is a greater potential for cross-contamination to occur. Newer model evidence vacuums have addressed this issue, but if your agency has not replaced older vacuum equipment, you must be aware of the potential for cross-contamination and take extra precautions to prevent it from occurring. If CSI protocols require that evidence vacuums be used, ensure that all procedures are followed to enhance the integrity of the evidence and reduce the possibility of a defense attorney attacking the admissibility of the trace evidence in court.

At most crime scenes, you will need to collect trace evidence where it is located. If you are using nondisposable forceps to recover items,

FIGURE 5.15
Tape lift with hair and fibers collected from a fabric upholstered sofa.

such as hairs or fibers, be sure to clean the forceps with a bleach solution between picking up each item to prevent cross-contamination. It is often more time- and cost-effective to use disposable tweezers or forceps to collect trace evidence. Adhesive or fingerprint tape is often used to retrieve hairs, fibers, and other trace evidence from clothing or other locations (see Figure 5.15). Place the adhesive side of the tape on a piece of clear acetate after you have taken photographs of where the evidence is located and prior to making any alterations to the crime scene. If acetate is not available, cut the sides of a Ziploc®-type plastic bag and open it out to use in place of clear acetate. When you have secured the trace evidence and taped it to the inside of the plastic bag, be sure to seal the edges.

When the clothing of a suspect or victim is located, it must be obtained in a manner that will protect against the loss of trace evidence. If the clothing is being worn, the person should stand on a clean piece of butcher paper and remove clothing one article at a time, and then each piece should be individually packaged. The paper should also be folded up, secured inside a paper bag, and submitted as evidence to the crime lab. When clothing is found in a pile, you should spread out clean paper and then individually wrap each piece of clothing with paper between the folds to prevent cross-contamination. After you have folded each item, include the paper you were working over in the package as well. This will ensure that you have not lost any trace evidence that may have fallen from the garment as you were folding it for packaging.

IMPRESSION EVIDENCE

The crime scene may yield many types of physical evidence, including **impression evidence**. Included in this category are fingerprints, palmprints, nose or ear prints, toolmarks, and footwear and tire impressions (see Figures 5.16 and 5.17). Fabric imprints, such as those left by perpetrators wearing gloves or socks, are also found at crime scenes. Impression evidence may be found in unlikely places, and the CSI should be diligent in examining surfaces such as counters, desks, chair seats, and the tops of furniture. Evidence found in these locations must be preserved through photographs and sketches, because the locations are too large and impractical to transport the entire item to the crime lab for processing and comparison purposes. It is sometimes possible to cut out the portion of the item containing the impression and transport it to the crime laboratory without taking the entire item from the scene.

It is important for the CSI to identify, preserve, and collect the physical evidence and then assist the prosecutor in getting the evidence

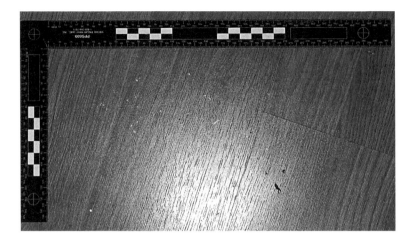

FIGURE 5.16
Dusty footprint photographed with direct lighting. Note that the footprint cannot be seen clearly when photographed this way.

FIGURE 5.17
The dusty footprint from Figure 5.16 photographed with "grazing" light (light held at an angle to the surface).

admitted in the courtroom. The analyst will take the stand and testify as to the examination and comparison techniques. Successful comparisons require partial or full impressions that are properly preserved and retrieved, as well as "known" standards (e.g., the suspect shoe or tire), and an examiner's expertise. Manufacturers provide reference files for designs used in soles and heels of shoes as well as tire tread patterns for the FBI laboratory.

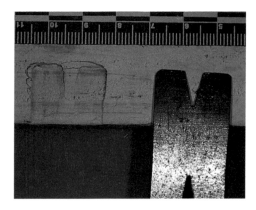

FIGURE 5.18
Marks on wooden frame of window compared against tool found in suspect's possession.

When one object impacts or impresses a second object, impressions may be created (see Figure 5.18). Examiners can compare unique characteristics of the impacting object, such as a screwdriver used to force open a wooden window. Striations present on the screwdriver may be observable on the window frame, and if accurate documentation and evidence collection occurred, this impression evidence can be linked to a unique source. Again, linking the suspect to the scene through the use of impression evidence can provide investigative leads to the detectives. Mikrosilt is a silicone casting agent similar to putty that can placed in the impression to create a cast that is suitable for comparison to the suspected tools. The CSI should always make every effort to obtain suitable castings of impression evidence; however, depending on the type of crime being investigated, it may be necessary to cut out the section containing the toolmark or other impression evidence and submit it to the lab for comparison.

Forensic Podiatry

Impression evidence includes shoeprints as well as footprints. These types of impression evidence can be valuable to the investigation, and some basic information is applicable to both categories of pattern evidence. It is possible to match an impression left at a crime scene with the footwear of a suspect. Usually, these types of examinations are performed in the crime laboratory by a criminalist trained much the same way as a latent fingerprint examiner; this specialist is focused on comparisons of class and individual characteristics.

The evaluation of evidence relating to the human foot is called **forensic podiatry** or pedal evidence. This type of expertise usually requires someone who has a background in podiatric medicine and is familiar with the structure of the foot, ankle, knee, leg, and hip. These specialists are valuable assets when attempting to examine footprints—especially when there are bare footprints, but also for sock impressions.

The forensic podiatrist may be able to determine the primary wearer of suspected footwear, in the event that touch DNA is not identified on the shoes. This is a possibility when a shoeprint is matched to a crime scene, but the suspect denies ownership of the shoes. Specialized examinations include gait analysis or perhaps an estimation of an individual's shoe size or height based on physical characteristics of the footprints found at a crime scene.

Impression evidence such as shoe- and footprints is easily destroyed at a crime scene. First responders are not going to search an area for this type of physical evidence prior to rendering aid or securing the safety of an area. As soon as possible, the CSI should use oblique lighting methods to scan the area for potential shoe or footwear impressions and then protect that area as these impressions are considered transient evidence. Some chemical reagents may be used to enhance bloody footprints for photography purposes, including leucocrystal violet (LCV), amido black, and luminol. Again, the appropriate special lighting techniques must be employed to ensure proper photography of the evidence.

Footwear Impressions

It is easy to overlook the value of footwear impressions. In addition to providing useful information such as the physical characteristics of the shoe (such as size and unique tread patterns), this evidence may lead to determining the number of suspects and/or the paths to and from the crime scene. There is the potential that if proper evidence-gathering techniques are utilized to preserve the patterns, an experienced examiner may be able to provide sequencing. That is, in some instances, the sequence of events leading up to an event may be discernible through the detection of various layers and the order in which the patterns were left at the scene.

Footwear impressions are easily lost, and the CSI must take immediate action to preserve and gather this type of evidence. Weather, people, and vehicles are extremely likely to damage footwear impressions unless they are protected and documented early in the crime scene investigation. It is likely that this type of evidence may have already been destroyed during the response and rescue efforts conducted by first responders; however, the CSI is responsible for locating and preserving potential impression evidence as soon as possible after arrival on the scene.

There are two forms of footwear evidence: impressions and prints. Three-dimensional foot or shoe impressions should be photographed and then cast using dental stone. Be sure to take a full set of photographs without a scale, and then take a second set of photographs with a scale inserted into the picture to present an accurate depiction of the size and shape of the impression. Use oblique lighting techniques to highlight the ridges and grooves of the impressions from various angles before casting the impression. Dental stone is easy to mix and captures minute details of the impression (see Figure 5.19).

Shoeprints or footprints should also be photographed; however, depending on the location of the print, it may be possible to simply take the print as physical evidence if it is left on paper or other substrate that can be removed without difficulty. Package the evidence carefully to prevent folds or other damage to the impression while it is in

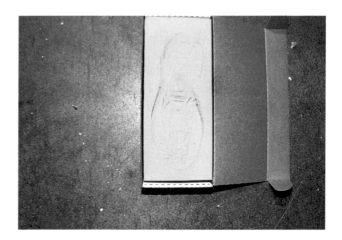

FIGURE 5.19
An example of a shoe impression preserved in biofoam.

transit to the laboratory for analysis. Depending on the type of crime that is being investigated, you might need to preserve the original impressions by cutting them out of the object where they are located. Be sure you have access to the proper equipment and safety devices necessary before beginning to dismantle or cut through a large item.

Footprint and shoeprint impressions are found on many different types of surfaces, and can be wet, dry, or in dust. Gel lifters are one of the best ways to attempt to lift and preserve these prints. Once the impression has been sufficiently documented with photographs, first without using an ABFO scale and then placing the scale next to the print, apply the gel lifter to the impression. Gel lifters are flexible, allowing you to apply gentle pressure to the back of the lifter to obtain a detailed impression. Remove the gel lift from the surface and carefully reapply the clear plastic protective cover over the impression. Take additional photos of the impression after it has been covered for supplementary documentation.

For a footwear examiner to perform a comparison, the suspect shoes must be submitted to the crime laboratory. It may be necessary for the detectives to secure a search warrant to obtain the suspect footwear. Shoes should be air-dried and packaged individually to protect any trace evidence or unique characteristics. Plastic packaging materials should not be used because this will lead to evidence degradation. Identify the location where the shoes were found; or if on a subject, be sure to document the wearer and date and time the shoes were obtained.

Tire Impressions

A tire tread analyst can examine the design of the tire impression and possibly determine the manufacture of the tire by the style of the

FIGURE 5.20
Tire impression in sandy substrate.

tread (see Figure 5.20). The FBI maintains a tire tread database that crime lab examiners can access for comparison purposes. This type of information can potentially lead the investigator to identify the make and model of a suspect vehicle, which will provide a link from the suspect vehicle to the crime scene.

The CSI must be diligent about identifying and preserving tire tread impressions or prints at the crime scene (see Figure 5.21). If the suspect vehicle is located, take appropriate photographs and make a sketch that clearly indicates the location of each tire on the vehicle. Be sure you have noted the make, model, and year of the vehicle as well as the VIN, color, and other distinguishing features. Use a flatbed or rollback-type tow truck to remove the vehicle from the scene and transport it to a secure facility for processing.

FIGURE 5.21
Pouring dental stone into an impression.

Bitemark Impressions

The term *bitemark* generally leads you to think about teeth impressions made in the skin when an animal or person bites down, catching skin and tissue between the upper and lower jaw. These impressions are an excellent source of physical evidence, but you should not overlook the possibility of bitemark evidence existing in a foodstuff or even chewing gum. All types of impressions can be analyzed and compared to suspect or victim dentition and used to corroborate or refute statements to investigators. Many times a victim will bite an attacker in a defensive effort, but often the assailant will bite the victim and leave evidence that can be preserved through photographs and other documentation.

Bitemarks can be potentially highly incriminating evidence because they can place the suspect's mouth on the victim's body at the time of attack. However, this evidence does not prove that the suspect committed the remainder of the attack, and other assailant(s) may have acted in concert or subsequent to the initial event. Bitemarks can be valuable evidence because the pattern of the teeth represented in the mark may be unique. In addition, saliva may have been deposited on the skin, making it possible for a DNA profile to be determined. Therefore, swabbing the area of the injury is important after you have completed taking photographs and documenting the bitemarks.

Antemortem bitemarks—those made on a living victim—are less distinctive than those inflicted on a victim after the heart has quit pumping blood (see Figure 5.22). Photographs of the injury site must be taken for several days after the initial injury to ensure that the dimensional integrity of the pattern is accurately captured. Postmortem bitemarks usually have well-defined indentations but no bruising because the blood was not circulating when the injury occurred. For both types of bitemarks, it is important to swab the area immediately to retrieve any DNA that might have been transferred to the victim from the assailant. You should not swab directly over the impressions, but should attend to the areas behind the teeth where the tongue and side walls of the mouth may touch the bitemark and where epithelial cells dislodge from the assailant.

Offensive bitemarks are usually more clearly defined and generally occur as postmortem injuries. Dimensions are not distorted, and the detail necessary for bitemark comparison is better defined when the victim is deceased or at least compliant. Victims who are defending themselves by attempting to bite their attacker may leave multiple bitemarks or cause tears in the skin. Teeth may leave scrapes or compression marks on the skin, and this is important when establishing linkages between victims and suspects.

FIGURE 5.22

Antemortem human bitemark.

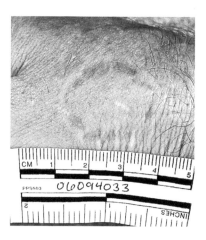

Proper photography techniques must be utilized to gather bitemark evidence. Photos should be taken both with and without an ABFO scale to provide a proper reference point for dimensional comparison by a forensic odontologist. Use oblique lighting so that details will be distinguishable in the photographs. Always take photos and swab for DNA prior to submitting the evidence for casting.

Although preserving bitemarks is difficult, special techniques are useful to supplement the photographs and videos that are made of the initial injuries. After swabbing the area for DNA, place a piece of clear acetate over the injury and trace the marks using a permanent marker. This rendition may be useful to the forensic odontologist when comparisons to a suspect's bitemark patterns are conducted. In the case of a deceased victim, the pathologist or medical examiner may decide to preserve the bitemark evidence by excising it from the victim for further study. This is a medical procedure designed to retard degradation of the impression.

It is important to involve a forensic odontologist at the beginning of any investigation that involves bitemark evidence. The skills and knowledge this expert can bring to the investigation will assist the CSI in acquiring the highest quality physical evidence and documentation, which is necessary for comparison of dentition and bitemark evidence. Medical personnel are trained to recognize bitemarks because they are commonly inflicted on victims of child or spousal abuse. If this type of evidence is not recognized and processed properly, critical information may be lost.

A forensic odontologist can examine and evaluate bitemarks to a reasonable degree of dental certainty. Four findings can be related to the examination of bitemarks provided a suspect has been identified:

- **Definite**—To the exclusion of all others (i.e., only the suspect could have made the bitemark impression)
- **Consistent**—No features present that will exclude the suspect
- **Possible**—Due to the nature of the injury, positive confirmation or exclusion of the suspect is not possible
- **Exclusionary**—Definitely not made by the suspect

Remember that food items found at a crime scene, such as apples or candy bars, may have bitemarks left in them by the perpetrator. In addition to the pattern evidence, saliva may be present that can establish a linkage among the victim, the perpetrator, and the scene.

Photographic Techniques

To locate footwear or other impression evidence at the indoor crime scene, darken the area and use a strong white light at an oblique angle. Alternate forensic light sources can also provide illumination that may assist the CSI in locating impression evidence more effectively than by just using a flashlight. Document the location of each impression and photograph each one individually to provide an accurate representation of the crime scene. Remember that this type of documentation may be useful for substantiating or invalidating victim/suspect statements later in the investigation. Because lifting or preserving all impressions may not be possible, you should always photograph each one individually. A photograph or lift provides a 2D reproduction of the print. Be sure the photographs accurately depict the location of the impression evidence in relation to the overall crime scene.

Inked Impressions

If suspect footwear is located, inked impressions of the shoes should be made by rolling ink on the bottom of the shoes, stepping inside the shoes, and walking on clean, white paper, Mylar®, or gel lifters (see Figure 5.23). If the impression to be compared was a bare footprint, the same techniques should be used for obtaining friction ridge details on the bottom of the foot. First, clean the feet and then apply printer's ink with a fingerprint roller. Direct the subject to take several steps on clean white paper, carefully documenting the time and location where you secured the comparison footprints. The suspect and the CSI should both sign the papers on which the inked impressions are collected.

Another method for obtaining footwear, footprints, fingerprints, palmprints, or tire prints uses common household supplies. Spray a nonstick cooking spray on the item to be printed; then step or roll the items on the paper or a Mylar sheet to create the impressions. Next, apply fingerprint powder to develop the ridge, shoe, or tire details. This procedure works well for agencies that have a limited budget; a can of nonstick cooking spray can always be purchased and kept in the crime scene response vehicles.

You might also need to create inked impressions of tires from suspect vehicles. Remove the tires, collect and preserve any trace evidence that may be found in the treads, and then apply ink to the tire tread using a fingerprint roller. Make sure you have sufficient clean paper available to roll the tire to secure tread impressions from the entire

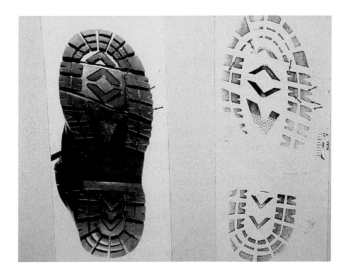

FIGURE 5.23
Inked footwear impression.

rotation of each tire. Mark each set of tire impressions as to the location on the vehicle. Properly photograph any anomalies noted on the tires and include this information in your documentation.

Casting and Lifting Techniques for Impression Evidence

If the impression is located on a surface that is easily transportable to the crime lab, it should be secured, protected, and collected as evidence. Casting footwear impressions can present some challenges—usually because of weather conditions. Wet conditions may dictate changes in the usual protocols for making and pouring casting material. **Dental stone**, which is composed of calcium sulfate (plaster of Paris) with potassium sulfate added for greater hardness, is most commonly used for casting footwear and tire impressions (see Figure 5.24). It is readily available, inexpensive, and easy to transport. After the cast has set for about 20 minutes, you should scratch your initials, date, and case-identifying information on the back of the cast. After any cast is retrieved, it should be allowed to air-dry for 24–48 hours before being stored in an evidence lockup. Never attempt to remove grass, sticks, or other debris from the cast. This may be valuable evidence, and it should be retrieved by the impression analyst conducting the scientific examination. Always use shock-absorbent packing material and never place the cast into a plastic bag. Photographs of the impressions should also accompany the cast to the crime lab for analysis.

An **electrostatic dust print lifter** is useful for preserving impressions left in dust and residue. A sheet of Mylar film is placed on top of the impression, and a roller is used to apply pressure. A high-voltage electrode applied to the film creates a charge and causes the dust to adhere to the film. This technique is useful on colored surfaces where an impression is visible but difficult to photograph or recover. As you conduct your initial crime scene assessment and locate fragile evidence such as imprints in dust or residue, remember that these types of transient evidence must be documented and preserved early in the investigation to prevent their loss or destruction.

Many agencies may not have access to an electrostatic dust print lifter, so the CSI needs to be familiar with other methods of preserving larger impressions. One such method is using a gel lifter (see Figure 5.25). After you have taken photographs of the dust impression, first

FIGURE 5.24
Dental stone cast of footwear.

FIGURE 5.25
A dusty shoe print being lifted with a black gelatin lifter. *Evident Crime Scene Products, www.evidentcrimescene.com.*

unaltered and then with a scale indicating size and dimension of the print, place a large gelatin or adhesive lifter over the print and slowly lift the impression. Avoid stretching or tearing the material so that you do not distort the original size of the print. Use clear acetate over the print to preserve the impression.

Dental impressions and casts should be made by a forensic odontologist or at least a practicing dentist. Molds or casts made of suspects' or victims' teeth must be examined by an expert in order to form opinions based on scientific knowledge as to whether they match bitemarks left on victims or in soft foodstuffs. It is testimony from these professionals that allows the jury to weigh the value of the forensic evidence in a criminal case.

Tire impressions should be cast using dental stone to preserve the impression and create a 3D model of the tire tracks. You should not pour the dental stone directly onto the impression; doing so may destroy a portion of the imprint. Use a spatula or piece of cardboard to baffle the flow of the dental stone into the impression. The cast should dry for 20 minutes, and name, date, and case number or other identifier should be scraped into the back of the cast. Dental stone casts will vary in thickness depending on the medium where the impression is created, so drying times will vary as well. Do not attempt to clean any debris from the cast once it is retrieved. Allow it to air-dry for two days before it is sent to the laboratory for comparison and always package it in paper and sturdy cardboard boxes.

Impressions in Snow

Forensic products are available that can assist in the preservation of snow impressions; however, you can also use dental stone to cast these types of prints. Never cover snow impressions with plastic; this could cause them to melt or degrade, making it impossible to preserve the original evidence. After taking initial photographs, make sure the impressions are visible in the photographs by lightly spraying gray primer paint into the impression to highlight the ridges and grooves. Do not hold the can too close to the impression because the compressed air may disturb fragile ridges, tread marks, or shoeprints.

Dental stone can be used with a potassium sulfate additive that speeds up the setting time and allows the casting to set in extremely cold conditions. Another commercially available product, Snow Print Wax®, is a wax that can be sprayed on the impression and allowed to set up for 10 minutes prior to using regular dental stone mixed with

FIGURE 5.26
Dried dental stone impression lifted from snow using Snow Print Wax.

cold water (see Figure 5.26). Either method can yield good-quality impressions if the impressions are allowed to dry for approximately one hour prior to the CSI trying to lift them.

Additional time—up to 48 hours—should be allocated for the entire cast to dry in a temperature-controlled environment.

Additional information on trace evidence can be gained by visiting the website hosted by the American Society of Trace Evidence Examiners (www.asteetrace.org). Another site of interest is the Association for Crime Scene Reconstruction at www.acsr.org. Finally, detailed data is provided by the American Society of Forensic Podiatry on the organization's website at www.theasfp.org.

Discussion Questions

1. What is trace evidence? List examples. Explain the general procedures for collecting this evidence.
2. Generally, why is preserving trace evidence important? What pitfalls should be avoided?
3. List several potential areas of trace evidence and the procedures for collecting/preserving each.
4. What special techniques are necessary for accurately photographing impression evidence, such as shoeprints?

CHAPTER 6

Bodily Fluid Evidence

KEY TERMS

CODIS (Combined DNA Index System)	Gas chromatography	Serology
	Mass spectrometry	Sexual assault nurse examiner (SANE)
	Mitochondrial DNA (mtDNA)	
Confirmatory test		Touch DNA
EDTA	Presumptive test	Toxicology
Epithelial cells	Prostate-specific antigen (PSA)	
Forensic biology		

What You Will Learn

The collection of bodily fluids can lead to a DNA profile that links multiple crimes to an individual. This is one of the latest yet most effective scientific advancements in the realm of scientific analysis being linked to criminal investigations. This chapter describes how the discovery of bodily fluids can be used to identify individuals at the scene of the crime.

MURDER IN THE NEW YEAR

Bodily Fluid Evidence

Chief Medical Examiner Sara Evans leaned back in her chair and answered her cellphone. "Investigator, why in heaven's name did I ever agree to give you my private cell number?"

Tom Smith chuckled, "Because I'm so irresistible?"

"Have you looked in a mirror lately?" the CME replied with a laugh. And before you ask me for a specific time when I can get any results to you, the answer is NO! One of my evidence analysts is out with the flu, and the other

DOI: 10.4324/9780429261657-6

one is working 12-hour shifts—so unless you can provide me with another analyst, you will have to wait your turn.

***

Ed Ellwenger sipped a mango smoothie as Tom handed Mavis Fletcher a cup of coffee. Pulling the top off the paper cup, she glanced at Tom with feigned disgust. "I bring you Starbucks, and you bring me Mel's. What gives?"

Tom shrugged. "You may have forgotten, Detective, that I'm not a high-paid detective, but only a lowly part-time, retired CSI."

Mavis Fletcher took a sip and looked at the crime scene technician. "Ed, I bet your smoothie tastes better than Mel's coffee."

Mavis pulled a file from her handbag. "What else have you found? Any word from the CME?"

"The sexual assault nurse examiner (SANE) collected a vaginal and semen swab from both victims. Blood work, a toxicology screen, and crime scene DNA analysis should be available soon," Tom replied.

Detective Fletcher's brow furrowed. "How soon?"

Tom Smith crumpled his paper coffee cup and tossed it in a trash can. "Not tomorrow. CME Evans informed me that we will have to wait our turn. I'll give her another call day after tomorrow. How about you? How did your initial interview go with the esteemed Dean Michael Sellers?"

Mavis took another sip of her coffee. "I must say I found Dean Sellers to be a potential but not necessarily definite suspect. He was a bit haughty, but became increasingly nervous and, more importantly, increasingly evasive as the interview wore on."

Ed sucked the last of his smoothie through his straw. "Did he have an alibi?"

"Sort of," Mavis replied. Said he spent the entire evening with Amanda, his wife. I'll talk with her tomorrow. Said he regretted his one-time indiscretion and the pain it had caused all who were involved, but that he and Amanda were engaged in marriage counseling with his pastor. Dean Sellers seems convinced that he and his wife are on the mend.

Tom Smith cocked an eyebrow. "A 'one-time' indiscretion, you say?"

Mavis smiled. "Yes. Michael Sellers has concluded that he succumbed in a moment of weakness to the charms of an attractive woman who worked for him."

Pulling a paper bag out of her purse, Mavis looked at her two colleagues. Dean Sellers was drinking a bottle of Perrier sparkling water during our interview. As luck would have it, he threw the empty bottle into his trash can when his phone rang, and he excused himself to engage in a brief chat with a colleague in the office next to his.

Tom Smith locked his fingers together and leaned forward in his chair. Well done, Detective. If you will complete the evidence submission paperwork, I will make sure this valuable piece of evidence is turned over to the lab for a DNA test to determine Dean Seller's profile. Then we can ask for comparisons to those found at the crime scene.

INTRODUCTION

Establishing linkages between a victim, a crime scene, and a perpetrator remains a primary purpose in the reasons for reconstructing a crime scene. Evidence deposited at a crime scene can take many forms, but the types of information that can be gleaned from laboratory tests on bodily fluids are well recognized and accepted by the courts. Dried stains are easily overlooked, and this chapter provides essential information concerning the information that proper collection and preservation techniques can provide from bodily fluid analysis.

Forensic biology is the nexus between the examination of physical evidence utilizing both cellular and microbiology subspecialties and determining if the findings can be applicable to a crime scene investigation. The scientific study and analysis of serums (blood, semen, saliva, sweat, or fecal matter) is called **serology** and is an essential step in the examination of physical evidence. These analyses cross multiple disciplines and include biology, chemistry, immunology, and genetics. At the crime scene, the most frequently encountered biological stains are blood, seminal fluid, and saliva; however, other substances, including vaginal secretions, urine, and feces, may also be discovered.

The serological examination begins in the crime laboratory with the location and identification of biological evidence, which is then analyzed to determine if there is a possibility of obtaining a DNA profile. Forensic serology deals most frequently with samples that are degraded or in stain form.

Toxicology is the study of bodily fluids, tissues, and organs for the presence of drugs or poisons. Forensic toxicology analyzes the adverse effects of chemicals on living organisms. Toxins take the form of a liquid, gas, solid, mineral, animal, or vegetable and are materials that could be life-threatening to organisms. The **presumptive test**, or screening test, is the first step of two processes the lab performs to check for the presence of a drug or poison. A **confirmatory test** is the second step. The most common confirmatory test is the **gas chromatography/mass spectrometry** (GC/MS) test (see Figure 6.1), which can unequivocally identify any organic chemical (drug or poison). Toxicological analyses are useful in establishing impairment or in relating the use of drugs to the commission of a crime. Forensic toxicology is also used to establish whether drugs were a contributing factor to or cause of death.

FIGURE 6.1
A gas chromatography/ mass spectrometry (GC/MS) unit.

The main sources of evidence submitted for toxicological analysis are urine, blood, hair, saliva, and sweat. Law enforcement officers are probably most familiar with urine and blood tests to determine levels of alcohol and other drugs in impaired drivers or those involved in motor vehicle fatalities. Workplace and pre-employment drug screenings use both urine screenings and hair examinations and generate an immense workload for private laboratories that perform toxicological examinations. Whereas a urine test can indicate recent drug usage, hair analysis provides a timeline that indicates drug use over a much longer period of time.

With all bodily fluid evidence, you must submit known and elimination samples from the victim, suspect, and other persons present at the crime scene. If a suspect has been identified, his or her DNA profile will be compared to the profile recovered from the physical evidence to determine if the fluids originated from the same individual. When a suspect is a convicted felon, his or her DNA profile should already be in a DNA database, so you might not need to submit another sample from this individual. If you do get a database hit, this gives you probable cause to obtain a new sample from the suspect for confirmation of the hit.

Bodily fluids, wet or dry, have been shown to carry diseases, so universal safety precautions must be utilized, including using personal protective equipment (PPE) when processing crime scenes where biological evidence may be present. Dry stains may flake and become airborne when disturbed or collected. These particles can be absorbed through your eyes, nose, mouth, open cuts, or chapped skin, so remember to protect yourself.

TOXICOLOGY

Blood samples must be drawn by a doctor, nurse, or other qualified medical staff member. The evidence must be sealed and refrigerated until it is transported to the crime laboratory for analysis. Both urine and blood samples will begin to deteriorate when removed from the body. Blood samples should never be frozen; however, it is permissible to freeze urine samples until they can be transported to the crime laboratory.

When you are processing a crime scene at which drug use—either by the suspect or by the victim—is suspected, it is important to look for evidence such as empty or partially filled bottles; envelopes; the contents of a medicine chest, nightstand, or drinking glasses; and the trash inside and outside the scene. You should draw a sample from partially filled glasses or bottles. If powders or liquids are present, collect and submit samples for analysis. Other items that you may encounter include poisons, acids, pesticides, petroleum distillates, volatile liquids, and metals (arsenic or mercury). If you determine the need to submit samples of these substances, handle with caution and place in leak-proof, spill-proof containers with proper labels on the exterior surface.

The National Forensic Science Technology Center has posted many useful videos on various topics. You can view these videos at www.youtube.com/user/TheNFSTC.

DNA TECHNIQUES AND THE IMPACT OF TECHNOLOGICAL ADVANCES

In England in 1984, Sir Alec Jeffreys discovered the first deoxyribonucleic acid (DNA) "fingerprints." The impact and significance of this research demonstrated that DNA profiling can distinguish every individual in the world (with the exception of identical twins). Recently, new and ongoing research labs using sophisticated test methodologies have determined that even identical twins have differences. In fact, research published in the journal *Nature Genetics* revealed that identical twins differ by an average of 5.2 genetic mutations (Jonsson et al., 2021).

DNA carries the genetic code that individualizes each person, and DNA can be easily obtained from blood, bone, urine, dandruff, earwax, fingernails, skin, sweat, hair, seminal fluid (with or without sperm), vaginal or rectal cells, and teeth. Regardless of the body tissue or specimen examined, DNA is the same in every cell, and it always remains the same.

The scientific community immediately adopted genetic profiling, and, only two years later, the first DNA tests were accepted in a US civil court. The benefits and uses of DNA analysis were quickly acknowledged in scientific journals and have become effective in both the identification of criminals and the exoneration of those wrongly accused of committing crimes. Using DNA analysis in forensic investigations provides the capacity to form strong association or exclusion of individuals as possible donors of biological evidence exchanged or left at the crime scene.

FIGURE 6.2
A computer-generated DNA profile.

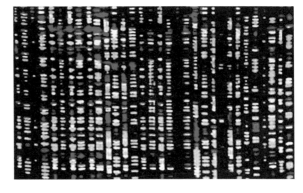

DNA is an organic compound found in the chromosomes of the nuclei of cells. This personal blueprint contains the unique genetic information of each individual's approximately 3 billion base pairs of chromosomes (see Figure 6.2). Only identical twins share the same genetic makeup. **Mitochondrial DNA**

(mtDNA) is transmitted only through the maternal line. The Y chromosome is transmitted through the paternal line and can be useful in resolving DNA mixtures in sexual assaults (XY = male; XX = female).

The analysis of mtDNA has assisted historians and researchers in confirming the identification of significant persons, including the human remains of Dr. Joseph Mengele, a Nazi concentration camp doctor who fled Germany to avoid prosecution; Russian Czar Nicholas II; and the remains of US soldiers from the Vietnam and Korean conflicts.

DNA AND CRIME SCENE INVESTIGATION

There is no accurate way to measure the impact of the discovery of DNA analysis on the responsibilities of the CSI. In 1998, the FBI established the **CODIS (Combined DNA Index System)** database, a central repository database containing DNA profiles of convicted felons from all 50 states.

The CODIS database enables federal, state, and local crime labs to exchange and compare DNA profiles electronically. The Forensic Index includes profiles from crime scene evidence. The Offender Index contains DNA profiles of individuals convicted of sex offenses and other violent crimes. All states have enacted legislation allowing the collection of DNA samples from every convicted felon to be entered into CODIS. Many states have also started collecting DNA from all arrestees (see Box 6.1).

Agencies also submit DNA samples from unsolved crimes in an attempt to match suspects and provide investigative leads to detectives working cold cases involving homicides and other serious personal assaults. If a suspect list has not been developed, the DNA profile developed from biological evidence can be searched against the DNA database in an effort to establish links among other cases and identify a common perpetrator. If CODIS identifies a match, DNA analysts are required to validate or refute the match by obtaining a new sample from the suspect.

The collection of DNA evidence is performed much the same as any other type of physical and biological evidence. The CSI must utilize the proper safeguards when dealing with potential biological evidence. Be sure to use PPE (see Figures 6.3 and 6.4) and label all samples with biological warning labels (see Figure 6.5). The PPE will

BOX 6.1

In June 2013, the US Supreme Court ruled it is legal to take DNA samples from everyone arrested for serious crimes. www.ksl.com/?nid5129&sid524199640.

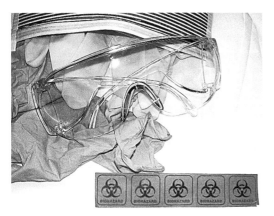

FIGURE 6.3
Personal protective equipment (PPE).

FIGURE 6.4
Different tasks require various PPE to ensure the safety of the CSI and prevent contamination of the crime scene.

protect the CSI from potential biohazards on the evidence, but it will also protect the evidence from potential contamination from the CSI's DNA. In fact, many laboratory personnel routinely wear masks while examining items with potential DNA evidence to eliminate the chance of sneezing or inadvertently spraying the item with their saliva. (See Chapter 2 for more information on PPE.)

It is important to remember that DNA itself does not make a case. A good investigation is still what leads to successful case resolution. State-of-the-art scientific techniques are useful only if the crime scene investigation is accurate, complete, and the evidence admissible.

FIGURE 6.5
Biohazard symbol labels must be attached to the exterior of every package containing potential biohazards.

DNA Probative Value

Not every item at a crime scene should be considered probative evidence. The facts of the case, along with other information, will assist in making the determination of what evidence should be tested in the lab. The best evidence occurs when DNA belonging to the victim or suspect is found where it is not supposed to be (see Box 6.2). Many laboratories use a triage system. They will accept only a certain number of items from each case in a single submission. They want to examine the most probative items first. Therefore, it is very important for the CSI to be in contact with the laboratory. If the first round of items does not yield any probative evidence, the lab will often accept additional items. DNA is a very stable molecule and can remain intact for many years. Maintaining the integrity of the crime scene and preventing contamination of physical evidence recovered at the scene or on the victim are essential to the credibility of the CSI and the subsequent lab analyses.

BOX 6.2 ADVANTAGES OF DNA ANALYSIS

DNA analysis can
- Identify a suspect
- Implicate or eliminate a suspect
- Place a known individual at a crime scene
- Refute a claim of self-defense
- Put a weapon in a suspect's hand
- Change a suspect's story from an alibi to one of consent

- Analyze unidentified remains
- Resolve paternity/maternity cases
- Link related cases
- Provide leads in cold or unsolved cases
- Be used to appeal convictions

FIGURE 6.6
Hat brims are an excellent source of touch DNA.

FIGURE 6.7
Shoes may contain epithelial cells or sweat, both useful for DNA testing.

Touch DNA

Touch DNA is useful to the CSI because items thought to have been handled by the perpetrator can be processed for latent fingerprints before being tested for DNA (see Figures 6.6 and 6.7). Fingerprint powders and other chemical processing agents have been found not to interfere with the forensic scientist's ability to retrieve **epithelial cells** necessary for analysis and creation of a DNA profile. Epithelial cells line the cavities of human organs, provide surface cover (skin), and are the most prolific types of human cells. They can be left at a crime scene in many ways, such as in urine.

However, there is the possibility of cross-contamination if the CSI uses the same powder and brush when processing different items for latent prints. It is important to place small amounts of powder into separate containers and to use disposable brushes to eliminate cross-contamination.

Because the tests to detect touch DNA are so sensitive, there is always the danger of contamination. Do not allow anyone to eat, drink, or smoke at the crime scene. Avoid touching anything unless you are wearing double layers of gloves, and the outer set should be changed each time you touch a new piece of physical evidence. Anyone with a cough or cold should be excluded from the scene. Elimination and reference samples are taken from anyone whose DNA may be at the scene of the crime. Most officers' and CSIs' fingerprints are already in the AFIS database for elimination purposes, and as DNA analysis becomes more readily available, agencies are beginning to require DNA profiles of other employees to be entered into the DNA database for elimination purposes.

Some laboratories limit the types of items they will examine for touch DNA. This is especially true if the touch DNA is found on items from too many potential sources—for example, a door handle of a bank. In this type of evidence, the chances that the lab will obtain a useful profile from a single individual are too small to warrant its examination. Therefore, it is important for the CSI to contact the laboratory to see what its policy is regarding touch DNA.

BLOOD

Is it blood? Presumptive tests for blood are initial screening tools that indicate—but are not specific for—the identification of blood (see Figure 6.8). The more common presumptive tests include leucomalachite green, phenolphthalein, o-tolidine (see Figure 6.9), tetramethylbenzidine (TMB), luminol, and MacPhail's reagent. Before conducting any presumptive tests, ensure that you have sufficient samples available. If you do not, preserve the stains and transport them to the laboratory for a complete scientific analysis.

Presumptive tests for the presence of blood can assist you at the crime scene in differentiating among rust, blood, chocolate, or other brownish-colored stains that could be misidentified as blood (see Figures 6.10a–6.10d). Using presumptive testing will also assist you

FIGURE 6.9

Positive reaction on an o-tolidine test—positive for the presence of blood.

FIGURE 6.8

A presumptive blood test kit for use by CSIs.

FIGURE 6.10A
Suspected bloodstain is rubbed onto filter paper.

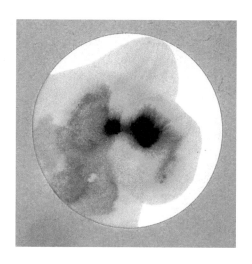

FIGURE 6.10B
A few drops of a presumptive blood test reagent (TMB) followed by a few drops of hydrogen peroxide will produce a green color reaction in the presence of blood.

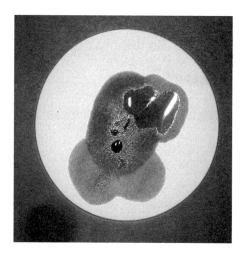

FIGURE 6.10C
A blank test is run to ensure that the reagent is not contaminated and giving false-positive reactions.

FIGURE 6.10D
A known (control) test is run with known blood to determine if the reagent is providing a true color reaction in the presence of blood.

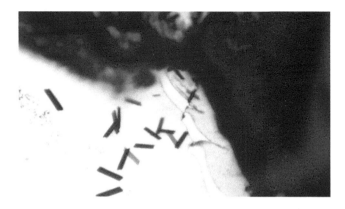

FIGURE 6.11
A microscopic hematin crystal test produces brown rhombic crystals in the presence of hemoglobin. In this case, this is a confirmatory result of blood.

in prioritizing the areas of the crime scene to process because it is important to collect bodily fluid evidence early in the investigation to prevent loss or deterioration of the physical evidence.

Always use swabs or filter paper to conduct presumptive testing and never place the chemicals directly on the stain. Following this procedure will prevent loss of the stain and allow you to collect it for submission to the crime laboratory. Positive and negative control tests should be performed on the chemicals to ensure validity before you test the unknown stains. All of these tests must be documented in your case notes and must include location, time, date, name of the CSI performing the tests, and which specific tests have been conducted. It is imperative to document the lot number and expiration date of all chemicals used.

Confirmatory tests and further characterizations of the stains are required to eliminate the false positives created by some organic compounds (see Figure 6.11). Once a stain has been confirmed to be blood, lab analysis can identify the origin of the blood. Is it human or animal? Usually, if a determination is made that the stain is not human blood, no further analysis is conducted. When it is important to establish the origin of animal blood, however, the crime laboratory can determine the animal family.

SEMINAL FLUID

Semen is composed of approximately 95 percent fluid and about five percent spermatozoa. The average male ejaculation is less than a teaspoon, but it contains about 200 million spermatozoa. UV light causes seminal stains to fluoresce. **Prostate-specific antigen (PSA)** is a substance that is present in semen and is usually not found in other

FIGURE 6.12
An alternate light source (ALS) may aid in detecting bodily fluids.

FIGURE 6.13
A control test on acid phosphatase shows the reagent is valid for presumptive testing for the presence of semen.

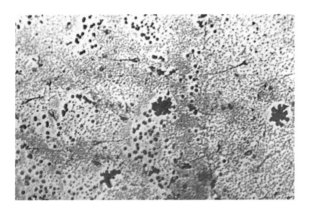

FIGURE 6.14
The acid phosphatase test for the presence of semen is positive when the color turns purple.

bodily fluids. It is also only found in higher primate species. Detection of PSA, also known as p30 protein, is indicative of the presence of semen.

An alternate or forensic light source can be used to locate possible seminal fluid (see Figure 6.12), and then a presumptive test (acid phosphatase) should be used if you have sufficient samples available. Before conducting any presumptive tests, you must conduct a positive and negative control test on the chemicals and include the results of these tests in your documentation. Touch a clean, sterile swab or gauze to the suspected stain, and then apply the reagent to the swab or gauze. This is a colorimetric test, and if the sample turns purple, it is a good indication of the presence of semen (see Figures 6.13 and 6.14).

Forensic scientists perform microscopic identification of non-motile spermatozoa or spermatozoa heads (they lose the tails when degradation begins) as confirmatory tests for seminal fluid. The absence of seminal fluid does not mean that a rape or sexual assault did not occur. Other physical injuries or trace evidence may be used to confirm that an attack did take place. Because rape is generally not a sexually motivated crime, often the rapist will not ejaculate, so there is no seminal evidence to recover. Sometimes, the suspect wears a condom, and this will eliminate the chances of finding seminal fluid on the victim.

In living persons, sperm heads have been detected in the vaginal cavity for up to seven days after ejaculation, in the anus and rectum for two to three days, and in the mouth for approximately 24 hours. These are generally accepted time frames and are provided only as a guideline for the investigator. They can vary immensely depending on many variables, such as the post sexual behavior of the victim, the amount of ejaculate, the number of spermatozoa deposited, and the inconsistencies among medical personnel with regard to gathering physical evidence.

You might need to collect and analyze the DNA of the victim's recent consensual partners, if any, when you are conducting a rape investigation. This step is required to eliminate the partners as potential contributors of DNA suspected to be from the perpetrator. All DNA samples must be obtained legally, and you must always seek consent or obtain a search warrant for every person—whether that person is a suspect, family member, partner, or other identified person. Most people will cooperate and allow you to collect buccal swabs. By law, DNA from family members or other people collected for elimination purposes cannot be entered into the CODIS database. If someone refuses to provide a sample, you will have to obtain a search warrant to secure the DNA. Of course, you should not forget that many times people who are uncooperative leave their DNA on a cigarette butt, chewed gum, or a can or bottle—which can make sample collection much easier. Don't forget to document every sample you collect for the investigation.

SALIVA

Saliva is an excellent source of DNA. It is often detected at crime scenes at which the suspect may have left cigarette butts or drunk from a can, bottle, or water glass. It may also be recovered from the skin of a victim who has suffered bitemarks made by the perpetrator. If bitemarks are found, the area should be swabbed in an attempt to recover DNA from saliva left by the perpetrator. Remember not to swab directly on or over the bitemarks but around the area to preserve the integrity of the bite impressions. Chewing gum, envelopes, and stamps are good physical evidence sources of saliva. When a suspect uses a ski mask to commit a crime and the ski mask is later found, saliva may be present around the mouth or nose opening. Other types of skin cells and hair that can be used to generate a DNA profile may also be found in the ski mask.

OTHER BODILY FLUIDS

Urine

During the course of the investigation of a serious or violent crime, both blood and urine samples should be collected by a medical staff member if a suspect is taken into custody. A search warrant may be needed to acquire the samples. Samples may also be needed to substantiate or refute claims by a suspect of being under the influence of a drug or other intoxicant at the time the incident occurred. Urine samples must be refrigerated immediately and delivered to the lab within two to three days for analysis.

Primarily composed of water and salts, urine stains are very diluted and have low cell concentrations. As a result, DNA analysis is not usually successful. Further, urine contains large amounts of bacteria, which cause degradation of the sample and hinder DNA analysis. Each laboratory has its own policy regarding the examination of urine evidence. It is best for the CSI to contact the lab before submitting any samples because urine is usually collected only for drug/toxicology screens.

Vaginal Secretions

Vaginal fluid may be located on a suspect's underpants or taken from pubic area swabs. It is possible to generate a DNA profile if a sufficient sample is available for testing. Vaginal secretions may be important when a victim alleges that objects were inserted into the vagina as part of a sexual assault. Before any evidence suspected of containing vaginal secretions is collected, a sample swab should be collected, air-dried, and secured in paper packaging to avoid loss of additional trace evidence such as pubic hairs or skin cells.

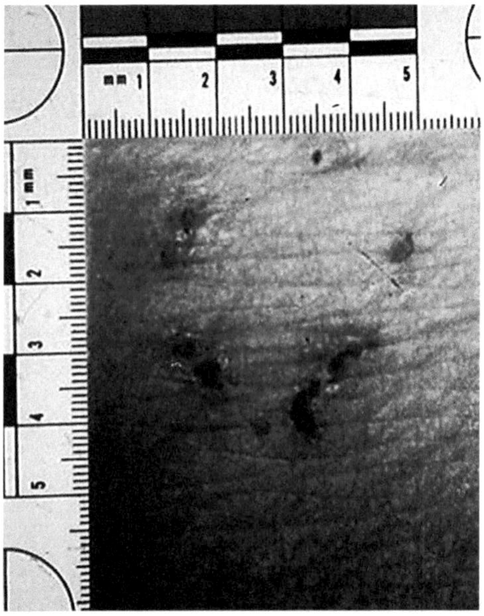

FIGURE 6.15
Bitemarks should be swabbed using the double-swab technique to collect saliva DNA.

SEXUAL ASSAULT: SPECIAL CONSIDERATIONS

Most forcible sexual assault victims survive the event, and the CSI is challenged to recover physical evidence that may be available only in minute amounts. The victim may bite in a defensive effort to escape the attacker. The victim may also suffer from bites made by the perpetrator. It is extremely difficult to document and preserve bitemark evidence; however, epithelial cells contained in the saliva left on the skin surrounding the area of the bitemark may be sufficient to result in a DNA profile. The amount of saliva may be very small, and it is important to maximize the quantity of salivary cells by using swabbing techniques to recover the evidence.

Many studies indicate a high success rate when a double-swab technique is used for retrieving saliva from the skin of a victim (see Figure 6.15). However, other research indicates that while double-swabbing may be preferable for certain complex surfaces, it may be more efficient to use a single wet swab (Hedman et al., 2020). Two swabs—one wet and one dry—are often utilized to ensure that the maximum sample of evidence is collected. First, wet a cotton swab with distilled or sterile, deionized water, and then swab the entire area around the bitemark pattern. Place this swab in an upright position to air-dry. Take a second dry swab and use the same pressure and movements to rotate the tip over the area to recover the remaining moisture on the skin's surface from the wet swab. Air-dry the second swab; then seal and submit the swabs for analysis. Hydrating the area with the first swab tends to cause more dried cells to adhere to the second swab, which increases the amount of DNA recovered from the saliva stains.

LOCATING, COLLECTING, AND PRESERVING BODILY FLUID EVIDENCE

At the Crime Scene

Suspect wet bodily fluid stains should be collected using clean, sterile cotton swabs or clean, sterile gauze patches. The swab stick can be wooden or plastic, but you should not use Q-tips or double-tipped swabs. Allow the swab or patch to air-dry before packaging. Remember to collect a known control swab as well. If the item is porous and not conducive to swabbing, you must cut out any stained areas and package them separately in paper or cardboard containers. In addition, collect adjacent unstained areas for control samples. Some laboratories do not require the collection of control samples. The CSI must contact the laboratory to determine if such samples need to be collected.

If dry stains are located, it will be necessary to collect samples by cutting out the stain or scraping the stains onto clean, sterile filter paper and then using a druggist fold to guard against loss of the evidence. Place this evidence inside a paper envelope to secure all contents. Never try to scrape a dry stain into a plastic bag, because if static electricity causes the airborne particles to scatter, the sample will be lost. If the scraping technique is used, the CSI must wear a mask because of the risk of breathing in the airborne particles, in addition to minimizing the chances of contamination. As with all biological evidence, place a biohazard label on the outside of the package so the forensic biologist conducting the analysis will be aware of the contents. See Table 5.1 in Chapter 5 for an illustration of a druggist fold.

If it is necessary to swab the dry stain, use a clean, sterile cotton swab and one to two drops of distilled or sterile, deionized water. Saturate the swab, but not enough for water to drip off the swab, and collect several samples. Always air-dry all swabs before packaging them. If the laboratory requires a control swab, simply moisten the swab with the distilled or sterile, deionized water and then air-dry it before insertion into the transport package. Clearly mark the control packages with the word "Control" on the label.

If a suspect is not available for collection of a DNA buccal swab, it is possible to gather samples in other ways. Ear plugs, chewing gum, hairbrushes, and cigarette butts are all good sources for acquiring samples from a reluctant contributor. Toothbrushes often contain mixtures of DNA, especially if multiple brushes are stored in close proximity to one another. Remember to address the constitutional issues and ensure that the evidence you are collecting is gathered legally. Acquire a search warrant if you cannot obtain a legal consent to search, so that all evidence will be admissible in the courtroom.

From a Victim or a Suspect

Physical evidence recovery kits (PERKs), also known as "rape kits," are designed by and provided to local law enforcement agencies by the state crime labs or their local jurisdictions (see Figure 6.16). The kits are usually available at hospital emergency departments. They

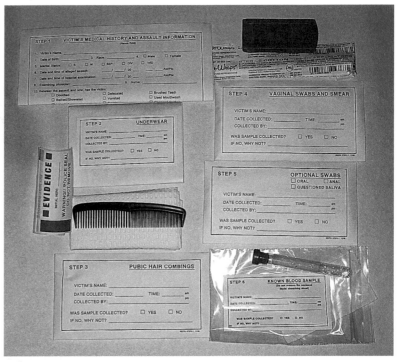

FIGURE 6.16
Typical contents of a PERK or rape kit.

contain the swabs, slides, test tubes, combs, and paper envelopes necessary for the collection of all samples. The purpose of the kits is to allow for the uniform collection of evidence from sexual assault victims regardless of the type of assault or the age or sex of the victim. The PERK contains everything necessary to collect sexual assault physical evidence, including secretions and trace evidence as well as known samples from the victim. PERKs that are specifically designed to collect known samples of suspects also are available for comparison by the crime lab analysts.

In larger jurisdictions, a **sexual assault nurse examiner (SANE)** or a member of the sexual assault response team (SART) may be available to collect evidence for the PERK. Otherwise, a physician or other trained medical staff member should collect the evidence, with the CSI taking control of the kit to preserve the chain of custody. The kit should be sealed and initialed by the medical professional conducting the examination, and should be refrigerated immediately and transported to the crime laboratory as soon as possible. Refrigeration does not prevent degradation of the evidence; it only slows down the degradation, so these kits must be submitted for analysis in a timely manner. Remember that biological fluids begin to degrade as soon as they leave the body. If bacterial growth or evidence contamination occurs, it may interfere with typing tests and make the physical evidence unusable.

FIGURE 6.17
Purple-top Vacutainer tubes contain EDTA, a preservative for blood sample collection.

Liquid blood samples from live victims must be taken by a doctor, nurse, or other qualified medical personnel and collected in a 7 mL purple-top Vacutainer tube, which contains the preservative/anti-coagulant **EDTA** (ethylenediaminetetraacetic acid; see Figure 6.17). If the victim is deceased, the blood will be drawn by the medical examiner or coroner. Gray- or red-topped tubes may be used if no purple tops are available. Make sure the samples are properly labeled (see Figure 6.18) and packed separately in a stable container surrounded with absorbent material before you leave the medical facility.

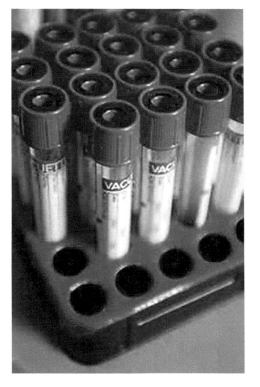

Collect all clothing worn by the victim at the time of the attack. Residual vaginal or seminal fluid or hairs may be present on the clothes that will be important to the investigation of the case. Medical personnel may have removed the clothing when performing rescue efforts, or the victim may have changed clothes prior to seeking medical attention. It may be necessary to enlist the assistance of family members

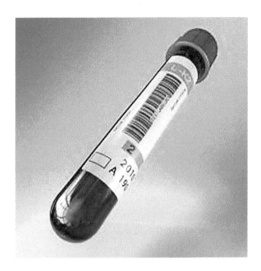

FIGURE 6.18
Ensure proper labeling of all evidence, especially vials of blood taken by medical professionals.

in retrieving the clothing, but it is of primary importance to a sexual assault investigation. Take photographs and make written notes concerning every piece of clothing and where it was obtained.

If the victim is deceased, the medical examiner or coroner will remove the clothing at the autopsy. Photograph the body at the crime scene and document the condition of all clothing. Once the victim is placed into a body bag, it is possible that bloodstain evidence may be destroyed. You must have an accurate record prior to releasing the body for transport to the morgue. Always air-dry clothing and then seal it in paper (not plastic) for submission to the lab. Remember to label packages with biohazard labels on the outside and indicate contents on the laboratory analysis request forms.

Collect DNA samples using buccal (oral) swabs and rubbing clean, sterile swabs on the inside surfaces of the cheek. Air-dry the swabs and place them into a sealed container. Buccal swabs do not need to be refrigerated. Properly label each container including the subject's name and other identifying information.

Bodily fluids may fluoresce under or absorb UV light. Once you have located the stains using the UV light, document and collect the evidence as you would with any other type of physical evidence. A laser or alternate light source works the same way as a UV light. None of these light sources will cause the stain to degrade or become contaminated. Remember that certain chemicals, such as detergents, can mimic bodily fluid stains under these lighting conditions. Be sure to collect standards as well as the stains for submission to the crime laboratory. It is necessary to use filtered photography to document the fluorescence caused by suspect stains because cameras without special filters cannot detect and record the fluorescence either digitally or when using regular film.

Alternate light sources (ALSs) use different wavelengths that may cause bodily fluids to be more visible. This is useful when you are examining dark or patterned surfaces. As discussed earlier in the text, protective eyewear must be worn when using an alternate light source, and the room should be darkened to enhance your ability to see the stains. Be sure to check joints, seams, and other openings because blood may have seeped or dripped into these openings and may not be readily visible to the naked eye. Remember that the appropriate colored filter must be placed on the camera lens to block out other lights when attempting to document stains located with an

ALS. While most bodily fluids fluoresce, blood absorbs the light and appears black when lit with alternate or forensic light sources.

When you are preparing clothing or other items such as bed linens for air-drying and submission, crime laboratories recommend the following steps to protect the integrity of the evidence:

- If air-drying articles, place them on or over a piece of clean paper. If any debris or trace evidence falls from an item while it is drying, it will be collected on the paper—which should also be folded and submitted with each individual article.
- Guard against cross-contamination. Do not allow stained areas to rub against or contact each other or another unstained area. Place several clean sheets of paper on the work surface and then lay the article of clothing on top. Use paper or thin cardboard as a barrier to separate the layers of clothing. Insert paper inside sleeves, pant legs, between the front and back of a shirt or jacket, and inside a dress. Fold the item loosely or roll it up using the sheets of paper on the workspace as the outer protective layer. Seal the rolled-up item with tape and place each one into a separate paper bag. Record all case-identifying information on the bag and apply biohazard warning labels to the outside of each package.
- Physical evidence can be contaminated by the CSI's sweat or saliva drops (sneeze or cough). Be sure to use proper PPE when processing the scene and packaging physical evidence.
- Laundering of clothes or bed linens does not always remove all traces of bodily fluids. Collect and submit these items for laboratory analysis because forensic biologists can utilize specific techniques to detect unseen trace evidence.

Luminol (3-aminophthalhydrazide) is a chemiluminescent compound used to determine the presence of blood in the absence of visual stains (see Figures 6.19a–6.19c). (*Chemiluminescence* is the emission of light without the emission of heat as the result of a chemical reaction.) It is very sensitive and can detect minute traces even when an effort has been made to wash away the blood. Luminol is sprayed on objects in a darkened room, and the luminescence is photographed with appropriate filters. Always collect visible stains before using luminol, because luminol can interfere with typing by diluting the sample and may limit the capacity of scientific analysis. Include control swabs of adjacent areas that do not luminesce. False positives are created with horseradish, household bleach, oranges, lemons, grapefruits, and radishes. Luminol is sometimes used as a presumptive test for visible blood, but its use should be limited to determining the areas that should be subjected to more thorough sampling. Proper PPE must be worn when using luminol because it is a lung and skin irritant.

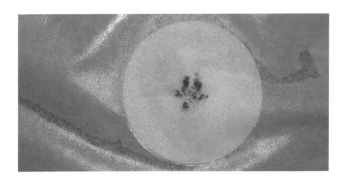

FIGURE 6.19A

Tests with luminol require that the test sample be sprayed with the reagent.

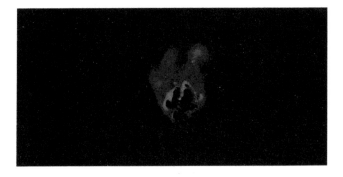

FIGURE 6.19B

A positive reaction occurs when a bluish glow emits from the suspected bloodstain. In this example, the camera exposure was 60 seconds.

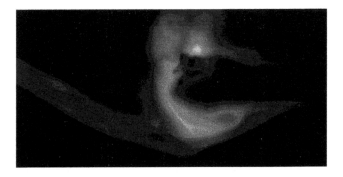

FIGURE 6.19C

The suspected sample must be re-sprayed with luminol to continue the glow, which may make the sample run. This is the same sample as in Figure 6.19b photographed at a 120-second exposure time.

Another blood visualizing agent is BLUESTARforensic®, which was developed to overcome some of the problems CSIs encountered with the exclusive use of luminol (see Figure 6.20). BLUESTAR lasts longer and does not require total darkness for blood stains to become visible. The area can be sprayed multiple times with BLUESTAR, and the luminescence intensity is higher than with other products (www.bluestar-forensic.com).

Fluorescein is another chemical that may enable the CSI to view bloodstains or patterns that cannot be seen under normal lighting conditions (see Figures 6.21a and 6.21b). An alternate light source

FIGURE 6.20
The crime scene in natural light and then after BLUESTAR® has been applied. *Photo courtesy of BLUESTAR-forensics.com.*

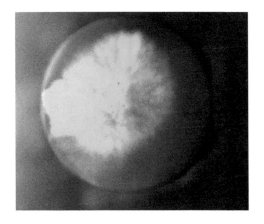

FIGURE 6.21A
A suspected bloodstain is sprayed with fluorescein reagent.

FIGURE 6.21B
Fluorescein reagent will fluoresce in the presence of blood using ultraviolet illumination.

is required to visualize the bloodstains or patterns. Unlike luminol, fluorescein does not react to household bleach. Neither luminol nor fluorescein has been found to interfere with DNA testing. Standard procedure, however, indicates that if blood is visible and can be collected without the use of either of these chemicals, they should not be used. If you need to enhance or identify stains or patterns that are not visible to the naked eye, collect evidence samples and cover the visible blood prior to spraying the area with either chemical. PPE must be worn at all times when using fluorescein.

Many evidence issues are shared between post-conviction cases and cold cases. Once again, a primary consideration is the potential for evidence to be contaminated as it is handled by attorneys, judges, and juries from the original trial.

Condom Trace Evidence

The advent of the CODIS database appears to have prompted sex offenders to begin using condoms when committing assaults. Just as burglars and other criminals use gloves to prevent leaving their fingerprints at the scenes of crimes, sex offenders often use condoms to prevent leaving seminal fluid evidence (DNA) at the scene of the crimes they commit. When a condom is discarded, valuable evidence is lost that cannot be retrieved. To overcome that problem, forensic scientists are now trained to detect trace evidence left by the condoms.

FIGURE 6.22

A condom package showing a fingerprint treated with fluorescing fingerprint powder.

Condom manufacturers have developed unique manufacturing formulas, including exchangeable trace materials that are contained in databases designed to allow cross-matching. Powders, lubricants, and spermicide content all contribute to trace evidence that can be detected and identified through various scientific analyses in the crime laboratory. Condom traces found inside a victim can provide evidence of penetration. Serial rapists tend to use the same brand of condom to commit repeated attacks, and the trace evidence can be utilized to link the perpetrator to multiple assaults. Discarded packages may have fingerprints on the outside (see Figure 6.22), and trace materials may be located on the inside of the package linking it to the victim and/or the suspect.

In collecting this type of evidence, the CSI must make one very distinct change in protocol. Everyone involved in the investigation, from the CSI to the medical personnel gathering evidence, must be sure to wear powder-free gloves. Many condom manufacturers use the same types of particulates, including cornstarch, talc, or silica, in the production of the condoms that are used in making latex or rubber gloves. The use of powder-free gloves ensures the integrity of the evidence and eliminates the potential for cross-contamination by another type of particulate material found on the gloves of those handling the evidence.

FIGURE 6.23
Human bone sectioned for DNA analysis.

USE OF DNA TO IDENTIFY VICTIMS

Items such as toothbrushes, cigarette butts, ear plugs, and hairbrushes were used to gather skin cells to build profiles of the victims of the September 11, 2001, terrorist attacks at the World Trade Center. Family members brought personal items of the victims to the New York City Medical Examiner's Office in the hopes of being able to claim the remains of family members who were lost in the terrorist attack.

Personal items can also be useful to build a DNA profile of a missing person, which can then be entered into a missing person database such as NamUs (www.namus.gov). Forensic anthropologists also collect bone marrow samples to submit to DNA laboratories to generate profiles of sets of unidentified human remains in an attempt to match them in the database (see Figure 6.23). These steps often bring closure to families and resolve cold cases for law enforcement agencies.

Discussion Questions

1. Generally, what is forensic biology? Specifically, explain what the study of serology entails.
2. What is the origin of deoxyribonucleic acid (DNA), and why is it considered an "individual" characteristic of a person? Why has DNA been accepted in courts?
3. What is CODIS, and why is it useful?
4. When you are investigating a sexual assault, what are the unique procedures that should be used, and why are they important?
5. What national database allows private citizens to query missing persons?

REFERENCES

Hedman, J., Jansson, L., Akel, Y., Wallmark, N., Liljestrand, R. G., Forsberg, C., & Ansell, R. (2020). The double-swab technique versus single swabs for human DNA recovery from various surfaces. *Forensic Science International: Genetics, 46,* 102253.

Jonsson, H., Magnusdottir, E., Eggertsson, H. P., Stefansson, O. A., Arnadottir, G. A., Eiriksson, O.,... & Stefansson, K. (2021). Differences between germline genomes of monozygotic twins. *Nature Genetics, 53*(1), 27–34.

CHAPTER 7

Blood Spatter Evidence

KEY TERMS

Bloodstain pattern analysis	Directionality	Point of origin or impact
Cast-off patterns	Impact spatter	Transfer stain
Contact stains	Passive stains	Wipe patterns
	Point of convergence	

What You Will Learn

Bloodstain pattern analysis is becoming a more frequent tool of CSIs. A specialist can properly identify many characteristics that assist in telling the story of the actions that occurred in a crime scene. Remember, there is no "L" in the proper usage of the term *blood spatter*.

MURDER IN THE NEW YEAR

Blood Spatter Evidence

Day 4 found Detective Mavis Fletcher, CSI Tom Smith, and Crime Scene Technician Ed Ellwenger back at the original crime scene. The house had been secured since they departed on the night of the murders, but to ensure admissibility of any additional evidence, Mavis had obtained a search warrant for the premises.

Tom Smith thrust a cup of hot chocolate into the hand of Officer Scott who was stationed outside the house. "Officer, you look like you could use a little sugar and chocolate pick-me-up. Long night?"

Scott rubbed his eyes and nodded. "Yes, sir. It was definitely long enough … not exactly action filled."

Mavis took off her gloves and walked to the spot in the kitchen where the couple was found. "Although we haven't received all the results we need, at least we have the blood work back."

DOI: 10.4324/9780429261657-7

Tom said, "Yeah, the BPA results confirm what you and I guessed. The HUI's spatter indicates Mrs. Morton was shot at close range, and perhaps Mr. Morton then shot himself in the heart."

"Perhaps?" Mavis queried.

"Yeah, perhaps," Tom replied.

> According to the evidence, the husband would have held the gun farther from his chest than would seem natural. Possible, but why, when one would think a person intent on shooting himself in the heart would simply press the barrel against his heart and pull the trigger.

Ed Ellwenger nodded in agreement. "And the position his body was found in could suggest he might have been trying to get away."

"Or not," the detective answered. "Blood spatter analysis offers us a clear picture of the wife's shooting but a somewhat more ambiguous result concerning Mr. Morton's demise."

Mavis Fletcher looked at her watch. "I will be interviewing Mrs. Sellers and the dean at their home this afternoon. After that, we'll see whether Michael Sellers stays in the 'maybe' suspect category or moves more in the direction of 'definite.'"

INTRODUCTION

Because blood is one of the most frequently encountered substances at a crime scene, its importance must not be underestimated. The position and shape of bloodstains may provide information about the circumstances of a crime. The nature of violent crime involves bloodshed, and a bloodstain pattern analyst (BPA) can provide many leads for the investigator. As more technicians are being certified, a wealth of information about the form of bloodstains is beginning to be utilized in the reconstruction of events (James, Kish, & Sutton, 2020).

FIGURE 7.1

Blood spatter characteristics used to determine direction of travel.

Bloodstain pattern analysis is the examination of the shapes, locations, and distribution patterns of bloodstains to provide an interpretation of the physical events that occurred at the crime scene (see Figure 7.1). Results of the analysis will also provide additional information that may be used by the medical examiner to establish the time of death of a victim.

The average male has five to six liters of blood in his body, and a female has slightly less, approximately four to five liters. The consensus is that a normal-sized individual must lose about 40 percent of the total volume of blood to produce irreversible shock and death.

While becoming a certified bloodstain pattern analyst requires years of training and practice, the CSI can learn to examine blood spatter at

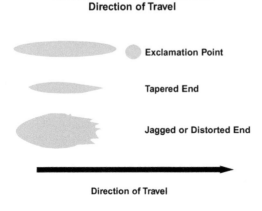

Characteristics Used to Determine Direction of Travel

Exclamation Point

Tapered End

Jagged or Distorted End

Direction of Travel

the crime scene and determine direction of travel and a general location for area of origin of the impact. This understanding is important, because the interpretation of blood spatter patterns and other evidence at crime scenes may reveal important investigative information, such as the positions of the victim, assailant, and objects at the scene; the type of weapon that was used to cause the spatter; the number of blows, shots, stabs, and so on that occurred; and the movement and direction of the victim and assailant after the bloodshed began. It may also support or contradict statements given by victims, suspects, or witnesses, and, most important, may keep an innocent person from being convicted.

Passive bloodstains are created by the force of gravity and can be found on a variety of surfaces, such as carpet, wood, tile, wallpaper, or clothing. A close inspection of the crime scene is required, and all stains must be documented. By applying the law of physics, mathematics, and trigonometry, bloodstain pattern analysis can provide information that will assist the investigator in determining what events occurred, who was or was not present, and the validity of a self-defense claim by the suspected perpetrator.

The crime scene may contain several areas where blood spatter is found. During the initial walkthrough, it is important to consider each location for analysis. In addition to the possible determination of the course and sequence of events, the reconstruction will allow the CSI to develop a plan for the collection of blood samples from the most logical sites after the scene has been documented. There is no need to sample every single blood drop. Careful analysis of the scene will result in accurate representative samples of blood being submitted to the crime laboratory for analysis.

THE NATURE OF BLOOD SPATTER EVIDENCE

A free-falling drop of blood forms a sphere and maintains that shape due to the force that pulls the surface molecules of a liquid toward the interior. This force creates surface tension and causes the liquid to resist penetration and separation. Regardless of the distance a drop of blood falls, it maintains the spherical shape because of the surface tension, which acts like an invisible outer skin.

A drop of blood will not break unless it strikes another object or surface or unless it is acted on by some force. When a drop of blood strikes a nonporous, smooth, and hard surface, such as a floor tile, it will create little, if any, spatter (see Figure 7.2). Falling or dripping blood is characterized by larger, more circular stains. Rough surfaces, like textured wallpaper, however, will break the surface tension with

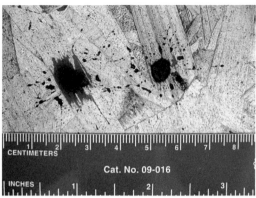

FIGURE 7.2
Blood droplets on linoleum floor.

FIGURE 7.3
Blood droplets on rough, porous surface.

rough edges that will produce spatter and irregular stains with serrated or spiny edges (see Figure 7.3).

Blood drops falling at a 90-degree angle will produce a circular stain of equal width and length. If it falls at an angle of less than 90 degrees, it will be more oval or elongated. When the bloodstain pattern analyst is determining the distance from which a drop of blood has fallen, it has been found that distances greater than 7 feet do not increase the diameter of the bloodstain. At distances less than 7 feet, the size or diameter of the bloodstain will increase with the distance from where it originates to where it falls.

By examining the edges of individual stains, the CSI can determine **directionality**, because the narrow end (or tail) of a stain usually points in the direction of travel. By using string to draw straight lines through the axes of the bloodstains, the CSI can establish a **point of convergence** (or area of convergence; see Figures 7.4 and 7.5). This convergence will represent the relative location of the source of the blood. A bloodstain pattern analyst can perform more detailed examinations and utilize 3D projections to determine an approximate location 90 degrees up from the 2D point of convergence. This will aid the investigation by identifying the angle of impact and the point of origin for the bloodstains. These findings will provide investigative leads that can corroborate or refute the statements of witnesses, suspects, or victims.

The size of blood spatters can be examined to indicate the velocity of the force that was applied. If a smaller (slower moving) force is involved, the spatter size will be larger. If a greater (faster moving) force is used, a smaller spatter will occur. Bloodstains smaller than a freely forming drop are referred to as "**impact spatter**." Historically, there

Point of Convergence

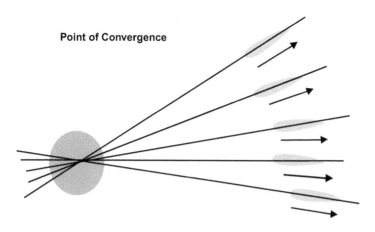

FIGURE 7.4
A diagram illustrating the point of convergence.

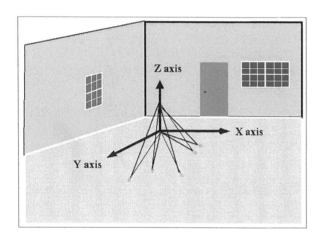

FIGURE 7.5
Diagram showing the use of stringing to determine the point of origin.

were three general patterns of blood spatter based on the correlation between the velocity of the impact and the size of the blood spatter. This terminology has largely been abandoned, though, in favor of simply classifying the spatter as impact spatter only until other factors have been established that will allow you to determine the type of activity that would create the observed spatter.

Low-velocity impact spatter (LVIS) results when blood is traveling at about 5 feet per second. A good example of LVIS is blood passively dropping into blood, such as a wound from an arm dripping into a pool of blood on the floor. The size of this type of blood spatter averages about 3 mm or more in diameter.

Medium-velocity impact spatter (MVIS) creates smaller spatter and is produced when the velocity of the force is between 5 and 25 feet per second. Blunt trauma, such as beating a victim with a fist, club, hammer, rock, or golf club, may result in MVIS spatter. Sharp trauma, including stabbing, would also create medium-velocity impact spatter that ranges in size from 1 to 3 mm in diameter. **Cast-off patterns** are created by blood being propelled by a force greater than gravity, as can happen, for instance, when blood is flung off a bloody object during a back swing.

High-velocity impact spatter (HVIS) occurs when the velocity of the force is above 100 feet per second and is generated by a gunshot, explosion, power tool, or automobile accident. HVIS blood spatter is almost mist-like and less than 1 mm in size (see Figure 7.6). Many mitigating factors can impact the size of HVIS spatter, including the caliber of weapon; location and number of shots; and impeding factors such as clothing, hair, boots, and so on.

With gunshots, there may be two different sets of spatter. Back spatter, or blowback, may be found on the weapon and the shooter. It is associated with an entrance wound. An exit wound can also create forward spatter, but there is usually more back spatter than forward spatter.

Current terminology utilizes five categories of bloodstains: passive stains, transfer stains, wipe patterns, contact stains, and miscellaneous patterns (ANSI/ASB, 2017). **Passive stains** are created by drips, flows, pools, and saturation stains. Drip patterns are formed when free-flowing blood drips from a stationary source. Rough surfaces cause the spheres of blood to spatter in irregular patterns with rough edges, whereas smooth surfaces, such as glass or ceramic tile, will not disrupt the spherical pattern of the blood drop.

FIGURE 7.6
High-velocity impact spatter.

Impact and projected spatter stains are the result of splashes, cast-off, arterial spurt, or gushing, as well as from the impact itself, and expiration (usually from the victim's mouth or nose). Cast-off occurs when blood accumulates at the area of impact and adheres to a moving object (see Figure 7.7). This object might be a weapon, but it can be anything in motion (e.g., a swinging hand or moving hair). As the object is repeatedly swung, centrifugal forces cause the blood to be flung off, resulting in cast-off patterns as the blood lands on walls or nearby items. These stains are round at the beginning of the trail (where the assailant was standing) and become more elongated as the trail continues. With blunt force trauma, the number of trails is indicative of the number of blows plus one. Remember, the first blow will not have cast-off because the blood is not present during the initial strike unless the weapon is an ax or machete.

Splash patterns may indicate movement of a victim after being injured. They are created when large volumes of blood are falling from a source, such as an injury. Arterial spurt may be small sprays or large gushes depending on the location of the arterial break and whether the injury is covered by clothing. Expiration bloodstain patterns occur only if the victim has blood in the mouth, nose, or airways or suffers an injury to the chest or neck involving the airways.

A **transfer stain** is created when a wet, bloody surface comes in contact with a secondary surface (see Figure 7.8). For example, a suspect with bloody hands might bump into a refrigerator door, leaving a palm impression on the surface. A recognizable image of all or a portion of the original surface may be observed in the pattern, such as a fingerprint, shoeprint, or even a weapon. Transfer stains occur from wipes, swipes, transfers, or contacts. A transfer stain may occur when a bloody object comes into contact with a secondary surface; for example, a knife may be carried away from the crime scene in a paper bag that is later discarded. On the inside of the bag, a transfer stain may be located that can subsequently be linked to the knife and the suspect (see Box 7.1).

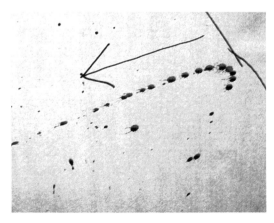
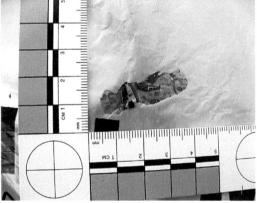

FIGURE 7.7
A cast-off blood spatter pattern. The arrow indicates the direction of blood travel from the instrument.

FIGURE 7.8
Transfer bloodstains on a plastic trash bag.

BOX 7.1 BLOODSTAIN PATTERN ANALYSIS EXPLAINED

Interesting photos and additional information on bloodstain pattern analysis can be found at http://forensicsciencesimplified.org/blood/principles.html.

FIGURE 7.9
Wiping blood patterns on a wall.

Wipe patterns are observed when a perpetrator attempts to clean up a crime scene by wiping away blood with a cloth (see Figure 7.9). **Contact stains** occur when a bloody fingerprint or shoeprint is left at the site of the attack.

The fifth category contains miscellaneous patterns, which can be void patterns, fly spot patterns, bubble rings, and perimeter or skeletonized bloodstains. A void pattern is created when an item is removed from the area after bloodstain spatter has been created. The void may clearly indicate the shape of the missing item, such as a credit card, piece of jewelry, or other article removed by the perpetrator. Drying times for blood are impacted by the temperature, humidity, air currents, and surface on which the blood has fallen. Bloodstains dry from the perimeter inward, and small spatters will typically dry within about 15 minutes. Skeletonized stains occur when the perimeter of the stain has dried and the center has flaked way, leaving the visible outer ring.

DOCUMENTING BLOODSTAIN PATTERN EVIDENCE

Often a bloodstain pattern analyst will not be available to examine the scene, so the documentation you create must allow the analyst to become familiar with the location through your work. Accurate measurements and photographs may permit the analyst to develop a reconstruction of the sequence of events that created the bloodstain pattern.

Video can provide an overall spatial relationship for documentation purposes and allows the viewer to observe the crime scene in a more dimensional perspective. However, you must corroborate these observations with scale drawings and accurately placed photographs for a more thorough analysis. Data such as the size and quantity of the blood drops, location, distribution, angle of impact, and characteristics of the target surface are essential to the accurate analysis of blood spatter. Because blood behaves according to the laws of fluid dynamics, a bloodstain pattern analyst can attempt to reproduce patterns under similar circumstances when accurate and complete documentation is collected by the CSI (see Box 7.2).

BOX 7.2 WHAT CAN A BLOODSTAIN PATTERN ANALYST TELL YOU?

A bloodstain pattern analyst can usually provide realistic and specific information, such as

- Position of victim or suspect—sitting, standing, lying down
- Evidence of a struggle
- Areas where stains are absent (voids in patterns), indicating someone or something blocked the path of the blood
- In-line stain patterns created by cast-off
- Sequence of events—movements of suspect or victim
- How many impacts and from what direction
- Indications that the scene was altered before the CSI arrived
- Whether stains or patterns are consistent with statements

The bloodstain pattern analyst may determine information that eliminates other avenues of investigation. By identifying whose blood is where, the analyst may prevent the need for additional costly lab analysis of blood samples.

FIGURE 7.10

CSIs using stringing and a protractor to locate point of origin.

Always include other information that may be useful to the bloodstain pattern analyst in your crime scene documentation. This includes information such as handedness of the suspect and victim (if known); physical descriptions of individuals, including injuries or physical limitations; and whether alcohol or other drug use is known. Also note features of the scene, such as any unusual physical characteristics; weather; and environmental conditions, such as whether the heat or air conditioning units are operational; the condition of blood pools and stains (wet, dry, or in the process of drying); and the presence of other fluids or substances in proximity to the blood.

The ability of blood to record physical actions and then yield evidence by interpretation of the stains is useful to CSIs, but only if the evidence is properly recorded through photography and precise measurements. As with any crime scene involving biological evidence, the CSI is reminded to utilize personal protective equipment (PPE) during the assessment and processing stages. Once the documentation stage is complete, it will be necessary to collect sufficient samples of the blood to submit for laboratory analysis. As the samples are collected, be sure they are accurately depicted on the diagram and in the photographs in the event the blood is from more than one individual.

Measuring techniques involve placing string at the base of each bloodstain and projecting the strings back to the point of convergence (see Figure 7.10). This simple stringing technique will yield a 2D model that will indicate an area of origin and can generally be completed by the CSI with assistance from another crime scene technician. Be sure to document all measuring and stringing exercises through video and photographs because these will be useful to the bloodstain pattern analyst in the final determination of the events surrounding the crime.

By measuring the width and length of the individual bloodstains in a pattern, the analyst can determine the angle of impact for that particular stain. Combining the area of origin with the angle of impact, the analyst can then use a protractor to create a 3D model to determine whether a victim was standing, lying down, or sitting when the impact that resulted in the blood spatter occurred. Each of these steps must be documented on an elevation crime scene sketch as well as in photographs and video.

DETECTING INVISIBLE BLOODSTAINS

Luminol can be used to locate blood at a scene where it is suspected that an attempt at cleanup was made. Remember that luminol does not provide a positive identification; it is instead used to determine the likelihood that blood is present. Do not use luminol on surfaces where blood is clearly present. Luminol and hemoglobin produce a chemical that phosphoresces (glows in the dark). It is sensitive and works well even on aged and decomposed bloodstains. Some cleaning agents (laundry detergent and bleach) and some painted surfaces may yield false positives as they react with luminol. Phenolphthalein is a confirmatory test that is often used by CSIs to eliminate false positives developed by luminol.

Although it is best to collect the entire object when processing a crime scene with bloodstained objects, this is not always possible. For example, if the pattern is contained on a wall or other immobile object, you must carefully document the stains and conditions and take control swabs from an unstained area in addition to the evidentiary swabs you are collecting. Control swabs must also be air-dried before being sealed for submission to the crime laboratory. A serologist will analyze some of the samples you collect to determine from whom it originated. ABO typing and DNA analysis are confirmatory tests conducted by the serologist in the laboratory.

When creating the sketches of the crime scene, in addition to the regular floor plan or bird's-eye view, you must include elevation drawings to accurately depict bloodstain patterns on vertical walls. Your photo logs should cross-reference the sketches to indicate where stains were located as well as the locations where samples were collected.

PHOTOGRAPHING THE SCENE

The use of proper techniques to document the location and condition of bloodstain patterns at the crime scene is essential for the bloodstain pattern analyst to make extrapolations and draw factual

FIGURE 7.11
Bloodstain analysis.

conclusions from the physical evidence. Use overall, midrange, and close-up photography techniques to ensure that you are accurately documenting the size, shape, and distribution of the individual stains as well as the overall patterns. Mount the camera on a tripod to ensure exact focusing and that the plane of the photograph is parallel to the surface being photographed.

Close-up photographs will depict the pattern of the stains and relative sizes. Remember that the first set of photographs should be taken without altering the scene, and then the scene should be photographed a second time with the appropriate measuring scales in place.

The midrange photographs should show the relationship of the stained area to the floor, corner of the room, or other recognizable features of the location. When you place the measuring scales in the photographs, position them so that the height of the stain pattern is easily discernible. In some photographs, you may need to insert an additional perpendicular scale at a right angle to document the horizontal spread of the stain pattern.

As a CSI, you must be cognizant of the fact that ceilings may contain important blood spatter patterns. Always remember to look up when you are conducting the initial walkthrough of the crime scene. Floors, too, may contain vital stain pattern evidence and should be carefully examined with a flashlight or forensic light source to ensure that all evidence is properly identified during the walkthrough and included in the collection phase (see Figure 7.11).

During crime scene processing, don't overlook items that may contain valuable bloodstain evidence, such as jewelry, eyeglasses, shoes, and clothing worn by the suspect or the victim. Sock or other fabric impressions may provide useful information as the reconstruction progresses and may assist in corroboration or refuting statements.

INTERPRETING EVIDENCE

Finding no bloodstains on the suspect or his or her clothing does not establish that the suspect was absent from the crime scene. Depending on the circumstances surrounding the crime, the suspect may have been wearing protective clothing—or may have been naked. The clothing that is being worn during questioning may not be the clothing that was worn during the commission of the crime. These findings, however, are essential to the overall investigation and subsequent prosecution of the crime because they may reveal preplanning or premeditation.

Bloodstain pattern evidence contributes to the overall investigation but may not be conclusive in and of itself. In combination with photographs, diagrams, and other physical evidence, bloodstain pattern evidence can provide a more complete explanation and allow the investigator to present a clearer picture of the scene. It may link the assailant to the victim by providing an explanation of how blood traveled in flight to land on the clothes of the suspect, and the location of the bloodstains may offer an explanation as to the position of both the victim and the suspect during the altercation. Consideration of the bloodstains at a crime scene will aid the investigator in determining whether statements made by the suspect, victim, or witness are consistent or inconsistent with the physical evidence.

The CSI must recognize the limitations of bloodstain pattern analysis. In some situations determining the point or area of origination is impractical or impossible to recreate with stringing methods. In these cases, a certified bloodstain pattern analyst should be consulted. In addition, forensic software specifically designed to assist the expert can be utilized to project the likely **point of origin or impact**. An experienced analyst can also study the crime scene to determine the sequence of events and may utilize additional enhancement techniques that could yield further physical evidence to the investigation. Remember that not all bloodstain patterns may still be visible, and through the use of latent blood visualization chemicals, supplementary evidence may be developed.

Bloodstain pattern analysis is a science because the stains and patterns can be reproduced under controlled circumstances. A certified analyst is capable of examining the crime scene and developing inferences based on years of training and experience, resulting in his or her acceptance as an expert witness. Similarly, the expert analyst can aid in the examination of clots of blood found at the crime scene or on items of clothing. In some investigations, it may be necessary to recreate the crime scene environment to determine the age of bloodstains or clots. These experiments are best left to the seasoned bloodstain pattern analyst because care must be taken to reproduce the environmental conditions as well as the circumstances surrounding the creation of the bloodstains.

Discussion Questions

1. Discuss the characteristics of blood spatter. Explain what can cause the spatter to be different given the same amount of blood.

2. Photographing bloodstains at a crime scene accurately is very important. Specifically, what should the photographs capture?
3. Is there a need for the CSI to include a diagram or sketch if photographs are taken properly? If so, why?
4. What tools are necessary for the point of convergence to be accurately determined?

REFERENCES

ANSI/ASB. (2017). *Terms and Definitions in Bloodstain Pattern Analysis* (Technical Report No. 33). Retrieved from https://www.aafs.org/asb-standard/terms-and-definitions-bloodstain-pattern-analysis

James, S. H., Kish, P. E., & Sutton, T. P. (2020). Principles of *Bloodstain Pattern Analysis: Theory and Practice* (1st Edition). Boca Raton, FL: CRC Press.

Firearms and Toolmark Evidence

What You Will Learn

Firearms can be individually identified with the proper examination. Various manufacturers of weapons and ammunition cooperate with law enforcement investigative units to establish databases and establish class and individual characteristics. Tools also leave identifiable markings. The similarities of weapon and toolmark identification are discussed in this chapter.

MURDER IN THE NEW YEAR

Firearms and Toolmark Evidence

Tom Smith parked his ancient Ford pick-up truck and looked at the eatery he was about to enter, the Bistro Café. He thought to himself. "Why would anyone choose to eat at such a restaurant like this when a 'Waffle House' is next door?"

Detective Mavis Fletcher looked up from her notebook as the CSI approached. "Tom, pull yourself up a chair. Since you were running late, I've already started. You can check out the menu and order at the cashier's station."

"No thanks, Detective," Tom replied, holding up his coffee mug. "I had a big breakfast. I'll just finish my coffee."

Mavis Fletcher smiled as she smacked her lips and returned to her lunch. "This cranberry–blue cheese spinach salad is delicious. You sure you don't want to try a bite?"

Tom took a sip of coffee. "Sorry, but it's against my religion to eat healthy. How did the interview with Mrs. Sellers go?"

The detective put her fork down.

> It was a useful interview. Although Amanda Sellers vouches for her husband, she was somewhat unclear on the details of her husband's whereabouts the whole afternoon and early evening. Apparently, she suffers from migraines and often takes a nap around mid to late afternoon. Her hubby seemed a little perturbed when she revealed that bit of information.

"That so?" Tom replied, putting his coffee cup down.

"When she noticed his displeasure, she quickly added that she and Michael were meeting with their pastor on a regular basis and were well on their way to repairing their relationship."

Tom drummed his fingers on the table. "Sounds a lot like what the dean told us a couple of days ago."

"It does at that," Mavis responded, wiping her mouth with her napkin. "That's not the half of it. Amanda revealed that someone broke into their home a month ago and took several World War II artifacts, including guns. Her husband added that he promptly reported the theft to the authorities."

"Seems like Amanda is either sleeping off migraines or talking a little too much. I don't suppose Michael was too happy about that revelation either."

Mavis speared a chunk of blue cheese. "Not particularly. One of the objects taken was a vintage German Luger, a semi-automatic nine mm pistol."

Tom Smith leaned back in his chair. "I do believe Ed dug a bullet out of the wall that matched the characteristics of nine mm ammo."

"That is correct. The only other circumstance involving a Luger was an accidental shooting two years ago when a member of some kind of local militia shot himself trying to quick draw."

Tom shook his head. "Vintage weapons can be tricky."

Mavis Fletcher looked at Tom. "I'll tell you what else is tricky—the whereabouts of Michael Sellers's allegedly stolen pistol."

Tom nodded. "Could his stolen property and the murder weapon be one and the same?"

"Could they, indeed?" the Detective replied. "An NIBIN search and test firing analysis of the striations and characteristics of the bullets could answer that question in short order. The shell casing will be entered into the NIBIN database for comparison."

INTRODUCTION

Establishing linkages between suspect, victim, and crime scene is important in every crime scene investigation. Associating bullets or other projectiles with the weapon that fired them is one important type of linkage in the field of forensic evidence. Similarly, connecting

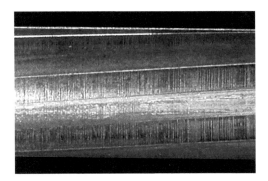

FIGURE 8.1
Revolver barrel showing lands and groove rifling.

FIGURE 8.2
Fragment of bullet showing lands and groove impressions.

a tool with the unique marks created by it can establish corroborating evidence that can lead to the identification of the perpetrator of a crime. This is the key to firearms and toolmark investigations: when a bullet travels through the barrel of a gun (see Figure 8.1), individual markings made by the **lands and grooves** on the inside of a barrel are created on the surface of the bullet (see Figure 8.2). These striations meet the definition of a toolmark—that is, an impression made on a softer surface (the bullet) by a tool or other object with a harder surface (the barrel's lands and grooves). By themselves, lands and grooves are not individual to a particular firearm; the markings created while rifling the barrel or through use and/or abuse are the individual characteristics examiners seek when performing their tests.

Firearms and toolmark examiners use comparison microscopes to complete forensic examinations of characteristics that are unique to a specific weapon or tool (see Figure 8.3). Some irregularities, impressions, abrasions, and striations are significant individual markings that provide sufficient evidence that the marks were made by a certain weapon or tool to the exclusion of all others examined. Because these two areas of crime scene investigation and microscopic examination are similar, they will be discussed in the same chapter.

There are two categories of firearms: handguns and long guns. Handguns include both revolvers and pistols; both are designed to be fired with one hand and are the weapon of choice in most firearms crimes. They are small and easy to conceal, and ammunition is still relatively easy to acquire. Rifles and shotguns are the most prevalent types of long guns, but this class also includes machine guns and any other weapons that are designed for being fired from the shoulder using both hands.

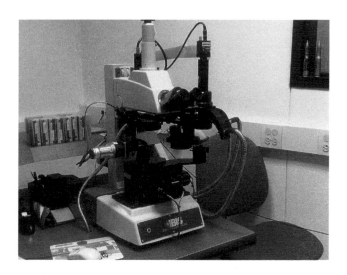

FIGURE 8.3

An NIBIN workstation with comparison microscope. A comparison microscope allows the viewing of specimens on two stages at the same time. It is commonly used to compare test bullets or toolmarks with questioned specimens.

BOX 8.1 QUESTIONS A FIREARMS EXAMINER CAN ANSWER

- What type and caliber of weapon was discharged?
- What was the sequence of events?
- Was the firearm functioning properly?
- At what angle and distance was the gun fired? (Usually, this type of examination must be conducted by a private trajectory analyst rather than a publicly funded laboratory.)

Firearms identification should not be confused with the term **ballistics**, which means the study of a projectile in motion. CSIs and detectives realize the value of working with firearms examiners because they can assist in the reconstruction of a shooting event (see Box 8.1).

Toolmarks are often found at burglary investigation scenes; however, they are prevalent in other types of crimes as well.

It is possible to find marks on many different surfaces, including wood, metal, paint, or any location where a soft surface has been impressed by a hard object. Some of the more common edges studied by toolmark examiners include those caused by saws, scissors, screwdrivers, knives, pry bars, tire tools, and tin snips (see Figure 8.4).

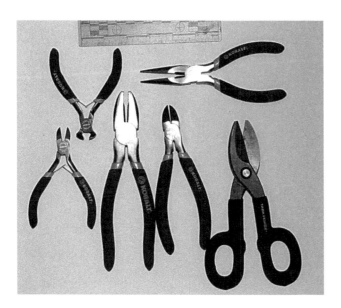

FIGURE 8.4
Various cutting tools that will leave microscopic striation marks.

BULLETS AND CARTRIDGE CASINGS

Several types of projectiles or bullets are used in the cartridges of ammunition, including lead bullets, semi-jacketed bullets, full-metal jackets, and shotgun slugs and buckshot, depending on the type of weapon and the target (see Figures 8.5–8.8). All types of cartridge ammunition include a projectile, powder, primer, and cartridge or shell case as the main components. Cartridges are referred to as either rim-fire or center-fire cartridges. This designation refers to the position of the primer in the base of the cartridge. When the trigger is pulled, the firing pin strikes the primer, which causes the

FIGURE 8.5A
A .22-caliber rim-fire cartridge.

FIGURE 8.5B
Base of .22-caliber rim-fire cartridge.

FIGURE 8.6A
A .40-caliber center-fire cartridge.

FIGURE 8.6B
Base of .40-caliber center-fire cartridge.

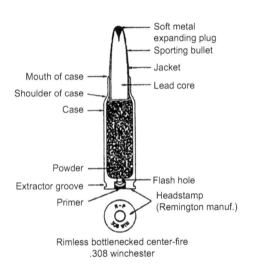

Soft metal expanding plug
Sporting bullet
Jacket
Mouth of case
Lead core
Shoulder of case
Case
Powder
Extractor groove
Flash hole
Primer
Headstamp (Remington manuf.)

Rimless bottlenecked center-fire
.308 winchester

FIGURE 8.7A
Anatomy of a cartridge.

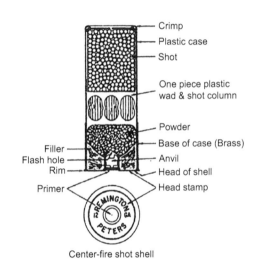

Crimp
Plastic case
Shot
One piece plastic wad & shot column
Powder
Filler
Base of case (Brass)
Flash hole
Anvil
Rim
Head of shell
Primer
Head stamp

Center-fire shot shell

FIGURE 8.7B
Anatomy of a shotgun shell.

detonation of a shock-sensitive primary explosive, which then ignites the gunpowder and propels the bullet down the barrel.

Bullets are generally made from lead, which is a soft, heavy metal. It can easily cause jamming in magazine-fed semi-automatic handguns; it can disintegrate or melt in the barrels of rifles with high-muzzle velocities; and it can also disintegrate, instead of penetrate, when striking harder surfaces. As a result, many manufacturers encase the bullet in a metal jacket. The jacket is usually brass, copper,

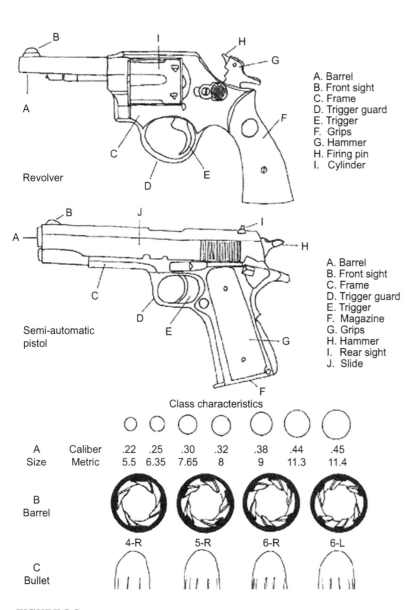

A. Barrel
B. Front sight
C. Frame
D. Trigger guard
E. Trigger
F. Grips
G. Hammer
H. Firing pin
I. Cylinder

Revolver

A. Barrel
B. Front sight
C. Frame
D. Trigger guard
E. Trigger
F. Magazine
G. Grips
H. Hammer
I. Rear sight
J. Slide

Semi-automatic
pistol

Class characteristics

A Size	Caliber	.22	.25	.30	.32	.38	.44	.45
	Metric	5.5	6.35	7.65	8	9	11.3	11.4

B
Barrel

4-R   5-R   6-R   6-L

C
Bullet

FIGURE 8.8
Revolver, pistol, and ammunition characteristics.

or an alloy, and this keeps the bullet from jamming, melting, or disintegrating. Jacketed bullets also reduce fouling or residue deposits in the barrel of the gun. There are many types of bullets, including wad-cutter, semi-wad-cutter, full-metal jacket, semi-jacketed, soft-point, hollow-point, Teflon-coated, and frangible bullets, and each has a particular use.

CLASS VERSUS INDIVIDUAL CHARACTERISTICS

Just as individuals have fingerprints that are unique, firearms have individual characteristics that allow forensic firearm examiners to determine if a bullet was fired from a particular weapon. Firearm identification is primarily concerned with the determination of whether a bullet, cartridge case, or other ammunition was fired, extracted, or ejected from a specific firearm.

Research and studies over the years have shown that no two firearms—even those consecutively made of the same make and model—will produce the same unique marks (striations) on fired bullets and cartridge cases (see Boxes 8.2 and 8.3). The barrels of most firearms, with the exception of zip guns and shotguns, are rifled with lands and grooves that twist down the length of the barrel and are designed to put spin on the bullet, add stability, and increase accuracy. Minor differences created by wear on the tools used in the rifling manufacturing process make every firearm unique. When a bullet travels through the barrel, the unique markings created by wear on the lands and grooves create scratches—known as **striations**—on the bullet. Individual characteristics can also be made by use, abuse, and wear and tear of a specific tool or firearm. These unique striations allow firearms examiners to match bullets to the weapons that discharged them.

If a suspect handgun is located and submitted for testing, the firearms examination includes test firing the weapon into a water tank (using similar ammunition) to create a (known) comparison sample and to check the firearm's operability (see Figure 8.9). The known

BOX 8.2 CLASS CHARACTERISTICS OF BULLETS

- Caliber (size)
- Number of lands and grooves
- Width of lands and grooves

- Degree of twist
- Direction of rifling twist

BOX 8.3 CLASS CHARACTERISTICS OF CARTRIDGE CASES DISCHARGED IN GUNS

- Caliber
- Firing pin location
- Relative location of extractor/ejector
- Primer type

- Extractor and ejector marks
- Firing pin size and shape
- Breechface markings

bullet and the bullets found at the scene or recovered from the victim are then placed side by side on a comparison microscope, where they can be examined to see if the striations match (see Figures 8.10 and 8.11). The breechface and firing pin impressions as well as the extractor, ejector, and possible chamber markings can also be compared if

FIGURE 8.9

A test bullet recovery water tank. Bullets are fired into a tank of water to prevent damage to the bullet. Water is a chosen test firing medium because it does not add to or subtract from the markings placed on a fired bullet by a rifled barrel. The bullet is then retrieved from the tank and used to compare with questioned bullets on a comparison microscope. *Knoxville Police Department.*

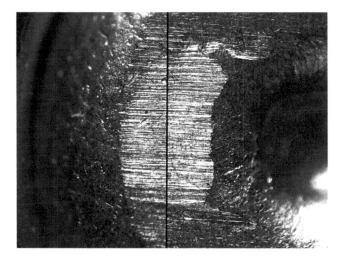

FIGURE 8.10

A comparison microscope examination of two cartridge cases showing machine markings (striations) made by the breech (rear) of the pistol that fired the cartridge cases. The firing pin impression can be seen on the right side of the photograph. *Knoxville Police Department.*

FIGURE 8.11
A comparison microscope examination of two bullets showing striations matching the lands and grooves of the bullets. *Knoxville Police Department.*

FIGURE 8.12
Two .45-caliber bullets fired from two identical pistols. The class characteristics match, but the microscopic striations do not.

cartridge cases are found at the scene of the crime or in the suspect weapon.

For pistols or rifles, ejectors and/or extractors also create markings on cartridge cases that can be examined against a test-fired cartridge case. The firearms examiner can render four conclusions concerning the comparison of a suspect weapon to recovered bullets:

- The bullet was fired by the suspect gun.
- Class characteristics and striations do not match; therefore, the suspect gun is excluded.
- Class characteristics match, but striations do not (see Figure 8.12 for an example); therefore, the results are inconclusive.
- The bullet had no microscopic marks of value and was unsuitable for identification.

LOCATING, COLLECTING, PACKAGING, AND SUBMITTING EVIDENCE

When any firearm is located, take immediate steps to secure it and take all safety precautions. You may not know whether the weapon is loaded, but you should treat it as a loaded gun at all times. Document the location of the weapon with photographs, notes, and appropriate entries on the crime scene sketch. After documenting its position, examine the firearm for trace/transfer evidence, such as latent fingerprint, hair and fiber, toolmark (defaced serial numbers), and blood spatter evidence.

If the firearm is a revolver, indicate the position of the cylinder as well as the chamber from which each cartridge or cartridge case was unloaded. This can be done by marking the cylinder on each

FIGURE 8.13
Cylinder open on revolver showing where cartridges were located.

FIGURE 8.14
Gunshot residue flaming on the front of the cylinder of a revolver.

side of the top strap (that part of the frame directly above the cylinder) and numbering each cartridge or cartridge case as it is removed. Do not etch or scratch any markings, as this could deface the firearm or, in some instances, destroy striations that could be used for examination. Laboratories recommend the use of a permanent marker. Some agency and laboratory protocols may not allow this procedure, however, and if the weapon is going to be processed for latent prints or DNA, you should preserve this information by photographing the cylinder and cartridges before they are moved.

Open the cylinder, keeping the chamber that was aligned with the barrel in the 12-o'clock position (see Figure 8.13). Photograph the front and back of the cylinder while it is in this position. This will allow you to document the cylinder gunshot residue (GSR) flash rings or flaming around the chambers on the front of the cylinder, as well as the cartridge headstamps that indicate the caliber and make of the cartridge case (see Figure 8.14). These pictures will also document the primer condition and the cartridge position in the back of the cylinder. After taking these photographs, remove each of the cartridges and place them on a sheet of paper in the same order and take additional pictures. Each cartridge should be assigned a unique identification number and packaged individually in protective material to preserve any latent prints or trace evidence.

A diagram indicating cartridge/cartridge case positions, caliber, manufacturer, primer color, primer conditions, and bullet type, if

1 = Remington-Peters spent

FIGURE 8.15

A hand-drawn diagram depicting the location of rounds of ammunition in a revolver.

applicable, should be made and included in the documentation that will be submitted to the crime laboratory (see Figure 8.15).

If the agency protocol requires physical marks to be placed on all cartridges and cartridge cases, it is recommended you use the first letter of your last name and a unique evidence number assigned to each particular item of evidence. The cartridge should be marked at the top of the casing by the mouth, and care must be given to ensure that you don't damage any ejector marks. For cartridge cases, these marks should be made on the inside top of the cases. The same procedure should be followed with ammunition recovered from magazine-fed pistols or other auto-loading firearms. Indicate which cartridge was recovered from the chamber and the position of each cartridge in the magazine. Enter all identifying information, and attach an evidence tag to the trigger guard of each firearm.

If agency protocol does not include marking each cartridge in the magazine of a pistol, document the position with photographs and then remove each cartridge and place it on a piece of paper in the same order as it was found in the magazine. Assign unique numbers to each item and take several photographs before packaging individually for submission to the firearms examiner. Remember that all packages containing ammunition must be labeled "LIVE AMMUNITION" and transported to the lab in the appropriate manner.

If the suspect weapon is a pistol, be sure to document the position of the safety and the hammer and whether the serial number has been defaced. If the pistol is magazine fed, the magazine must be removed first and then the chamber cleared. Initial the magazine and the cartridges following the steps previously outlined. Mark the cartridges according to their order in the magazine. Never wipe the firearm off or clean the bore, because you may remove trace evidence. Unless there is imminent danger of losing trace evidence, the CSI should leave any blood or foreign material (trace) attached to the firearm and affix a biohazard label to the outside of the evidence box.

When preparing firearms for transportation from the crime scene, use sturdy cardboard boxes and plastic ties to secure the weapon and prevent any damage or loss of trace evidence. If possible, the cylinder of a revolver should be secured in the open position, and if the weapon is a pistol, the slide should be locked back and open. Unless agency policy dictates otherwise, do not put a plastic-tie or zip-tie through the barrel because doing so may add extraneous markings if sand and/or grit is present.

Long guns should be collected following the same procedure as handguns. Make note of the position of the safety and the position of the hammer, bolt, or striker before moving the firearm. If the firearm is still loaded, the ammunition must be removed. Prior to removing the ammunition, be sure to note the order in which the loaded cartridges were in the firearm when it was recovered.

Bullets or bullet fragments may be classified as projectiles, components from a cartridge, or deformed bullets. Each item should be individually wrapped in clean paper or a plastic bag and placed in a rigid container to prevent additional damage from occurring during transit. On the container, indicate the source of each item, affix appropriate labels, and seal the evidence package.

Remember to check with your state or regional crime laboratory regarding proper protocols for firearms evidence. Forensic

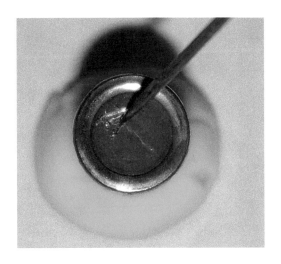

FIGURE 8.16
If bullets must be marked, they should be marked on the base so that microscopic striations are not damaged.

laboratories vary in their recommendations concerning the need to place an identifying mark on each bullet. Many labs do not want additional marks placed on the evidentiary item, and request that marks be placed on the container when it is sealed. If your lab does allow marking on the bullets, do not disturb the sides or cylindrical portion (bearing surface) of the bullet. Mark bullets only on the base or a deformed area with no striations (see Figure 8.16).

Cartridges are ammunition typically consisting of a bullet, primer, powder, and cartridge case. A cartridge case is the portion of the cartridge that contains the gunpowder and primer and into which the bullet is seated to complete the cartridge. Note that hand-loaded or reloaded ammunition might not include primers or powder in it, so while standard manufactured cartridges are generally encountered, it is possible to locate improperly loaded ammunition.

In the case of a pistol, the portion of the cartridge that is extracted and ejected from the chamber after the bullet has been fired is referred to as the "discharged cartridge case." Each cartridge or cartridge case should be wrapped individually in clean paper or a plastic bag and placed in a rigid container to prevent further damage. Indicate on the container where each cartridge or case was located. You should not mark cartridges or cartridge cases near the rim, head, or primer; you should place the mark near the mouth of the case. When sealing the packages, remember to note the contents of the package as "LIVE AMMUNITION," if applicable.

In the case of shotguns, recover as much of the shot material and wadding as possible (see Figures 8.17 and 8.18). Try not to damage the shot when collecting it for evidence. Package pellets and wads from different locations in separate containers, and clearly indicate the source of the evidence. You should not attempt to mark pellets or wadding.

FIGURE 8.17
An example of plastic wadding from a shotgun shell.

FIGURE 8.18
An example of pellets from a shotgun shell.

If a shot pattern is present at the crime scene, on a victim, or on an object that cannot be submitted to the laboratory (such as a wall, car, or house), a scaled photograph should be taken first. While every effort should be made to acquire the section or area where shot evidence is located, it is sometimes not physically feasible to do so (e.g., on a concrete bridge). Take measurements, make a video, and record written notes before attempting to remove the shot material.

Articles of clothing that are going to be submitted to the crime laboratory for testing to determine the presence of gunpowder residue must be air-dried before packaging if they contain wet blood. Place cardboard or paper under, inside, and over the garment to separate layers, sleeves, pants legs, or cuffs and prevent cross-contamination or loss of trace evidence. The site of the bullet hole and the surrounding area should be sandwiched between two pieces of cardboard or paper in a fixed position. Fold or roll the item; then seal and place it into a paper bag to prevent loss of evidence. Indicate the contents of the package and identifying information, and affix biohazard labels on the outside of the package if any blood is present on the item. Do not use plastic bags if the item of evidence contains blood or other body fluids.

A firearm recovered from under water should be packaged in the same water in which it was found in a sealed plastic bag to keep the weapon from rusting. Differences in pH, organic materials, etc. may be different, so use of the same water is critical. This bag should be packed in a sturdy box and properly labeled and sealed. It should be hand delivered to the laboratory to prevent any damage to the weapon or the packaging.

SAFETY TIP

Remember that if a rusted firearm is recovered from water, it may be rusted shut and loaded, so extreme care must be taken to ensure safe transport and packaging.

You must remember to use caution when recovering fired bullets and shot pellets from the ceiling, walls, floor, furniture, or body of a victim to prevent them from being altered in any way. When bullets are embedded in wood or some other material, it is recommended that a portion of the material be secured so that the bullets can be removed at the laboratory. You should never try to pry a bullet out of an object with a sharp tool or pocketknife unless you have been properly trained to do so. Correct procedures for bullet removal do not allow hard objects to come in contact with the surface of the fired bullet to ensure no extraneous markings are placed on the bullet.

Fired cartridge cases may contain marks left by the firing pin, ejector, extractor, magazine, chamber, and breech face. Firearms examiners can compare these marks and match them with test-fired cartridge cases from the evidence weapon as well as other fired cartridge cases found at the crime scene, on a suspect, in a suspect's vehicle, etc., to establish more linkages in the investigation. If you are investigating a case in which a shotgun was used, it is possible that more than one shot was fired and more than one size of pellet may be found at the scene. It is important to keep the recovered pellets from each shot separated whenever possible.

Like the brass cartridge case, the brass portion of the fired shotgun shell may display identifying markings. Sometimes the shotgun shell's body may have markings. Most have information printed on the shell's body that includes the size of the shell, load, amount of shot (expressed in ounces), and sometimes the type of shot.

In some instances, the wadding from shotgun shells could be in the victim, provided the weapon was held close enough (usually within 10 feet). If not, a careful examination of the scene will reveal at least part of the wadding. The wadding can bring to light very interesting information for the investigator, such as the make of the shotgun shell used, the gauge of the gun, the approximate position from which the shot was fired, and the size of the shot that was loaded in the shell (unless the shotgun was reloaded). You can expect to find the wadding within a distance of 0 to 40 feet from where the shot was fired. When recovering wadding from the scene, place it in individual containers and label appropriately.

TRAJECTORIES AND MEASUREMENTS

The importance of documenting all the critical aspects of ballistics-related evidence found at a crime scene cannot be overemphasized. Accurate documentation of this evidence can assist with the reconstruction of the events of the crime. Discharged cartridge cases, ejection patterns, gunshot residue patterns, and ballistic damage patterns (in the form of bullet holes or ballistic impact marks) can all assist the CSI with a possible reconstruction of the positions, movements, and sequence of events of the crime.

At the scene of a shooting, the CSI will be confronted with many items that appear to be ballistic damage evidence. You will have to determine what is or is not such evidence. Simple chemical tests for lead and other metals associated with bullets can be performed on the damaged sites if there is a question as to whether a hole or impact site was actually made by a bullet or if it was made by a secondary projectile. One such test is the sodium rhodizonate test for lead. The materials needed for this test consist of an appropriate-sized sterile filter paper with a plastic or Mylar film backing, 10 percent acetic acid, and a solution of sodium rhodizonate and deionized water. This solution should preferably be mixed fresh at the scene because it has a very short shelf-life. Before this test is performed at any of the sites, the evidence must be thoroughly documented in the same manner as other physical evidence.

As with any chemical field test, positive and negative control tests should be conducted on the reagent to make certain the test is working properly. This entails testing the reagent on a known lead sample and on a blank. The known lead sample should produce a positive reaction and the blank a negative one. These control tests should be documented with written notes and also photographed. Once the reagent is deemed to be working properly, it can be used on the questioned specimen. Care must be taken to limit any alterations to the various sites during the testing. The test is performed by placing a drop or two of the acid on the paper side of the filter paper and then carefully placing the acid-wet paper on and in the sites. Remove the paper and place a drop or two of the sodium rhodizonate on the paper. If trace amounts of lead are present, a dark red to purplish color will appear instantly on the filter paper. A similar test can be performed (in the same manner as previously described) for copper, using dithiooxamide. Once the tests are completed, they should be documented in the written notes, and photographs should be taken of the test results next to the test site. These types of field tests should not be performed on possible ballistic-damaged clothing in the field. This type of testing is always better performed in a laboratory.

Discharged cartridge case patterns (ejection patterns) can aid in identifying where a shooter was standing when the weapon was fired if they have not been disturbed or altered by emergency personnel. Accurate documentation in the form of photographs (long, medium, close-up, and overhead views of the entire pattern), written measurements of the discharge, the precise location of cartridge casings at the scene utilizing one of the standard measuring techniques, and a sketch showing the discharged cartridge casing positions plotted on a 2D plane drawn to scale (see Figure 8.19) are all required to assist in the reconstruction. If a suspect firearm is recovered, a series of ejection pattern tests can be performed by firearms examiners utilizing the firearm and the same type of ammunition associated with the scene and the firearm. It is preferable to submit suspect ammunition, if possible, to use for these testing purposes. If suspect ammunition is not available, some labs will not perform this examination because "similar" ammunition may be from different lots, and powders may have changed slightly, which may alter the patterns derived from laboratory testing.

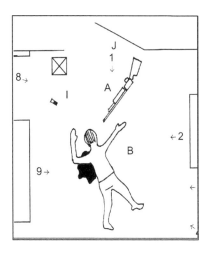

FIGURE 8.19
A crime scene sketch depicting the location of a spent shotgun shell to help establish the location of the shooting.

Other factors to consider when formulating the tests are the shooter's height or suspected height; the shooter's hand position and grip; the angle, trajectory, and sequence of shots; any movement of the shooter; weather conditions; and type of ground surface at the scene. These factors must be duplicated as closely as possible to the pattern found at the crime scene for the ejection pattern tests to be fair and accurate. These tests should be documented in the same manner as the scene, and a video should be made of actual test fires from several vantage points.

Other questions may arise with ballistic damage evidence:

- Which damage indicates an entrance or an exit hole?
- What is the sequence of events and shots fired?

Some of the answers can be obtained by the field tests and the presence of visible gunshot residue. Other possible ballistic damage evidence will require careful examination of the damage, which includes the detailed measurements that were taken prior to the chemical tests and a good understanding of the physics involved in creating the damage, such as the size, shape, and characteristics of both the damaged article and the bullet.

Certain basic effects occur when a cylindrical object impacts another surface. The energy on the impact side will cause the impacted surface to come under compression, and the opposite side of the impact will come under tension. The edges of the impact site under compression will typically tend to be more clearly defined, with somewhat smoother edges and an inward punch-like appearance. This is known as a "collar abrasion," which is similar to what one would see when drilling a hole with a drill bit. The opposite side of the impact, which is under tension, will actually break or fracture first, causing uneven, rough, damaged edges.

A good example of this would be using your two thumbs to apply pressure away from your body, at a single point on the center of the same side of a pencil, while pulling the ends of the opposite side of the pencil toward your body. The thumb side is under compression and the opposite side is under tension. When enough force is applied to overcome the tensile strength of the pencil, the opposite side of the pencil, which is under tension, will splinter and break with rough sharp edges. The exits will also have some sort of cone-like appearance caused by the tension break. This coning effect is typically prevalent with bullet holes in plate glass, making a determination of entrance and exit relatively easy (see Figure 8.20; also see Chapter 5).

Due to the laminate on automobile safety glass, determining from which side a window was fractured may be harder to differentiate, but it still follows the same basic physics as previously described. A thorough examination of the damage will show the classic concave coning caused by the side under tension breaking on the exit side of the glass. A glass-free ring of the plastic laminate will be exposed in the exit crater, while the glass on the entrance side will either be covering the laminate or have noticeably less laminate exposed than the exit side. One more item that might assist with the determination of entrance and exit location is to look for some curling in the laminate. The laminate curl will typically follow in the direction of the force that broke through it.

Another method of determining the direction in which a bullet passed through glass is to scratch your fingernail across the glass fractures on either side of the glass. Several types of glass fracture patterns occur when glass is broken. The two most commonly seen are radial and concentric fractures. **Radial fractures** begin at the center of the impact site and propagate outward like an asterisk and occur on the exit side of the glass due to the tension breaks (see Figure 8.21). **Concentric fractures** are a series of circular cracks that surround the impact site and move away from the site, with each circular fracture increasing its diameter as it propagates outward, like the ripples in water when a stone is dropped (see Figure 8.22). The concentric fractures occur on the impact side of the glass, after the radial fractures, because tension has now been transferred to the impact side of the glass by the bowing of the glass caused by the force of the bullet passing through it. By scraping your fingernail across the glass, you will feel only one type of fracture pattern present for each side of the glass. The side with the concentric fractures is the side the bullet entered, and the side with radial fractures is the side the bullet exited.

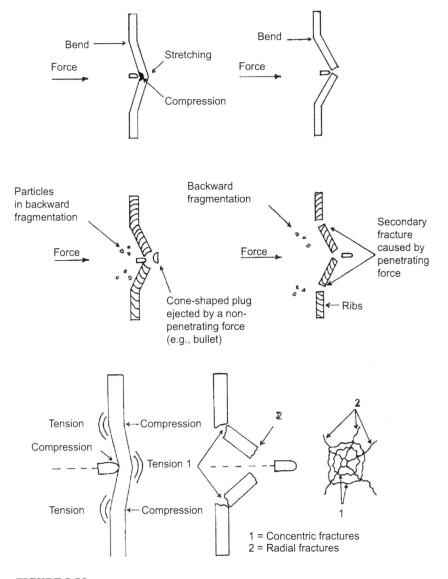

FIGURE 8.20
Effects of bullets on glass.

These same glass fractures can also possibly assist the CSI with determining angles, directionality (up, down, left, or right), and sequence. For example, a bullet passing through glass at 90 degrees typically leaves a circular hole with radial and concentric fracture patterns evenly dispersed around the bullet hole. However, a bullet passing through the glass at an angle will create more of an elliptical-shaped hole with radial and concentric fracture patterns concentrated more to the side of bullet hole toward which the bullet is traveling, and less (or none) on the side of the hole from which the bullet came.

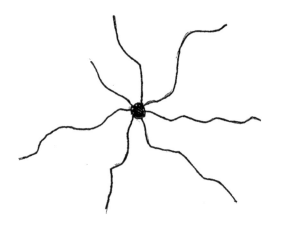

FIGURE 8.21
Diagram showing radial fractures in glass.

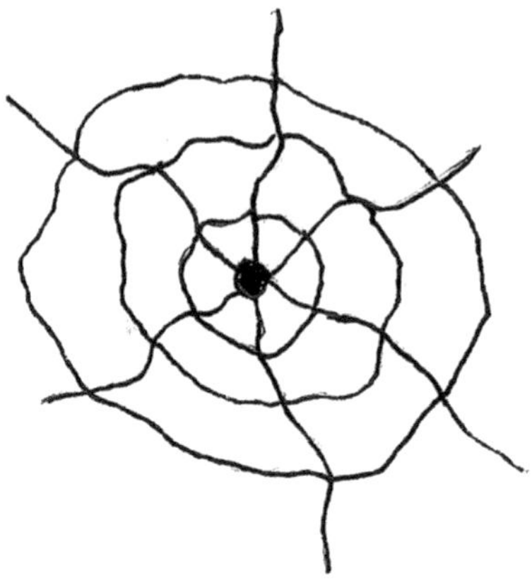

FIGURE 8.22
Diagram showing concentric fractures in glass.

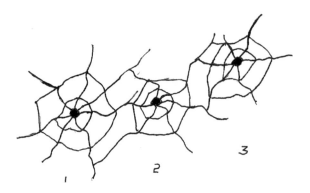

FIGURE 8.23
Diagram showing multiple bullet holes in glass, demonstrating termination points. The numbers represent the order in which the bullets entered the glass.

The concentration of the fractures is directly proportional to the angle of impact. With regard to sequencing multiple bullet holes in glass (see Figure 8.23), this may be possible to determine by viewing the radial-fracture line-termination points. The first bullet hole in the glass will have radial fractures that are unimpeded and terminate on their own. The next subsequent bullet hole will have its radial fracture terminated where it came in contact with the radial fractures of the first bullet hole, and so on for any other subsequent bullet hole in that glass. Radial fractures cannot pass over another radial fracture and continue onward. By carefully examining the radial fractures for each bullet hole and determining where they terminate, you may be able to establish the sequence of shots fired.

Another important source of ballistic reconstruction information is the ballistic **trajectory**, the path a bullet takes when a weapon is discharged. This information, obtained from the scene, can be extremely helpful in locating a shooter's positions and movements, and in determining the possible sequence of the shots. The ballistic trajectory information can be obtained from a number of sources, such as GSR patterns found on surfaces, the bullet wounds of victims, and ballistic damage con-

SAFETY TIP

One note of caution concerning trajectory calculations: If the bullet's flight path has been altered, for whatever reason, it could cause deflection of the bullet's trajectory or cause the bullet to tumble, which could seriously undermine some reconstruction efforts.

sisting of bullet holes/bullet impact marks on surfaces. The detailed measurements of the physical evidence can be utilized to calculate angles of impact or entry, in the same manner as bloodstains, because a spherical or cylindrical object (blood, GSR, or a bullet) is striking a surface, which in turn will a leave a geometric pattern (a bloodstain, GSR pattern, bullet hole, or bullet impact mark) from a true circle to an ellipse in or on the surface that is directly proportional to the angle of impact or entry. This is a basic application of physics and the language of physics and math (specifically, geometry and trigonometry).

Before any attempt is made at determining a trajectory, all items must be documented in the same manner as previously outlined for discharged cartridge cases. A special note must be made about the proper photographic documentation of GSR, ballistic wounds, and ballistic damage, especially if the CSI does not have the training and experience to perform the ballistic trajectory calculations and will be relying on a firearms examiner to perform these calculations. You must ensure that a scale is always present in the photographs and that the lens of the camera is parallel to the surface and at 90 degrees to the ballistic damage evidence. Use bracketing with the flash unit at an oblique angle around the ballistic damage. It is highly recommended that a tripod be utilized to ensure accuracy.

If you have completed training and have access to a forensic light source, the items/surfaces should be examined under various wavelengths of the forensic light source and photographed appropriately when a significant fluorescence is observed. Once the photographs have been completed, the CSI must take detailed measurements of the GSR patterns, bullet wounds, and ballistic damage, including bullet holes/bullet impact marks, specific diameters, lengths, and widths. Care must be taken to ensure that no alterations occur to the aforementioned items while you are taking the measurements.

Once these angles have been calculated and whether a bullet hole occurred upon entrance or exit has been determined, the CSI can calculate and document the trajectories utilizing a variety of commercially available trajectory kits.

Laser Protractor Kit

Once the angle has been calculated, in the case of GSR on a stationary surface, a bullet hole, or a bullet impact mark, a specially designed zero-base **laser protractor kit** is set to the calculated angle and placed in the appropriate location at the site of the pattern. The laser is then projected to a possible terminal point (forward or reverse). If these points are located, they must then be documented with written notes and measurements, photographed, and plotted on a sketch. One more set of measurements must be taken, showing the angle of the surface containing the ballistic damage. Another non-laser, zero-base protractor is typically used to find this point. The trajectories should be documented; several methods of photographic documentation can be employed:

1. Utilize photographic fog (an aerosol haze containing mineral oil) to visualize the lasers (see Figure 8.24) and photograph the illuminated trajectories from several vantage points.
2. After identifying the terminal points, mark them. Then, utilizing reflective photographic strings or colored strings stretched tightly and secured between the sites—bullet hole(s) and terminal points (forward and reverse)—take photographs of the trajectory strings from several vantage points.

FIGURE 8.24
Green laser trajectory measured with photographic fog to record laser beam angle.

Laser Trajectory Rod Kit

The laser trajectory rod kit consists of a variety of items needed for determining trajectory:

- A set of brightly colored trajectory rods, with female screw connectors
- At least two end rods (one end of which has a blunt rounded tip and the other a female screw connector)
- Several double-sided male screw connectors (attaches rods to rods, rods to tripod base plates, rods to eye-hook string attachment)
- Several plastic bullet hole–centering guides with rubber O-ring stoppers
- Several aluminum blunt-tip probes with female screw connectors
- Several plastic eye-hook string attachments with male screw connectors
- Two trajectory lasers with male screw connectors (connects to rods or base plates)
- Several brass tripod base plates with female screw connectors
- An angle finder (which finds the up–down angles)

The kit can be customized to any configuration needed, but it does not have a zero-base protractor to obtain angles off the surface containing the ballistic damage evidence. Utilization of this kit does not require the user to perform the trigonometric calculations. The kit is very easy to use and is effective with ballistic-damaged surfaces that have clearly identifiable entrances and exits, such as might be found in a standard stud wall. It also works well with a single bullet hole and a ballistic impact termination mark.

When using such a kit, the CSI must carefully place the centering guides in the bullet holes, making sure not to damage the holes; place the rod or rods through the guides; and place an O-ring over the rods to keep the rods from slipping through the centering guides (see Figures 8.25a and 8.25b). At this point, the angle finder can be placed on the rod, and the up–down angle can be found. A zero-base protractor is now used to find the angle–off the surface.

All this information must be included in the written notes and should be photographed. For short trajectories, a series of rods can be screwed together to show the entire trajectory. It may be necessary to set up a tripod with a base-mounting plate to assist in keeping the rods and/or rod/laser combinations true. If long trajectories are present, the CSI can attach lasers to rods, and the possible terminal points, forward and reverse, can be located and documented.

These kits can also be used with two lasers attached (front and back) to the tripod-mounting base plates. The tripod can then be positioned between two associated bullet holes that are separated by a suitable distance. The laser is aligned with the two bullet holes, and the possible terminal points are located. A note of caution about using lasers over extremely long distances: the longer the distance, the less likely your laser trajectory will be accurate, because lasers are true and straight and cannot account for factors such as windage, elevation, and/or gravitational drop-off associated with a parabolic trajectory.

Once these points have been found, they should be documented as outlined previously for the laser protractor kit. The trajectories must be documented; several methods of photographic documentation can be employed that are similar to those provided for the laser protractor:

1. Leave the laser on the rods and utilize photographic fog to visualize the lasers. Photograph the illuminated trajectories from several vantage points.
2. Identify and mark the terminal points. The lasers can be removed from the rods and replaced by the plastic eye-hook string attachments. Utilizing reflective photographic strings or colored strings stretched tightly and secured between

FIGURE 8.25A
Bullet hole through window of car.

FIGURE 8.25B
Inside of car showing trajectory rod through bullet hole.

the sites—bullet hole(s) and terminal points (forward and reverse)—photograph the trajectory strings from several vantage points.

DISTANCE DETERMINATION

When the patterns found on evidence are compared to test patterns produced by the suspect firearm using suspect ammunition (whenever possible) or the same type of ammunition as that found in the weapon or at the scene, an approximate firing distance and angle (muzzle to target) can be established (see Figures 8.26a–8.26f). The distance from the end of a firearm (muzzle) to a shooting victim or an object can be determined by examining the area around any bullet entrance wound, bullet entrance holes, or bullet impact marks for the presence of a pattern of gunshot residue. Gunshot residue is projected at a high velocity out of the muzzle, chamber, breech, trigger, or any other area of the firearm where there is an opening; and it may embed, pass through, or adhere around bullet entrance wounds, bullet entrance holes, or bullet impact marks. This same principle applies to shot pellet pattern dispersal, creating the ability to determine a muzzle-to-target distance, which is sometimes expressed in a range of yards. This is a reminder that some firearms examination labs will

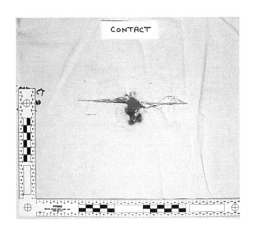

FIGURE 8.26A
Distance determination test of a .50-caliber saboted bullet fired in a .50-caliber muzzle-loading rifle. Contact with the target shows minimal powder marks on the fabric. Commonly used in muzzle-loading hunting rifles, a sabot is a plastic sleeve that holds a smaller bullet so it can be fired from a larger-caliber firearm. A bullet encased in a sabot will typically not have any identifying characteristics on it that may lead back to a specific firearm; however, the sabot may contain striations if fired through a rifled barrel.

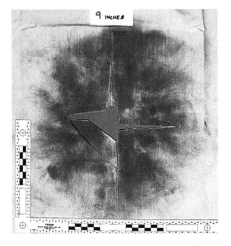

FIGURE 8.26B
At a distance of 9 inches, there is considerable burning and gunshot residue appearing on the test fabric.

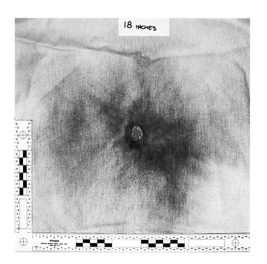

FIGURE 8.26C
At a distance of 18 inches, there is still considerable burning and gunshot residue adhering to the test fabric.

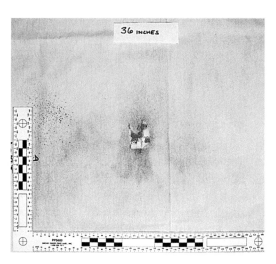

FIGURE 8.26D
At a distance of 36 inches, gunpowder residues are dissipating but are still visible on the test fabric.

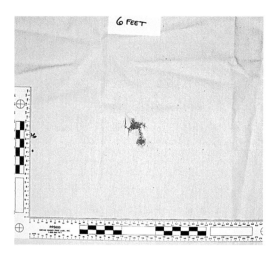

FIGURE 8.26E
At a distance of 6 feet, the powder has dissipated considerably and the sabot has entered the test fabric just above the bullet entrance.

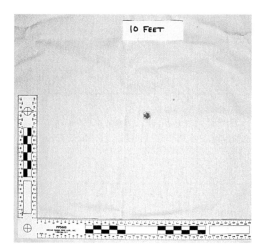

FIGURE 8.26F
At a distance of 10 feet, there is minimal powder residue and the plastic sabot has bounced off the test fabric.

not perform these types of pattern tests if suspect ammunition is not available.

The absence of powder residues may be due to one of the following:

- A shot may be fired beyond the maximum distance at which residues would have been deposited.
- Excessive blood may wash away any gunshot muzzle residue originally present.
- There may have been an intervening object (such as a pillow) between the gun and the target.
- Improper handling of clothing may have dislodged residues.
- In the case of a contact shot, the powder residues can be introduced into the wound and may be visible under the flaps of the skin surrounding the entrance wound.

There may be evidence of a cylinder flash pattern on a contact wound if a revolver was used. If the muzzle was in direct contact with hard skin (bone directly under the skin), there will be blowback of GSR and a star-shaped entrance wound that is easily mistaken for an exit wound (see Figure 8.27). Examine this type of wound for burning

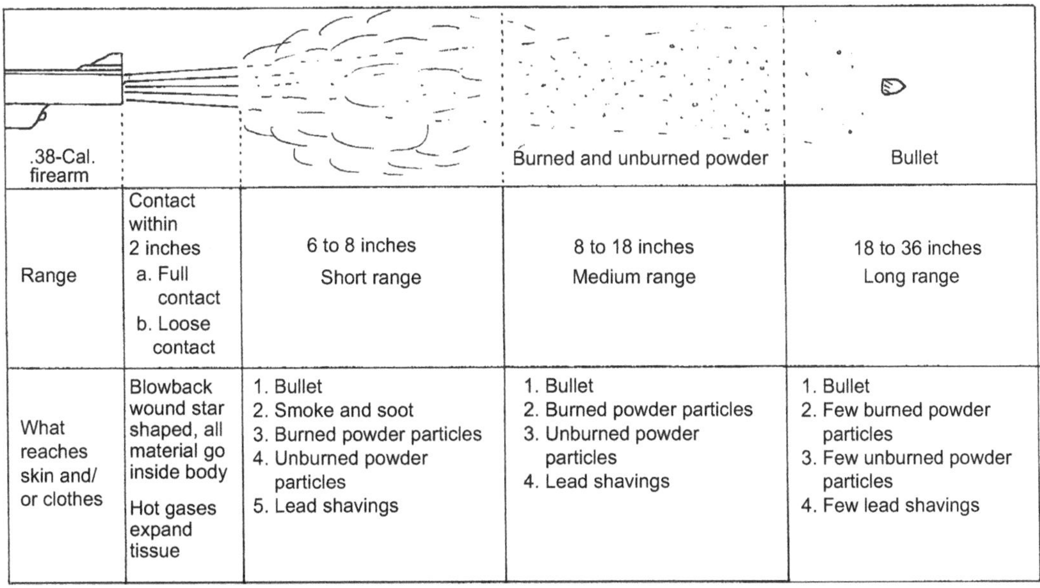

.38-Cal. firearm			Burned and unburned powder	Bullet
Range	Contact within 2 inches a. Full contact b. Loose contact	6 to 8 inches Short range	8 to 18 inches Medium range	18 to 36 inches Long range
What reaches skin and/ or clothes	Blowback wound star shaped, all material go inside body Hot gases expand tissue	1. Bullet 2. Smoke and soot 3. Burned powder particles 4. Unburned powder particles 5. Lead shavings	1. Bullet 2. Burned powder particles 3. Unburned powder particles 4. Lead shavings	1. Bullet 2. Few burned powder particles 3. Few unburned powder particles 4. Few lead shavings

FIGURE 8.27
Diagram showing how gunshot residue travels from the barrel of a firearm.

and powders under the flaps of the skin. Finally, if there is direct muzzle-to-clothing contact, the clothing will have GSR, burning, and tearing present. **Tattooing** is the term used to describe the physical defect caused by the penetration of the skin by gunpowder particles. This is another reason why it is critical to locate and confiscate clothing from victims to ensure that valuable evidence is not discarded or washed down the drain when clothes are laundered.

NATIONAL INTEGRATED BALLISTICS INFORMATION NETWORK (NIBIN)

Expended bullets and cartridge cases possess unique characteristics, or signatures, that can be captured and stored digitally. These digital microscopic images are stored in a nationwide computer database that is maintained by the Bureau of Alcohol, Tobacco, Firearms and Explosives. This database is known as the **National Integrated Ballistics Information Network (NIBIN)**. The Integrated Ballistics Information System (IBIS) equipment digitally captures images of fired bullets and fired cartridge cases and compares them to the images of test-fired ammunition from recovered firearms and other evidence cartridge cases and bullets (see Figure 8.28). When a hit is found, a firearms examiner must confirm the accuracy of the hit.

The database uses an algorithmic equation that allows each signature to be compared to others in the system. It assigns a numeric value, which is shown as a percentage of a likely hit to items found in the database. To make a hit, a firearms examiner must microscopically compare the bullets and/or cartridge cases to determine if they

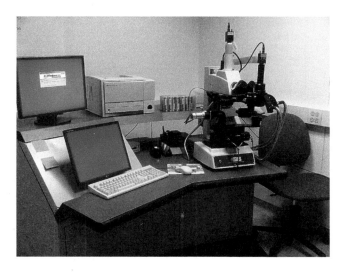

FIGURE 8.28
An NIBIN examination station.

originated from the same weapon. NIBIN provides examiners across the country with the ability to associate previously unrelated crimes, which can generate investigative leads, arrests, and convictions.

GUNSHOT RESIDUE TESTING

Gunshot residue (GSR) is composed of the deposits of unburned or partially burned gunpowder particles, primer residues, and soot that remain after a firearm is discharged. Primer residue includes barium, antimony, and lead and is produced from the ignition of the primer. When the primer is hit by the firing pin or striker of the gun, a small explosion is created that lights a propellant, causing gases to form that force the projectile(s) through the barrel of the firearm. GSR and the projectile (bullet or slug) are expelled through the barrel of a firearm, as well as any other opening found in the firearm, when it is discharged. GSR may be found at the site of the entrance wound. At the same time, some GSR may escape from the rear of the weapon and be deposited on the shooter's hands or clothing.

GSR is important to the CSI because its presence may reveal a shooter, and it may indicate a possible muzzle-to-target distance. GSR is fragile trace/transfer evidence and must be processed carefully to avoid loss of the residue and substantive information.

A positive test does not mean that a person fired a weapon; GSR can be transferred to the hands, clothing, or other objects in proximity to a gun when it was discharged through handling of the gun or any number of other ways. Similarly, a negative test does not mean that the person did not discharge a weapon. GSR is easily removed from the hands by washing or putting the hands into pockets or can even be rubbed off when a person is being handcuffed. Tests have shown that GSR deposits are not detectable on a subject's hands after four to six hours have elapsed from the time a gun was fired.

Because GSR trace evidence is so fragile, it can be easily lost, so care must be taken to identify its potential locations as quickly as possible to preserve samples for crime laboratory analysis. If clothing is suspected of containing GSR, it should be confiscated and submitted for alternate light source, microscopic, and chemical examinations. If a victim is deceased, place paper bags on the hands and secure them to prevent loss of trace evidence (see Figure 8.29). Never use plastic bags because moisture will cause the deposits to be lost more quickly.

FIGURE 8.29
Bagging the hands of a deceased victim may prevent the loss of transient evidence.

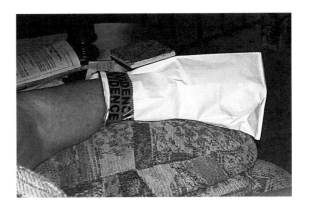

Many variables impact gunpowder residue. The type of firearm and ammunition as well as the barrel length, weather conditions, and distance of the weapon to the target all affect the probability of locating GSR as physical evidence.

SERIAL NUMBER RESTORATION

All new and legally manufactured firearms are stamped with serial numbers that are maintained in files by the firearms dealers who sell the weapons. The serial numbers are marked onto the firearm and may be placed on metal tags, which are molded into the frame (see Figures 8.30 and 8.31). The numbers may appear in more than one location. When a serial number is impressed into a metal object, the metal underneath the characters is compressed and hardened. Serial numbers are sometimes removed by grinding, scraping, or drilling away the impression until it is no longer visible or by stamping other digits or letters over the original number.

Firearms examiners are often able to restore original serial numbers through a variety of chemical processes and other restoration techniques that cause the original numbers to become visible because of the displacement of the metal structure underneath. Magnaflux® (magnetic particle inspection), chemical etching, ultrasonic cavitation, and other procedures can be conducted at the crime laboratory in an attempt to recover the original serial number. These processes have also been used successfully on engine blocks, heavy equipment, and other metal surfaces.

More recently, organic solvents and heat processes have been found to reveal the serial numbers effectively on plastic items as well. It is not always possible to retrieve a complete serial number either in metal or plastic, depending on the degree and method of alteration or obliteration, but even a partially restored serial number can provide possible investigative leads for the detectives to track the owner of an item and possibly link a suspect to a crime scene.

FIGURE 8.30
Location of serial number on the frame of a pistol.

FIGURE 8.31
Location of serial number on the frame of a revolver.

Serial number restoration is time consuming and requires the use of various chemical processes. PPE and laboratory safety equipment must be used, and it is recommended that all weapons without serial numbers be submitted to the crime laboratory for the firearms examiners to process. Three chemical reagents that are utilized at the laboratory are Frye's reagent, nitric acid, and acidic ferric chloride. The determination of which process an examiner will use depends on the type of metal used to manufacture the weapon as well as the application method of the serial number.

TOOLMARKS

A toolmark is any impression, cut, gouge, or abrasion left on an object that is softer than the object or tool that caused the marks. Although toolmarks are generally associated with property crimes, they can also be found in homicide investigations in which a toolmark is left in a victim's bone (e.g., a knife mark or bullet damage).

According to the Association of Firearm and Toolmark Examiners (AFTE), toolmark impressions are divided into two categories. **Compression marks** are the most common marks encountered at the crime scene and are typically the type of evidence that will be found at a burglary scene (see Figure 8.32). When a tool is pressed into a softer material, it will leave an impression that usually contains a clearly identifiable outline of the tool, which is a class characteristic. An example of a compression mark at a crime scene may be found when a screwdriver is used to pry open a window in a wooden sill. Enough force is applied to the screwdriver that it leaves an impression in the wood. If the impression is clear, there may be individual characteristics found in the softer material that can be used to match the tool with the impression if it is located.

The second type of toolmark defined by the AFTE is striated (also referred to as friction, abrasion, or scratch marks). These types of marks are produced when a tool is placed against another object with pressure applied. This results in the tool moving across the object, producing a striated mark (see Figure 8.33). Again, these marks can produce class and individual characteristics.

An example of a sliding toolmark would be the mark formed by sliding a screwdriver or pry bar along the edge of a door as the perpetrator seeks the locking mechanism inside the frame.

The generally recommended procedure for evidence collection of toolmark impressions is to document, cast, and then (whenever practical) collect the item

FIGURE 8.32
Example of a compression mark.

FIGURE 8.33

Example of a cutting
toolmark.

on which the toolmarks are located. Photographs are useful to the examiner and provide an overall view of the crime scene, but even high-quality macrophotography does not provide enough clarity for positive comparison to a suspect tool.

Trace evidence may be located on suspect tools and may provide a link to numerous crime scenes. Paint chips, safe insulation, metal shavings, and tissue or blood are just some of the many types of trace evidence that may be found on suspect tools. Handle all tools carefully and package them securely to keep from dislodging potential trace evidence.

If a suspect tool is located, it should never be fit into the toolmarks found. This action may alter the toolmark and create doubt as to the veracity of the original impression. Keep all suspect tools separate and package them individually in cushioned materials to protect any trace evidence and prevent additional damage from occurring to the edges that will be examined.

Testing and Comparison Techniques

A cast of the toolmark should always be made using one of the commercially available silicone rubber materials as casting agents. These products have a thick consistency and can easily be placed into the toolmark and left to airdry while other areas are processed.

Always make a cast of the toolmark prior to attempting to remove it for transport to the crime laboratory. Removal of the object with the toolmark may mean cutting away a portion of a larger item, for example, a windowsill. In some instances, this is just not feasible. Therefore, comparisons can be made using casts and photographs when necessary (see Figure 8.34). Department policy and officer discretion regarding the type of crime and value of the object that is going to be removed must always be taken into consideration by the crime scene investigation team.

FIGURE 8.34

Example of a tool being
compared to a Mikrosil
cast.

After the suspect tool has been checked for trace evidence, the toolmark examiner will make several test toolmarks that will be microscopically compared with the tool and the toolmark evidence submitted from the crime scene. It is important for the comparison toolmarks to be made at the same angle and while holding the suspect tool in as close as possible to the same manner as the mark was made. A series of tests may need to be performed to identify how the toolmarks were made.

Photographs will assist the examiner in understanding the overall crime scene, and midrange pictures will depict any furniture or other items that may have restricted the perpetrator's movements as the marks were being made. Close-up photographs will aid in the exact placement of the tool against the surface and angle of placement.

Examiners are looking for individual characteristics that result from wear or damage or that occurred during the manufacturing process or from use and/or abuse of the tool. Some individual characteristics arise from the misuse of a tool out of its ordinary intended usage, corrosion, or damage. Newer tools may be individualized due to irregularities or random imperfections during the manufacturing process. These imperfections are unique to that tool and distinguish it from all other tools (AFTE Glossary, www.afte.org).

Discussion Questions

1. What is meant by the term ballistics? Discuss the possible information that can be obtained from a handgun or long gun and its projectile.
2. What characteristics make each firearm unique?
3. What is a laser trajectory rod kit, and what is its use?
4. What is the significance of the presence or absence of gunshot residue?
5. How do tools attain individual characteristics that make them unique and identifiable?

CHAPTER 9

Arson and Explosives

KEY TERMS

Area of origin	High explosives	Association
Arson	IEDs	(NFPA)
Burn patterns	Low explosives	Serial fires
CBRNE	National Fire	Spoliation
Fire triangle	Protection	Trailers or streamers

What You Will Learn

Technology has paved the way for investigating fires and incidents where explosive devices have been deployed. Arson and CSIs now use various types of equipment to locate accelerants or remnants of explosive materials. Arson may be used in an attempt to cover up another crime, and it is up to the CSI to maneuver in this very difficult type of crime scene to document and recover evidence that may have been destroyed by heat, fire, and other destructive means.

MURDER IN THE NEW YEAR

Arson and Explosives

The phone rang.

"Ten p.m.," Tom Smith muttered to himself. "And right in the middle of the Normandy invasion on the Military History Channel."

Tom muted the sound with his remote and picked up the phone.Tom, Mavis here. I think we caught a break. I was checking the police logs on the day and night of the murder-suicide and noticed that an elderly neighbor called in what she thought might be an act of arson on the back of the Sellers's property. Two uniforms investigated, and Michael Sellers said he was burning some trash.

DOI: 10.4324/9780429261657-9

Looking at the police report Mavis Fletcher handed him, Tom cleared his throat. "Burning trash at midnight? A bit odd, wouldn't you say?"

> "And that's not all," the detective continued. Matt Powell, our computer analyst, came across something interesting when checking out James Morton's laptop. He found a DVD taped under the computer hutch. When he loaded and activated it, he noticed some entries about a College of Arts and Sciences foundation. The file displayed a list of donors and their donations as well as various transactions. The long and short of it is that Matt seemed to think there was a lot of activity going on for a foundation of that nature. Some of the expenditures seemed questionable at best.

Tom Smith pulled a toothpick out of his pocket and stuck it in his mouth. "Let me guess. Our erstwhile dean was in charge of said foundation."

"Bingo," Mavis replied. "We need a search warrant for the Sellers's property and the dean's office, and I already have the paperwork prepared. Meet me at Judge Abernathy's office at 8:30 tomorrow morning."

INTRODUCTION

The fire scene investigation is one of the most dangerous crime scenes that a CSI will typically work. Environmental health concerns and the danger of collapse due to the continuing deterioration of physical structures must remain the primary safety concerns as you complete the assessment of the crime scene and determine additional resources that will be necessary to complete the investigation.

Special safety equipment must be worn during the investigation of a fire, and these safeguards will impact the procedures you must follow while collecting evidence and maintaining your own personal safety. Many items that have been burning may emit toxic fumes for a period of time after the fire has been extinguished, so it is very important to remain in close contact with the fire scene commander to determine when working conditions are safe. Fire suppression crews on the scene must continue to monitor the quality of the atmosphere in the structure. The CSI should enter the structure with the appropriate breathing apparatus only after the atmosphere has been declared safe by the monitoring agency.

FIGURE 9.1
Fire suppression efforts will impact the crime scene.

Evidence may be contaminated or cross-contaminated by volatile accelerants or the effects of fire suppression and overhauling (see Figure 9.1). Precautions must be taken to protect against further contamination or increased hazards to your health. It may be necessary to secure the fire scene and enter only after environmental concerns have been identified and addressed, so do not rush in to begin the investigation without proper clearance from health, safety, and fire officials.

Additional factors must be noted as you travel to the scene of a fire. Because the fire department is reacting in the rescue mode, some activities conducted by firefighters to suppress the fire may cause additional damage to any physical evidence. Dealing with the preservation of potential forensic evidence is secondary to their primary purpose of protecting lives and suppressing fires (see Box 9.1). It is your responsibility to document the scene on arrival, take photographs, and secure additional information from firefighters as to the actions they took in the areas you will be processing as a crime scene (see Figures 9.2 and 9.3).

Unlike most other crime scene investigations, a fire or explosion scene involves many different activities occurring simultaneously— particularly if there is an active fire in progress. It is essential to form a team and establish a responsibilities matrix. Overall scene security and the safety of all personnel are of paramount importance. There are many mitigating circumstances that are constantly changing and must be monitored to ensure the safety of all team members.

BOX 9.1 A SIGNIFICANT PUBLIC HEALTH PROBLEM

According to the Centers for Disease Control and Prevention (CDC), deaths from fires and burns are ranked as the third leading cause of fatal home injury. In 2010, there were 2,640 fire-related deaths equally on average, a fire-related fatality in the United States every 169 minutes.

FIGURE 9.2
The crime scene investigation of a house fire reveals an ashtray in the hand of a victim.

FIGURE 9.3
A mobile home destroyed by an accidental fire.

Darkness, steam, the danger of collapse, hot spots, and other hazards, including leaking gases, live electrical lines, or water, can place additional demands on the rescue and recovery efforts and compromise the overall success of the investigation. These factors may affect the continuity of the fire investigation.

At the scene of an explosion, responders and CSIs must be aware of the possibility of secondary devices and unexploded residues. There are usually two scenes at the place where a bomb has exploded: the crater area and the area outside the crater. Bomb technicians arriving on the scene of an explosive investigation may inadvertently contaminate the crime scene unless preventive steps are taken to maintain the integrity of the scene. If it is not possible for the technician to wear Tyvek® apparel prior to entering the scene, swabs of the boots worn should be taken to establish a baseline before the technician enters the perimeter of the scene. Bomb technicians will be able to assist CSIs in discerning whether the device was constructed with high or low explosive materials; identify components, containers, and odors; and assist with safety concerns including X-rays of bodies or other devices present at the post-blast scene.

In the past, fire investigators have taught that damage to a structure from fire is significant because fire doubles in size every 60 seconds. Today, with the fuel load in buildings, fire grows far more quickly than doubling every 60 seconds, so the time taken for the burning fire and resulting smoke to be noticed, 911 dispatch called, and the responding fire department to get to the scene and begin suppression quite often results in considerable damage very quickly. Many rooms flash over in less than five minutes. In the past, arson investigators might look at this extreme damage and feel the fire could not have been accidental. That is no longer the case, and this means the scene examination must be performed with even more attention to detail because of the severity of the fire damage (NFPA, 2021).

CRIME SCENE PROCESSING

It is important to begin taking photographs and video as soon as possible. Note the weather conditions as well as the direction and color of smoke and flames. While the color of smoke and flames is subjective and may not be a reliable indication of the true conditions, your notes should reflect your observations on arrival at the scene. Continue to take photographs, because the crime scene will evolve. Extensive damage will reduce the amount of physical evidence, so photographs will be essential in documenting the scene. Always take photographs and videos of the onlookers at the fire scene. Oftentimes an arsonist will join the audience to observe the results of his or her criminal activities. It is normal for many arsonists to return to the scene within 24 hours of starting the fire to review the extent of the damage. Bystanders may be taking still pictures and video of the scene with their cellphones. Often, this digital evidence will offer important information that may tell a story about the incident prior to the arrival of fire suppression personnel. People showing up asking questions about the fire should be documented. Caution should be used when dealing with these people because history has shown that they may intend to harm the investigator or CSI conducting the scene review.

In contrast to other crime scene investigations, in which you begin working from the center outward, the investigation of a fire scene almost always requires the CSI to work from the area of least damage inward to the area where the most destruction has occurred. This sequence of examination will lead to the suspected area of origin of the fire and provide the evidence that can assist with the determination of the cause of the fire.

Area of Origin

Fire is a chemical process that requires heat, fuel, and oxygen (air), which are commonly referred to as the fire triangle (see Figure 9.4). With a continued supply of these elements, the fire can have an uninhibited chemical chain reaction, which adds a fourth element and is called the "fire tetrahedron." If any one of these elements is removed, the fire will go out. As mentioned earlier, careful examination of the entire fire scene to determine the place of origin may begin from the area of least destruction and proceed inward toward the area where the most destruction is observed. The arson investigator will rely on this physical evidence as well as statements made by witnesses regarding events leading up to the discovery of the fire to determine the area of origin of the fire, that is, the general location(s) where the heat ignited the first fuel.

As the area of origin is examined, it is important to systematically identify and eliminate probable accidental ignition sources. Once all natural or accidental heat sources have been eliminated from consideration, it is probable that this is an incendiary fire and that an accelerant was used to start and fuel the fire. This is not a conclusion for the CSI to develop; arson investigators must take additional steps to determine whether the fire was incendiary or accidental. Arsonists quite often utilize on-site ordinary combustibles to start their fires. The resulting damage creates patterns that investigators can use to locate the area of origin.

FIGURE 9.4
Fire triangle.

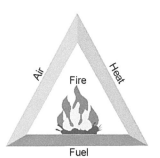

Burn Patterns

As fire travels, it leaves indications of the direction it has taken. Burn patterns (also known as "fire patterns") are visible effects, such as charring, smoke and soot deposits, changes in the character of materials, and the consumption of consumables, that may indicate the ignition source of a fire.

The three modes of heat transfer are convection, conduction, and radiation; together, these modes produce many of the fire patterns found in a structure. Another common phenomenon found in fire scenes that is often mistakenly identified as a second or multiple point of origin is "drop down." Drop down occurs when a material on the wall or ceiling is ignited by the super-heated gases created from the fire, and the ignited material drops down to the floor, creating a burn pattern resembling an ignition point. Rising hot gases form a cone-shaped plume, and when the plume encounters a vertical surface, such as a wall, a V-pattern will be visible on the surface (see Figures 9.5 and 9.6). In the flame zone, the pattern will resemble an inverted V. This pattern can be analyzed to determine the width of the base of the fire and can provide valuable information as to the availability of combustible materials consumed by the fire.

Ventilation greatly impacts the spread of the fire and affects intensity and movement patterns. These patterns should be documented with photographs and elevation drawings because they will contribute to establishing the area of origin of the fire. Fire patterns can be found on any surface (both vertical and horizontal) exposed to fire, smoke, or hot gases but are most often observed on walls, floors, and ceilings (see Figure 9.7).

Trailers or streamers are any ignitable liquid or solid or a combination of these used to move fire from one point to another. These

FIGURE 9.5
V-patterns on wall.

FIGURE 9.6
V-pattern on metal siding (inside).

FIGURE 9.7
Burn patterns (pour pattern) on floor indicating that an accelerant was used.

paths link separate fire locations and are generally observed along the floors that connect separate fire sets.

Impact of Fire Suppression on the Crime Scene

Fire scene investigation challenges the CSI because so much of the evidence is destroyed by the fire. Secondarily, the efforts of firefighters to suppress the fire with water hoses and other techniques will cause additional destruction of physical evidence. After the flames have been extinguished, firefighters begin the process of overhaul, which is the inspection and movement or removal of debris to ensure that smoldering embers are not allowed to rekindle the flames. Evidence may be destroyed during this process, so whenever possible, it is recommended that the area of origin not be overhauled until an arson investigator has arrived on the scene.

Documentation of the condition of the burned area and collection of physical evidence should be completed before the area is overhauled.

This is not always possible because every fire scene is different and poses unique dangers to the firefighters and CSIs. Intentionally set fires may have more than one area of origin, and the absence or presence of contents in these various areas must be documented as soon as possible after the fire has been extinguished and the area is safe to enter.

WHY INVESTIGATE FIRE SCENES?

Physical evidence recovered at the scene of a fire may be relevant to determining the origin, cause, spread, or responsibility for the fire (see Figure 9.8; see also Box 9.2).

Oftentimes a motive for an incendiary fire will be discovered as the investigation progresses. A suspect may be identified based on patterns or trends detected: for instance, if fires appear to be clustered in geographic areas, if they are set during the same time periods (days of week), or if similar materials and methods are noted in fire locations. Two or more incendiary fires attributed to an individual or group are classified as **serial fires**.

According to the FBI's National Center for the Analysis of Violent Crime (NCAVC), the motives for setting fires can be both expressive and instrumental and may include vandalism, excitement, revenge, profit, extremism and terrorism, and concealment of another crime. Vandalism results in property damage. Common targets may include schools and other educational facilities.

There are four identified categories of excitement-motivated fire-setters. They range from thrill-seeking, attention-seeking, and recognition to sexual gratification or perversion (see Box 9.3). Their fires include targets of various sizes, and these arsonists may be the ones who remain in the crowd to observe the effects of their crimes. Quite often, gangs will use fire as a rite of initiation and, after ignition, members will stay and observe incoming fire trucks and the initial suppression efforts.

FIGURE 9.8
Residence fire suspected of being caused by arson.

Revenge-focused fire-setters act because of a real or perceived injustice, and their actions may be focused toward individuals, institutions, or society in general. This type of arsonist may be a disgruntled employee, the victim of a social snub, or someone responding to a personal rejection. Fires started by arsonists who are profit driven are usually attempts to defraud an insurance

BOX 9.2 THREE PRIMARY REASONS FOR THE INVESTIGATION OF FIRE SCENES

- The point of origin must be determined to establish the cause of the fire: accidental (e.g., a product failure or a person falling asleep with a lit cigarette), natural (i.e., act of God), incendiary (i.e., arson), or undetermined.
- There may be public safety issues concerning product reliability, and the investigation can assist with uncovering areas of concern for manufacturing defects or misuse of these products.
- Owners may be in violation of state or local fire codes and/or building codes, which has placed the lives and property of others in jeopardy.

BOX 9.3 MOTIVES OF THE ARSONIST

- Vandalism
- Excitement
- Revenge
- Profit
- Extremism
- Concealing another crime

company, eliminate competition, or escape building code requirements. They may also be an attempt to destroy records, create intimidation, or commit extortion.

Extremist fire-setters are usually well organized, and they target political or economic institutions. Terrorism and civil disturbances are included in this category; however, business or property owners seeking to defraud insurance companies may sometimes take advantage of these situations to set fire to their property, hoping that these crimes will be associated with extremist-motivated groups.

These brief descriptions are provided as an overview of the various motivations for arsonists. The arson investigator and case detectives will conduct in-depth inquiries into these crimes. The CSI, however, is more likely to be involved in incendiary fire investigations involving the motive of crime concealment.

Covering Up Another Crime

Arson is the willful and malicious burning of another's property or of one's own property for some illegal purpose. According to the UCR, there are approximately 10.9 arson offenses for every 100,000 inhabitants (2019). It is important to document pre-fire conditions because this information may be important in determining whether the fire was intentionally started. The presence of a fuel or ignition

FIGURE 9.9
Burned living area.

source does not create a fire. There must be a sequence of events that allows the fuel and ignition source to combine and result in a fire.

Electrical devices (e.g., appliances), the general upkeep of the area, and the presence of easily ignitable materials may be key indicators that a fire was intentionally set. You should locate any smoke detectors and determine their position and whether the detectors were in working condition at the time of the fire. You should also check for burglar alarms, missing documents and files, the absence of valuable items in the debris, and whether the area of origin of the fire was in an area where records or computers were located.

The amount of fire damage is a consideration in determining if the cause of the fire was an incendiary action. If there is a large amount damage that is inconsistent with the known available fuels and the room or area did not reach flashover or full room involvement (see Figure 9.9), this should be documented in the CSI's notes. Other signs of an incendiary fire include timers or delay devices, the unusual presence of ignitable substances, and irregular burn patterns consistent with the presence of ignitable liquids being poured throughout the area. An absence of personal items, or if the entry is blocked or obstructed, would indicate the need for additional inquiries to be conducted by the arson investigator.

If the arsonist was intent on covering up another crime, such as a burglary or murder by burning a body, sabotage inside the structure or building may have occurred in an effort to increase the amount of destruction and eliminate physical evidence. Other issues that may indicate that the fire was the work of an arsonist include financial records showing economic problems, unpaid taxes, liens, obsolete equipment, or substandard building condition.

PRODUCT RELIABILITY

The determination of the circumstances and factors that allowed heat, fuel, and oxygen to combine and result in a fire is necessary when attempting to assign legal responsibility or culpability for the fire. The fact that the design or manufacture of a product is found to be flawed generally has serious ramifications, including the immediate need (in some cases) for product recall, or at least the issuance of warnings to owners/ users of the product. Consideration should be given to spoliation issues when working in the area of a product that may have been the cause of a fire. It is also possible that the device or equipment is safe, and human actions have introduced factors that allowed the fire to occur. Electrical appliances are manufactured under strict guidelines with precautions taken to ensure the public safety; however, the introduction of unsafe working conditions or the lack of common sense and disregard for operating instructions in the application/use of the appliance can result in fire scenes that must be investigated.

FIGURE 9.10
The fuel load of a building can impact the damage in residential fires.

Code Violations

Materials, design, and quality of construction have significant impacts on the fire safety of buildings. Fire-resistant designs for electrical and mechanical engineering systems, floor plans, and ventilation systems are approved for individual buildings in an effort to maintain a safe environment for occupants. Building owners are responsible for keeping the property up to standards and are subject to financial penalties as well as criminal charges for failing to observe fire, life safety, and building code requirements. In addition to structural maintenance, early warning systems such as sprinklers and alarms and safe storage conditions for materials that constitute a fire/life safety hazard are also subject to inspection by fire marshals. Violations of code offenses can range from fees and penalties to jail sentences. The failure to sustain a safe working and living environment for occupants is considered a serious offense and may lead to closure of the building. Local and state agencies employ fire marshals to conduct inspections of facilities and empower them to issue citations, make arrests, and force evacuations of locations that are found unsafe for human occupancy (see Figure 9.10).

MOTOR VEHICLE FIRE INVESTIGATION

The same type of fire scene investigation must be conducted for a vehicle fire as is performed for a building or residence; however, the footprint of the scene will be more compact. The area of origin of a motor vehicle fire is determined by the burn patterns on the body panels and the interior of the vehicle. A thorough examination of the vehicle is necessary and includes, but is not limited to, examining the remains of a battery and components such as the drive shaft and transmission to ensure that the vehicle could have been driven to the scene of the fire.

FIGURE 9.11

Vehicle fire following a car bomb explosion.

A vehicle has many ready sources of fuel because flammable or combustible liquids are contained within the fuel tank as well as under the hood (transmission, power steering, and brake fluids). If the vehicle was running at the time of the fire, there are many possible potential sources of ignition, including electrical circuits and hot surfaces such as the catalytic converter or manifold. Because modern vehicles have so many combustible components, it may not always be possible to ascertain whether the fire was intentionally set. At the time of arrival of the first responders, the CSI should determine what was on fire or what part of the vehicle was on fire (engine, interior, trunk, or entire vehicle) and whether there was anything present that indicated the cause of the fire (see Figure 9.11). Inquire of firefighters whether they observed anything unusual and identify who reported the fire so investigators can conduct further interviews.

Post-crash fires can occur when battery and starter cables are severed and contact a grounded surface in the presence of easily ignited combustibles or ignitable liquids. Lamp filaments in broken bulbs and mechanical sparks also can be responsible for igniting fires. Recreational vehicles and trailers usually contain additional electrical power sources that may cause a fire, and these systems must be inspected for failure when conducting a motor vehicle fire investigation. The upholstery fabrics used in modern vehicles are highly flame retardant, so it is difficult to start a fire with a burning cigarette; however, the foam urethane used to manufacture car seats does burn readily once ignited. Fires do occur when cigarettes or burning matches are placed in ashtrays that contain other combustible materials.

It is also important to establish what items would normally be present in the vehicle. Determine whether it was used as a business, delivery, or personal automobile. The presence or absence of items may provide additional investigative leads, including the possibility that the fire was set to cover up a robbery or other criminal act. Ascertain ownership of the vehicle, and determine who was in control of the vehicle at the time of the fire. Additional information that you should include in your documentation includes the odometer reading, the last service date and location, what equipment was on the vehicle (radio and other accessories), how far the vehicle had been driven, when the vehicle was last fueled, and any unusual damage or unreported damage. Locate the Vehicle Identification Number (VIN), which is on the dash panel on the driver's side. If the VIN is not observable, check the additional locations on the vehicle where the number is stamped, including the engine side of the firewall (bulkhead).

Most important, it is necessary to determine if there are any victims in the vehicle. Depending on the intensity of the fire, this may not be readily discernible, and it may be necessary to enlist the assistance of a forensic anthropologist to search the vehicle to resolve any question of whether human remains are present. A vehicle may or may not be the scene of death of an individual whose remains are found inside. The crime scene search must include both the interior and exterior of the vehicle as well as the surrounding area where the vehicle was burned. Pre-establish a relationship with a local towing company so that the burned vehicle can be transported and secured in a towing compound for further and more intense ongoing review. Because many vehicle arsons occur in the hours of darkness, transporting the vehicle to a towing compound ensures a better look at the remains in daylight hours while maintaining a solid chain of custody of the evidence. If a vehicle has been moved from the scene of a fire, you must visit the location of the fire to look for additional evidence.

There are also safety issues concerned with the examination of a motor vehicle that has burned. The toxic fumes released from materials in automobiles have been known to cause serious injury and even death to responders who have inhaled them a short time after extinguishment of the vehicle fire. Undeployed airbags and other reactive seat restraint systems must be disengaged before you begin to work inside a vehicle. Fuel leaks, electrical energy remaining in the battery, lubricant drips, and broken glass also pose safety-related concerns to the CSI. Various types of fuels are used in modern vehicles, including pressurized gases (propane and natural), solid fuels, and electrical cells. It may be necessary to include a vehicle engineer as part of the crime scene investigation team when unusual fuels are encountered.

COLLECTION AND PRESERVATION OF ARSON EVIDENCE

The goal of a fire investigation is to identify the location at which the fire began (origin) and then determine the reason that the fire started (cause). The procedures used to establish the origin and cause of a fire incident often require specific training and education beyond that available to the CSI, and many state agencies and local fire departments have designated and specially trained arson investigators.

CSIs, however, must be prepared to investigate fire scenes. They may need to assist arson investigators or investigate in the absence of arson investigators because evidence is transient and deteriorating conditions can lead to the destruction of the crime scene before an arson investigator can arrive (this is particularly true in rural areas). The National Fire Protection Association (NFPA) has established standards that dictate the knowledge, skills, and abilities that arson investigators must master. These standards are contained in NFPA 1033, and although CSIs are not required to meet these standards, they contain excellent protocols and should be used as a reference point. In addition, many states have adopted their own standards and offer training and certifications in fire investigations.

There are many potential contaminants on the fire scene, including debris and dirty tools. With the exception of CBRNE crime scenes (scenes involving weapons of mass destruction—chemical, biological, radiological, nuclear, and explosive), no other crime scene has the potential of becoming more compromised because there are so many people tasked with so many concurrent responsibilities. The CSI must continue to utilize crime scene protocols but must keep in mind that many factors may impact the order in which evidence should be identified and collected. The physical state and characteristics of potential evidence, including fragility and volatility, present additional challenges on a fire scene.

Once the areas of origin of a fire have been located and all potential causes eliminated, the CSI must be able to recognize and locate possible evidence of arson (or the lack thereof), specifically ignitable substance residues (ISRs). The identification of the point(s) of origin and fire patterns can assist with places to search for possible ISR samples, but the question becomes how to safely conduct an effective search. Several validated methodologies can be employed. They include the use of certified accelerant-detection K-9 dogs, electronic detectors, and forensic and alternate light sources. Note that all these ISR detection tools/tests are considered presumptive field tests, with the possible exceptions being the Fourier transform infrared spectroscopy (FTIR) and gas chromatography/mass spectrometry methods (discussed later). The confirmation of the presence and identity of an ISR will typically come from analytical tests performed by certified forensic laboratories.

Accelerant-Detection K-9

Time and time again the accelerant-detection K-9 (ACD) has proven to be invaluable in locating minute amounts of ISRs at fire scenes (see Figure 9.12). These dogs are typically trained to detect numerous ISR hydrocarbons used as an accelerant for arson. To be certified as ACDs, the K-9s and their handlers must pass a rigorous series of tests to ensure that the K-9 is not making false-positive or false-negative hits. Most ACDs are trained by the Bureau of Alcohol, Tobacco, Firearms and Explosives (ATF) and complete a rigorous program before they are certified. The training includes providing food as a reward, and the only time the dog will eat when it is on the scene or being trained is when he hits on an accelerant. To maintain their conditioning, the dogs are trained on a daily basis. Once the ACD certification has been issued, the K-9 and the handler will require continuing training and annual proficiency testing.

One of the biggest advantages of the ACD over electronic detectors is the ability of the ACD to distinguish between actual accelerant ISRs and those caused by the fire debris. Once the dog identifies a sampling location, the CSI should follow the appropriate protocols for the documentation, collection, and packaging of the specific samples. Another advantage of using ACDs is that they perform nondestructive screening, which means they work off the vapors and do not require a sample to be drawn and subjected to an analytical process that will destroy it. ACDs can also be used as part of a quality control/quality assurance (QA/QC) program for the ISR collection and packaging equipment, as well as a QA/QC check of the samples and controls collected.

FIGURE 9.12
Accelerant K-9 assisting at the scene of a residential fire.

Electronic Detectors and Instruments

CSIs and fire investigators employ several types of electronic chemical detectors that utilize different technologies to assist in locating possible ISRs in a fire scene investigation. All these detectors require an electrical energy source (hard line or batteries), the use of an internal pump to draw the sample (air or liquid) into the detector (with the exception of FTIR), and a QA/QC program for training on the detector's use and maintenance/calibration. In addition, these detectors, like the ACDs, can be used as part of a QA/QC program for equipment and collected samples. With the possible exception of gas chromatography/mass spectrometry and the FTIR, these detectors typically cannot differentiate between ISRs and the pyrolyzed (i.e., changed chemically due to heat) fire scene debris.

Metal Oxide Transistor

The metal oxide transistor measures a decrease in electrical resistance caused by the ISR, displacing oxygen molecules from a heated semiconductor between two electrodes. The amount of resistance is measured and is directly proportional to the concentration of the ISR.

Photoionization Detectors

Photoionization detectors (PIDs) can be used to detect the presence of organic or inorganic vapors without destructive testing. Ultraviolet (UV) light is directed into an ionization chamber, which involves

FIGURE 9.13
LIS unit.

FIGURE 9.14
MiniRAE unit.

the absorption of the UV light by gas molecules leading to ionization. The gases will be detected and measured by the analyzer, and the results will be displayed on a digital monitor. PIDs are able to detect low gas concentrations and provide a fast response.

Laboratory instrumentation services (LIS) and trace gas analyzers are still utilized through the fire service and are nondestructive analyzers. The LIS is a portable instrument used to detect, measure, and provide a direct reading of the concentration of a variety of trace gases in many atmospheres (see Figure 9.13). Other technology being utilized includes the MiniRAE 2000, which is much smaller than the older LIS units and more portable (see Figure 9.14). This is the smallest pumped, handheld volatile organic compound monitor currently available on the market. The MiniRAE has a photoionization detector that can be used for trace gas detection as well as other security applications.

Flame Ionization Detectors

The flame ionization detector (FID) draws the suspect vapor into the unit and mixes it with hydrogen. The mixture is then introduced to a flame, which ionizes the molecules. The greater the ionization, the greater the amount of ISRs present in the vapor.

Fourier Transform Infrared Spectroscopy

Fourier transform infrared spectroscopy (FTIR) is a detector that emits an infrared beam of electromagnetic energy into a suspect vapor (see Figure 9.15). The detector then measures the amount of energy being absorbed by the suspect vapor, and a spectrum is produced

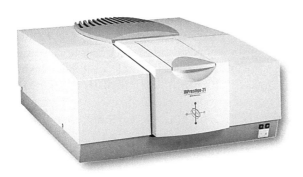

FIGURE 9.15
FTIR unit.

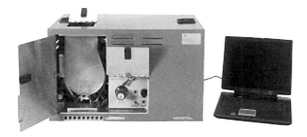

FIGURE 9.16
A portable gas chromatography/mass spectrometry (GC/MS) unit.

FIGURE 9.17
GCMS laboratory instrument.

that is compared against a known library of spectra of various chemical compounds for the identification. Each spectrum is unique to a specific chemical compound, just as a fingerprint is unique to an individual. This is a confirmatory identification method.

Gas Chromatography/Mass Spectrometry

Gas chromatography/mass spectrometry (GC/MS) is a portable field version of a highly respected laboratory identification system (see Figures 9.16 and 9.17). A liquid sample or a vapor sample can be placed into the GC, which will separate the components of the sample. The GC cannot specifically identify the chemicals present by run times alone, so the GC will push the separated chemical components into the MS where the components enter a vacuum chamber. The components are then subjected to a high-energy electron beam. This beam causes the molecules of the components to obtain a positive charge, which makes the molecules break up into tiny fragments. The fragments are separated by their mass. This pattern of fragmentation, known as the "mass spectra," is then compared against a known library of mass spectra for its identification. As with FTIR, when the samples are properly analyzed, no two substances have the same fragmentation pattern, so the mass spectra pattern is unique to a specific chemical compound.

Forensic Light Source/Alternate Light Source

Forensic light source/alternate light source (FLS/ALS) devices are electronic tools that exploit the properties and nature of light between the ultraviolet (UV) 180 to 400 nm band and the infrared (IR) 700 nm band of the electromagnetic light spectrum to assist CSIs with locating and documenting physical evidence. A forensic light source is made up of a powerful lamp and filters that allow it to produce the various wavelengths of light. These wavelengths of light can cause the visualization of evidence. When evidence interacts with the various wavelengths of light, four possible effects can occur with respect to the evidence: It may (1) fluoresce (evidence glows), (2) absorb (evidence darkens), (3) cast shadows, or (4) reflect (small particle evidence revealed through oblique lighting techniques). It has been found that the FLS/ALS will cause many types of ISRs to fluoresce from several light wavelengths, and the fluorescence strength is directly proportional to the strength of the absorbed light.

PRESERVATION OF EVIDENCE

Spoliation refers to the destruction or alteration of evidence or the failure to preserve property as evidence in pending or potential litigation (whether civil or criminal). In a majority of cases, the CSI and the arson investigator will not be able to determine immediately whether the fire was caused by deliberate actions or is accidental (resulting from negligence or a natural occurrence). For this reason, every scene must be processed as though it were a crime scene to prevent spoliation from occurring. When evidence is properly identified, collected, preserved, and submitted for analysis, the investigation is completed accurately, and outcomes are left up to the courts.

In addition to the traditional physical evidence collected at a crime scene (fingerprints, bodily fluids, footwear impressions, toolmarks, etc.), other evidence includes ash and soot debris, porous and nonporous materials, and flammable residues. It is essential to use clean/sterile, airtight containers such as new Teflon®-lined metal containers, glass jars with Teflon-lined silica septa caps, polyester or nylon evidence bags (e.g., Soplaril®), or a combination of these containers to gather and protect the physical evidence. Space must be left in the can, bottle, or bag for the volatile materials, so the can or bottle should never be filled more than two-thirds full, and the bag should be the appropriate size. Seal the can, bottle, or bag and affix the appropriate labels on the exterior. Indicate contents on the label so that the forensic scientist assigned to the case will know what is inside and how to extract samples safely for analysis.

FIGURE 9.18
Kerosene heater located at the area of origin of a house fire.

When you are investigating a fire, the presence or absence of combustible or flammable materials and how the ignition source and the fuel came together are major factors. Some sources of ignition include power cords, irons, lights, matches, burning cigarettes, lightning, stoves, and heat sources such as floor or kerosene floor heaters (see Figure 9.18). Even if the ignition sources are melted beyond recognition, they must be identified and collected for the appropriate lab analysis. Consult with your laboratory technicians for recommended practices regarding the submission evidence samples for testing.

Collect liquid samples using a clean, sterile eyedropper, syringe, or pipette. If a suspected liquid accelerant is found in its original container, the liquid should be removed from the container and prepared for submission to the laboratory for analysis. The accelerant should be placed in new, clean, Teflon-lined metal containers; glass jars with Teflon-lined silica septa caps; polyester or nylon evidence bags; or a combination of these containers. The original container should be handled carefully to preserve any latent fingerprints or other trace evidence that might be present on the outside of the container.

It is also acceptable to absorb liquid samples with clean, sterile cotton balls or gauze pads and then seal them in an airtight container. If you are looking for samples of liquid accelerant near the area of origin of the fire, be sure to check grooves in flooring, between tiles, and under the edges of floor covers or door facings because the accelerant will spread toward the lowest point in the room and is often not fully consumed during the fire. Often liquid residue can be recovered in these areas because it is the vapor and not the liquid that is burning.

Comparison samples must also be submitted to the crime laboratory. Cut or collect uncontaminated specimens and seal them in the same manner as the suspected contaminated evidence. When possible, collect comparison samples from areas that were not touched by fire or intense heat. Soil samples must also be collected in the case of outdoor fire scenes. To slow down the degradation of any bacterial agents present in the soil, seal and freeze samples until they can be transported to the laboratory for analysis.

The majority of arson fires are started by petroleum distillates such as gasoline and kerosene. There are several telltale signs of arson, including evidence of separate and unconnected fires, streamers or trailers indicating fuel paths that link fires together, and severe burning found on the floor as opposed to the ceiling. As discussed earlier, through detailed scene processing, one may be able to determine that the fire was either accidental or incendiary. Acts of God are termed "providential" and fall under accidental causes. If the cause cannot be determined, the fire should be called "undetermined" and the case filed administratively pending receipt of further information.

RECOVERY OF BURNED BODIES

Chapter 20 of the National Fire Protection Association publication *Code 921: A Guide to Fire and Explosion Investigation* emphasizes the importance of investigating every fire scene that involves serious injuries and a fire and/or explosion that has immediate fatalities. This is crucial to the inquiry because many deaths occur weeks and even months after the event took place. Every death investigation that is linked to a fire or explosion should include an autopsy to determine manner and cause of death. This information is critical to the arson detectives because it may provide additional investigative leads in the case. The probable cause of a fire should never be published until conclusive results have been obtained from the autopsy.

If a fire victim is located at a scene and there is no chance for resuscitation, firefighters should attempt to minimize damage or destruction of any physical evidence that may be on or near the victim's body. If at all possible, straight-streamed hoses should not be used because the force of the water will di-minish or obliterate potential trace evi-dence. In some cases, it will be necessary to move the body—for example, if there is imminent danger that the structure will collapse or if there is uncontrollable fire nearby. If a victim was moved prior to your arrival on the scene, you must document this fact and talk with the firefighter or other party who moved the victim from the original location. All fire scenes with fatalities must be treated from the outset as a crime scene. Two separate yet concurrent investigations will be conducted: one for the fire origin and cause and the second to determine the cause of the fatality.

FIGURE 9.19
Body found in a burned building.

When circumstances permit the body to be left in place, document the scene with photographs and video as soon as possible (see Figure 9.19). Burn patterns may be visible on the victim's clothing, and can assist in determining the origin of the fire. Once the body is removed, photograph the area where the body was found. At this time, you should also complete diagrams or sketches with accurate measurements and dimensions. It may also be helpful to re-create the outline of the body using chalk or string because the investigation may continue for several hours or days.

Adult human bodies are not easily destroyed by fire. Studies reveal that in order for a body to be reduced to ashes, it must be exposed for several hours to temperatures ranging from 1,800 to 2,000°F. Even then, there are many bone fragments and remnants of teeth that do not disintegrate. The bodies of small children and infants, however, can be totally consumed by flames and heat because there is much less mass and calcification.

The body may be covered under layers of debris and may be burned or unburned. It is essential that the CSI participate in a systematic search of the area where a victim was found or is suspected to be lo-cated to identify, collect, and preserve all forensic evidence. Remem-ber that critical evidence as to the origin of the fire or circumstances of the fire could be located within arm's reach of the victim, so it is imperative to restrict access of nonessential personnel to this area.

Identification Techniques
The identification of victims at a fire scene is a challenge that will require information from many sources. Visual identification is the

most unreliable means and should be utilized only to begin the verification process. Clothing and jewelry provide additional information, but it is easy to substitute clothing and personal belongings. X-rays are the most positive means of identification; in the case of severely damaged bodies, antemortem and postmortem dental records can provide positive victim identification.

Fire deaths may require the assistance of a forensic anthropologist or odontologist to ensure recovery of the entire body and ascertain the position of the victim at the time of death. A forensic anthropologist may also be called to the scene to examine bones and determine if they are human or animal. As tissue and muscle are consumed by fire, it becomes more difficult to differentiate between large animal and human bones.

Fire victims are often found in a crouching pugilistic (or boxer) stance, which results from the effects of the fire on the body. This should not be misconstrued as a defensive or escape posture. The crouching position occurs as the muscles shrink and then dehydrate from the bones, causing the body to assume a stance with flexed elbows and knees and clenched fists.

The cause of death is the event, injury, or illness that is responsible for death occurring. Examples of causes of death at a fire scene include smoke inhalation, burns, trauma (including gunshot wounds and stabbings), asphyxiation, carbon monoxide poisoning, or heart attack. The manner of death will be determined by the medical examiner after an autopsy is completed. It may be accidental, homicide, natural, undetermined, or suicide. If victims are located in a fire or explosive scene, the question "Why did they not escape?" must be answered by the investigation.

BOMB SCENE INVESTIGATIONS

Most bomb scene investigations will begin locally; however, the resources of the ATF and other federal agencies are available on request. Multiagency task forces allow smaller organizations to pool their resources when investigating crimes involving firearms or explosives, providing enhanced access to investigative tools and expertise. The ATF maintains the Arson and Explosives Incident System (AEXIS) and the Bombing Arson Tracking System (BATS) databases. These secure sites allow law enforcement and arson investigators to report and share information on bombing incidents, including photographs, and to analyze similarities among improvised explosive devices and incendiary devices being used nationwide. According to BATS, there were 428 bombing incidents reported in 2020.

FIGURE 9.20

A blast scene can contain hundreds of pieces of potential physical evidence.

FIGURE 9.21

Bomb robot investigating a suspicious package.

Of primary concern when investigating a bomb scene is maintaining safety and ensuring that there are no secondary devices in place that can jeopardize the lives of first responders (see Figure 9.20). A CSI should not approach the crime scene until it has been searched and declared safe (see Figure 9.21). Even then, there remains the potential of structural damage that may endanger the investigators, and just like a fire scene, assessment of the safety of the location must be ongoing. Hazards may include damaged gas lines, downed utility lines, and the chance that fires may erupt. It is essential for the CSI to remain in contact with the incident commander throughout the crime scene investigation. The recovery of evidence is always secondary to the safety of all personnel.

An explosion is the sudden and rapid escape of gases from a confined space, usually accompanied by high temperatures, violent shock, and loud noise. There are three types of explosions: mechanical, chemical, and nuclear. A mechanical explosion occurs when pressure builds up in a container until the pressure exceeds the structural resistance of the container. Chemical explosions are the result of fuel and oxygen supporting a rapid combustion. Atomic explosions are produced by fission, splitting of the nuclei of atoms, or fusion, which forces the nuclei of atoms together under great pressure. This section focuses on mechanical and chemical explosions because they are the most likely to occur.

The two broad categories of explosives are low explosives, which burn rather than explode, and high explosives, which are detonated by shock and do not have to be confined to explode. Examples of low explosives include black powder and smokeless powder. Both black

FIGURE 9.22
Pipe bomb.

and smokeless powders are often used to make pipe bombs and are available for purchase through many retail outlets. To explode, low explosives must be confined in a container and are usually initiated by safety fuses, but it is possible for them to be set off by friction.

High explosives are subdivided into three groups based on their sensitivity: primary, secondary, and tertiary explosives. Primary explosives detonate forcefully and are extremely sensitive to heat, shock, or friction. Primary explosives are generally used to manufacture blasting caps and are not often used as the main charge. The majority of high explosives are considered secondary explosives. These explosives, which include dynamite and military-grade explosives such as C-4 and TNT, require a detonating device or initiating explosion such as that found in a blasting cap (see Figure 9.22). The last group is the least sensitive explosive type. These explosives, called tertiary explosives, require a booster or a secondary high explosive to cause detonation. Examples include ammonium nitrate soaked in fuel oil (ANFO) and urea nitrate soaked in fuel oil.

The flash or fireball that occurs at detonation usually causes the fires that are associated with explosions (see Box 9.4). This may create additional injuries or damage around the point of origin.

Locating and Collecting Evidence of Explosive Devices

The presence of a crater will indicate the origin of the blast, regardless of whether high or low explosives were used to manufacture the device. Soil samples must be gathered from all areas surrounding the crater, and a systematic scene search should be conducted to locate remnants of the detonating mechanism. As you develop the perimeters of an outdoor blast scene investigation, remember to check rooftops, gutters, ledges, and trees for debris and take samples from street signs and streetlights because they are excellent sources for explosive residue.

Post-Blast Investigation Techniques

The CSI must be aware of the many chemicals and other easily obtainable items that can be combined to create a deadly homemade device. In addition to pipe bombs, the determined bomb-maker can

BOX 9.4 WHAT HAPPENS WHEN AN EXPLOSIVE IS DETONATED?

When explosives detonate, three events occur:

- The blast pressure effect occurs when a powerful detonation (shock) wave moves outward at a massive speed and creates tremendous overpressures and primary blast injuries.
- Air rushes back into the void created by the positive pressure, causing tertiary blast injuries from blunt trauma.
- Fragmentation of the container and dispersal of shrapnel that was enclosed in the device cause secondary blast injuries (see Figure 9.23).

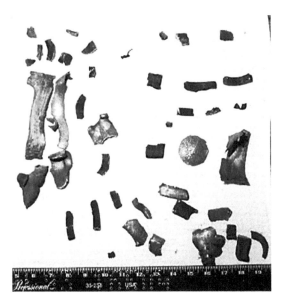

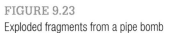

FIGURE 9.23
Exploded fragments from a pipe bomb

FIGURE 9.24
Bomb technician in protective equipment.

create improvised explosive devices (IEDs) in suitcases, backpacks, boxes wrapped to resemble presents, and so on. The list is virtually endless.

CSIs assigned to process a post-blast scene should be properly trained as bomb technicians so that they can accurately identify fragmentation and other types of physical evidence (see Figure 9.24). Blasting caps or other detonators as well as batteries, flashbulbs, and match heads may be present at the scene. Remote detonators such as cellphones or walkie-talkies may yield DNA as well as fingerprint evidence.

FIGURE 9.25A
Car destroyed by a homemade bomb.

FIGURE 9.25B
Car explosion showing mapping of debris.

Each room or area should be treated as a separate crime scene (see Figures 9.25a and 9.25b), and clean protective clothing should be donned prior to entering the next search area. Evidence should be separated by room or area as well, so that an accurate reconstruction can be compiled. Assign a letter to each room and issue sequential numbers for evidence located in each room.

For every questioned sample, a control sample must be collected and submitted for analysis. The proper method for gathering residue samples is to utilize a dry cotton gauze pad, cotton ball, or swab first and then follow with a second pad, ball, or swab dampened with methanol/ethanol. You should attempt to locate residue from all surfaces that face the origin of the blast.

Process all areas that were likely to be touched by the suspect for latent prints and other trace evidence. If a suspect is identified, collect all clothing, jewelry, glasses, or other items that may contain residue or trace evidence. Seal everything individually in paper bags.

The FBI, ATF, and state or local laboratories should be contacted prior to packaging and transporting explosives or hazardous materials. If liquid samples are collected for submission to the laboratory, the container with the sample should be inserted into a second, larger canister and surrounded with absorbent material to protect the primary container. Affix appropriate labels on the outside of the canister that identify the contents as hazardous materials. Remember that the transportation of hazardous materials requires special conditions, and you may not be able to ship this evidence to a laboratory.

Discussion Questions

1. What is the primary initial question an arson investigator is trying to answer?
2. Discuss what is meant by burn patterns and what characteristics affect them.

3. What are the different types of explosions? Explain each. What are the different categories of explosions? Describe each.
4. Why has modern building construction altered the way fire investigations are conducted?

REFERENCES

National Fire Protection Association (NFPA). (2021). *Code 921. Guide for fire and explosion investigators.* Quincy, MA: NFPA.

Uniform Crime Report. (2019) Retrieved from: https://ucr.fbi.gov/crime-in-the-u.s/2019/crime-in-the-u.s.-2019/topic-pages/arson

United States Bomb Data Center - Explosive Incident Report. (2020). Retrieved from: https://www.atf.gov/file/155141/download

CHAPTER 10

The Electronic Crime Scene

KEY TERMS

Bullycide	Faraday bag	Phishing
Computer crime	Hackers	PROTECT Act of
Crime scene staging	Identity theft	2003
Cyberbullying	International Mobile	Script kiddie
Cybercrime	Equipment	Spyware
Cyberstalking	Identity (IMEI)	URL (uniform
Cybertailing	Internet protocol (IP)	resource locator)
Digital evidence	Internet service	
Digital forensics	providers (ISPs)	

What You Will Learn

Electronic gadgets dominate our lives. From iPods to smartphones, tablets to infotainment units on our vehicles, we live connected lives. All this convenience also allows more access for hackers and cyberattacks to occur, thus expanding the potential crime scene to the virtual world. CSIs must know how to identify, preserve, and collect evidence that will be further examined by digital analysts.

MURDER IN THE NEW YEAR

The Electronic Crime Scene

The computer analyst handed Detective Fletcher and CSI Smith each a folder.

"Matt Powell, computer analyst, at your service."

DOI: 10.4324/9780429261657-10

Mavis Fletcher opened the folder and began to review the documents. "Well, Matt Powell," she said to the computer analyst, "what did you find?"

The computer analyst smiled at the detective. "I found some interesting stuff on both the Morton's laptops and Michael Sellers's desktop. We are still doing digital forensics analysis—extracting and analyzing relevant data—but what I can tell you is that an interesting picture is emerging."

"How interesting?" Tom Smith said as he stuck a piece of gum into his mouth.

"We were able to break the encryption on the Sellers's desktop that confirmed James Morton's laptop was used in the misuse of the foundation account. At best, the dean was using the funds for personal expenses ranging from purchasing a time-share at Hilton Head to a one-week trip to Maui. By the way, his password for that account was 'honeymoon photos.'"

"Were there any?" Tom quipped.

"Were there any what?" Matt asked.

"Photos."

Matt scratched the back of his head. "No—no photos, but besides misusing foundation funds, Sellers was also harassing Morton's wife."

Mavis looked at Tom. "Cyberstalking and bullying are both on the rise, but usually we see that type of behavior among teenagers. We need to keep open minds and remember these types of crimes are not limited to the teens."

Matt Powell leaned back and placed his hands behind his head. "There is one more interesting twist. Apparently, Mr. Morton was something of a computer whiz himself. From the timing of the messages and activity, it seems Morton may have infected Sellers's computer with spyware that came from in an e-mail that Seller thought was from Morton's wife. With the spyware, Morton gained access to Sellers's computer, including his 'honeymoon photos' file."

Tom Smith leaned forward. "What about Morton's suicide note? Whose printer produced that note?"

The computer analyst shrugged, "It came from the Morton's home printer."

Detective Fletcher began writing in her notebook. "Of course, since it was typed and not signed, we don't know for sure who the author is."

"Normally, we can tell you the account that was logged into the computer at the time the letter was printed. Every transaction leaves a trace! In this instance, however, we can only tell you that James Morton's account was the last to log into the system," said Matt.

Mavis Fletcher put her pen and notebook in her handbag and looked at the two men sitting across from her. "Gentlemen, it looks like Mr. Morton could have been building a case against the dean. What we now have is a possible motive for murder."

Tom nodded in agreement. "Particularly in light of the evidence Ed found in the dean's firepit. The remnants of a jumpsuit and residue that suggests a pair of latex gloves were part of the kindling for Michael Sellers's late-night bonfire. For once, the rain was our friend."

"Yes, indeed," Mavis replied, "Calls and text messages to Mrs. Morton's smartphone support the digital forensics. Well done, Matt."

"Why, thank you, Detective. Glad to be of help," Matt responded with a smile.

INTRODUCTION

Computers and technology permeate our everyday environment, and it is impossible to measure the extent of the impact the Internet has on today's world. You have probably used a computer several times today in ways you take for granted. Did you buy gas, stop at the ATM, make a purchase, drive down an interstate with traffic-monitoring equipment, read a text message, tweet, or make a phone call? And, because technology is abundant in our lifestyles, so is digital evidence—any data stored or transmitted using a computer is probative in nature and can be used to generate investigative leads. CSIs are not expected to be technical experts in digital evidence, but do need to be able to identify, document, and preserve the evidence at the electronic crime scene. Digital forensics is the controlled extraction and analysis of digital evidence from a wide range of electronic media for obtaining evidence relevant to an investigation.

Although technology can aid the investigator, the criminal element of society is also utilizing technology to avoid getting caught and to commit even more offenses. Advances in digital capacity far outpace the capabilities of law enforcement officers to detect and apprehend the perpetrators. It is more likely than not that those involved in criminal operations are utilizing cellphones, computers, and the Internet. The variety of crimes committed through the use of technology spans the spectrum from embezzlement, money laundering, fraud, corporate espionage, identify theft, stalking, exploitation, and obscenity.

Digital data is being transmitted all around us—from the wireless signals utilized by high-speed Internet and networks to fiber-optic cables to satellites. Every transmission leaves a trace on the system from which it is generated to the device it was transmitted to. Digital evidence examiners can analyze the data and establish both class and individual characteristics just as with other forensic evidence. This electronic evidence can be used to facilitate investigation of all types of crimes, ranging from the investigation of online fraud, identity theft, child pornography, cyberstalking, and Internet predators, to traditional crimes such as drug dealing, homicide, and missing persons.

The proliferation of GPS-enabled devices, including smartphones and infotainment units in vehicles, has created a new field of investigation and digital evidence. GPS forensics includes the process of acquiring, examining, and analyzing GPS devices for evidence of a criminal act or gathering data that may assist in an investigation (www.gpsforensics.org). Most GPS devices have an internal hard drive or an SD card slot and allow pictures, audio and video files, as well as documents to be stored. Sometimes an analyst can retrieve the last journey where the GPS was used. Even if the route was updated multiple times during a trip, the analyst can testify in court that the device was in the locations from which the GPS obtained a satellite lock.

CYBERCRIME: THE INTERNET AGE

While the Internet provides access to countless resources, it also makes millions of users vulnerable to becoming victims of cybercriminals (see Box 10.1). The ease of accessing the Internet now extends to smartphones, laptops, gaming devices, tablets, e-readers, public kiosks in cybercafés, and other unmonitored locations. Net-enabled mobile devices have provided easy access to millions of unsuspecting victims. Around 90 percent of teens in the United States actively participate in social networking sites such as Facebook. There are now more than 2.7 billion monthly active users of Facebook in 2020, an increase of 11 percent in one year (www.facebook.com/iq/insights-to-go), and, of those users, more than 81 percent of active users access Facebook utilizing a mobile device (www.statista.com/statistics/377808/distribution-of-facebook-users-by-device/). This proliferation of electronic devices and victims makes it possible for a single perpetrator to commit many crimes against a large number of people from anywhere in the world.

Computer crime consists of a myriad group of offenses defined by state and federal statutes and includes unauthorized access, software piracy, alteration or theft of electronically stored information, transmission of destructive viruses or commands, child pornography, predatory activities, etc.

Cybercrime is a term referring to technology-assisted crimes that generally involve the use of the Internet. These crimes basically consist of traditional crimes such as fraud, stalking, and theft combined with new techniques made possible by technology. Digital evidence is any type of data that is transmitted or stored that can support (or refute) allegations of offenses. Digital evidence can also be used to establish intent or alibi; however, it is only one component of the successful investigation.

BOX 10.1 EXPONENTIAL GROWTH OF TECHNOLOGY

A 2021 study conducted by Pew Research revealed that 85 percent of all American adults currently own a smartphone with the largest population of users in the 18–29 age bracket (www.pewresearch.org/internet/fact-sheet/mobile/). More than 72 percent of smartphones are Android devices, making those users a better target (https://gs.statcounter.com/os-market-share/mobile/worldwide), and more than 480,000 malicious Android programs were identified in 2020. Over 90 percent of users access the web from mobile devices rather than from computers (www.statista.com/topics/779/mobile-internet/#:~:text=In%202020%2C%20the%20number%20of,mobile%20device%20to%20go%20online).

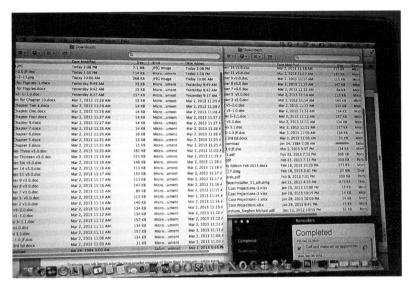

FIGURE 10.1
Millions of electronic fingerprint records are generated daily by today's technology.

Just like other crime scene investigations, every electronic or digital forensics case is unique and can present unforeseeable challenges to the CSI and case detectives. Physical evidence is identified, collected, and preserved at the crime scene and then submitted for analysis by forensic examiners, who are sometimes called "digital evidence examiners." Electronic devices such as GPS units and smartphones should not be examined in the field because every power up or keystroke can change the data contained on the device. Only well-trained forensic examiners should attempt to recover data from the devices. A Faraday bag is a specially designed bag that prevents devices from communicating with networks, whether Wi-Fi or cellular phone signals. Devices that connect to a mobile network should be transported and stored in a Faraday bag. Several sizes are available, thus enabling you to protect devices of any size. iPhones and iPads use the iCloud application to "find my phone," and the user can select "remote wipe" to secure data. Using a Faraday bag will prevent a remote wipe of the device.

Data can exist in storage media, primary or secondary memory, volatile memory, or virtually in the cloud. A digital crime scene can be identified as the electronic environment where digital evidence can potentially exist.

If a computer is involved in a crime scene, be sure to limit access to the computer to decrease the likelihood of changing the evidence. Once a forensic copy of the evidence is made, the data can be examined from the copy, and detailed scrutiny can establish linkages, determine the sources of data, and identify the pertinent data.

Internet service providers (ISPs), such as Time Warner Cable, Comcast, Verizon, and Charter, use authentication servers to verify passwords and record which **Internet protocol (IP)** addresses are assigned to specific users each time they sign in online. IP addresses may be static or dynamic. An example of an IP address is 122.55.741.1, and it can be traced to a particular computer if it is assigned to a defined location every time that unit connects to the Internet. Network administrators manually assign static IP addresses, whereas various automatic methods assign dynamic IP addresses. Although dynamic IP addresses are assigned automatically, they still create a digital signature that can be authenticated by a digital forensics investigator (see Figure 10.1). The system and application logs provide essential information to the cybercrime investigator, and ISPs are required to cooperate with law enforcement investigations. It is possible to use event logs to determine which account was using a computer at a specific time. With the number of users growing exponentially, the ISP cannot store the information forever. Most will retain any new logs with a preservation request and not delete the information for a specified length of time.

For example, when using a computer for creating, downloading, viewing, printing, encrypting, or deleting files, a user leaves traces in the computer's system and application logs for real-time activity. Corroborating evidence, such as video from surveillance cameras and confiscation of printouts obtained during specific sessions, can be used to link a suspect to a specific computer even in a public location.

The system and application logs provide essential information to the cybercrime investigator, and ISPs are required to cooperate with law enforcement investigations. Many freely available software tools and protocols, such as WHOIS, allow investigators to view the IP addresses or domain name system (DNS) server along with the registrant's identity. This information is not always accurate but can make corporate identity issues a concern to those who are not involved in illegal Internet activities.

FIGURE 10.2
The widespread popularity of Internet devices creates even more opportunities for digital crimes to be committed.

Although digital evidence can rarely prove conclusively that a victim or a perpetrator was in a specific place at a specific time, a preponderance of the evidence can be determined by the trier of fact (judge or jury). IP addresses are not unique to the individual but to the computer that is assigned the IP address at the specific time. Other sources of digital evidence are computer-based diaries, contacts, spreadsheets, GPS coordinates, and the web browser's history of sites visited and downloaded files. Many of these applications require a specific username and password combination to gain access. The fast-paced development of new software applications combined with the proliferation of e-devices creates new methods for criminals to commit illegal activities faster than law enforcement officials can solve cases (see Figure 10.2).

Prevalence of Cybercrime

There is no real way to know how much computer crime is being committed. Thefts of service, fraud, cyberbullying, and cyberstalking have catapulted computer crimes into a category whereby victims may never be identified and the total cost of the crimes never discovered. Every type of criminal offense presents challenges to the investigation.

Some computer crimes may not be reported simply because victims do not want the inconvenience of having their computer confiscated and examined, or they are afraid of the embarrassment of being "taken for a ride." Corporations may discover internal or external hacking attempts—or even successful intrusions—but will not report them because they do not want the publicity or resulting investigations by outside entities.

A computer network breach could result in negative press, leading to decreased confidence in the corporation and a loss of income or customers. In 2012, the State of South Carolina's Department of Revenue databases were hacked. More than 3.6 million Social Security numbers and other identifying information were stolen. At least 387,000 credit and debit cards were also compromised in an attack that was described by the US Secret Service as one of the largest breaches against a state agency computer system. To understand the impact of this digital crime, you need to know that the three major credit reporting bureaus use Social Security numbers to provide credit information for *everyone* applying for credit in the United States. Computer crime has created a new group of people: cybervictims.

Worldwide access through the Internet presents the problem that some criminal offenses in the United States are not violations of the law in other countries. Multijurisdictional issues create tangles of venue concerns; the perpetrator may be located thousands of miles away from where the victim lives. Having the victim travel for court appearances to ensure prosecution may not be possible due to the victim's age, financial considerations, or—in the case of international crimes—the inability of the victim to enter or leave foreign countries.

IDENTITY THEFT

Millions of people fall victim to **identity theft** each year, making it one of the fastest growing high-tech crimes. In 2020, identity theft topped the list for consumer complaints filed with the Federal Trade Commission (www.ftc.gov/news-events/press-releases/2021/02/new-data-shows-ftc-received-2-2-million-fraud-reports-consumers). Identity theft reports have almost doubled since 2019 with approximately 1.4 million reports of identity theft. Offenses involving identity theft occur when the perpetrator pretends to be another person for the purpose of committing crimes. Identity theft carries low risk for the perpetrator and the potential for high return; it is easy to commit and difficult to detect initially. Every individual is subject to becoming a victim if he or she does not take adequate measures to safeguard personal information. Although traditional theft of identification still happens frequently (purse snatching, burglaries, etc.), digital evidence investigations have found that Internet users do not take enough precautions to guard against the theft of personal information. According to the US Census Bureau, approximately 92 percent of US households have a computer, while 85 percent of US households report having Internet access (www.census.gov/newsroom/press-releases/2021/computer-internet-use.html). A lack of vigilance allows perpetrators to compile extensive data on individuals and commit identity theft very easily. Lifelock provides information concerning identity theft and mitigating strategies. To review the information, go to www.lifelock.com/learn/.

The Identity Theft and Assumption Deterrence Act of 1998 established identity theft as a federal offense (www.ftc.gov/node/119459). A variety of crimes are covered by this act, including the following:

- **Credit card fraud**—This type of fraud involves using existing cards to make purchases or obtain cash advances or using personal identification to establish new credit card accounts.
- **Utilities fraud**—The most prevalent type involves telecommunications and subscription fraud.
- **Bank fraud**—This type of fraud involves emptying existing accounts and opening new accounts with stolen identification or redirecting automatic deposits or making unauthorized electronic withdrawals.
- **Loans**—This type of fraud involves fraudulently obtaining personal, automobile, and home loans.
- **Government documents**—This type of fraud involves generating false documents such as birth certificates, driver's licenses, and passports; acquiring access to federal benefits such as Social Security or veterans' checks.

Identity theft also occurs when perpetrators obtain databases containing hundreds or even thousands of accounts with personal information, as discussed in the case of international hackers gaining access to credit card processing databases under the control of the South Carolina Department of Revenue. These offenses occur through no fault of the victims, and investigations are usually initiated when consumers begin to complain about unauthorized transactions on their accounts. These types of cybercrimes can occur thousands of miles away from the victims, so physical contact or close proximity is not necessary for someone to be a cybervictim.

SPYWARE

Spyware is a self-installing software program that exploits vulnerable computers by monitoring the Internet activities of the computer user and providing this data to third parties. Spyware is usually embedded into software programs that are offered as free downloads, and once it gains access to the operating system, it collects information such as website visits, launches pop-up advertisements, and even records keystrokes in an attempt to intercept passwords or credit card numbers. Microsoft Windows [C0]-based machines are particularly susceptible because Internet Explorer is the most popular web browser, and it is tightly integrated with the operating system. Spyware can also change the configuration of a laptop, may alter the user's ability to change settings, and can cause the computer to crash.

Users may not be aware of the presence of spyware on their computers. Newer variants of spyware can be downloaded without end users knowing that they have downloaded anything. When a system slows down and as users begin to experience sluggish performance, spyware should be suspected. Spyware is designed to be difficult to remove, making it arduous for you to change your settings back to the way they were originally arranged. Detailed information about spyware/malware prevention is available from Microsoft at support. microsoft.com/en-us/topic/how-to-prevent-and-remove-viruses-and-other-malware-53dc9904-0baf-5150-6e9a-e6a8d6fa0cb5. Many commercial anti-spyware programs are available that can be used to identify and remove the spyware.

INTERNET CRIMES AGAINST CHILDREN

Criminals usually feel safe on the Internet, and with more than 5 billion users, the Internet greatly enhances the reach of predators (www.internetworldstats.com/stats.htm). Criminals can now commit a crime in a foreign country without ever having a passport, and Internet access allows predators to commit sexual crimes without ever physically coming into contact with the victim.

The most common Internet crimes against children involve the solicitation of minors for sex and the creation, possession, and distribution of child pornography. In the United States, most criminal Internet activity falls under the jurisdiction of federal agencies such as the Department of Justice and the Federal Trade Commission, although the states carry the burden of enforcement. In 2020, Internet Crimes Against Children investigations led to more than 109,000 arrests and over 85,600 forensic examinations (https://ojjdp.ojp.gov/programs/internet-crimes-against-children-task-force-program).

Pornography

The type of illegal pornography created, collected, or distributed reflects the motive of the offender. Clues as to the identity of the suspect may be gleaned by studying online profiles he or she creates. These virtual identities may seek young victims (cybervictims), many of whom do not realize they are being exploited. This provides predators with the ability to lurk inside the victims' homes through the Internet.

The **PROTECT Act of 2003** modified federal pornography laws to define the possession of child pornography as being in possession of contraband (www.gpo.gov/fdsys/pkg/BILLS-108s151enr/pdf/BILLS-108s151enr.pdf). (PROTECT stands for Prosecutorial Remedies and Other Tools to end the Exploitation of Children Today.) Child pornography is any image that depicts, in a sexually explicit manner, a prepubescent human being.

Under federal law (18 U.S.C. 2256), child pornography is defined as any visual depiction, including any photograph, film, video, picture, or computer-generated image or picture, whether made or produced by electronic, mechanical, or other means, of sexually explicit conduct, where

- The production of the visual depiction involves the use of a minor engaging in sexually explicit conduct;
- The visual depiction is a digital image, computer image, or computer-generated image that is, or is indistinguishable from, that of a minor engaging in sexually explicit conduct; or
- The visual depiction has been created, adapted, or modified to appear that an identifiable minor is engaging in sexually explicit conduct.

Predators

Internet predators have a perception of safety and believe they can remain anonymous because they can alter their identity, age, gender, and physical appearance to potential victims. By donning various personas, pedophiles can troll cyberspace, entering chat rooms looking for children who are expressing loneliness or low self-esteem or who are "just having a bad day." The chat room environment appeals to children, particularly those of middle-school age, because it provides them with the ability to communicate with many people in real time. Thus, predators are able to begin relationships and convince victims that they care about them. Such efforts to groom these victims are often successful because many children in the 21st century spend a large part of their lives in the virtual world.

Before the Internet became embedded in our everyday lives, child predators had to troll for their victims in public venues, such as malls, parks, and schoolyards. Now, children are exposed to predators in the privacy of their own homes. This false sense of security sometimes lowers the inhibitions of predators to act on impulse. Sexual predators who travel to meet victims acquired online are referred to as "travelers." The Internet has made the world smaller and created a virtual venue without boundaries for child exploitation.

CYBERSTALKING, CYBERBULLYING, AND OTHER HARASSMENT

Cyberstalking takes the traditional crime of stalking and adds the complexity of the Internet to the situation. The perpetrator will develop a fixation and obsession with a victim that usually causes the perpetrator to reveal himself or herself to the victim. A stalker wants to exert power over the victim, primarily through generating fear. Once the stalker determines that he or she has the capacity to frighten and control a victim, his or her actions become bolder.

These actions of the perpetrator are observable, and a thorough and objective analysis of digital evidence can establish the modus operandi of a perpetrator as well as the motive for committing the offense. While increased vigilance on the part of local law enforcement has increased the number of cybercrime investigators, advances in the technical expertise of the stalkers and the ease of access to victims have also increased the number of occurrences of the crime.

Victimology, the study of the ways in which the behavior of crime victims may have led to or contributed to their victimization, becomes important when investigating cyberstalking and may lead to the identification of the perpetrator. By developing information, including the choice of tools and the location, time, and method of approach, the investigator may determine the significance of facts and link other victims to the stalker.

Victims unintentionally reveal personal information, including photographs, addresses, and hobbies, which creates a target-rich environment for Internet harassment. Chat rooms and applications such as Kik and Whisper open the door for perpetrators to monitor and select victims. Harassment includes establishing a pattern of behavior and places the victim in constant fear of physical danger. Annoyance or vague threats are not considered harassment.

Bullycide is a term used when someone takes his or her life as a result of being bullied and is a serious issue for law enforcement and CSIs. Children and teens who are victims of bullies at school are constantly bombarded with online attacks—through vicious comments, tweets, social networking sites, and posts of unflattering photos. Approximately 59 percent of students report being cyberbullied, and with 95 percent of teens using the Internet, the number of potential victims and digital crime scenes is staggering (https://dataprot.net/statistics/cyberbullying-statistics/).

Open Source Intelligence (OSINT) is the process an investigator uses to follow a perpetrator through various computer networks in an attempt to identify the suspect. Even if investigators are not able to locate the source computer, digital evidence can be retrieved from network activities that may lead to identification of the suspect. Digital evidence examiners can follow the cybertrail to find related evidence on the Internet, commercial systems, and private networks. They can obtain information from online chat networks and utilize e-mail headers that may link suspects to victims or digital crime scenes. Combined with video camera recordings, the digital evidence can be used to show that intent existed (*mens rea*) to commit a crime or establish premeditation of an act. Data mining is the process of collecting digital evidence from multiple sources and importing that data into analytical software to link perpetrators to victims in a graphical depiction. This pictorial evidence can be used to convince a jury of events that are difficult to document in narrative reports.

FIGURE 10.3
John Halligan shows the web page devoted to his son, Ryan Patrick Halligan. After being bullied online by classmates for months, 13-year-old Ryan took his own life in 2003. Most states now make explicit reference to cyberbullying in their anti-bullying laws. *AP Photo/Toby Talbot.*

Cyberbullying takes place when victims are threatened or harassed by Internet users using available technology (see Figure 10.3). Cyberbullies create false profiles and use social networking sites as well as instant messaging (IM), texting, and cellphones to intimidate their victims. Posting online rumors and posting anonymous comments can lead to various criminal activity. Surveys of victims indicate that at least 50 percent of the time, victims are acquainted with the cyberbully in the real, offline, world. This is a growing crime that has led some victims (usually teens) to attempt suicide (bullycide), run away from home, or succumb to the suggestions of cyberbullies and predators. The National Crime Prevention Council offers more information about this crime atwww.ncpc.org/resources/cyberbullying.

Fifteen-year-old Amanda Todd's death captured international headlines in 2012 when she posted a video on YouTube only four hours before committing suicide. Amanda was a victim of repeated cyberbullying attacks on Facebook and other social media. Her nine-minute video and subsequent death was the culmination of more than a year of taunting and online attacks by an as-yet-unidentified tormenter. Twenty full-time investigators were assigned to this case. You can read more about the ongoing cyberbullying investigation at https://abcnews.go.com/ US/bullied-teen-amanda-todds-death-spurs-fake-fundraising/ story?id=17507029.

The difference between cyberbullying and cyberharassment is the age of both the victim and the perpetrator. For cyberbullying, they both have to be underage. The crime has to have a minor on both sides or at least to have been instigated by a minor against another minor. Once adults become involved, the crime is plain and simple cyberharassment or cyberstalking. Adult cyberharassment or cyberstalking is never called "cyberbullying."

Social Networking Sites and "Sexting"

The online social scene, characterized by pages on Facebook, Twitter, Instagram, and other similar sites, has increased the availability of victims for online predators. Due to the proliferation of mobile devices in the modern era it has also increased the reach of predators and the damaging effects of sexting, such as revenge porn. The ease of access has also increased with Pew Research finding that in 2020 85 percent of Americans own a smartphone, meaning there is constant access to social media for a vast majority of Americans (www.pewresearch.org/internet/fact-sheet/mobile/).

Unsurprisingly the Covid pandemic has also played a part in smartphone usage during 2020 with a 20 percent increase of smartphone usage since 2019 due to social distancing and travel restrictions (www.forbes.com/sites/johnkoetsier/2020/08/17/weve-spent-16-trillion-hours-on-mobile-so-far-in-2020/?sh=f61a5966d61d).   This has resulted in an increase to approximately 4.3 hours a day on mobile devices for the average American. While this increase may be due to the pandemic, smartphones are continually increasing in popularity over other forms of Internet usage.

FIGURE 10.4
QR code on a T-shirt.

Personal information, photographs, and lists of friends have provided easy access to millions of people, creating a predator's paradise with instant access to the next victim. Unsuspecting victims post personal information that easily allows Internet predators to threaten, intimidate, and coerce people around the world.

Other methods that predators use include Omegle, which can instantly connect the user to a stranger to chat. This site does not require users to register, and there are ways to reveal personal information. Sites such as these are attractive to young Internet users who are lured by the ease of making new friends. Another site, WhatsApp, is an encrypted anonymous messaging app with approximately 2 billion users. This site allows texting, photo exchange, and VoIP (Voice over Internet Protocol) at no charge to those who want to reach out and establish new acquaintance in complete anonymity. Skype is a peer-to-peer technology that permits users to communicate with instant messaging and voice chat. In 2021, there were more than 300 million active monthly users. Skype allows users on all platforms (i.e., Windows, iOS, Android, Linux, and others) to make calls using a wireless Internet connection.

Law enforcement agencies are also dealing with the crimes involving *sexting*, which is the use of mobile devices to send sexual messages, pictures, or video. These data transmissions are illegal when involving minors, and teens are not aware of the potential consequences of their actions. There is growing concern that this type of information is readily accessible to predators and can lead to many more serious offenses, including hazing, blackmail, cyberbullying, and child pornography. The threat also extends to adults such as through revenge porn, where photos or videos are distributed to the Internet without permission of the parties involved.

One final innovation that has permeated advertising and is a useful law enforcement tool is QR (Quick Response) codes that can be included on any type of print material, from newspaper and magazine ads, to T-shirts (see Figure 10.4).

The code is scanned using a smartphone with a QR reader application and will automatically take the user to a web page for more information. It can be a valuable investigative tool to distribute information about searches for lost children or wanted persons, for example, and it costs very little to utilize.

COMPUTER INTRUSIONS: HACKERS

Determining how an intruder gains access to a target computer or network can provide cybercrime investigators with a clear sense of the suspect's skill level, intent, and motive. If the offender needed a high level of skills to gain access to the target computer, it is important to determine how that knowledge was obtained and who possessed the skills. "**Hackers**" are professional computer experts who use their skills to overcome technological issues. Perpetrators who infiltrate computer networks are commonly known as "**black-hat hackers.**" The location of the hacker can often be determined by the motive relative to the targets they attack (see Box 10.2). Hackers seek to invade computer networks, whereas virus writers create tools to damage and destroy computer systems.

BOX 10.2 MOTIVES FOR HACKERS

- **Revenge**—To inflict injury or damage
- **Hacktivism**—To advance a political or social agenda
- **Profit**—To achieve personal gain or extortion
- **Pride**—To demonstrate who is in control or to release a virus
- **Curiosity**—To prove oneself because hacking is intellectually challenging

Outside Hackers are usually induced by profit and the feeling of accomplishment when they are able to breach security or obtain proprietary client information. Computer virus developers create and unleash the virus to gain fame and notoriety or to seek revenge against some perceived wrong. Writing and releasing computer viruses can cause disruption and/or denial of services, destroy files, shut down a server, bring a halt to e-commerce, and trigger many other destructive activities. *Profit-driven hackers* may be seeking credit card account information, digital goods, or access to intellectual property. Many profit-driven hackers may establish a back door to the system that allows undetected entrance to and from the network so they can quietly access files. They may be electronically transferring funds or altering or destroying records. In some instances, hackers choose to attempt to extort money from the corporations they have infiltrated using ransomware. Ransomware is typically where the company being attacked has had their data encrypted and are no longer able to access their data. The infiltrator then will request money in return for an encryption key that will decrypt the company's data, typically in cryptocurrency.

The novice hacker who has no legitimate access to the computer network under attack may be motivated by the intellectual challenge of penetrating a secure network just for the thrill of accomplishing that feat. He or she may simply pick a target and monitor traffic until a vulnerable computer system is discovered. Once inside the system, the hacker elevates computer access privileges—the maximum point being the gain of entry to all resources on the system. This type of hacker may be seeking access to movies, music, or games that are protected intellectual property. The term **script kiddie** is used in a derogatory manner to refer to inexperienced hackers who use open-source programs or tools to search for vulnerable computers on a network. These hackers do not have the skills necessary to write their own code and are scanning networks for PCs without firewalls and stealing password files or crashing systems. The goal of script kiddies is generally malicious vandalism, and these offenders can be compared to online gangs. Penetration of unsecured personal computers and password files, however, can lead to many more serious cybercrimes.

Inside hackers are usually performed by disgruntled employees who may be seeking revenge by abusing computer systems that they are authorized to access. Their actions include disabling critical technology, sifting through payroll records, forwarding confidential information to competitors, and altering employment files. In business hacking investigations, insider threats whether intentional or not intentional are frequently involved in breaches and other security incidents.

Criminal hackers are outsiders who seek access to computer networks with malicious intent. They seek personal gain and may release a virus to cripple or destroy the compromised networks. They may be motivated by revenge or a desire for fame, and sometimes they are referred to as "crackers" because they have cracked a system with criminal intent. Estimates for 2019 include over 15billion compromised records resulting from 7,098 reported breaches (www.securitymagazine.com/articles/91728-more-than-151-billion-records-exposed-in-2019). Hackers do not have to be present to commit their crimes—most cybercrimes have international origins, and prosecution may rely only on the digital information captured on the laptop or smartphone of the unwilling victims.

Ethical hackers are those who constantly seek out weaknesses in networks in an effort to prevent security breaches and are known as **"white-hat hackers."** Corporations spend millions of dollars each year in an attempt to make their computer networks more secure. Many universities and computer instruction schools now offer ethical hacking courses that are designed to help computer professionals seek out and be aware of how and where hacks come from. This type of training teaches network administrators how to find potential vulnerabilities within their own networks.

Unsolicited e-mail (known as spam) is the number-one generator of victims being sent to bogus websites created for phishing purposes. Cybercriminals will make slight changes to a **URL (uniform resource locator)** so that unsuspecting users will go to a fake site as opposed to the real site. Many people are familiar with *.com* at the end of a URL, so if the real website has *.org*, *.gov*, or one of the other less common extensions, the phony website will be set up by the same name as a *.com* and send the user to the bogus site.

SCAMS

The potential audience for Internet scams is large, while the investment necessary to create a scam is very small. The prevalence of Internet scams proves that perpetrators are convinced that the chance of getting caught is low, the likelihood of being prosecuted is minimal, and the probability of making money is high. **Phishing** is an Internet fraud scheme that utilizes fake e-mail or pop-up messages that

BOX 10.3 PROFESSIONAL ORGANIZATIONS FOCUSING ON CYBERCRIME

- High-Tech Crime Investigation Association—www.htcia.org
- InfraGard—www.infragard.org
- American Registry for Internet Numbers—www.arin.net
- National Center for Missing and Exploited Children— www.missingkids.org
- National White Collar Crime Center—www.nw3c.org
- Violent Crimes Against Children International Task Force—www.fbi.gov/investigate/violent-crime/cac/international-task-force

- Computer Crime and Intellectual Property Section of the US Department of Justice—www.justice.gov/criminal-ccips
- Anti-Phishing Working Group—www.apwg.org
- International Crime Complaint Center—www.ic3.gov
- International Association of Computer Investigation Specialists—www.iacis.com
- United States Secret Service Cyber Investigations—www.secretservice.gov/investigation/cyber

appear to be legitimate websites. The messages usually indicate the business is seeking updated personal or financial information and lures unsuspecting users to reveal financial or authentication data. These criminals are experts at designing fake e-mails and websites, and countless numbers of victims provide information and do not realize they have been scammed until unauthorized charges appear on statements or a bank account is cleared out. Unwilling models for these phony websites include Netflix, PayPal, Google, and other Internet-based companies (see Box 10.3).

PROCESSING THE ELECTRONIC CRIME SCENE

As with any crime scene investigation, standard procedures and protocols should be followed when responding to the scene of a cybercrime investigation. Whenever possible, an experienced digital evidence investigator should participate in processing the crime scene to minimize the chance of corruption of the original data. In reality, however, experienced digital investigators are not available in every agency. The information here is provided as a guideline for the CSI so that the best possible crime scene and evidence preservation can be provided as local law enforcement agencies transition to the effective new technologies used to commit crimes.

As with other types of crime scenes, photographs and documentation are essential for providing a true and accurate representation of the electronic crime scene. The CSI should maintain evidence logs and preserve the chain of custody throughout the process. Create a sketch indicating the location of cables, connections, and peripheral equipment. Use color-coded labels to indicate where each cable is connected and make these notes on the sketch to aid forensic examiners in recreating the exact configuration of the system. Determine if there is a wireless network in place and locate the router. Photograph it in place and note the status of lights and digital indicators that may be present on the unit. Unplug the power to the router to prevent any remote access to the system from occurring.

There are many types of electronic crime scenes in addition to home offices. Agency investigators may be specially trained in forensic technology, the use of scientific techniques to solve criminal cases by identifying, collecting, preserving, and processing evidence that may be used in the course of an investigation of a crime or accident. Forensic technology is also used in the recovery of information from erased computer hard drives, shredded documents, flight data recorders, etc. Do not overlook these valuable sources of data when you are documenting a crime scene. Evidence may be contained on computer hard drives, servers, USB flash drives, CDs, DVDs, and other media storage devices. Flash drives now come in all shapes and sizes, so do not miss important data that may be stored on a USB flash drive that resembles a Lego, cartoon character, or even a plastic bracelet (see Figures 10.5a and 10.5b).

There are special considerations when beginning to process a computer crime scene, including the determination of whether the system is powered up when you arrive. One of the first things a CSI should do after photographing is to determine if any active programs are erasing or changing data on the device. If there is any active program that may affect the data, either attempt to stop the program or pull the plug from the back of the device to save as much data as possible. If the system is off, feel the chassis to determine whether it is warm, which would indicate recent use. Do not turn on anything that is turned off—doing so creates immediate changes to the data— and *do not do anything you have not been trained to do*. Likewise, if the

FIGURE 10.5A
Flash drives come in all shapes.

FIGURE 10.5B
Do not overlook possible key evidence.

system is on, do not power off or turn off the system. Doing so may begin processes running in the background and will alter data and transaction logs.

Take photographs of the monitor screen to document open files before any action is taken to secure the computer. Enlist the assistance of more experienced digital evidence examiners so that you do not create, alter, or destroy data files on the computer. If any changes are made, account for them in your documentation and keep detailed logs of actions taken. It may be possible to determine by looking at the monitor screen whether or not the computer is on a network or is a standalone device. It also may be possible to determine if the device uses encryption such as Bitlocker, Veracrypt, etc., by looking at the right-hand side of the toolbar. The entire scene must be documented before evidence collection begins (see Figure 10.6). When only one computer is located, it is referred to as a "single-scene seizure." If the illegal activities have been taking place on a network, such as in a business situation, it may be a "multiple-scene seizure," and the CSI should work with the network administrator to complete the documentation as well as secure the computers that may contain digital evidence. These computers must be isolated from any interaction with the network after seizure.

When you are processing the cybercrime scene (see Figure 10.7), it is essential to use antistatic packaging materials for securing the physical evidence. Styrofoam may produce static electricity and should not be used to package equipment. You also must ensure proper transportation of physical evidence. Due to the volatility of electronic equipment, it must be treated as fragile cargo; kept away from drastic temperature changes; and protected from water, fumes, dust, magnetic fields, and two-way radios to ensure the integrity of the evidence. Electronic evidence stored on media can deteriorate over

FIGURE 10.6
Find the nine devices in this crime scene that store data.

FIGURE 10.7
Important information including passwords may be written on pieces of paper on the desk under the keyboard or in the trashcan.

time, and arrangements for environmentally controlled and secure storage conditions should be arranged in advance.

When processing the crime scene where the computer is located, do not overlook evidence such as scraps of paper and printouts that are in trash containers. Perpetrators who use several ISPs or other accounts may write usernames and passwords or phone numbers on bits of paper and tape them to the bottom of the keyboard, mouse pad, or other easily accessible area for quick retrieval.

As you collect papers or printouts, seal them in plastic bags and label each one separately (see Figure 10.8). All photographs should be collected and preserved as physical evidence. Backgrounds in photographs may reveal critical information, including location identification, the time of year (season), other participants or victims, and family members or acquaintances of alleged predators. When collecting software, check for signs of physical damage to the media prior to sealing it in an antistatic package. Seasoned offenders have been known to store digital files on CDs that are kept in the microwave if they should need to quickly destroy libraries of pornography or other evidence of criminal activities.

The chain of custody is just as important with digital evidence as it is with physical types including documentation. CSIs must preserve and maintain the integrity of digital evidence as well as physical evidence so that it will be acceptable under the criminal rules of evidence.

Internet Crimes against Children (ICAC) task forces have reported many instances of finding firearms in the immediate vicinity of the computer. The cybercrime investigator should be aware that a weapon could be within reach of a suspected perpetrator being searched. The presence of a firearm not only creates an officer safety issue but could also cause the suspect to commit suicide to avoid detection or arrest.

FIGURE 10.8
Seal and label each piece of evidence separately. Document each package with a photograph.

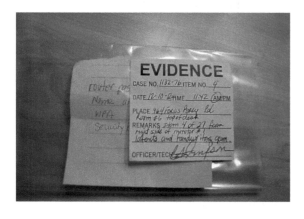

If multiple rooms are involved in a crime scene investigation, assign each room an individual letter and sequentially number each piece of physical evidence related to that specific room. Evidence logs must establish a chronology that demonstrates who had access to the media at all times. Secure digital (SD) cards are manufactured in various shapes and capacities. Micro SD cards can be smaller than a fingernail and hold 1 TB of data making it extremely easy to miss during a crime scene investigation. Do not overlook these valuable pieces of evidence when collecting the obvious printouts and software at the digital crime scene.

A diligent CSI should remember that flash drives are so common in today's digital society that they could be easily overlooked. Again, care must be taken to preserve the integrity of digital evidence, and the use of antistatic packaging materials is another way to protect data from accidental erasures. When the digital examiner takes custody of the evidence, duplicate copies will be made to be used as investigative tools, and the original devices will be secured to maintain the veracity of the original evidence.

COMPUTER HARDWARE

As a CSI, you must approach the scene of a cybercrime investigation just as you would any other crime scene. Be aware of the potential for trace evidence—including latent fingerprints or DNA. You might need to process the hardware for latent fingerprints, so be sure to wear latex or nitrile gloves when labeling and collecting evidence at this type of scene. Be sure to note the position of the mouse in photographs and written documentation because this information can be important in establishing the handedness of the perpetrator and may establish an additional linkage from the suspect to the crime scene (computer).

Individual Computers

If a computer is powered up, photograph the screen and make a list of all files and applications that are open. When possible attempt to collect the RAM using RAM capture tools such as Magnet RAM capture, FTK Imager, Goldfish, etc. Not only does RAM contain valuable evidence, but it can also contain passwords or recovery codes that are essential in breaking encryption such as Bitlocker or Filevault. In addition, it is important to check and document the system time and date. Individual computers enable users to manipulate this information, which may be done deliberately in an attempt to disguise the creation times/dates of files as well as to establish alibis.

After documentation of the computer is complete, do not perform a system shutdown. Instead, disconnect the power cord from the chassis and then the wall. Seal every opening in the chassis with evidence tape, including the CD drive, floppy disk drive (if applicable), and any drive bays. If you are seizing a laptop computer, be sure to remove the battery and check for the presence of a secondary battery pack. Always take the power supply or battery charger for the device you are seizing.

Network and phone cables should be disconnected from the chassis and their connection ports should be documented. Never try to connect with the computer that is going to be confiscated once disconnected. Devices may communicate via data cables, memory cards, or wirelessly through Bluetooth technology.

Remove the chassis cover and photograph the interior of the computer, including all cables, hard drives, and other connections. If necessary, disconnect the hard drive from the power plugs to guard against the accidental boot of the hard drive.

Network Computers

Seizing an individual computer requires the knowledge, skills, and ability to secure as much of the digital evidence as possible along with all the hardware and peripherals that are co-located with the computer. However, capturing evidence that resides on a network demands a detailed plan, the cooperation of the system administrator, and experienced digital evidence investigators. In a network environment, you might need to seize evidence that was created by badge readers, credit card scanners, biometric data ports, and other remotely located hardware devices. Audit trails, applications, and firewall logs are also essential to the investigation.

The distributed nature of networks makes it difficult for offenders to destroy all digital evidence, but it also may make determination of a single machine (the crime scene) more complicated.

Network evidence searches are very different from seizing an individual computer, and you must remember to isolate the suspect machine with minimal disruption to the network. You may accomplish this by simply disconnecting the network cable from the computer, but you should coordinate and consult with the company's network administrator before taking this step. While you may not be able to retain data that exists in the memory (RAM) of the machine, network activity logs can provide digital evidence to assist in the investigation. If it is not possible to remove the individual computer, attempt to perform a live forensic acquisition using reliable imaging tools such as FTK imager or Digital Collector. This methodology will bypass most encryption but may be affected by the type of security settings such as Apple's M1 chip. These actions must be documented in your written narrative, as changes will be made to the original hard drive when it is duplicated. You should avoid pulling the plug on a company network because it may cause irreparable damage to the system, disrupt legitimate business, and create liability for both yourself and your agency.

Peripheral Equipment

When collecting equipment at the scene, be sure to confiscate all peripheral equipment, including tape drives, scanners, printers, digital cameras, and power strips. Items such as digital and video cameras, scanners, DVRs, smart speakers, smart health monitors, etc. may be useful in proving the perpetrator was creating and distributing pornographic or other illegal materials over the Internet. Digital cameras have both internal and external memory capacity, and the date and time on the system clock of such a device must be verified by the investigator. If the system clock is incorrect, all data on file creation will also be wrong. This could lead the forensic examiner to the wrong conclusions if the data is not verified.

Cables must be photographed in place and a color-coded label placed on each end of the cable, indicating the port to which it was connected. Any unused ports should be labeled "unused" and clearly indicated on the system diagram. Trace and collect all cables; they may lead to additional hidden hardware, such as a server or other storage device in another room or building.

Collect all software and hardware manuals or other system documentation that may assist the forensic investigator in recreating the computer environment. Be sure to check the roof and other outside areas for a satellite uplink.

Printers and photocopiers may have internal storage or printer spool files that may be lost when the power supply is eliminated. Scanners may create distinctive characteristics when digitizing images that can link the device with the files it created. Be sure to take these peripherals when packing up the cybercrime scene—after you have documented the location and type of connection and have included them on the sketch.

VIRTUAL EVIDENCE

There are few people who are fully aware of the amount of information retained by their computers. The Internet has created a virtual storehouse of data that can be mined and used for prosecutorial purposes when collected and secured following established protocols. Be cautious of attempts to obfuscate incriminating evidence or being manipulated by crime scene staging when looking through digital evidence. **Crime scene staging** occurs when perpetrators attempt to plant or fabricate digital evidence that will implicate someone else. Staging itself can reveal information about the offender, including the level of technical skill, economic status (indicated by access to various technologies), and IP address of the source computer.

When you arrive at the cybercrime scene, it is important to accurately document the state of the computer at the time you begin the on-scene investigation. In documentation and collection, always proceed from the most volatile to the most persistent evidence. This is known as the order of volatility. For example, the most volatile data to collect includes RAM and least volatile would include the hard drive and other storage media. It is important to be aware of any attempt to connect or alter evidence on the device during collection either through Bluetooth (an industrial specification for wireless personal area networks) or through the Internet which may allow the perpetrator to activate remote destruction of potentially incriminating files. Take photographs and documentation of any e-mails, instant messages, apps, programs, etc. that are currently active on a live computer before turning off the device. If circumstances allow, video any ongoing instant messaging or chat room activities that may be beneficial for future prosecutorial use. Data that is stored in the cloud or online, such Google and Dropbox, can be halted and collected using preservation requests and subpoenas.

Even if a user successfully erases an e-mail from his or her computer, it is likely that the message still exists in a recipient's electronic mailbox, on the hard drive, or somewhere on the Internet. Multiple copies of the erased message may exist and may be located. Data analysis by forensic examiners includes the recovery of data that has been deleted, camouflaged, or otherwise hidden from view. Reconstruction of data fragments usually provides much more information than what is actually written in the text of deleted e-mail messages or files. Information such as time, date, origin, recipient's name, headers and footers, file names, and the date the message was last accessed will provide valuable leads for the detectives conducting the investigation.

The International Association of Computer Investigation Specialists provides certified training based on a series of core competencies in the field of computer/digital forensics. Read more about this specialized training at www.iacis.com.

Cellphones and Smartphones

When you are investigating a crime scene, it is generally recommended that you leave a mobile device in the condition in which it was located; that is, if it was powered on, leave it on. If a mobile device is powered off, leave it off. Remember, however, that you must document information such as call logs, open Internet browsers, and apps immediately because this information may be lost if the battery charge is exhausted. Display this information, write it down, and photograph it. Do not dial the numbers from this device because doing so will alter digital files in the memory and on the network. Make sure to document, when possible, the make, model, serial number, IMEI, etc. of the mobile device. The **International Mobile Equipment Identity (IMEI)** is a number that is unique to every mobile device and is used to identify devices. It can be printed on the phone underneath the battery or the edge of the SD card slot. The first five numbers are used to identify the manufacturer and type of phone. In order to prevent locking out the phone it may become imperative to keep the phone on and in an unlocked state for the duration of transportation. If the CSI it properly trained they may be required to stop the screen from locking out by manipulating the phones auto-lock settings. Live acquisition of the device using Cellebrite UFED or other tools may be required depending on the case. After all information has been recorded, pack the cellphone for transport in a Faraday bag, a bag that is specially designed to block radio transmissions, and keep the phone powered on, if the unlocked state is required, using the appropriate power cord and supply. If power cords and equipment manuals are available, confiscate them with the phone.

Tablets and Other Mobile Devices

Handheld computing devices can be used for multiple tasks and are purchased more frequently than laptops or PCs. Most are capable of synchronization with a personal computer and communicate via various types of technologies. They are valuable items of physical evidence because they may contain backup files that relate to criminal activities, photographs, GPS locations, e-mail access, contact lists, memo pads, and calendars. With removable memory cards, they can contain libraries of text, image, audio, and video files. These types of data may provide linkages from the suspect to the victim or the crime scene, and this evidence must be collected properly. When confiscating a handheld electronic device, leave the device powered on because it may have a lockout function that requires a password to reactivate. It may be necessary for a trained Crime Scene Investigator to disable the auto-lock feature of the mobile device. If power cords and connection cables are present, take custody of them. You may need to use a Faraday bag for transportation as some tablets are connected to a cellular network or be vulnerable to potential manipulation from wireless technology such as Bluetooth. Bluetooth technology is based on radio transmission and can connect to a handheld device from a range of up to 25 feet.

Fax and Digital Answering Machines and Caller-ID Devices

The information contained in fax and digital answering machines and caller-ID devices must be documented at the scene. The CSI must verify the number of the phone line to which any machine is connected. Write down, print out, and photograph (if possible) the speed dial list, as well as the last number dialed. Once the device is powered off, the last number dialed is not retrievable. Include the user manuals, if available, for future reference.

Biometric Technology

Biometrics have been integrated into many forms of technology today such as the facial recognition or fingerprint scanner on smartphones. In many cases it has been used as a method of providing multifactor authentication for increased security. Many organizations now use some type of biometric technology to strengthen security aspects. Banks use hand and finger geometry to provide unescorted access to the safety deposit box area. Iris and handprint scanners are becoming more accepted in high-tech buildings. Facial recognition software has been deployed for federal and state agencies providing homeland security and border crossing protection. Biometrics generally encompasses automated methods of recognizing an individual based on measurable anatomical and physiological characteristics. The overall implementation of a biometric system simply adds another level of authentication to personal identification. There are several other types of recognition methodologies being tested including speaker recognition, dynamic signatures, retina, gait/body traits, and facial thermography. More information can be gained at www.biometrics.gov.

DIGITAL CRIME SCENE ANALYSIS

Forensic evidence examiners will reconstruct the cybercrime scene utilizing the photographs, sketches, and written documentation provided by the CSI. They will attempt to recreate the network connections and begin to analyze the data that is stored on a forensically obtained duplicate of the hard drive. The original data files are not used for examination so as not to destroy the original evidence. The examination should always be done from the images obtained from the suspect's hard drive. When imaging, it is important that any digital evidence is attached to a tool or computer that is actively being write-blocked. **Write blocking** is where tools or software is used to prevent digital evidence from being compromised and ensures the integrity of the evidence. Hardware and software write blockers are essential to the digital evidence examiner. Before this process begins, the forensic examiner will authenticate that the copy is an exact duplicate of the original device to ensure the integrity of the data using hashing, a string of alphanumerical values that accurately represents the data that can be used to determine no alterations were made.

Experienced examiners can retrieve deleted files and/or fragments of data left by deleted files, and once the data is recovered, they will begin a process of harvesting the usable data to establish evidentiary information relevant to the case investigation. By studying the location of files on disks, the forensic examiner can determine the types of hardware used to create the files (such as a webcam—or digital camera). The times the files were created may be essential in linking a suspect to a victim to prove that an offense was committed. Digital evidence examiners can also determine what software was used to create the files and if the files were redistributed. Such information may result in additional criminal charges against the perpetrator.

Just as in an examination of biological evidence from the crime laboratory, scientific analysis will result in laboratory reports of findings that are admissible in court. Forensic evidence examiners are subject-matter experts and will provide expert testimony in court proceedings.

Discussion Questions

1. What is identity theft? Describe several ways it is accomplished.
2. Why do people become hackers? Explain the common reasons.
3. Describe the procedure for seizing a computer and its associated equipment.
4. Identify some of the most common forms of digital crimes.
5. Why is computer crime severely underreported?

CHAPTER 11

Documentary Evidence

Electronic signature	Graphology	Thin-layer
ESDA (electrostatic	Handwriting	chromatography
detection	complexity	(TLC)
apparatus)	Line quality	Trash marks
Exemplars	Simulated signature	
Forensic linguistics	Statement analysis	

What You Will Learn

Examining questioned documents and determining authorship of signatures continue to be specialized areas in criminal investigations. This chapter presents the examination of questioned documents and related topics to demonstrate the variety of criminal activities used to exploit victims. Financial fraud, forged documents, blackmail, threatening communications, and profiling based on handwriting are some of the topics covered in this chapter.

MURDER IN THE NEW YEAR

Documentary Evidence

Dean Michael Sellers clasped his hands together in an effort to maintain self-control. In spite of his efforts, his flushed face, and the bead of sweat breaking out on his forehead said otherwise.

> How dare you insinuate I would misuse foundation money or, even worse, have anything to do with the demise of James and Margie Morton? You are attempting to destroy a 30-year academic career devoted to excellence, and I will not stand for it!

DOI: 10.4324/9780429261657-11

Detective Mavis Fletcher reached across the desk and handed Michael Sellers a list of questionable expenditures. "Can you enlighten me on the nature of these transactions and withdrawals and how they relate to the foundation?"

Michael Sellers's right temple began to throb as he reviewed the document. Sellers reached into his desk drawer and pulled out a handful of papers. "I did not want to resort to this," he sputtered,

> but you leave me little choice. As you can see, these unauthorized expenditures which correspond with your list are signed by Mrs. Morton on my behalf without my knowledge or permission. My discovery of these papers led to her decision to resign. Given my lack of impropriety, I wanted to spare the poor woman … and of course, myself, any further discomfort.

The dean threw his hands into the air. "I had hoped especially to spare the Morton children from having their mother's reputation besmirched any further, but I feel I have no other recourse but to turn these papers over to you."

Mavis Fletcher looked over the authorizations. "Why didn't you provide us with this evidence during our initial interview?"

Her question went unanswered.

The detective rose to her feet. "I will be in touch, Mr. Sellers."

The dean stood up. "That's Dean …"

Mavis smiled. "That's right … I'll be touch, Dean Sellers."

*****

Mavis Fletcher handed CSI Tom Smith a hot dog.

"A foot-long chili-dog all the way! What's the occasion?" Tom exclaimed.

The detective wiped some mustard off Tom's chin with a paper napkin. "We have just been handed another piece of the puzzle."

"Or another nail in Michael Sellers's coffin," Tom replied. "You reckon he's contacted a lawyer yet?"

Mavis ran her hand through her hair. "With all his academic excellence and his large ego, I'm not sure he has concluded where this train is heading. He should have contacted a lawyer, but I wouldn't bet on it."

Mavis handed Tom the paper napkin. "Do you realize you eat like a pig? Anyway, I just got off the phone with Larry Ryan."

Tom took another bite. "The certified document examiner over in Townsend?"

"One and the same," Mavis Fletcher replied.

> Seems our dean has just as inflated a view of his forgery skills as his academic or, should I say, criminal prowess. He tried to pass off the phony paperwork he gave me last week as being the handiwork of Mrs. Morton. Larry says otherwise. He compared the signatures of Mrs. Morton, Michael Sellers, and the alleged authorization signatures and indicated that there were ample indicators that the forgeries were a rather clumsy attempt by the dean to forge the victim's signature.

INTRODUCTION

Documents recovered from a crime scene are often a crucial form of physical evidence. Documentary evidence includes items that indicate motive, such as love letters, financial records, personal diaries, and threatening letters. Sometimes, documents found at a crime scene, such as maps, phone numbers, and indented writings on a pad of paper, may yield information about other suspects, victims, and/or locations. Documentary evidence may be questioned or unquestioned. A *questioned document* is one for which the authenticity of the document itself is in question (i.e., counterfeit documents or forgeries) or for which the identity of the writer is in question (e.g., anonymous threat letters and suspect suicide notes). An *unquestioned document* is one for which authenticity is not questioned or the identity of the writer is not in dispute (e.g., personal letters, diaries, and financial records).

Documents found at a crime scene may have evidentiary value based on their content. Content is both graphic and linguistic. The graphic aspect is the substance and symbols (letters and/or drawings). The linguistic features may provide investigators with clues as to the identity of the perpetrator, character, personality, motive, and so on. Another aspect of documents is their configuration, that is, the medium employed to create the document (e.g., ink, typewriting, blood, paper).

An evidentiary document is almost anything involving written communications and is not limited to paper writing surfaces. Questioned handwriting and drawings appear on walls, mirrors, cars, and even bodies. Additionally, questioned communications are not limited to handwriting. Driver's licenses, birth certificates, passports, currency, and typed and printed documents are frequently forged or altered. Questioned documents may be stored on a computer's hard drive, in an electronic e-mail, as a text on a phone, or written on a digital tablet. While paper-based documents are still widely used, questioned electronic documents are prevalent and include electronic signatures and electronic tablet writing. Because of the diversity of questioned documents, an interdisciplinary investigative approach involving chemistry, physics, psychology, physiology, and information technology is necessary. For example, ink and paper are chemically analyzed, while the psychophysiological process of handwriting is applied to handwriting identification and behavioral questions. Information technology is utilized in investigating computer crimes related to questioned documents.

Documents recovered in crime scene investigations include anonymous notes, suicide notes, altered documents (such as checks), bank robbery notes, ransom notes, drug recipes, or pawn receipts.

FIGURE 11.1

William George Heirens, the Lipstick Killer, wrote on a wall with lipstick.

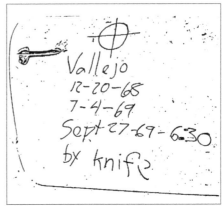

FIGURE 11.2

The Zodiac Killer left writing on a victim's car door.

Handwriting or drawings can appear in a variety of places at crime scenes, including on mirrors, doors, cars, walls, the body of the victim, and other unusual surfaces. William George Heirens, dubbed the Lipstick Killer, wrote a message on the wall at one crime scene using lipstick (see Figure 11.1). The Zodiac serial killer wrote several anonymous notes and ciphers. One was written on a victim's car door (see Figure 11.2). In the Black Dahlia case in Los Angeles in 1947, the perpetrator wrote on the body of the victim using lipstick. Unusual materials may be used for "ink," such as blood or feces. In the Tate/LaBianca murders, Charles Manson's "family" used victims' blood to scrawl "Helter Skelter" and "Pig" at the crime scenes, and a knife was used to carve "War" onto the body of one victim. A package mailed by Jack the Ripper contained an anonymous note and the kidney of one of his victims, but the Ripper sometimes wrote with red ink to give the impression that he was writing with blood.

Questioned documents can also be lethal. A packaged bomb mailed by the Unabomber is an example of a dangerous questioned document. Biohazardous documents have included a spate of anonymous letters sent through the US mail in 2001 that contained lethal amounts of anthrax and the poison ricin mailed to President Obama and Senator Wicker in 2013.

PROCEDURES FOR HANDLING AND RECORDING EVIDENTIARY DOCUMENTS

In securing questioned documents or handwriting at a crime scene, the CSI should first photograph the location of the document as found to preserve the contextual reference of the document at the scene. Paper documents are preferably handled with white cotton gloves. Latex gloves have been known to leave fingerprint impressions on paper documents, especially if the gloves are thin and have foreign residue on the fingertips. Cotton gloves may be worn over latex gloves to prevent such contamination. Paper documents should be handled as little as possible and secured in a way to prevent any further handling, folding, marking, or impressions on the document. Documents may be placed in acid-free paper bags or envelopes or in cellophane or glassine envelopes.

Paper documents can be tested for latent impressions and indentations, so it is important that notes are not written on top of the document. This is especially important if latent and fingerprint analysis is to be conducted. Plastic sleeves can create moisture that can interfere with latent and fingerprint analysis. Additionally, the way a document was folded or handled may have relevance to the inquiry surrounding the document. Care should be taken in preserving the questioned document exactly as it was found at the crime scene without adding marks, folds, or wear. If an investigator's initials must be placed on a questioned document, they should be made as inconspicuous as possible and in an area that has little or no writing or printing. However, it is preferable that an investigator's initials are not placed on a questioned document at all. The document can instead be sealed in an envelope with initials and labels placed on the envelope to protect the integrity of the chain of custody. To prevent indentations from appearing on the evidentiary document, the investigator should place his or her initials and case file information on the envelope before placing the evidentiary document into the envelope.

In processing a crime scene, the investigator should photograph any handwriting or drawings that cannot be physically removed as evidence. For example, anonymous communications, such as bomb threats, may be found in bathroom stalls or on mirrors. It is important that good-quality, high-resolution, close-up photographs are taken of the fine details in the handwriting. These types of photographs are used not only for handwriting examination and comparison, but also for courtroom exhibits. Blurry photos or photos taken too far away prevent the document examiner from analyzing the fine detail that is crucial in such investigations. Scratched lettering or symbols on car or wall surfaces may require special lighting techniques so that the writing is visible in the photograph. Always include a scale in such photographs. Measurements should also be made and recorded, such as height from floor and/or ceiling and relationships to other objects at the scene.

To initiate an investigation of a questioned document, it may be beneficial to secure other materials from the crime scene, such as computers, printers, seals, paper, notepads, checks, other nonquestioned documents, and writing instruments. The CSI should note where the document was in relation to the crime or if the document could have been produced by the suspect or victim. For example, in a suicide case, verify whether the alleged suicide note was written with materials that were accessible to the suicide victim at the scene of the crime.

Sometimes documents that have been burned may have evidentiary significance. Handling and preserving charred documents must be done carefully to prevent the document from breaking into fragments. Spraying a fine mist of clear varnish or clear-coat and placing charred documents in a box with loosely packed cotton may help prevent further deterioration of the document. Charred documents should be transported to the laboratory in person rather than by mail or shipping service. No matter how carefully a charred document is packaged, it is likely to be destroyed if sent to the laboratory by mail.

An initial thorough examination of the note using document examination standards of practice is necessary to preserve the evidence. The examiner should compare the handwriting to that of any potential suspects and gather other evidence from the source document such as latent impressions, fingerprints, or preprinted material. For example, the back side of the document may be written on preprinted notepaper that may identify the location of the perpetrator. In addition, the type of paper, watermarks on the paper, and specialized print or writing styles can provide further clues to the identity of the writer in anonymous writing cases.

INVESTIGATIVE TECHNIQUES FOR EXAMINATION OF DOCUMENTS

In criminal investigations, following proper process and protocol when examining evidential documents serves to preserve the evidence so that it can be analyzed before the document is subjected to destructive testing. Although fingerprints can be developed on documents, remember that this type of testing partially destroys the document. Therefore, the document should be examined and photographed prior to fingerprint development. All avenues for testing must be explored. Destructive ink or paper testing should be conducted only after other nondestructive tests have been performed to determine whether the question can be adequately answered through nondestructive means. Document examiners rely on methodological standards to standardize their examination procedures. One method that has been extensively used is Analyze, Compare, and Evaluate (ACE). This method is used in the standards developed for document and handwriting examination published by the Scientific

(a)

(b)

FIGURE 11.3

Date obliterated using a bleaching compound. The top photograph (a) shows the date as "94,"
but the bottom photograph (b), under ultraviolet illumination, shows the original date as "97."

Working Group for Forensic Document Examination (SWGDOC),
which are widely relied upon by document examiners in the United
States. Published standards include procedures for both destructive
and nondestructive tests in handwriting, ink, paper, alterations,
toner and inkjet technology, impressions, and indentations. The
SWGDOC standards are gradually being revised and republished
by the Academy Standards Board (ASB) and the National Institute
of Standards and Technology (NIST). Scientists and researchers
have published other methodological approaches including use of
probability scales based on likelihood ratios and modular methods
(Found & Bird, 2016; Taylor et al., 2020).

Simple nondestructive lighting techniques can be used to answer
many document questions. Both short-wave and long-wave ultraviolet (UV) light can reveal chemical erasures (see Figures 11.3a and
11.3b). In check-washing cases, exposing the check to UV light allows the investigator to detect the presence of certain chemicals used
to alter the document. UV light can also detect different paper types
in a document. In a multipage document, the individual pages can
be observed and compared using UV light to determine if all the
pages fluoresce with the same color and intensity.

Infrared (IR) light also can be used in examining and differentiating
ink. Ink formulas may react to IR light differently. Some absorb or
reflect at varying levels. Two ink entries made with a black ballpoint
pen may look like the same ink to the unaided eye. Under IR light,
however, one ink entry may be opaque (visible), whereas the second

FIGURE 11.4
Infrared photography was used to decipher obliterated writing and to render it as shown in the lower photograph.

is transparent (not visible). The different reaction to the IR light indicates that the two entries were written with different inks. IR light also can be used to recover obliterated material. For example, an ink entry obliterated with a second pen can sometimes be recovered with IR light. IR and UV lights are also useful for quickly determining the authenticity of documents such as currency, passports, and identification cards. These documents are frequently embedded with security devices that are visible under IR or UV light.

Other nondestructive lighting techniques include oblique and transmitted lighting. Oblique lighting (side lighting) can help make latent indentations visible. This technique can be helpful in determining what was written on top of notepads or documents found at crime scenes. Transmitted lighting (backlighting) is performed by placing a light behind the document.

Infrared photography was used to decipher obliterated writing in Figure 11.4a and to render it as shown in Figure 11.4b (such as on a lightbox) to make the document more transparent. If parts of the document have been obliterated or otherwise covered by black marker or a white-out liquid, backlighting can frequently make them visible. Backlighting also is useful in detecting erasures, determining the opacity of paper, and in visualizing watermarks.

Sophisticated methods for developing latent impressions on documents are available. Documents can be processed on an electrostatic detection device, which can develop latent fingerprints and other latent impressions such as handwriting, typing, or marks. It is important for electrostatic detection examination to be performed prior to any destructive testing such as fingerprint (ninhydrin) testing because ninhydrin not only dissolves ink on the paper but also makes the paper fibers expand, thus eliminating latent indentations on the paper. Latent indentations are important because they can record information that was written on top of the document. For example, sometimes forgers may practice signatures on top of the targeted questioned document. Or an anonymous note may have been written on a pad of paper found in the suspect's home or work. The note may carry clues in its latent impressions of the notes written on top of the paper. Or a blank notepad may be found at a crime scene, and the impressions on the notepad (which can run several pages deep) may carry important clues about whether a questioned document was written on that notepad. Although some indentations can be seen using oblique or side lighting (see Figure 11.5), use of electrostatic detection equipment, such as an **ESDA (electrostatic detection apparatus)**, is a more sophisticated and sensitive method for developing latent impressions.

Other tests can also be performed on documents to help solve investigative questions. Microscopic analyses are frequently conducted on questions involving ink or paper. Semi-destructive techniques, such as **thin-layer chromatography (TLC)**, can be used to determine if two inks are the same. Other ink tests can be performed to determine ink chemistry and the approximate date when an ink entry was written. However, these techniques require chemical testing with sophisticated instrumentation and should be conducted in a laboratory.

FIGURE 11.5

Moderate contrast, combined with side lighting, helps to decipher illegible indentations on paper.

MACHINE-PRODUCED DOCUMENTS

Although typewriters have largely been replaced by computers and other electronic devices, it is still important to know about typewriter technology for when older documents are questioned. Typewriters are also still used today in prisons, including by inmates, and within funeral homes, in government work, and widely used in countries in South America and in India. In 2013, it was reported in the press that the Russian government purchased typewriters for its intelligence agency. Typewriter make and model may be determined by examining the font style and method of recording (e.g., keys, element, fabric, or carbon ribbon). The individual typewriter that produced a questioned document may be identified if specimens for comparison are collected from the suspect typewriter.

The investigator should submit the original questioned typed document along with the suspect typewriter to the laboratory. If the suspect typewriter itself cannot be submitted, specimens made on the typewriter should be taken, along with the ribbon. Most newer typewriters use a single-pass carbon film ribbon that can be read to see if the questioned text is present. Specimens taken from the suspect typewriter should include the same combination of words and spacing as contained on the questioned document.

Photocopied documents are frequently encountered as questioned documents. Photocopied documents may have features that can identify a particular copier used to create the questioned photocopy. Marks on paper created by "grabbers," the mechanical apparatus that pulls paper through the copier, may be identified. In addition, **trash marks**, small particles of toner appearing in the same location on multiple copies, may identify a particular copier as producing the questioned document. Comparison copies on blank paper from the suspect copier may show evidence of matching grabber and trash marks.

Most computer-generated documents are printed on laser or inkjet printers. Many printing and copy machines are multi-function units that print, scan, copy, and fax. Identifying print process is one way to analyze documents or parts of documents that are produced from different machines. For example, a multipage document, such as a legal will or contract may be altered by replacing one of the pages. One way of detecting a difference in the page is by examining the print process using magnification that is sufficient to examine the fine detail in the print. Determining the machine, use techniques similar to identifying photocopy machines through print marks that are produced through minor defects in the printing process. High-quality color printers are used to create documents that are passed as "originals." Original signatures are scanned and then digitally placed on a new document. The signature can be colored blue so that it looks like original ink to the unaided eye. A microscopic examination helps in determining if the ink is writing pen ink or if it is created through a laser or inkjet print process. Color printers are also used to create counterfeit money.

HANDWRITING IDENTIFICATION

Many document questions involve handwriting identification. Handwriting identification mostly involves comparison of questioned writing with samples of suspects' known writing. Known writing samples may be collected at the crime scene or collected from other sources. Frequently, comparison handwriting samples are collected directly from the suspect. However, these types of samples are problematic, because they may be self-serving or manipulated by the suspect. A suspect's natural writing habits are more effectively demonstrated on what is known as normal-course-of-business documents. These samples can be found on checks, rental agreements, mortgages, deeds, driver's licenses, identification cards, passports, social security cards, credit cards, and other documents. Time-matched or contemporaneous handwriting standards are preferable when comparing handwriting.

It is necessary to examine more than one handwriting standard when performing handwriting comparisons. It is a handwriting identification principle that no two people write exactly alike, and the individuality of handwriting has been established in research studies (e.g., Srihari et al., 2002). However, no two writings—even written by the same person—are exactly alike either. A collection of standards is necessary to establish the writer's natural range of variation. Handwriting identification is founded on a pattern-based principle. Although no two signatures are exactly alike, there is a pattern parameter within which the collection of signatures falls. Range of variation differs among writers (see Figure 11.6). For example, a comparison of the signatures of two writers can demonstrate how one writer has a wider range of variation than another writer. When two signatures are exactly alike, it is indicative that one of the signatures is not a natural signature but a copy or tracing of an original signature. Genuine signatures can be transferred to other documents through copying, tracing, or digital methods. The signature appears genuine because it is a copy of a genuine signature. However, if the original source signature can be identified and matches perfectly, then it is evidence that the signature was transferred to another document. In such cases, the signature may be genuine, but the document it was transferred to is not.

FIGURE 11.6

Comparing the range of variation between two writers. Both writers were instructed to write three consecutive signatures using the same pen and paper. The writer on the left has considerably less variation between signatures than the writer on the right, who has an uneven baseline and randomly leaves out letters. The appearance of individual letters can also vary (note the second writer's variance in the uppercase letter B).

In some handwriting identification cases, collecting an adequate number of contemporaneous comparison standards may be difficult. To answer the question of how many comparison standards are enough, it is usually best to collect as many as possible. Due to range of variation and internal and external conditions that can affect handwriting, one or two comparison signatures rarely will be enough to answer handwriting identification questions adequately. When examining distorted handwriting or graphic disturbance, unusual or extraordinary conditions need to be addressed. Was the writer in an awkward position or writing on an unstable surface? Was the writer affected or impaired by medications, alcohol, or other drugs? Was the writer physically or mentally impaired? Unusual conditions can have a dramatic impact on the writer's natural range of variation (see Figure 11.7). Collecting standards written under similar conditions is preferable.

In some cases, finding a collection of normal-course-of-business writings is not possible. In these cases, request exemplars are taken from the suspect(s). **Exemplars** are standards of known handwriting used for comparison purposes. Although standard texts can be used for taking handwriting samples, the best request exemplars are those that are similar in composition to the questioned document. For example, if the questioned document is a check, then the request exemplar needs to be written on a check blank. If the questioned document is a signature written in a box, then the request exemplars need to be signatures written in boxes.

The procedure for taking request exemplars from suspects is important. First, the questioned document should not at any time be shown to the suspect. To help prevent the possibility of the suspect writer intentionally disguising or altering the writing in the request exemplars, several exemplars should be taken under various conditions. Text can be dictated to the suspect writer instead of copied. The writer is instructed to write in his or her normal writing and then instructed to write as fast as possible. Samples should be taken of writing with both the dominant and nondominant hand. In questioned document cases involving anonymous notes or handwritten text, both handwritten and handprinted exemplars are taken. So that the exact contents of an anonymous note are not dictated to the writer, one can dictate a variation of the note's content that contains the same words and letter combinations. It is important to take numerous exemplars because it is more difficult for a person to disguise or alter handwriting the more the person writes. If graphic disturbance or disguise is suspected

FIGURE 11.7

The two signatures are written by the same person. The top is a normal specimen, while the bottom specimen was written on an uneven surface.

in the questioned document, the suspect writer can be asked while writing request standards to disguise his or her writing or to write in unusual or awkward positions such as placing the paper on the wall, writing on a clipboard while standing, or writing on the lap with no support. Request exemplar sessions should be personally witnessed, and individual writing tasks should be timed.

Several forms are used to collect request handwriting exemplars from suspects. Although these forms may be good for screening several suspects, they are not particularly well suited as comparison standards to identify or eliminate a writer of a questioned document. Document examiners need to compare the same word and letter combinations found on the questioned document with known exemplars. Case law has established that the taking of handwriting exemplars for identification purposes is not a violation of the Fourth and Fifth Amendments of the US Constitution, nor does it require the presence of counsel (*United States v. Cotner, United States v. Hollins, Gilbert v. California,* and *United States v. Wade*).

Inadequate exemplars would include documents for which the identity of the writer is not established. Informal notes or cards that are not signed are usually not adequate sources for exemplars. Additionally, investigators need to be cautious about the documents used as comparison standards so that contaminated standards are not used for comparison purposes. For example, in elder abuse fraud, if a document is questioned, other comparison signature sources may not be reliable because the suspected writer may have access to the elderly person's bank accounts and other financial documents. The suspected forger may even have a power of attorney to sign for the elder person. The investigator needs to proceed with caution in such cases to ensure that questionable documents are not part of the comparison standard collection. Be aware that notarized signatures do not automatically ensure that a signed document is valid as notary seals can be stolen, the document improperly notarized, or the notary committed the forgery. An important task in handwriting identification is determining whether a questioned signature is a forged or **simulated signature** (see Figure 11.8). Several different methods are used to simulate handwriting. In signature forgery, when an original model is not available to the forger, a simple simulation of a signature is written. This type of forgery makes no attempt to simulate the genuine writer's signature. This can happen in cases in which checks are stolen and signed with the check holder's name, but the signature model is not available to the forger. It can also occur during transactions when the signature is written on a digital tablet, but the forger

FIGURE 11.8
The top signature is genuine. The bottom signature is a freehand simulation. Note the differences in line quality, spacing between letters, and variation of pressure pattern. The top signature looks smoothly executed while the bottom signature appears drawn.

makes no attempt to imitate the signature. A second type of forgery is an imitation of a signature that is drawn by the forger with a model available. This type of forgery is usually practiced prior to writing it on the questioned document and is known as a *freehand simulation*. A third type of forgery is a tracing of the signature. A model of the signature is placed underneath or on top of the targeted document and then traced. Finally, a fourth method of forgery is copying or digitally transferring the signature onto the questioned document. In this type of forgery, an original is not available.

Professional document examiners make a comprehensive examination of handwriting elements. Harralson and Miller (2018) describe Huber and Headrick's 21 "discriminating elements of handwriting" that are organized into four categories: style, execution, consistency, and expansion/proportions (p. 82). SWGDOC identifies several handwriting elements, as listed in Table 11.1. When forged signatures are examined, forgeries are frequently detected by the **line quality**, which refers to the level of fluency and smoothness of the handwriting. In traced forgeries, the forms and spacing of the signature will be executed accurately, but the line quality of the signature reflects a slowly drawn quality, which is an important indicator of simulation.

In signature examination, fluently written, complex forms are more difficult to simulate. **Handwriting complexity** refers to the number of complex moves necessary to create a signature or handwriting consisting of the number of intersections and turning points. When signatures are examined, the complexity of the signature needs to be determined to ascertain the level of confidence with which the examiner can make an opinion. Some signatures are so simplistic that they are easy to imitate. Alternatively, it would also be easy for the genuine writer to disguise his or her own signature.

Table 11.1 Handwriting Identification Elements

Abbreviation	Method of Production
Alignment	Pen hold/pen position
Arrangement, formatting, positioning	Overall pressure/patterns of pressure emphasis
Capitalization	Proportion
Connectedness/disconnectedness	Simplification
Cross strokes/dots	Size
Diacritics/punctuation	Skill
Direction of strokes	Slant or slope
Disguise embellishments	Spacing
Formation	Speed

Freedom of execution	System
Guidelines of various forms	Tremor
Type of writing	
Handedness	Range of variation
Initial, connecting, terminal strokes	Patching/retouching
Legibility	Slow, drawn quality of the line
Lifts, stops, hesitations of writing instrument	Unnatural tremor
Line quality	

Source: Adapted from SWGDOC Standard Guide for Examination of Handwritten Items, 2013a.

The characteristics of handwriting, which have identifying features, may also be masked or changed in such a way that the handwriting cannot be identified. Disguise is produced in a variety of ways, such as by using a computer or typewriter so that no handwriting can be analyzed; cutting out letters from print to create the words or letters in a note (commonly seen in ransom note cases); using the nondominant hand, which gives the handwriting an awkward and immature appearance; use of a different handwriting style, such as print script or calligraphy in place of cursive; or the deliberate altering of handwriting forms. In the deliberate alteration of handwriting, frequently the disguise is superficial merely changing the obvious features in the handwriting such as slant, size, and certain letters such as capitals (see Figure 11.9). Using ornate, grotesque, or inconsistent letter forms is another typical way of disguising handwriting. Whether analyzing handwriting for identification or profiling purposes, the investigator should look past the obvious features of disguise to analyze the pattern produced in the subtler movements of the writing. Frequently, numerals and punctuation are overlooked when disguise is employed.

An **electronic signature** is a symbol, sound, or process attached to or logically associated with a record and executed or adopted by a person with the intent to sign the record. In the United States, in 2000, a bill called the Electronic Signatures Act was passed, acknowledging digital signatures as legally binding to contracts. Digital and electronic signatures are in widespread use internationally. However, the law does not distinguish between a digital cryptographic signature and a biometric or dynamic signature. Legally, they are both considered electronic signatures, even though they are very different processes. The digital cryptographic signature is not a handwritten signature. It is an encrypted code electronically attached to a document and has nothing to do with handwriting or signature dynamics. Examination of

FIGURE 11.9
Forgery or disguise? The top signature is questioned, while the bottom signature is representative of the writer's genuine signature. Although the differences between the two are readily apparent, disguise on the part of the genuine writer needs to be considered.

FIGURE 11.10
Examples of three electronic signatures written with different writing implements: first signature written on digital ink pad with stylus; second signature written on digital tablet with no visual feedback using stylus; third signature written on a pressure-sensitive pad with finger. Due to no visual feedback, the second signature is more connected than the first signature. The problems with the third signature were partially caused by the finger sticking to the pad.

digital signatures requires the skill of a forensic computer expert. Biometric or online digital capture of handwritten signatures is accomplished through electronic recording of handwriting on a digital tablet with a stylus pen, mouse, or finger. While some electronically captured signatures allow for the recording and analysis of temporal characteristics that are not typically available in the examination of static paper and ink signatures, the low-resolution images captured by many electronic signature systems have limited identifying features useful for forensic analysis.

From a practical perspective, most digitally captured signatures encountered in document examination cases are static images rather than recordings. Many recording devices are handheld units, and this fact increases the awkwardness of writing conditions. In a publicized case in Tennessee, a police officer forged the signatures of motorists on a handheld digital signature device when filling out citations for moving car violations. A document examiner was provided with the static signature images recorded on the digital device for examination. Alternatively, biometric signature verification systems verify the user through identification of handwritten movements and features that are loaded into the system's database. Biometric handwriting verification systems are sometimes used as part of a security system that verifies the identity of a user entering the system.

Due to the complexities involved with digital and electronic signatures, a methodology has been developed to help document and handwriting examiners determine the limitations in analysis of both static, paper-based electronic signatures and biometric signatures (Harralson, 2013). Some of the limitations involve writing device constraints that cause writers to alter their signature (see Figure 11.10) and/or the quality of the hardware and software capturing the signature.

In offering opinions, professional document examiners rely on probability scales that provide degrees of certainty in document examination. The SWGDOC Standard Terminology for Expressing Conclusions of Forensic Document Examiners (2013b) recommends a nine-level scale that ranges from identification to elimination: identification, strong probability, probable, indications, no conclusion, indications did not, probably did not, strong probability did not, and elimination. Factors that preclude document examiners from providing definitive opinions on document cases frequently involve inaccessibility of original questioned documents for examination, insufficient or unreliable standards, graphic disturbance caused by unusual external or internal conditions, or limitations caused by the handwriting (such as overly simplistic forms). Any of these factors can limit the certainty of the document examiner's opinion.

COURT ACCEPTANCE OF DOCUMENT EXAMINATION

Questioned document examiners, also known as *forensic document examiners*, have been accepted as expert witnesses in courts for decades. In the 1990s, the courts began to scrutinize many disciplines in the traditional forensic sciences due to the lack of empirical evidence to substantiate claims that were previously accepted on face value. The claim that handwriting was, like a fingerprint, a unique human identification characteristic had never been empirically studied. In the 1995 case *United States v. Starzecpyzel*, the court ruled that testimony provided by a document examiner qualified as technical rather than scientific knowledge. After publication of numerous empirical studies on the reliability and scientific nature of document examination, the courts began to accept document examiners as scientific experts. In 1999, in *United States v. Paul*, the US Court of Appeals for the 11th Circuit upheld the court's admission of document examiners testifying on the scientific nature of handwriting evidence.

Additionally, newer court rulings have helped solidify the field's acceptance, such as the *Pettus v. United States* case in the District of Columbia Court of Appeals (2012). During the trial, it was challenged that handwriting identification does not meet the trial court's test of general acceptance of a particular scientific methodology. The challenge was supported by statements made by a report commissioned by Congress and published by the National Research Council of the National Academies (2009) that criticizes pattern-based forensic evidence. However, the court ruled that forensic handwriting examination satisfied the bedrock admissibility standard of *Frye*, and the forensic document examiner's testimony was admitted (*Frye v United States*, 1923). In defending the field's scientific acceptance during court testimony, the document examiner cited many of the principles relied on by document examiners in the field.

Scientific Validity and Reliability

Statistical studies conducted on handwriting identification lend support to its scientific validity. Studies have shown that handwriting is unique and identifiable (Lytle & Yang, 2006; Marquis, Schmittbuhl,

Mazzella, & Taroni, 2005; Srihari, Cha, Arora, & Lee, 2002; Srihari, Huang, & Srinivasan, 2008). Other studies have statistically explored a range of variation to identify and quantify intra-writer variation (Jindal, Kaur, & Chattopadhyay, 1999; Ling, 2002; Marquis et al., 2005). Statistical probability studies on the uniqueness of identifiable characteristics were conducted by Zimmerman (1998). Statistical methods that can be used by examiners have been proposed by Strach (1998) and Found, Rogers, and Schmittat (1994). Bayesian multivariate models and likelihood ratios have been proposed in the assessment of handwriting evidence (Hepler et al., 2012; Linden et al, 2021). Computerized software systems have been developed—including FISH (Franke et al., 2003), CEDAR-FOX (Srihari et al., 2008), and FLASH ID (Walch et al., 2008)—that have handwriting databases and automated examination features and can produce statistical analyses. These software systems are not meant to replace the examiner, but to assist in the examination process while providing statistical support for opinions proffered.

Published expert proficiency studies prove the ability of document examiners in distinguishing between genuine and simulated handwriting and in matching handwriting samples (Found & Rogers, 2003; Found, Sita, & Rogers, 1999; Found et al., 2001; Kam & Lin, 2003; Kam, Fielding, & Conn, 1997; Kam, Wetstein, & Conn, 1994; Kam et al., 2001; Sita, Found, & Rogers, 2002). Compiling the error rates from the published studies, document examiner error rates were in the range of 0.04–9.3 percent. Some of the studies also showed that document examiners exhibited more skill than laypersons in performing handwriting identification (layperson error rates were in the range of 26.1–42.86 percent).

The research published thus far has demonstrated document examiner reliability on tasks including both handwriting and signatures. Further, difficult tasks have also been tested, including studies on the detection of simulations produced by expert penmen (Dewhurst, Found, & Rogers, 2008) and distinguishing between simulation and disguise (Bird, Found, & Rogers, 2007; Found & Rogers, 2008). These studies have helped to define when caution needs to be exercised in expressing handwriting opinions.

HANDWRITING AND FORENSIC PSYCHOLOGY APPLICATIONS

Handwriting has been referred to as *brain writing*, and analysis of an individual's unique handwriting characteristics can be as identifiable as his or her fingerprint. Due to the involvement of the brain and the central nervous system in the production of the handwriting as well as its cultural influences, script can tell a great deal more than a fingerprint about a person and his or her written communications. The scope of this section focuses on specific techniques investigators can use in analyzing written communications as behavioral evidence. In analyzing handwriting for criminal profiling applications, a multidisciplinary approach is most effective, integrating theories from forensic psychology, graphology, and linguistics.

For most criminal investigations involving handwritten notes or other forms of communication, a combination of profiling from handwriting and analysis of the statement or content is utilized. Reading the written communication from a content perspective can provide clues. Does the writer identify gender or make some other reference that indicates gender? Does the linguistic content reveal information about locality or cultural identifiers?

Content needs to be judged especially carefully because it is always possible that the writer has made misleading statements to misdirect the intended reader. In some anonymous communications, the writer may provide information regarding the motive for a crime. In analyzing anonymous communications, ask what is the purpose of the communication? How does the writer approach the communication? What does the writer intend to be understood? The intent and purpose of the communication may be very different from the factual evidence with respect to the crime.

PHYSICAL PROFILING

Handwriting analysis can be especially useful in cases in which the identity of the writer is in question, such as in anonymous note cases. Handwriting can provide details that can help build a profile of the writer regarding age, gender, handedness, literacy, occupation, health, and behavior.

> Through searching evaluation of the thought content, graphic forms, indications of writing training, experience and usage, arrangement and modes of expression, grammatical ability, word usage, etc., the document examiner is frequently able to catalogue highly descriptive personal and personality characteristics of the writer.
>
> **(Conway, 1978, p. 155)**

Age

Although age cannot be conclusively determined from a writing sample, handwriting styles that are formal and exhibit an adherence to traditional penmanship principles are more likely to have been written by an older person. Current trends show that penmanship is not practiced in schools as much as it used to be, and the writing styles of recent generations tend to be more graphically independent from penmanship norms and/or exhibit limited graphic maturity. In addition, printing styles are less likely to be seen in an older population that adheres to traditional penmanship principles. Age can also affect the fluency of handwriting. Degenerative disorders such as Parkinson's disease create tremor and disfluency in handwriting. Other degenerative disorders affecting the muscles in the hands, such as arthritis (also frequently found in an older population), can create significant problems involving handwriting disfluency. Conversely, immature forms of handwriting, such as very round writing with limited fluency, can indicate the handwriting of a younger person such as a child or a teenager. Circle i-dots or other stylistic graphic forms are frequently seen in the handwriting of teenagers. Gang symbols can be employed by younger writers along with graphic references to symbols. A study on assessing age from handwriting samples showed that untrained judges could determine elderly handwriting with better-than-chance accuracy. Another study found that younger subjects wrote faster than older subjects.

Gender

It has been frequently stated in handwriting literature that the biological sex of the writer cannot always be accurately determined from handwriting.

Instead, the masculine and feminine tendencies of the personality are expressed in handwriting. For example, some men may have feminine personality characteristics that resemble feminine handwriting features, and vice versa. However, research has shown that

Table 11.2 Most Frequently Rated Handwriting Characteristics of Male and Female Handwriting

Male	Female
Messier, scruffier	Tidier, neater
More slanted	More rounded
More scribbling out, mistakes	Circles instead of dots
More spiky, angular	Bubbly, curlier, curvier
All over the place	Much easier to read, clearer
Smaller handwriting	Very uniform, more regular

Source: Adapted from Beech & Mackintosh (2005).

laypersons have a better-than-chance ability to determine gender from handwriting. Some of the handwriting attributes assigned to masculine and feminine handwriting may be influenced by cultural perceptions. The judges in the Burr study (2002) reported that women had "large, rounded, and carefully executed writing," whereas men had "a sloping, spiky style that appeared confident and hurried" (p. 698). This could be explained by the theory that females have better fine motor skills than males. Another study explored sex differences in handwriting as related to sex hormones. The raters in the study provided several descriptions of male and female handwriting (see Table 11.2). Exploring the male and female brain during handwriting using functional MRI, it was found that there were neurological differences between the two genders. The study further showed that females have better writing quality than males (Yang et al., 2020).

Handedness

Contrary to popular belief, not all left-slanted handwriting is necessarily written by left-handed writers. More valuable in assessing the handedness of the writer is the direction of the writing stroke. For example, some left-handed people cross t-bars and other letters from right to left. Although there are a greater number of right-handed people in the population, the number of left-handed people may be increasing as the stigma of left-handedness has decreased in recent decades. Many left-handed people are also ambidextrous. Always keep in mind that some writers may intentionally use the nondominant hand to disguise their handwriting.

Literacy and Occupation

The literacy of the writer can dramatically affect the fluency and skill of the writing. Those with unskilled handwriting produce uncoordinated and inconsistent forms. Factors that assist in establishing literacy include spelling, punctuation, and grammar. Poor handwriting and graphic skills have also been correlated with criminal behavior. However, it has not been clearly established whether limited graphic skill was a cause of limited literacy among criminal populations, as "handwriting apparently reflects the socio-economic status of the writer" (Nevo, 1986, p. 214). From a social perspective, it is probably a combination of both the effects of literacy and social conditions impacting certain classes that may contribute to criminal behavior. These cultural and social factors can be seen to some extent in handwriting. Alternately, the handwriting of a highly literate or educated person can be seen from the skill or fluency of execution with handwriting and composition skills. However, it is not uncommon in anonymous note cases for some educated people to mask their level of literacy by pretending to have less skill in both handwriting and composition. It has even been said that educated or literate people are typically the ones who write anonymous notes. The Zodiac Killer, profiled as educated and literate, attempted to mask his literacy level by misspelling words and consciously limiting vocabulary. The Zodiac Killer was not consistent in the use of the ruse, however, because he would demonstrate his masked literacy level by inconsistently using more complex words in other notes. While those with handwriting and literary skills can sometimes successfully mask their level of skill by adopting a style of someone with less skill, those with limited literacy cannot successfully adopt a more sophisticated style. In addressing literacy in handwriting, culture and language should also be considered. What may appear to be unskilled handwriting may be attributed to the writer using English as a second language. Cultural influences can help distinguish some handwriting styles.

Assessing vocational aptitude is frequently employed by handwriting experts in personnel screening. For profiling purposes, certain handwriting indicators provide clues as to the writer's profession or training (past or present). A linear type of block print script is often used by drafters, architects, and engineers. Some writers who work with numbers, such as accountants, bookkeepers, and bankers, use a checker-type numeral 2. Employing some of the techniques of graphic symbolism could help the investigator assess the vocational aptitude of the writer, which may give clues as to the writer's occupation, past work experience, and training or education.

Physical and Mental Health

Indications of the writer's physical and mental health may be assessed from an examination of the handwriting (see Figures 11.11a and 11.11b). Obvious features of tremor need to be carefully examined by a handwriting expert to ascertain the cause of the tremor. Tremor in handwriting can be caused by external environmental conditions, such as writing surface, or could be attributed to complications involving a neurological degenerative disease. An extensive study on the influences of nearly 600 types of medications on handwriting was conducted by Wellingham-Jones in 1991. The influence of marijuana and alcohol on handwriting has also been studied. In terms of mental health, erratic, illegible forms can be indicative of degenerative mental health, often seen in elderly people with advanced forms of Alzheimer's disease and dementia.

Although handwriting experts need to be cautious about making statements about state of mind from handwriting samples, changes in handwriting can be examined and compared to other samples that can corroborate evidence regarding extreme emotional states

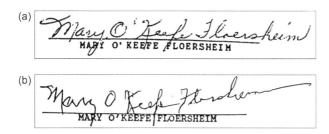

FIGURE 11.11
Signatures from an elderly woman. The top signature (a) was written when she was relatively healthy. The bottom signature (b) was written after she was diagnosed with advanced-stage Parkinson's disease and dementia. The irregularity of the handwriting in the bottom signature reflects the state of her mental and physical health.

and mental and physical health. Handwriting studies related to schizophrenia, obsessive-compulsive disorder, and depression have shown that there are correlations between handwriting and mental disorders. It has also been shown that graphologists can distinguish between the writing of healthy controls and suicidal patients using handwriting criteria such as falling lines, disconnected letters, weak line quality, internal variation, and changeability (Mouly et al., 2007). Neurological research into the forensic application of cognitive status based on distorted handwriting showed that handwriting variables such as spatial problems and spelling errors could be correlated with neuropsychological scales associated with dementia (Balestrino et al., 2012). This type of handwriting examination would be useful in forensic cases in which the person signing the document in question is deceased (e.g., probate matters in which the decedent's will is in question).

BEHAVIORAL PROFILING

When handwriting samples are available, a behavioral profile of a suspect can be enhanced by examining a writing sample's graphic symbolism. Although there have been mixed results regarding research and validity in handwriting analysis as a technique for personality assessment, the schools of thought utilizing a consistent and established method have found better success. In a study comparing the Five Factor Model of personality with graphological traits, significant correlation was found between behavioral indices and graphological characteristics. Handwriting characteristics were shown to predict basic personality correlates including openness to experience, conscientiousness, extraversion, agreeableness, and neuroticism (Gavrilescu & Vizireanu, 2018). Graphology techniques founded on the structured principles of graphic expression offer clues in behavioral profiling, which help support or enhance traditional criminal profiling techniques. This guide is for preliminary investigative techniques and does not address all the limitations and variables that can occur in handwriting. Further, one handwriting factor should never be analyzed in an isolated fashion; instead, like most profiling techniques, the sum of the parts provides a complete profile and should be weighed with the physical evidence available.

In analyzing handwriting, three foundational principles of graphic symbolism are examined: arrangement, form, and movement. Arrangement addresses the organized use of space by the writer through analysis of writing size; proportion of writing forms; spatial arrangement of the margins; and spacing between letters, words, and lines. Form determines the writing style, along with the connective structure of the forms, which can show the structure and expression of the personality. Movement reveals the energy dynamics of the writer in terms of pressure, speed, and direction. Table 11.3 demonstrates a few of the graphic indices used in **graphology**, the field of psychology that profiles the personality and behavior of an individual based on his or her handwriting characteristics. A behavioral profile of the writer is created through the systematic analysis and interpretation of graphic indicators. From a criminal investigator's perspective, graphological analysis of available handwriting specimens can help corroborate or enhance the criminal profile. A criminal profiling model used by the FBI distinguishes between organized and disorganized crime scenes. The method (organized or disorganized) in which an offender approaches a crime or leaves a crime scene is used to profile the offender.

The behavioral characteristics of the organized and disorganized types are easily recognized in handwriting samples. The Zodiac Killer's handwriting, found in anonymous notes that he mailed, was organized and careful in terms of its arrangement, form, and movement (see Figure 11.12). Planning and organization also typified the Zodiac Killer's crime scenes. Conversely, Charles Manson's handwriting is disorganized and chaotic, not dissimilar to the method in which he orchestrated his "family's" mayhem and murder sprees (see Figure 11.13).

Although handwriting analysis can be used to assist in profiling, it cannot definitively predict criminal or deviant behavior. In fact, as behavioral evidence analysis, it is equivocal and dependent on the physical evidence available. Much has been written in handwriting analysis literature about identifying danger signs in handwriting as a tool for predicting criminal behavior. Forensic psychology research has shown that one of the primary indices for predicting criminal behavior stems from impulsivity (action without foresight). Impulsivity in handwriting is seen through strong rightward movement, erratic and disorganized handwriting forms, and speed. Even when

Table 11.3 Graphic Indices of Expression

Arrangement	
I believe I would be Wide spacing/small letters (introverted; observant)	*working as a team is key.* Narrow spacing/large letters (extroverted; interactive)
Form	
helping Garland writing (feeling, social, adaptable, conforming)	*demand* Arch writing (sensing, protective, creative, practical)
Management Angle writing (thinking, analytical, directed, ambitious)	*lecture* Thread writing (intuiting, spontaneous, quick, abstract)
Movement	
I have been Slow/leftward movement (methodical; reflective)	*STREAMLINE* Fast/rightward movement (quick; progressive)

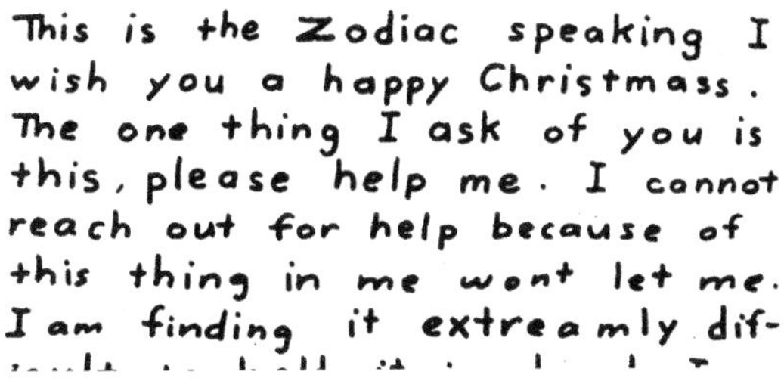

This is the Zodiac speaking I wish you a happy Christmass. The one thing I ask of you is this, please help me. I cannot reach out for help because of this thing in me wont let me. I am finding it extreamly dif-

FIGURE 11.12

A taunting, anonymous note typical of the Zodiac serial killer. Note the contrived handwriting style indicative of disguise, and purposely misspelled words "Christmass" and "extreamly." The cautious, slow writing style also indicates someone who uses forethought and planning

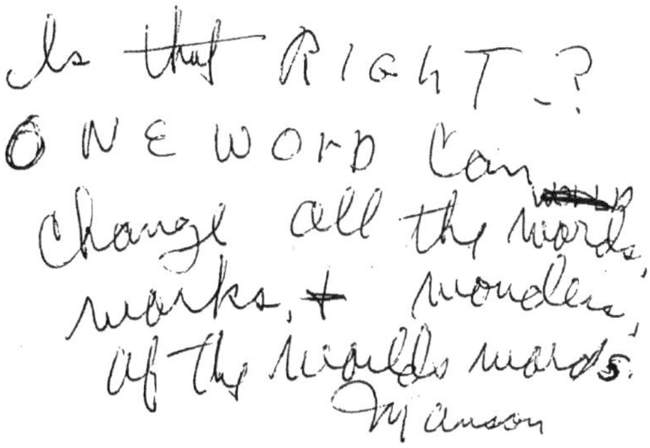

FIGURE 11.13

Inconsistent arrangement, form, and movement in the handwriting of Charles Manson.

handwriting danger signs are evident, if there is high impulse control (ability to delay immediate gratification), it can offset the possible danger signs evident in the handwriting. In a research study involving the Five Factor Model, Thomas et al. (2020) found specific handwriting features associated with risk-taking behavior including heavy pressure, irregular margins, rightward trend, wide letter spacing, and ascending baselines.

A systematic method for analyzing danger signs in handwriting was established by Iannetta, Craine, and McLaughlin (1993). In their method, danger signs are divided into primary indicators of dangerousness, facilitators, and inhibitors. Each handwriting factor is numerically weighed and scored so that the level of dangerousness based on handwriting factors is given a quantitative measure. In all, they list 33 indicators of dangerousness. Table 11.4 illustrates the most significant danger signs. To predict dangerousness accurately, several danger signs need to be present in the handwriting sample and compared to other signs that facilitate or inhibit potential dangerousness. Some psychotic killers exhibit controlled and organized handwriting styles that do not show strong indicators of violent or criminal tendency. It has been theorized that these types may have two personalities and that their handwriting can change when engaged in a psychotic episode. This theory is supported by cases in which individuals with dissociative identity disorder significantly change their handwriting during varying phases of personality manifestation. This issue can create problems not only in profiling but also in handwriting identification cases.

Table 11.4 Handwriting Signs of Dangerousness

Clubs	Slashes	Tics
Dot grinding	Weapon-shaped letters	Intense pressure
Muddiness	Disguised letters	Unexpected angles
Open-bottom circles	Letters drop below baseline	Distorted d's

FORENSIC LINGUISTICS, STATEMENT ANALYSIS, AND HANDWRITING

Forensic linguistics is the analysis of written or spoken language as applied to issues of law. In assessing linguistic style in a suspect text, specific areas, such as syntax, spelling, abbreviations, phrases, and text arrangement, are systematically analyzed and compared to a suspect's language. Forensic linguistics is frequently used as an identification aid in determining authorship of questioned written or spoken text. **Statement analysis**, the examination of stress as indicated by the written word, is used in determining the veracity of a statement. Anonymous communications are linguistically analyzed for identification purposes as well as for determining the threat level from the communication. Investigators utilized forensic linguistics in solving the Unabomber case.

Statement analysis can be used in conjunction with handwriting examination as a tool for determining the veracity of a handwritten statement. As in polygraph examinations, stress caused by deception can create a graphic disturbance in handwriting. Mostly, the graphic disturbance is seen in differences in the writer's regular graphic pattern, which can include changes in size, spacing, slant, pressure, and formation. Unusual breaks, patching, or overwriting may be found in parts of deceptive phrases.

It has been demonstrated that stress or extreme emotional states related to or causing stress influences handwriting movement. Van Gemmert and Van Galen's (1997) research on the effect of stress on graphic tasks showed increased neuromotor noise in the human information-processing system. Conditions such as pressure, reaction time, and movement time in graphic tasks were affected by stress. Longstaff and Heath (2003) noted that writers with tremor or motor-system degradation had a harder time adapting to writing conditions in which mild stress was introduced. A study by Halder-Sinn, Enkelmann, and Funsch (1998) found that differences in handwriting occurred when subjects wrote under acceleration/stress conditions: slant of descenders, horizontal extension, exactness of lines, and distance of i-dots. In a case study reported by Walters and Hening (1992), when the patient was startled, his or her handwriting became bigger, showed inconsistencies, and exhibited tremor.

Dick, Found, and Rogers (2000) reported that stress associated with deceptive behavior also caused graphic disturbance in signatures. Responses to questions that were designed to elicit deception versus honesty showed differences in graphic movements in "measures of reaction time, writing pressure, movement time, pause time and

Table 11.5 Handwriting Signs of Dishonesty

company	*lasting*	*ovusumy*
Slow writing speed	Unnatural writing structure/style	Unstable, thready, formless structures
selling	*pamm*	*with*
Touching up letter formations	Letters written as other letters	Blobbed or punctuated writing
Jam	*coupny*	*allow*
Pen lifts	Important parts of letters omitted	Oval letters open at the baseline

THE TRUTH MUST ALWAYS BE ACCURATE

Marked initial emphasis

changes in acceleration" (p. 15). Another study showed that subjects' handwriting changed (pressure and stroke length and height) when writing true versus false statements (Luria & Rosenblum, 2009). There are differences in spatial and temporal measurements between deceptive and truthful statements which are observed as wider writing spaces and slower writing speed in deceptive statements (Luria et al., 2014). Additionally, changes in slant and distortion in key words or sentences can indicate deception. A handwritten statement prepared by a murder suspect may show signs of deception due to changes in margins and slant. The clues indicating deception in critical areas of the statement could help investigators interrogate the suspect.

Signs of dishonesty shown in handwriting can be used in conjunction with statement analysis. Saudek (1978) describes 10 signs of dishonesty (see Table 11.5). He found through his experiments on diagnosing dishonesty in handwriting that at least 4 of the 10 handwriting features must be present in the handwriting specimen. Figures 11.14 and 11.15 not only indicate alterations in the writers' natural style in critical parts of the statement, but signs of dishonesty and dangerousness are also present throughout the handwriting samples.

(a)

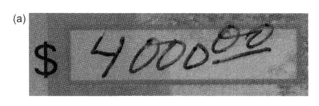

(b)

FIGURE 11.14

The top photograph shows numerals written with a black ballpoint ink on a questioned check that appears to look the same to the unaided eye. When using an IR viewer (bottom photograph), however, parts of the number "disappear," indicating that the original number was "100" before it was altered to "4000."

Examination of graphic disturbances in statement analysis, together with behavioral profiling techniques, can aid the criminal investigator in formulating appropriate questions and techniques for interrogation of suspects (see Figure 11.16). The effectiveness of statement analysis is also dependent on the kinds of questions that the investigator asks. For example, when the investigator has suspects prepare written statements, more information will be provided voluntarily if the suspect is requested to answer open-ended questions, such as asking the suspect to give an account of everything he or she did on the day of the crime.

QUESTIONED DOCUMENT CASE STUDY

In September and October 2001, the first cases of anthrax bioterrorism occurred in the United States when letters containing anthrax were mailed to congressional leaders and members of the news media. The anthrax note case presents the opportunity to apply many of the multidisciplinary investigative techniques described in this chapter, including document examination, handwriting identification, psychology, graphology, and linguistics. As part of the investigation of this case, the FBI publicly released a profile of the author of the anonymous notes. The main suspect in the mailings, Bruce Edwards Ivins, died of an apparent suicide in 2008 when he learned that the FBI was planning to arrest him for the crimes. The case remains officially unsolved.

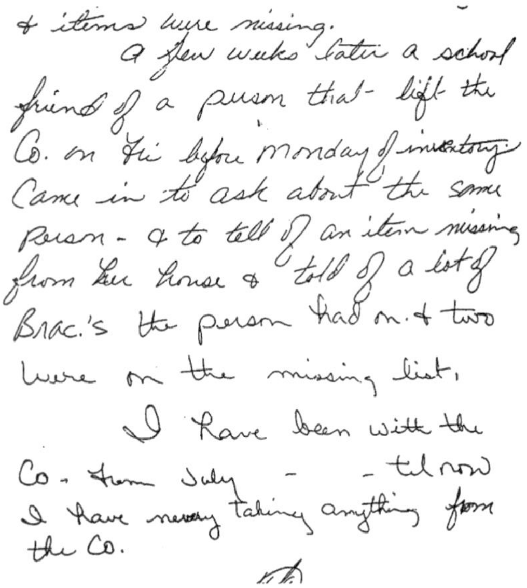

FIGURE 11.15

Written statement of an employee suspected of stealing money and merchandise. Note how the handwriting changes in the last paragraph of the statement. Change in slant, wider spacing, distortion (in the word "never") are evident in critical parts of statement. *Reprinted with permission from Handwriting Analysis and Detection of Deception (p. 12), by L.M. McDaniel (2006). Elijay, GA: Author.*

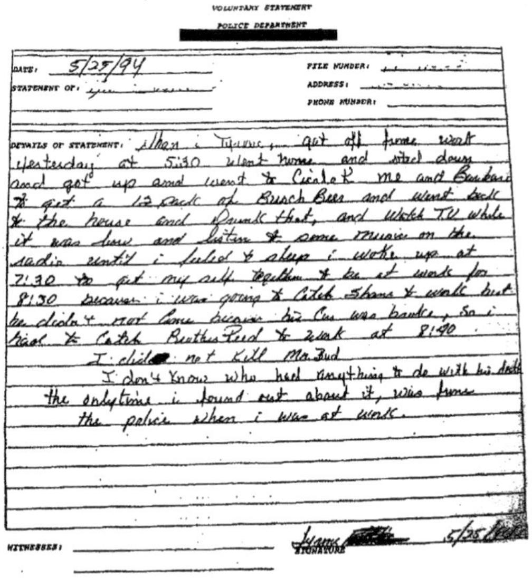

FIGURE 11.16

Handwritten statement of murder suspect. Note the changes in handwriting toward the end of the statement (margins indented, blotted out word, change in slant). The most critical phrase of the statement "I did not kill Mr. Bud" (line 12) stands out in the note, with wide indentations of space on either side of the phrase. During interrogation, the suspect broke down and admitted to murdering his friend for money. *Reprinted with permission of S. Tschirhart.*

A comparison of the handprinted text of the notes using handwriting identification principles established that the same person wrote the notes and corresponding envelopes (see notes in Figure 11.17). The FBI's analysis of the handwriting indicated the following distinctive characteristics: use of dashes in writing dates, a formal numeral 1, separation of the word "cannot" into "can not," use of block-style lettering with larger emphasis on the first word of each sentence, a downward slant on the handwriting of the envelopes, and use of prestamped envelopes.

The FBI's behavioral profile indicated that the writer was an adult male with a scientific background who may be working in a laboratory. According to the profile, he has an "organized, rational thought process" and selects victims deliberately. He is nonconfrontational, holds grudges, and vows revenge. He may anonymously harass other perceived enemies. He prefers to be alone. He was "mission oriented" when he mailed the anthrax letters, but also became secretive with unusual patterns of activity. After the

FIGURE 11.17

The examination of the infamous anthrax letters in 2001 involved forensic document examiners, graphologists, and linguistics experts to determine the possible identity of the writer.

offense, "he may have exhibited significant behavioral changes" such as anxiety, mood swings, withdrawal, and an altered physical appearance.

Although CSIs rarely perform examinations on documents, they are required to collect and preserve such evidence in the proper fashion. For example, testing a document for latent fingerprints using ninhydrin may damage the ink on the document and interfere with ESDA examinations. The CSI may also be called on to collect known specimens (exemplars) for comparison purposes. This step may entail procuring handwriting specimens from suspects as well as locating contemporaneous specimens of a suspect's known writing. In cases involving typewriting, machine-produced documents, xerographic reproductions, and computer printers, the CSI may be required to procure known specimens from the machine in question for comparison purposes. Knowing what a forensic document examiner needs to conduct an examination will make collection and preservation of this evidence more efficient and effective.

Discussion Questions

1 What evidence can be found using documents?
2. Describe how documents must be collected, stored, and accounted for in order to be used in court.
3. What characteristics of handwriting analysis can be useful in court proceedings?

REFERENCES

Balestrino, M., Fontana, P., Terzuoli, S., Volpe, S., Inglese, M. L., & Cocito, L. (2012). Altered handwriting suggests cognitive impairment and may be relevant to posthumous evaluation. *Journal of Forensic Sciences.* doi:10.1111/j.1556–4029.2012.02131.x.

Beech, J. R., & Mackintosh., I. C. (2005). Do differences in sex hormones affect handwriting style? Evidence from digit ratio and sex role identity as determinants of the sex of handwriting. *Personality and Individual Differences, 39,* 459[C0]468.

Bird, C., Found, B., & Rogers, D. (2007). Forensic document examiners' opinions on the process of production of disguised and simulated signatures. In J. G. Phillips, D. Rogers, & R. P. Ogeil (Eds.), Proceedings of the 13th biennial conference of the International Graphonomics Society, 11 14 November (pp. 171174). Melbourne, Australia: Monash University.

Burr, V. (2002). Judging gender from samples of adult handwriting: Accuracy and use of cues. *Journal of Social Psychology, 142*(6), 691[C0]700.

Conway, J. V. P. (1978). *Evidential Documents* (3rd Edition). Springfield, IL: Charles C. Thomas.

Dewhurst, T., Found, B., & Rogers, D. (2008). Are expert penmen better than lay people in producing simulations of a model signature. *Forensic Science International, 180*(1), 50–53.

Dick, D., Found, B., & Rogers, D. (2000). The forensic detention of deceptive behavior using handwriting movements. *Journal of Forensic Document Examination, 13,* 15–24.

Found, B., & Bird, C. (Eds.). (2016). *Documentation of forensic handwriting method: A modular approach.* Macleod, Vic, Australia: Victoria Police Forensic Services Department & Forensic Science South Australia.

Found, B., & Rogers, D. (2003). The initial profiling trial of a program to characterize forensic handwriting examiners' skill. *Journal of the American Society of Questioned Document Examiners, 6,* 72–81.

Found, B., & Rogers, D. (2008). The probative character of forensic handwriting examiners' identification and elimination opinions on questioned signatures. *Forensic Science International, 178*(1), 54–60.

Found, B., Rogers, D., & Herkt, A. (2001). The skill of a group of document examiners in expressing handwriting and signature authorship and production process opinions. *Journal of Forensic Document Examination, 14,* 15–30.

Found, B., Rogers, D., & Schmittat, R. (1994). A computer program to compare the spatial elements of handwriting. *Forensic Science International, 68,* 195–203.

Found, B., Sita, J., & Rogers, D. (1999). The development of a program for characterizing forensic handwriting examiners' expertise: Signature examination pilot study. *Journal of Forensic Document Examination, 12,* 69–80.

Franke, K., Schomaker, L. R. B., Vuurpijl, L. G., & Giesler, S. (2003). FISH-new: A common ground for computer-based forensic writer identification. In: *Proceedings of the 3rd European Academy of Forensic Science triennial meeting* (Vol. 136, Suppl. p. 84). Istanbul, Turkey: Forensic Science International.

Frye v. United States, 293 F. 1013 (1923).

Gavrilescu, M., & Vizireanu, N. (2018). Predicting the Big Five personality traits from handwriting. *EURASIP Journal on Image and Video Processing, 2018*(1), 1–17.

Gilbert v. California, 388 U.S. 263 (1967).

Halder-Sinn, P., Enkelmann, C., & Funsch, K. (1998). Handwriting and emotional stress. *Perceptual and Motor Skills, 87*, 457–458.

Harralson, H. H. (2013). *Developments in handwriting and signature identification in the digital age.* Waltham, MA: Anderson.

Harralson, H. H., & Miller, L. S. (2018). *Huber and Headrick's handwriting examination: Facts and fundamentals, second edition.* Boca Raton, FL: CRC Press.

Hepler, A. B., Saunders, C. P., Davis, L. J., & Buscaglia, J. (2012). Score-based likelihood ratios for handwriting evidence. *Forensic Science International, 219*(1–3), 129–140.

Iannetta, K., Craine, J. F., & McLaughlin, D. G. (1993). *Danger between the lines.* Kailua, HI: Author.

Jindal, D., Kaur, H., & Chattopadhyay, P. K. (1999). A metric analysis of handwriting: A study of signatures. *International Journal of Forensic Document Examiners, 5*, 105–107.

Kam, M., Fielding, G., & Conn, R. (1997). Writing identification by professional document examiners. *Journal of Forensic Sciences, 42*(5), 778–786.

Kam, M., Gummadidala, K., Fielding, G., & Conn, R. (2001). Signature authentication by forensic document examiners. *Journal of Forensic Sciences, 46*, 884–888.

Kam, M., & Lin, E. (2003). Writer identification using hand-printed and non-hand-printed questioned documents. *Journal of Forensic Sciences, 48*(6), 1391–1395.

Kam, M., Wetstein, J., & Conn, R. (1994). Proficiency of professional document examiners in writer identification. *Journal of Forensic Sciences, 39*(1), 5–14.

Linden, J., Taroni, F., Marquis, R., & Bozza, S. (2021). Bayesian multivariate models for case assessment in dynamic signature cases. *Forensic Science International, 318*, 110611.

Ling, S. (2002). A preliminary investigation into handwriting examination by multiple measurements of letters and spacing. *Forensic Science International, 126*, 145–149.

Longstaff, M. G., & Heath, R. A. (2003). The influence of motor system degradation on the control of handwriting movements: A dynamical systems analysis. *Human Movement Science, 22*, 91–110.

Luria, G., Kahana, A., & Rosenblum, S. (2014). Detection of deception via handwriting behaviors using a computerized tool: Toward an evaluation of malingering. *Cognitive Computation, 6*(4), 849–855.

Luria, G., & Rosenblum, S. (2009). Comparing the handwriting behaviours of true and false writing with computerized handwriting measurers. *Applied Cognitive Psychology.* Retrieved from: http://dx.doi.org/10.1002/acp.1621

Lytle, B., & Yang, C. (2006). Detecting forged handwriting with wavelets and statistics. *Rose-Hulman Undergraduate Mathematics Journal, 7*(1), 1–10.

Marquis, R., Schmittbuhl, M., Mazzella, W. D., & Taroni, F. (2005). Quantification of the shape of handwritten characters: A step to objective discrimination between writers based on the study of the capital character O. *Forensic Science International, 150*, 23–32.

McDaniel, L. M. (2006). *Handwriting analysis and detection of deception.* Ellijay, GA: Author.

Mouly, S., Mahe, I., Champion, K., Bertin, C., Popper, P., de Noblet, D., & Bergmann, J. F. (2007). Graphology for the diagnosis of suicide attempts: A blind proof of principle controlled study. *International Journal of Clinical Practice, 61*(3), 411–415.

National Academy of Sciences (2009). *Strengthening forensic science in the United States: A path forward.* Washington, D.C.: National Academies Press.

Nevo, B. (1986). Basic rhythms and criminal disposition in handwriting, by H. Honel: Critical review and reanalysis. In B. Nevo (Ed.), *Scientific aspects of graphology: A handbook* (pp. 203–215). Springfield, IL: Charles C. Thomas.

Pettus v. United States. (2012). *DCCA 8-CF-1361.* Retrieved from http://legaltimes.typepad.com/files/08-cf-1361_mtd.pdf

Saudek, R. (1978). *Experiments with handwriting (Reprint).* Sacramento: Books for Professionals.

Sita, J., Found, B., & Rogers, D. K. (2002). Forensic handwriting examiners' expertise for signature comparison. *Journal of Forensic Sciences, 47*(5), 1117–1124.

Srihari, S. N., Cha, S.-H., Arora, H., & Lee, S. (2002). Individuality of handwriting. *Journal of Forensic Sciences, 47*(4), 1–17.

Srihari, S., Huang, C., & Srinivasan, H. (2008). On the discriminability of the handwriting of twins. *Journal of Forensic Sciences, 53*(2), 430–446.

Strach, S. J. (1998). Proposed probability conclusions in handwriting comparisons. *International Journal of Forensic Document Examiners, 4*(4), 313–317.

SWGDOC (Scientific Working Group for Forensic Document Examination). (2013a). *Standard for Examination of Handwritten Items.* Retrieved from https://www.swgdoc.org/index.php/standards/published-standards (accessed November 12, 2021).

SWGDOC (Scientific Working Group for Forensic Document Examination). (2013b). *Standard Terminology for Expressing Conclusions of Forensic Document Examiners.* Retrieved from https://www.swgdoc.org/index.php/standards/published-standards (accessed November 12, 2021).

Taylor, M., Bird, C., Bishop, B., Burkes, T., Caligiuri, M., Found, B., Grose, W., Logan, L., Melson, K., Merlino, M., Miller, L., Mohammed, L., Morris, J.J., Osborne, N., Ostrum, B., Saunders, C., Shappell, S.H., Srihari, S., Stoel, R., Vastrick, T., Waltke, H., & Will, E. (2020). *Forensic handwriting examination and human factors: Improving the practice through a systems approach.* NIST Interagency/Internal Report (NISTIR), National Institute of Standards and Technology, Gaithersburg, MD, [online], Retrieved from https://doi.org/10.6028/NIST.IR.8282 (Accessed November 14, 2021).

Thomas, S., Goel, M., & Agrawal, D. (2020). A framework for analyzing financial behavior using machine learning classification of personality through handwriting analysis. *Journal of Behavioral and Experimental Finance, 26,* 100315.

United States v. Cotner, 657 F.2d 1171 (10th Cir. 1981).

United States v. Hollins, 811 F.2d 384 (7th Cir. 1987).

United States v. Paul, 175 F.3d 906 (1999).

United States v. Starzecpyzel, 550 F. Supp. 1027 (S.D.N.Y. 1995).

United States v. Wade, 388 U.S. 218 (1967).

Van Gemmert, A. W. A., & Van Galen, G. P. (1997). Stress, neuromotor noise and human performance: A theoretical perspective. *Journal of Experimental Psychology: Human Perception and Performance, 23,* 1299–1313.

Walch, M. A., Gantz, D. T., Miller, J. J., Davis, L. J., Saunders, C. P., & Lancaster, M. J. (2008). Evaluation of the individuality of handwriting using FLASH ID—A totally automated, language independent system for handwriting identification. *Proceedings of the American Academy of Forensic Sciences, 14,* 388.

Walters, A. S., & Hening, W. A. (1992). Noise-induced psychogenic tremor associated with post-traumatic stress disorder. *Movement Disorders, 7*(4), 333–338.

Wellingham-Jones, P. (1991). *Drugs and handwriting.* Tehama, CA: PWJ.

Yang, Y., Tam, F., Graham, S. J., Sun, G., Li, J., Gu, C., Tao, R., Wang, N., Bi, H.-Y., & Zuo, Z. (2020). Men and women differ in the neural basis of handwriting. *Human Brain Mapping, 41*(10), 2642–2655.

Zimmerman, J. (1998). Counting handwriting characteristics. *International Journal of Forensic Document Examiners, 4*(4), 318–322.

CHAPTER 12

Motor Vehicles as Crime Scenes

KEY TERMS

Chop shop	National Insurance	Point of impact (POI)
Driver's point of view	Crime Bureau	Skid marks
GPS	(NICB)	VIN

What You Will Learn

Motorized vehicles transport us to every type of activity we can imagine. Whether it is a car, snowmobile, boat, or other type of motorized vehicle, the growth of criminal activities grows exponentially with the addition of new types of transportation. This chapter discusses the concerns linked with processing a motor vehicle and how to investigate these categories of crime.

MURDER IN THE NEW YEAR

Motor Vehicles as Crime Scenes

Tom Smith popped the last of the hotdog in his mouth. "Want to hear some more good news?"

"By all means," Detective Fletcher replied.

"Ed Ellwenger phoned me 20 minutes ago and told me Officer Scott ran down a hunch that paid off. Apparently, the dean rented an SUV from Hertz in St. Matthews, 60 miles away, the day before the murders and turned it in three days later."

Mavis rubbed her chin. "Hardly a coincidence, I would think."

Tom wiped his mouth with the napkin. "Hardly. But I saved the best for last. Ed checked the GPS system, and it puts Sellers at the Mortons's house within the time frame the murders took place. He also did a tire impression, and it matched the cast he took at the crime scene."

DOI: 10.4324/9780429261657-12

Mavis Fletcher quickly scribbled something onto her notepad. "Looks like we're getting close to an arrest warrant. It's beginning to appear that our murder-suicide is, in fact, a double homicide with more to do about a financial affair than an extramarital one."

The detective closed her notepad and looked at Tom. "Why don't you meet me at the medical examiner's office tomorrow morning for her update on the autopsy?"

Tom grinned. "Sounds like a plan, Detective."

INTRODUCTION

Motor vehicles are an integral part of everyday life, and they are also involved in an increasing number of crimes, ranging from minor traffic offenses to homicides. They can be crime scenes on wheels, and the challenges they pose to CSIs are numerous. Vehicles present the CSI with the necessity of conducting a confined space search and the need for both interior and exterior evidence collection processes. Not all vehicle searches are performed to collect evidence of criminal activities. Many times the CSI will process a vehicle for the purpose of documenting and collecting physical evidence that may later be used to determine fault in a civil process rather than guilt in a criminal proceeding. The protocols and systematic processing remain the same, however, because final prosecutorial actions have not been determined at the time of the investigation.

PHOTOGRAPHY

When documenting the scene of an accident or other type of motor vehicle crash, the CSI must take photographs that accurately depict the **driver's point of view** as well as the point of view of other passengers at the time of the crash. You should carefully collect measurements that document the height of the driver and each passenger and then place the camera on a tripod at that height and take photographs of the scene in a 360-degree span (see Figure 12.1). Pay particular attention to any obstructions, such as hedges, unmown median grass, signs, or other physical barriers that may have impeded the view of the driver. These photos will be used to establish the conditions that existed at the time the crash occurred. It is also important to take photographs from the point of view of any witnesses outside the vehicle. This will allow the investigator to establish the credibility of the statements from witnesses based on the angle of view they had of the crash site.

Skid marks, which are created when the brakes on a motor vehicle are applied quickly to slow down or stop a vehicle's motion, are often present at the site of a motor vehicle crash. These marks require accurate measurements and photographs to document their location. Skid marks provide valuable information for the traffic accident reconstructionist and can be used to determine speed, distance, and other variables that may have contributed to the accident. The **point of impact (POI)** will usually yield valuable trace evidence and must be documented both on the sketch and in the photographs.

It is sometimes difficult to determine the exact POI, so the CSI should utilize the skills of traffic accident investigators as well as corroborating statements from witnesses to validate the location in documentation and photographs. Photograph the scene at the POI as well as at the final resting place of the vehicles (because they may travel several more yards before stopping after a crash occurs; see Figures 12.2a and 12.2b). Debris in the roadway, including substances such as battery acid, glass, coolant, and oil, should be noted on the sketches and photographed. All fluids present on the roadway, whether or not they are from the vehicles involved in the crash, should be photographed because they may have contributed to the accident.

FIGURE 12.1
Camera on tripod capturing view of driver.

Document the position of all light switches when you conduct your search of the vehicle. Do not turn on any switches in an attempt to determine whether the automobile's lights are functional because

FIGURE 12.2
Photos showing skid marks and gouge marks in pavement.

this will destroy any evidence the crime lab examiners may be able to find when they examine the lightbulb filaments. It is often possible for lab examiners to determine whether breaks in the filaments occurred when the light was turned off or were activated at the time of the crash. These vital pieces of evidence should be documented and collected for submission to the crime lab and will be used to substantiate claims of whether the lights were turned on when the crash occurred (see Figures 12.3a and 12.3b).

It is important to note any other items that may have contributed to the crash, including cargo inside the passenger compartment. Items being hauled may suddenly shift and obstruct the view of the driver. Often emergency responders will remove these items as they seek to render first aid to victims, and they may be moved clear of the vehicle by the time the CSI arrives on the scene. It is important to talk to the first responders to determine the condition of the vehicle when they arrived and any steps that were taken that may have altered the state of the vehicle since the time of the crash.

FIGURE 12.3A

The question at hand was whether the taillights of a vehicle were on or off at the time of the accident. Investigators pulled the bulbs from the rear of the vehicle. One bulb was shattered, but the filaments were intact.

FIGURE 12.3B

The filaments showed heavy deposits of tungsten oxide and melted glass, which forms when oxygen is introduced to a hot filament. This proves that the lights were on at the time of impact.

Photograph each seatbelt and shoulder harness. It is common for first responders to cut through these safety devices as they attempt to extract victims from wreckage. Also photograph the dashboard and door panels of the vehicle to document airbag deployment or failure of the system to deploy. It is possible for mechanics to test the systems to determine whether a mechanical failure contributed to the accident, but the condition of the interior of the vehicle must be documented at the time of the accident investigation.

Once the car has been moved to a secure location, it is important to complete the documentation process. Take photographs under the hood of the car to accurately depict fluid levels (if visible), hoses, and lines. If mechanical failure or equipment tampering is suspected, be sure that a reputable automobile mechanic is present to conduct the initial inspection. The vehicle should be placed on a lift so that accurate photographs can be taken of the undercarriage as you search for additional trace evidence. As a part of this undercarriage inspection, include photographs of all tires as well as the front and rear bumpers.

HIT-AND-RUN CASES

The prosecution of perpetrators of hit-and-run cases hinges on the cross-transference of trace evidence from the suspect vehicle to the victim (see Figure 12.4) and vice versa. Hairs, fibers, glass, paint, soil, fingerprints, or other impression evidence, as well as possible blood spatter or other tissue fragments, must be identified, collected, and preserved. The suspect vehicle may not be identified or located

FIGURE 12.4
A pedestrian victim of a hit-and-run driver.

for hours, days, or even weeks after the crime has occurred. The CSI must remain diligent in the search for trace evidence that can create linkages among the suspect, victim, and the crime scene. In some instances, many vehicles of the same color, body style, and make will be examined before the investigator determines the correct suspect vehicle. Photographs and subsequent documentation for each vehicle must be maintained by the CSI to ensure that credibility of the search process is established.

An increase in car crash research shows drivers who text while in control of a motor vehicle are 23 times more likely to

SAFETY TIP

Please view this video to realize the impact of texting while driving: www.youtube.com/watch?v5vOTbAbKoL28. There is also a printable PDF available from the Federal Communications Commission at http://transition.fcc.gov/cgb/consumerfacts/driving andtexting.pdf.

be involved in an accident (VA Tech Transportation Institute, 2009, July). Receiving and sending text messages can distract a driver's eyes for an average time of 4.6 seconds each time. If the vehicle is traveling at 55 mph, it will advance the length of a football field (100 yards) before the driver's eyes return to the road. The report also revealed that drivers who were texting were 23 times more at risk than undistracted drivers. At the time of writing, 39 states have enacted a full text messaging ban for drivers, while a number of states have a full ban on cellphone use by drivers. There is no national ban on texting or making calls on a cellphone (at this time). You can visit www.ghsa.org/html/stateinfo/laws/cellphone_laws.html for specific state information.

In 2010, 3,092 people were killed in crashes involving a distracted driver, and an additional 416,000 were injured in motor vehicle crashes involving a distracted driver (www.distraction.gov). In 2011, at least 23 percent of auto collisions involved cellphones. They included talking on the phone, reaching for the phone, texting, and surfing the Internet (www.textinganddrivingsafety.com).

Do not overlook the need to process the car crash crime scene just as you would follow standard operating procedures for other cases. Most people now drive with a cellphone within arm's reach. The fact that a cellphone is present in a vehicle crash does not automatically prove that a distracted driver in that vehicle caused the crash to occur. You do not need the cellphone to obtain the activity records from the phone service provider, but you will need a search warrant. How does this type of digital evidence enter into crime scene investigation?

It is becoming more likely there may be a global positioning system (GPS) or other satellite communication device in the vehicle (such as OnStar). These navigation systems contain information that may be useful to an ongoing investigation because they create an electronic record of location, time, and speed. Many car manufacturers now employ remote services such as OnStar, which provides turn-by-turn directions, accident detection, and roadside assistance, and they cooperate with law enforcement agencies to identify the location of vehicles that have been stolen or otherwise involved in a criminal investigation. Technology continues to positively influence and provide additional tools to CSIs and other investigators when vehicles are involved. More detailed information on these and other systems are available at www.onstar.com or www.gps.gov.

TRACE EVIDENCE

The collision of a motor vehicle and a human being or other object creates many forms of trace evidence. The importance of trace evidence must be emphasized, even though advances in DNA analysis have claimed the attention of most CSIs and detectives. Trace evidence, when properly identified and collected, can provide valuable information and investigative leads in many types of cases, including hit-and-runs, car thefts, kidnappings, and homicides. To assist in the identification of trace evidence, the FBI Laboratory maintains reference collections of human and animal hairs, natural and man-made textiles and fibers, seeds, woods, and feathers. These databases are in addition to the ballistics, fingerprints, and paint samples files that are available for state crime laboratories to query.

TYPES OF PHYSICAL EVIDENCE

Paint and glass fragments are two of the most common types of physical evidence associated with hit-and-run investigations. Both, if properly collected and in adequate amounts, can lead to the identification of the type of vehicle involved in the crash. It is important for the investigator to determine the point of impact and examine the area for any debris that may have been left at the scene. An accident reconstructionist is often utilized to establish the location if it is not readily identifiable on initial arrival.

If the crash involves two vehicles, paint transfer and glass from headlights or lightbulbs are usually present. If the investigation involves a pedestrian, there may be hair, fibers, tissue, blood, or other physical evidence either at the scene, left on the vehicle, or retrieved from the victim.

Paint consists of pigments and additives combined with a binder. This composite is then mixed with a solvent. After application, the solvent evaporates and leaves a layer of opaque color on the surface. Forensic chemists can analyze the layers of paint to determine the manufacturer and identify the make, model, and year of manufacture of most automobiles. In addition to the clear-coat and color, carmakers apply various layers of primers to the vehicle as it passes through the assembly process. These primer layers can also be analyzed to assist in the determination of the original vehicle color.

The FBI maintains the National Automotive Paint File, which is a database of paints related to all makes, models, and manufacture year of automobiles. State crime labs have access to this database for querying purposes. This type of information is valuable to investigators,

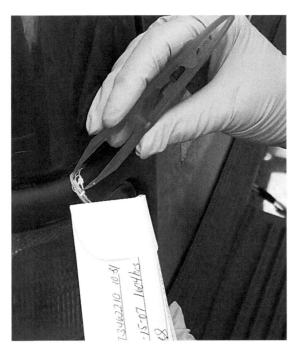

FIGURE 12.5
Valuable fiber evidence may be found when a suspect vehicle is thoroughly processed.

particularly if a suspect vehicle has not been identified. Individualization is possible if sufficient samples are available for analysis, but usually only class characteristics of paint samples can be determined.

Glass fragments found at the scene, on the victim, and on the suspect's clothing may provide linkages essential to successful prosecution of the case. Crime lab analysts may be able to piece together fragmented edges and match irregularities and striations that lead to individualized characteristics. This match can lead to positive identification that glass fragments originated from the suspect vehicle. Tempered glass is found in the side and rear windows of cars, and windshields are composed of laminated glass. Manufacturers place unique identifiers on all pieces of glass, and if an automobile window has been replaced, this information will be different on the new piece of glass. The CSI should always check the windows for consistent markings if a suspect vehicle is identified and glass fragments are part of the trace evidence.

Car parts ripped from a vehicle may be found at the scene of a crash. It is important to gather these pieces of evidence. Many of them carry identifying numbers, or it may be possible to match the parts to suspect vehicles.

Hair and fiber trace evidence may be found on the undercarriage or in damaged areas of a vehicle (see Figure 12.5). Fragments of fabric are often ripped from the clothing of a pedestrian victim. These can become individualized evidence if the edges of the cloth can be matched to the victim's clothes. Although single fibers are only class evidence, they may still be used to establish a link between the vehicle and the victim and should not be overlooked at the crime scene. Some synthetic fibers may contain special characteristics that make their presence at a crime scene unusual. In these instances, the importance of fiber trace evidence may become increasingly important in linking a victim to a crime scene.

Hair from the victim may be embedded in a windshield or other glass areas. This evidence is especially important when the investigator is trying to determine who was operating a motor vehicle when this fact is being contested. Remember that hair analysis can identify the racial origin and location of the body from which the hair came.

Soil samples may be useful trace evidence found on a suspect vehicle. Be sure to collect samples from under each of the four fenders to demonstrate that a complete investigation was conducted so that any linkages established through the soil samples will be admissible (see Figure 12.6). Soil samples may be associative evidence because examination yields only class characteristics, but every effort must be made to identify or eliminate suspect vehicles from the investigation.

Pattern evidence may be created by the vehicle on the victim's body or object that was struck. For example, a tire print or the imprint of a vehicle logo, grill work, or hood ornament can be documented and used for future comparison by a forensic examiner. Pedestrian fatalities usually involve a fracture of the leg; in many instances, bruising patterns around this injury may include the imprint of the bumper or other unique feature of the vehicle. It is also important to document the location of the injuries on the lower extremities and then gather measurements of the vehicle, including height from the bumper to the ground. Although this information may not present confirmatory evidence, it can provide corroboration that the suspect vehicle could have caused the injuries to the victim. Similarly, items of clothing the victim was wearing at the time of impact may create impression evidence on the vehicle. Marks from belt buckles, buttons, snaps, jewelry, or fabric impressions should be documented and preserved for future comparisons.

FIGURE 12.6
A CSI collecting soil samples from under a vehicle.

COLLECTION TECHNIQUES

Paint chips or fragments should be collected with disposable forceps and scalpels if possible. When disposable tools are not available, be sure to clean instruments between sample collections to eliminate the possibility of cross-contamination. Always collect known standards of paint by scraping down through all layers from the primer to the top-coat in an area close to the point of impact. This will help you identify contradictions in weathering, other layers of paint, and so on that may be present on a different portion of the vehicle. Securing samples of all the layers will increase the probability that a match can be made.

Collect the samples in paper; then use a druggist fold (see Table 5.1 in Chapter 5) to secure the edges and place the sample inside a rigid container to prevent any damage during transit. Do not use plastic bags to collect paint samples because static electricity will make it difficult to remove the samples at the crime laboratory.

The forensic examiner will first attempt a microscopic physical match by trying to piece together paint chips as if in a jigsaw puzzle, because a match would provide the most conclusive results. If this is not possible, the known and unknown samples will be compared for layers. To date, a scientifically accepted number of layers of paint to be matched in order to conclude the samples originated from the same source has not been determined by the courts. If the samples are too small for the analysis, they will be chemically analyzed to determine the original components of pigments and binders.

When collecting glass fragments from the suspect vehicle, you should remove samples from as close as possible to the point of breakage. One square inch is sufficient for the control sample, and it should be taken from an area adjacent to the breakage point. Do not forget to collect glass samples from side mirrors as well. Use solid containers with shock-absorbent padding to seal the evidence and avoid further breakage.

Imprint evidence (pattern wounds) from vehicles, such as bumper marks, unique logos, or tire prints, may be found on the body of the victim. These forms of impression evidence must be documented through photographs because they cannot be submitted to the lab for comparison purposes. Be sure to take photographs of the suspect vehicle and then insert a ruler or tape measure into the second set of pictures that clearly depicts the height of the bumper from the ground or the location of the logo in relation to other physical damage to the vehicle.

STOLEN VEHICLES

Auto theft crime rates have been showing an overall decline in recent years. The **National Insurance Crime Bureau (NICB)** conducts annual reviews of National Crime Information Center (NCIC) data for all 360 metropolitan statistical areas and compiles lists of the top ten makes and models of stolen vehicles in each location. This information is available on the NICB website under the "Hot Wheels" report. Older vehicles, such as the 1995 Honda Civic, continue to rank as the leading types of stolen automobiles.

Chop Shops

The Anti-Car Theft Act of 1992 defines a **chop shop** as any building, lot, facility, or other structure that is used for receiving, dismantling, destroying, or concealing passenger motor vehicles or parts that were illegally obtained (see Figure 12.7). The act prohibits the removal or falsification of **VINs** (vehicle identification numbers) and attempts to alter, deface, or destroy the identification of illegally obtained vehicles. The parts are usually worth more money than the vehicle, and once they are separated from the chassis, most do not have individual serial numbers so they cannot be linked to the original vehicle.

Salvaged vehicles have either been wrecked, burned, stripped, or are not worth repairing because the costs would exceed the fair market value of the vehicle. Car thieves purchase these salvaged vehicles from scrap yards for the VINs. Chop shop operators engage in a practice known as "salvage switching," whereby they remove the VIN plates from the salvaged vehicles and place them on stolen cars of the same make and model. VIN switchers will then create fraudulent vehicle titles and resell the car to unsuspecting victims.

In some cases, vehicles are stolen and all the parts are stripped off them, leaving the chassis abandoned. After the remnants of the vehicle are recovered by law enforcement, the stolen car report is canceled and the chassis is sent to the salvage yard. Chop shop owners will then purchase the chassis (with the title) and reassemble the vehicle, using the parts they removed when the car was stolen.

Car thieves generally operate in a geographic area commonly referred to as the "rip area." This location is in the vicinity of their chop shop or somewhere they can deliver stolen vehicles in a quick and convenient manner before the theft is reported by the victim.

FIGURE 12.7
Police credit a high-tech locating device on a stolen car with finding stolen autos at a "chop shop." *AP Photo/ George Widman.*

VIN Locations

The VIN is located on the left (driver) side of the dashboard, the driver side door jamb, and the engine block. You can also find a VIN on the title and the vehicle insurance card. Auto theft investigators are trained to check additional hidden locations where complete and partial VINs are included on vehicles, such as on the frame and inside

FIGURE 12.8
Automobile VIN plate secured on the dashboard by rosette-type rivets.

the trunk area. American vehicle manufacturers began using the VIN in 1954. Since 1981, the National Highway Traffic Safety Administration has required a 17-character fixed format. American-manufactured vehicles are required to have VIN plates attached to the dashboard using rosette-type rivets (six rose petals on each rivet; see Figure 12.8). Imported vehicles have metric-style pop rivets that are smaller and distinctive. Screws are occasionally used to mount VIN plates in imported cars, but they are never used in American-manufactured vehicles.

Manufacturers also embed electronic VIN numbers in various locations on a vehicle. Some makes and models have as many as six different computers and over 50 microprocessors from which this information can be retrieved. Auto theft detectives are trained and have access to obtain this information, which should be provided on supplemental reports when vehicles so equipped are involved in criminal investigations. A Federal Standard (SAE J1978) recommends storage of the VIN electronically. On-Board Diagnostics (OBD) is a 16-pin connector generally located under the dash near the steering column. Some do not retrieve the VIN but can provide other diagnostic information. The downside to relying on the OBD is that these on-board computers can be changed out. The International Association of Auto Theft Investigators offers additional training to law enforcement agencies (www.iaati.org).

VINs are used to track a vehicle from date of manufacture until it reaches the salvage yard. The VIN identifies the vehicle type, the factory where the vehicle was manufactured, and the year and week in which it was built. Each VIN is unique, and it is illegal for any two vehicles manufactured within the same 30 years to have the same VIN number.

Every digit in a VIN has a specific purpose. The first character identifies the country where the car was made; for example, the United States is signified by the number 1 or 4, whereas Japan is signified by the letter *J*. The second character may be a letter or number; it denotes the manufacturer such as Audi (*A*) or General Motors (*G*). Additional information, including body style and engine type, is coded into digits 3 through 8, and the 9th digit is a check digit that provides a method of cross-reference for validity. The model year of the vehicle is indicated by the 10th character, and the assembly plant is identified by the 11th digit. The remaining numbers and characters are unique to the vehicle and identify the sequence in which it came off the manufacturing line. The letters *I*, *O*, and *Q* never appear in a VIN.

Vehicle manufacturers must issue a manufacturer's certificate of origin (MCO) for each vehicle, which includes all identifying information concerning a specific vehicle. The MCO, which is more commonly known as the title, must accompany the vehicle through every transaction and is specially designed to thwart illegal copying or alterations. Various security features are incorporated into the design and printing of the vehicle title, including the use of sensitized security paper, complex combinations of ink colors, and a background security design that makes counterfeiting difficult to accomplish. The National Motor Vehicle Title Information System is a database that allows law enforcement and appropriate agencies to inquire about any vehicle or title. The system was designed to reduce auto theft and fraudulent titling of stolen cars. Car dealers, insurance companies, and private citizens can inquire about odometer readings, reported values, and other information pertinent to making a decision about purchasing a specific vehicle.

Various serial numbers appear on passenger cars, multipurpose vehicles, trucks, buses, trailers, incomplete vehicles, and motorcycles. The locations of these numbers can be determined by contacting local dealers and service departments. Every piece of construction or farm equipment has a unique product identification number (PIN), and all watercraft have a hull identification number (HIN) assigned to them by the manufacturer.

Electronic Vehicle Tracking and Recovery

Electronic tracking of stolen vehicles is available through the LoJack Corporation and its unique relationship with law enforcement. LoJack is the only vehicle tracking and recovery system that is completely integrated with law enforcement.

LoJack works on an FM radio signal, which allows penetration through obstacles that normally block out GPS signals, thus allowing recoveries in areas such as chop shops, underground garages, buildings, and shipping containers.

Police tracking computers (PTCs) are donated to law enforcement by LoJack and installed in cruisers, helicopters, and airplanes. Once the stolen vehicle is entered into the National Crime Information Center (NCIC) database, a signal is sent to the Vehicle Locating Unit that has been installed in the vehicle to a LoJack tower, which turns it on. The locating unit then emits a silent signal to the police vehicle, allowing the stolen vehicle to be tracked to its location.

LoJack is the only auto, truck, motorcycle, and construction equipment theft recovery system that is automatically activated and directly tracked by law enforcement.

Odometer Tampering

Odometer tampering is a federal crime, and it is estimated that annually more than $4 billion is lost due to odometer fraud. Disconnecting or resetting odometers, operating a vehicle with a nonfunctional odometer, and falsifying disclosure statements are also federal offenses. Vehicles with damaged or tampered odometers must be sold or transferred with a "True Mileage Unknown" statement, and the title will also reflect that the mileage is inaccurate.

PROCESSING EXTERIOR SURFACES OF VEHICLES

When you arrive to process a vehicle, the usual rules apply: consider where the most transient evidence may exist. Do not just jump into the car and take a look around! The areas most likely to have been touched by the suspect are the rearview mirror, steering wheel, gearshift knob or lever, door handle, glove compartment, windows, and possibly the trunk lid. Minimize the loss of trace or transient evidence by keeping people out of the vehicle. Most agencies will have a secure indoor location where vehicles can be taken for processing, and this is where the crime scene search should take place.

Before the vehicle is moved, document the location of the vehicle by using fixed points in your sketch, such as power poles with numbers on them, global positioning system (GPS) coordinates (if available), or buildings. **GPS** is a satellite navigation system that provides accuracy in location by providing longitude, latitude, and altitude in any kind of weather for any location in the world. Many first-responder agencies are now equipped with handheld GPS receivers, and the information they provide should be included in your crime scene documentation. Because vehicles are mobile and can be easily moved to another location, GPS coordinates are important when dealing with them and will help to establish venue and jurisdictional responsibilities.

Photograph the area where the car was found. Remember to take pictures of the VIN and the odometer. You should also examine and photograph the hidden serial numbers that are embedded on the chassis and engine block for future reference. When it is not possible to photograph the VIN plate, create a tape lift (see Figures 12.9a and 12.9b). Rub fingerprint ink over the numbers on the plate and place a piece of fingerprint tape or a lifter over the number to record the impression. Place the inked impression on an index card or piece of paper to preserve the numbers and then take photographs of this evidence.

Do not allow the vehicle to be removed until you have collected any soil samples or trace evidence (e.g., glass fragments). Remember to check

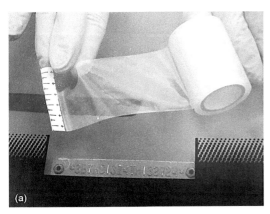
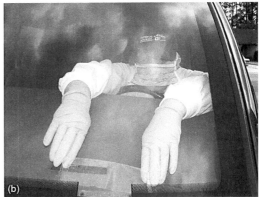

FIGURE 12.9
CSI creating a tape lift of the VIN of a vehicle. (a) Place ink or fingerprint powder on VIN. (b) Place tape over the inked/powdered VIN to create an impression.

for an entry/exit path to or from the vehicle in case the perpetrator tossed down any evidence. Take photographs and document the contents of the glove compartment, consoles, and trunk. Do not forget to check for hidden compartments, such as those built into vehicles used for moving drugs or weapons across state lines or national borders.

If you suspect that a vehicle was utilized to move a body, you should remove the seats and the carpeting both in the passenger compartment and in the trunk to check for bloodstains or other trace evidence. An alternate light source should also be used on the vehicle to check for the presence of body fluids, and this will require the vehicle to be in a darkened and secure area such as a garage. Luminol may also be used to check for traces of blood (see Figure 12.10). This process also requires a darkened location to view and photograph positive reactions. Be sure you are working in a well-ventilated area if you spray luminol because luminol's fumes are toxic.

FIGURE 12.10
Luminol being sprayed into the vehicle interior.

In the case of a hit-and-run investigation, the car will probably need to be placed on a hydraulic lift so that a complete examination of the undercarriage can be done. This will make photography of the vehicle easier because it allows the photographer to fully light the underside of the vehicle so as not to overlook any trace evidence. Hair, fibers, skin, and blood may be found on the bottom of the vehicle. Glass fragments and paint samples from various locations on the vehicle should be collected and labeled as known samples for submission to the crime laboratory.

Latent Fingerprints

When possible, it is advisable to process a vehicle in a secure and environmentally controlled location, such as a garage. It is possible to use powder and chemical processes on a vehicle that is outdoors, but it is easier to overcome obstacles such as weather-related issues if the vehicle is moved indoors. However, in circumstances such as car burglaries or vandalism, moving the vehicle is not usually part of agency protocol, so you must process the vehicle where it is located.

Sunlight and other weather concerns can cause fingerprints to deteriorate quickly on a vehicle. When metal is heated and exposed to sunlight, the perspiration and grease that compose latent print impressions will begin to evaporate and become difficult to detect, lift, and preserve. The combined effects of hot days and cool evenings will also take a toll on the quality of latent fingerprints on both the interior and exterior of a vehicle. Remember that the most likely places for a suspect to touch a vehicle include the rearview mirror, gearshift knob or lever, windows, glove compartment, and trunk lid. Follow standard procedures for determining the processing techniques. The most frequent method is fingerprint powder.

Superglue fuming is another useful tool for locating latent prints in a vehicle because it is easy to seal up the interior of the car or truck for fuming purposes. If you are going to fume the exterior of a vehicle, it will have to be placed inside a tent or other similar close quarters to achieve maximum exposure to the fumes.

Remember that if a vehicle is recovered wet, it must be allowed to dry before processing. If the exterior is cold, it should be slowly warmed to room temperature before you attempt to process for latent fingerprints.

Trace Evidence

You may not be able to collect enough glass to enable a reconstruction of broken fragments; however, adequate sample collection can make it possible for the forensic scientist to individualize the fragments to a common source. This is often important in cases of hit-and-run or burglary investigations. Whether a small-time burglar or a hit-and-run assailant, it is essential to place the suspect at the scene of a crime. Control samples from areas adjacent to locations with recent damage must be collected and submitted to the lab to assist in establishing linkages.

Always package glass fragments in solid containers to avoid further breakage. If you have collected the suspect's clothing to submit for examination, package each piece separately in paper and sealed bags to secure against loss of trace evidence. Remember to separate the layers of clothing (inside sleeves, pants legs, etc.) with paper or thin cardboard to prevent cross-contamination.

Direction-of-impact examinations require the CSI to gather all remaining glass in the headlight or reflector—and, if possible, indicate interior and exterior surfaces. The presence of dirt, paint, grease, or putty may indicate a particular exterior surface. With microscopic examination, it is possible to determine whether a light was activated at the time the impact occurred.

Transferability between the suspect, a suspect vehicle, and the scene makes soil samples valuable associative evidence that provides yet another linkage in the investigation. Even if you have not identified a crime scene, gather soil evidence where the vehicle is found—it can always be compared whenever a crime scene is determined. Remember not to be misled by the color of soil; it is always darker when wet and must be examined under controlled laboratory conditions.

It is important to gather control samples when you are collecting soil samples. In most cases, only the top-surface layer of soil will be picked up during the commission of a crime, so that is all you need to include in the evidence collection. Usually, about a tablespoon is all that the lab requires for a comparative analysis. All samples should be packaged and clearly labeled in individual containers. You should not make any effort to dislodge soil from garments or shoes. Submit the entire item to the crime lab wrapped in paper and secured inside a paper bag.

Cross-transference of fibers can occur in a hit-and-run case or in the course of a burglary attempt. The CSI has no way of measuring the value of individual evidence and should collect all fibers found at a crime scene. The evidentiary value of fibers is related to the forensic scientist's ability to trace their origin. The best possible circumstance is to match the torn edges of cloth together because then the evidence becomes based on individual characteristics instead of class characteristics (which is all most fiber comparisons can provide).

To collect fiber evidence (see Figure 12.11), fold the suspected surfaces inward, wrap in paper, and then secure in paper bags. Do not combine pieces of evidence; if you are submitting a rug or piece of carpet,

FIGURE 12.11
Fibers and other trace evidence being recovered from vehicle.

carefully fold and protect the surface. If you think a body may have been wrapped in a blanket or carpet, try using adhesive lifts on exposed areas of the body to try to locate fibers (or hairs). If you have a single fiber that you are afraid may be lost in transit, carefully remove it with a clean forceps and place it in a small folded piece of paper that is then secured inside another container.

It is not difficult for a forensic scientist to establish whether hair is of human or animal origin. Hair from different parts of the body varies significantly in physical characteristics, and you must submit adequate control samples of hair for forensic examination. A handy guideline would be to pull a total of 50 full-length head hairs from all areas of the scalp and a minimum of two dozen full-length hairs from the pubic area. Hair is class evidence; it is not usually possible to determine that a questioned hair came from a particular individual to the exclusion of all others, unless there are adequate skin cells attached that can be used for DNA analysis. The examiner can usually determine the race of the person from whom the suspect hair came, but age and sex cannot be determined except with infant hair.

Using an evidence vacuum to collect trace evidence in a vehicle is a standard procedure in many agencies. There is a high potential for cross-contamination unless the vacuum and filters are carefully changed before moving to the next grid area inside the vehicle. Submit the filter with the vacuum bag to ensure that the forensic scientist will have every bit of trace evidence collected for each grid. This procedure is generally reserved for major case crimes or when a vehicle is suspected of being used to transport a victim during the commission of a crime.

Stolen Property

Car thieves are not the only people who commit auto theft. Many times car owners are the perpetrators of the crime. Vehicle theft fraud occurs when an owner takes actions to report the car missing or tries to destroy the car so an insurance company will cover the losses. Cars are found burned, hidden, submerged, or driven off cliffs in many fraud investigations. Another scam is for an owner to hide a vehicle, report it stolen, and then accept a settlement from the insurance company. This is commonly known as the "30-day special," because it usually takes about 20 days for the insurance settlement check to arrive.

Frequently vehicles are reported stolen after the driver has been involved in an accident and leaves the scene without reporting the crash to the authorities. This is often the case when the driver was intoxicated or under the influence of illegal drugs and is trying to avoid arrest. When law enforcement officers locate the abandoned vehicle and contact the owner, the owner denies any knowledge of the accident or vehicle damage. This type of investigation is sometimes referred to as a "scapegoat case" because the driver/owner is seeking to avoid criminal charges and to keep from paying for any property and vehicle damages.

Contraband Search

The first step in conducting the search of a vehicle is to ensure that you have a valid right to proceed with the search. If it is not possible to obtain a consent to search from the owner of the vehicle, secure the vehicle until the case detective acquires a search warrant.

When you are preparing to search a motor vehicle, it is a good idea to don a pair of heavy work gloves for the preliminary search to protect yourself from hazardous items such as knives, syringes, or other sharp-edged items that may have been discarded under seats or between cushions. When possible, utilize canines trained to search for drugs or explosives prior to beginning a physical search. If a search dog alerts on a particular area of the vehicle, a separate search should be conducted focused on that area prior to advancing to the remainder of the vehicle.

If the vehicle is a passenger car, divide the interior into four grids: front left (driver), front right (passenger), left rear, and right rear. The trunk is also a separate grid. It is much easier to document, photograph, and sketch the search areas when using an organized grid, particularly when you are working in a confined space such as the passenger compartment of a motor vehicle. In some instances you might need to process the driver's grid at the scene to collect trace evidence prior to the car being moved to a secure location for thorough processing. Moving a vehicle means someone has to enter the driver's side before the vehicle can be towed or loaded onto a car hauler.

MOTOR VEHICLES AS WEAPONS

There are many facets to consider when discussing the use of a motor vehicle as a weapon. The average American car weighs about 4,000 pounds, and a tractor-trailer truck can weigh as much as 80,000 pounds. Add an impaired driver or a driver experiencing road rage, and the results can be deadly. Mechanical failures—whether deliberate or accidental—are also factors that must be considered at the scene of a motor vehicle crash. Mentally unstable drivers intent on

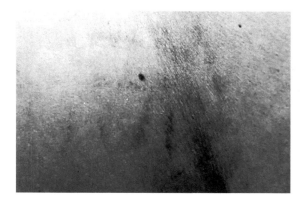

FIGURE 12.12A

Murder victim of a hit-and-run showing tire prints on abdomen of victim.

committing suicide do not consider whether the attempt to end their life will also endanger others on the roadway. Finally, terrorists can use motor vehicles as conveyances for explosives, as occurred at the bombings of Oklahoma City's Murrah Federal Building in 1995 and New York's World Trade Center in 1993. In this post-9/11 world, car bombs create crime scenes on a daily basis in the Middle East.

Documenting Injuries

Pattern injuries made when a vehicle comes into contact with a human being must be documented by photographs and written notes (see Figures 12.12a–12.12c). As the days pass from the time of the incident, abrasions and contusions will change color, swelling will subside, and a clearer image may develop on the skin of the victim (if living). It is usually recommended that a series of photographs be taken over the span of about one week to document the aging of a wound. Obviously, this practice will not take place on a deceased subject; in cases of deceased victims, the medical examiner will document the injuries during the initial observations of the body prior to autopsy. You should make arrangements to take additional photographs of the deceased victim at the funeral home after embalming has been completed but prior to the application of any funeral makeup because impression evidence often becomes more visible and easier to photograph once the embalming process has occurred.

FIGURE 12.12B

Through use of UV wavelengths of the alternate light source, a clear depiction of tire prints can be seen.

FIGURE 12.12C
Comparison of the UV prints on the body and the tire tread on the suspect vehicles is evidence that the suspect vehicle is the vehicle involved.

If there were multiple occupants in a vehicle involved in a crash, the position of each occupant must be determined and included in the documentation. Pay attention to the seat belts: Were they in use at the time of the crash? Talk to the first responders to determine if seat belts were removed when life-saving procedures were initiated. Many times the driver or occupants will be ejected from the vehicle, and it will be difficult to determine the position of each victim prior to the crash. When this situation occurs, it is up to the lead investigator to locate witnesses who can substantiate occupant positions. This may become a critical component of later criminal prosecution or civil litigation.

If a child is a victim of a motor vehicle crash, the presence or absence of a child safety seat must be documented when processing the vehicle. Carefully photograph the position of the device in the seat and determine if the child safety seat was correctly installed in the vehicle. Remember that the presence of a child safety seat does not automatically guarantee that it was being used at the time of the crash.

ACCIDENTAL DEATH—SUICIDE—HOMICIDE

Motor vehicle crashes claim the lives of thousands of people each year. Most of these deaths are ruled accidental, but some may be attributed to suicide or homicide, and some may be due to mechanical failures or road defects. It is essential to conduct the investigation of every crash involving a fatality the same as any other death investigation because the immediate cause of the crash may not be determined for weeks after the event occurred.

It is necessary to work closely with the medical examiner's or coroner's office because the autopsy will determine the cause and manner of death. Many car crash victims die as a result of blunt force trauma, much of which must be documented by the medical examiner when the investigation moves to the autopsy suite. Duplicate photographs and charts created by the medical examiner should be placed in the investigative file maintained by the case detective.

If a suicide note is found in a vehicle, photograph it and then protect any latent fingerprints by placing the note in a Ziploc-type bag. Make copies of the note for both the investigative file and the medical examiner's file. The original note should be submitted to the laboratory for chemical processing to determine if latent prints are present and to determine the identity of the individual who made those fingerprints.

Discussion Questions

1. What unique documentation is required of a vehicle that is involved in a crime scene?
2. You arrive on the scene of a known stolen vehicle. You are preparing to process the vehicle to retrieve any evidence possible to help identify the perpetrator. List what your procedures would be.
3. What unique documentation is required when motor vehicles come into contact with humans?

REFERENCE

http://www.vtti.vt.edu/featured/0413-distracted-driving.html. *The VTTI Driver Distraction in Commercial Vehicle Operations Study,* Virginia Tech Transportation Institute, Blacksburg, VA, July 2009.

CHAPTER 13

Death Investigation

KEY TERMS

Adipocere	Manner of death	Mummification
Algor mortis	(MOD)	Postmortem interval
Autopsy	Medical examiner	(PMI)
Cause of death (COD)	(ME)	Rigor mortis
Coroner	Medicolegal death	Skeletonization
Defensive wounds	investigation	
Livor mortis	(MDI)	

What You Will Learn

Death investigation always graces the most glamorous of TV crime shows. In fact, while we attempt to conduct a thorough investigation every time a human death is involved, there are many times when death occurs through undetermined causes. This is the most detailed chapter in the book and offers an insight for CSIs so that they will form a professional relationship with local medical examiners and coroners in an effort to simultaneously investigate and evaluate death scenes.

MURDER IN THE NEW YEAR

Death Investigation

Chief Medical Examiner Sara Evans joined Detective Fletcher and CSI Smith in her conference room. Opening her file, she leaned back in her chair.

> Mr. and Mrs. Morton died from gunshot wounds. Based upon entrance and exit wounds and casing, it appears the weapon is consistent with a small caliber bullet; however, you can never discern the caliber from the wound

DOI: 10.4324/9780429261657-13

size. Although the evidence concerning Mr. Morton's wound somewhat challenges the assumption that it was self-inflicted, the characteristics still fall within the range of possibility. You will need to check with a firearms expert to find out whether or not the specific weapon can be identified from physical evidence at the house. My crime scene consists of the bodies and the information I can determine from my medical examination of the victims during autopsy.

The CME leafed through several pages of the report. "Oh yes, seminal fluid analyses revealed that Mr. and Mrs. Morton had intercourse about an hour before they were killed."

Tom Smith looked at the CME and Detective Fletcher. "Sounds like the Mortons may have been on the mend and the dean was the odd man out."

Sara Evans closed her file. "One final thing—Mr. Morton had a pretty severe bite mark on the right side of his neck. We should have results on it tomorrow."

INTRODUCTION

A death investigation is the most complicated crime scene a CSI will process. Your observations of the victim on arrival at the scene and the documentation of those observations will play a very important role as the investigation moves through its various stages of completion. Determining how long a victim has been deceased is important in establishing the timeline that will be developed as the final events leading up to the death of the individual are reconstructed. This chapter provides you with the information needed to observe and process the death investigation crime scene accurately.

The protocols the CSI must follow for conducting the death scene investigation are the same established procedures used for every crime scene. Depending on the complexity of the scene, you may determine that additional resources are necessary, but the steps remain the same. Remember that not all deaths are homicides, but so that you do not miss subtle ones, you must investigate them as if they are homicides until the facts indicate that a homicide has not occurred.

Death investigations require additional authorities to be notified. In some jurisdictions, the medical examiner or coroner will be summoned to the scene; in other jurisdictions these officials will begin their investigation once the body arrives at the morgue. There are limitations to the actions a CSI can take related to processing a body before it is removed from the crime scene. You must be familiar with those protocols because they vary widely among cities, counties, and states. In the end, local custom often trumps best practices.

Begin your case notes by logging all dispatch information and the conditions of the scene when you arrived. Next, secure the scene, establish outer perimeters, and assign personnel to maintain the security and entry/exit logs. Conduct the initial crime scene assessment with the detectives and develop your plan for conducting the crime scene search. Often, death investigations will require, in addition to the medical examiner/coroner, the expertise of various disciplines, such as forensic anthropology and bloodstain pattern analyses (ANSI/ASB, 2021). Be sure the proper notifications are issued and that these resources are dispatched to the crime scene as you begin to conduct the investigation.

As with other crime scenes, indoor locations are easier to control and the environment is generally more constant than that of outdoor locations. Outdoor scenes require additional staffing and equipment. The weather conditions can greatly impact your ability to conduct the search for physical evidence. Circumstances may require the assistance of a specially trained rescue and recovery team, for example, an underwater recovery effort or a potential booby trap. Assist teams must be notified so that they can respond to the scene while your documentation process is under way.

Even to those well experienced in forensics investigations, the intersection of medicine and the law is unique. A 2009 National Academy of Sciences (NAS) report on the status and needs of the nation's forensic system included a separate chapter on the medicolegal death investigation process, indicating that medical forensics is different from other disciplines. Even so, all forensics investigations share many features. As noted by Sir Arthur Conan Doyle through Sherlock Holmes, three traits are required for excellence in investigation: observation, deduction, and knowledge. By knowing what might be of importance in a case, the investigator can make certain deductions about the nature of a given case. The ultimate responsibility of the scene forensics investigator is to document objectively, to the extent feasible, all pertinent positive, negative, and equivocal findings. These data are then available to assist in formulating conclusive opinions about the causative events. The opinions that are formed all hinge on the quality, quantity, and veracity of the scene and case documentation. A vital element, medicine, is the context; diagnoses are directly correlated to not only the laboratory results and the physical examination (the "evidence") but also to the circumstances, the patient's history. Without such context, a homicide might be missed, a suicide mistaken for an accident, or an innocent convicted for a crime he or she did not commit. *Context is everything.*

In medicolegal death investigations, forensics scene personnel come into direct interaction with the medical world. A basic understanding of the medical thought process and how different medicolegal systems are structured is fundamental to understanding how forensic investigations can be most effective. The most important principle in all forensics is to preserve as much evidence as possible, with analyses proceeding from noninvasive to minimally invasive to fully invasive to least destructive, and finally, if necessary, to most destructive.

At present, there is a push toward the concept of *evidence-based medicine* (EBM). This is the application of the scientific method (hypothesis testing based on experimentation and observable data collection) to medical decision making (i.e., making treatment choices among alternatives). EBM is being touted as a radical innovation in the practice of medicine. And it was when EBM first came into use more than 100 years ago. The general concept of scientific decision making based on theorizing and observable data is nothing new or outside the routine practice of medicine. The essence of all forensic scene work relies on documentation with this specific purpose in mind: to provide information that preserves the pertinent data (recognized, obscure, and covert) for potential later use, as necessary—in short, armed with foresight, providing probative evidence to later be placed into context.

MEDICOLEGAL DEATH INVESTIGATION

Conducting a **medicolegal death investigation (MDI)** is a statutory responsibility in cases of sudden, unnatural, unexpected death; these statutory duties are delineated in myriad ways in various jurisdictions. Although highly variable, as a rule of thumb, approximately 1 percent of any large population will die in any given year. Of those, some 20–50 percent will be cases requiring an MDI. At present there is no single national standard system for the investigation of sudden death; MDI Systems (MDIS) vary dramatically from one jurisdiction to the next. Except in a few locales (e.g., Texas with its justices of the peace), the official charged with leading the death investigation is either a coroner or a **medical examiner (ME)**. Some jurisdictions combine the two positions into a single Office of the Medical Examiner/Coroner (ME/C). Usually, the term **coroner** refers to an elected official and often has no minimum requisite educational standard. The ME, on the other hand, is generally an appointed office staffed by someone with a medical background, typically a physician but not necessarily a specialist in the medicine of sudden death and injury (forensic pathology). Roughly half of the US population is covered by approximately 239 ME systems, and the remaining half by coroners (see Box 13.1). Not surprisingly, the former tends to be in large population centers and the latter in more rural settings. In large part, this is related to cost effectiveness and the availability of medical specialists. Some estimate the break-even point for a cost-effective ME system is at 100,000 citizens. In the final analysis, it comes down to "you get what you pay for." Putting a price tag on justice, a fiscal reality of governance, is an arduous and controversial task. The population, as the payor, ultimately makes the decision of which system to utilize; however, this should be an informed decision based on a careful analysis of all parameters.

BOX 13.1 STATE DEATH INVESTIGATION SYSTEM BY TYPE: UNITED STATES*

Medical Examiner Systems (22)

A   State medical examiners (19)
  - Alaska
  - Connecticut
  - Delaware
  - District of Columbia
  - Iowa
  - Maine
  - Maryland
  - Massachusetts
  - New Hampshire
  - New Jersey
  - New Mexico
  - Oklahoma
  - Oregon
  - Rhode Island
  - Tennessee
  - Utah
  - Vermont
  - Virginia
  - West Virginia

B   District medical examiners (1)
  - Florida

C   County medical examiners (2)
  - Arizona
  - Michigan

Mixed Medical Examiner and Coroner Systems (18)

A   State medical examiner and county coroners/ medical examiners (7)
  - Alabama
  - Arkansas
  - Georgia
  - Kentucky

  - Mississippi
  - Montana
  - North Carolina

B   County medical examiners/coroners (11)
  - California
  - Hawaii
  - Illinois
  - Minnesota
  - Missouri
  - New York
  - Ohio (Ohio has one county medical examiner system—Summit County)
  - Pennsylvania
  - Texas
  - Washington
  - Wisconsin

Coroner Systems (11)

A   District coroners (2)
  - Kansas
  - Nevada

B   County coroners (9)
  - Colorado
  - Idaho
  - Indiana
  - Louisiana
  - Nebraska
  - North Dakota
  - South Carolina
  - South Dakota
  - Wyoming

---

* Centers for Disease Control and Prevention, www.cdc.gov/ EPO/dphsi/mecisp/summaries.htm.

Most frequently, the performance of the autopsy falls to the ME or the coroner's designee. In the latter case, the coroner typically contracts with a local practitioner for the service. Although, technically, any physician could conduct an autopsy, this is a recipe for disaster. Just as for other disciplines, the medical subspecialty of forensic pathology exists for a reason. Would one want a dermatologist performing brain surgery? This may seem trivial or petty, but it can have devastating effects on the justice system. Most physicians know precious little about the process of the autopsy—save for perhaps observing one or two while in medical school. Thus, possessing an MD hardly qualifies a physician to interpret an autopsy, let alone perform one. Regrettably, because of the scarcity of MEs, the CSI attempting to get answers in a case may turn to the local physician, who is, after all, a "real" doctor. The danger here is that one doesn't know what one doesn't know. When you are seeking a medical opinion, it is reasonable to seek out the best qualified expert available. The ideal for MDI is that a board-certified forensic pathologist (BCFP)—with four years of medical school, four to five years of internship/residency in pathology, and one to two years of subspecialty fellowship in forensic pathology—be available to conduct every examination. At present, there are only approximately 400 full-time actively practicing MEs in the country. To provide complete national coverage by BCFPs, twice as many would be needed. Some US counties do not even have a single physician in residence, let alone a subspecialist in an esoteric discipline such as forensic pathology.

As a practical matter, to ensure that MDI autopsy examinations proceed, many systems contract with local pathologists (physicians specializing in the laboratory study of disease) to perform autopsies. While not ideal, in many instances, that is the only available option. As recently as the mid-1970s, lay forensic scientists or technicians were conducting autopsy examinations on a regular basis in the United States. By today's standard, this would be *prima facie* medical malpractice. With a gradual increase in the understanding of the significance of the forensic autopsy, the bar of expectation has been raised. Practitioner accreditation and certification are now the endorsed, if not expected, baseline criteria. Regrettably, change is slow to come with a prior trend toward ME MDIS now stagnated due to the value added by competent professionals being muted by jurisdictional funding realities.

A certain level of basic expectations is assured by certification of the individual practitioner and accreditation of the office. The National Association of Medical Examiners (NAME), a professional organization for MDIs with MEs at the core, accredits ME offices. Only a fraction of US ME offices meet this criterion, although that number continues to gradually increase, and has recently spread to other countries. The American Board of Pathology is the only consensus provider of board certification of forensic pathologists in the United States. The American Board of Medicolegal Death Investigators (AB-MDI) provides certification for MDI practitioners. Remember, however, that the absence of accreditation and/or certification itself does not automatically mean an investigation is flawed or that the practice is substandard, but accreditation is intended to reflect that certain basic resources, personnel, and procedures are in place to meet expected case needs. Similarly, subspecialty certification documents that the individual has met a certain level of training and has demonstrated practical application of knowledge by successfully completing rigorous testing. The MDI process is an opinion; all parties will not necessarily agree on the conclusions reached. Debate and discussion about varying points of view should strengthen the ultimate confidence in a specific case. This once again speaks to the importance of data and context as the cornerstones of opinions and diagnoses.

Structure and Bias

The determination of the need for, and appropriate extent of, an examination properly rests with the medical professional charged with determining the cause and manner of death. In practice, this should be the ME or the contracted pathologist, who would be the one to render opinions based on observations. This is not a legal determination. The quality of the conclusion is predicated on the value of the evidence.

Another consideration is potential bias by the structure of the overall MDI. Some argue that any MDI should be completely removed from all law enforcement association. In many, if not most, areas, this is simply not practical. The only available scene investigative personnel, especially in rural areas, may be police or sheriff staff. The major concern, as noted by the 2009 NAS report, should be that the investigative section is administratively autonomous from the end user. The key is to remove the formulators of opinion (forensic labs and medical examiner or coroner) from those relying on those opinions for legal purposes (law enforcement personnel and attorneys). Because the raison d'être for the forensic sciences is to provide scientific information to assist with an investigation, it would be counterproductive to remove that investigative tool from those directly utilizing the information. Any potential bias should be avoided to the extent possible, but it should be recognized that the possibility of bias remains. The potential for concern should be obvious in law enforcement–associated fatalities, in which allegations often follow that excessive force was used, resulting in death. Likewise, a defense-hired medical expert might be tempted to shade an opinion in light of his or her employer's desired outcome. Objective neutrality is challenged by the necessities of the end user.

An investigation must rise above the possible desire for a conviction or win at the outcome of the case. In the American justice system as it currently exists, the criminal defendant is presumed innocent unless proven guilty. Superimposing neutral objective science on this framework becomes problematic. For example, an initial scientific opinion based on testing is considered more reliable if subsequent experiments find the same result. If repeated testing reaffirms an original conclusion to a reasonable degree of scientific certainty, then, in a perfect scientific-based legal system, all those affirmations of scientific fact, regardless of which side retained the expert, would be automatically admitted as probative. In reality, under the present rules, the defense would not want to admit scientific results from retained experts that support the prosecution and tend to incriminate their client.

Authorization

Cases requiring an MDI are delineated by code and typically involve sudden, unexpected, suspicious, and/or unnatural death. Different jurisdictions may expand the case selection criteria to include those occurring within a fixed time period following admission to the hospital or to those associated with surgical procedures. Because MDI cases are mandated by code, the ME is given authority to conduct the exam regardless of the next of kin's consent or denial. Ethical MDI practice should consider the true need for and extent of examination in each case, and then weigh the greater good against the individual harm given the case's specific parameters. A limited dissection or an external examination may accomplish enough to allow the statutorial duty of the MDI to be satisfied while recognizing the emotional needs of the survivors. In some areas, the law may also allow or even mandate exceptions—for example, based on religious grounds, a next of kin can in some areas prohibit an otherwise mandated autopsy from being conducted. An undercurrent behind such legal codicils is the failure of the MDIS to recognize legitimate concerns expressed by the users. Public outcry may trump best practices if those charged with providing the service of MDI fail to accommodate and address reasonable concerns where feasible.

Sometimes attorneys or law enforcement personnel may have a different point of view than the ME with regard to the need for and proper extent of an autopsy. What should remain immutable is the independence of the ME in making the ultimate decision. A dangerous and needlessly partisan situation may arise in which the medical portion of MDI is co-opted by nonmedical interests. An example of such potentially opposed medical and legal purposes involves organ/tissue procurement. In some jurisdictions, law enforcement personnel or attorneys have opposed procurement from homicide victims for fear of the potential loss of evidence. The reality is that procurement efforts go to great lengths to document the state of the body and individual organs. In those instances in which a diseased organ is removed for donation, a thorough examination with extensive documentation is made available and the postdissection tissue can be returned to the ME, if needed. The authorization of the procurement is a medical decision and hinges largely on the experience and comfort of the ME based on individual case circumstances. Ultimately, the needs of justice will dictate the proper resolution of a specific case.

One fundamental purpose of the MDI is to answer questions. In formulating responses, investigators should bear in mind that there are two types of data: fact and opinion. A report for a postmortem examination should clearly delineate these two information sets. The autopsy report should include a thorough factual description of wounds found. The significance of the various wounds and potential associated effects would be opinion, and thus should be included in a separately designated section (often titled "Opinions," "Diagnoses," or "Findings"). In a case in which there are numerous wounds, the specific absence of injuries to the decedent's arms (defense wounds) would have potential import to the investigators. The presence of these injuries is a fact, while the interpretation of the same—whether defensive or offensive—is based on case-specific parameters. There are a great many negative or absent findings and, for the sake of brevity, in the absence of an affirmation, findings are generally considered to be "normal" or "negative" unless specifically stated to the contrary. A prudent investigator should bear in mind the absence of expected negative and/or unexpected positive findings and, if unsure, should confirm concerns with the ME. There is always the possibility that certain elements were overlooked or were inconspicuous during the course of the examination. A detailed case review, including scene and autopsy photographs in particular, may uncover more subtle latent elements of an examination (see Box 13.2).

In formulating opinions about a case, many MEs choose to invoke *lex parsi-moniae* (the law of parsimony), which basically states that the simplest explanation to explain all circumstances is usually the best. Scenarios with complicated chains of events can be exploited by those speculating on possible answers as opposed to probable or likely ones. In a medicolegal criminal case, the occurrence of truth (primary truth) involves the interaction of the victim(s), the perpetrator(s), and the crime scene(s). The subsequent investigative revelation of that truth (secondary truth) requires successful interplay between the witness(es), scene(s), evidence, and investigation. This secondary truth is not exactly what happened but what the evidence indicates happened. It is often incomplete but represents the best that can be derived from the known data.

In court, this investigative conclusion is determined by the interplay between the judge, attorneys, and jury; the arbiter of fact finds the tertiary truth, in that it is twice again removed from the actual event. The case presented in court filters out that which is not allowed as evidence and is editorialized upon by both sides in the partisan process of adjudication. Thus, the ultimate finding of "fact" in court may bear little relation to what actually did happen—a guilty person may be acquitted because the proof of the primary truth, as conveyed through the investigation of the secondary truth and presented as

BOX 13.2 WHAT CAN WE FIND OUT FROM A MEDICAL EXAMINER'S AUTOPSY?

- Identification of the deceased individual
- Cause of death
- Manner of death
- Time of death
- Presence of disease or poisons
- Nature and number of injuries
- Presence of an environmental or health threat to the general population

tertiary truth in court, was insufficient to convince the jury to a reasonable degree of certainty.

The Death/Injury Scene

In investigating fatalities involving foul play, time is critical. Expedient reliable information is an investigative asset for detectives, while the passage of time favors the perpetrator. The more valid data investigators have, the better they can allocate their resources to effect an appropriate resolution to their investigation.

Different systems establish different roles for providers at the death scene. Effective interaction between the ME/C, law enforcement, and others at the scene is essential to ensure success. In many jurisdictions, the autopsy pathologist does not regularly attend the death scene. As such, the pathologist may be of little help in processing a death scene. By contrast, other jurisdictions require a physician to respond (not necessarily an ME), for example, to all homicides or all suspicious deaths or all high-profile deaths. In the latter situation, an experienced practitioner often provides directly relevant, region-specific opinions that may be helpful; however, this falls short of the ideal of a properly trained and qualified MDI. The ideal MDIS must work within jurisdictional and logistical constraints to achieve the best possible outcome.

FIGURE 13.1
Three overlapping strata to arrive at autopsy diagnosis.

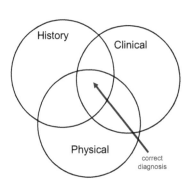

Preparation

To arrive at an ultimate valid conclusion, the autopsy, like any other medical procedure, employs three overlapping strata to arrive at a diagnosis: (1) history, (2) physical, and (3) clinical (see Figure 13.1). Even though each approach could reach the right answer independent of the others, where all coincide, one has the best likelihood of having arrived at the correct diagnosis.

Differential diagnosis is a concept employed by physicians whereby the rank order of likely potential diagnoses is established. Even remote possibilities may be viable alternatives at some point in the thought process. As new data is received, certain possible diagnoses become more or less likely and so move up or down or even off the list of differential diagnoses until one is left with a conclusive diagnosis. Diagnosis is an opinion and may be held to various degrees of certainty—reasonable certainty in criminal matters or reasonable probability in civil matters. There is no precise or reproducible quantitative metric to determine certainty versus probability, except that the latter is simply "more likely than not."

To arrive at the final opinion with regard to the facts associated with an individual case, one may benefit from considering the various levels of certainty regarding the relative potential lethality (certain, potential, marginal, none, or unknown/undetermined) of a specific physical (gross autopsy and/or microscopic), historical (scene and/or past or present medical or other data), or clinical (toxicology and/or other lab testing) finding (see Figure 13.2). The strongest opinions are those that consider all elements. Some tests will be superfluous (e.g., the concentration of a specific drug likely has little direct bearing on the cause of death in a fatal gunshot wound of the head). The circumstances surrounding a specific case might warrant such testing, but a blanket approach by which "all autopsies get complete toxicology" seems rarely justifiable and is particularly burdensome when lab systems are facing severe budget constraints. Think of the postmortem examination as managed health care in its earliest and purest form. Testing is performed to the extent deemed medically prudent. In some cases, it may be vital to prove a negative test result to properly classify the death.

Cause of death classification

Relative Significance	Pathology		Toxicology	Scene	History	Clinical
	Gross	Micro				
Lethal						
Potentially lethal						
Marginal						
None demonstrable						
Undetermined						

FIGURE 13.2
Levels of certainty regarding lethality of physical, historical, and clinical findings. Adapted from Hirsch & Adams (1993).

The Autopsy

The process of a thorough medicolegal **autopsy** is more than simply a physical evisceration and examination of the organs. The process involves a series of steps with the ultimate goal of determining the cause and manner of death. History is an essential step in the medical diagnostic arsenal. Based on historical information, the MDIS office makes a determination as to whether an exam is indicated and what the extent of such an exam should be. Some cases may be released based solely on the history; for example, a 65-year-old with a history of coronary artery disease or a terminal cancer patient probably does not need a thorough MDI-level exam. Each consult should be weighed on its own merit: people with natural disease can still die an unnatural death, but the presence of natural disease does not ensure a natural death. Furthermore, history helps in the appropriate triage of a case, ensuring that the appropriate indicated specimens are collected and tests requested. Not all analyses are necessary or helpful in all cases. Certain rare diagnoses may require very specific sample collection, handling, and processing, costing time and money that would cripple the system if applied to every case. For example, tests for anaphylaxis (overwhelming lethal systemic allergic reaction) need a blood sample collected in a specific way as soon as possible. The confirmatory test is not cost effective in the vast majority of cases but is essential when called for. The physician responsible for the totality of the case should determine such particulars on a case-by-case basis, and the ME requires the person's medical history to make such decisions appropriately.

If a case is accepted, the next step is a complete detailed external exam (see the left side of the circle in Figure 13.3), documenting all pertinent positive and negative findings, including the clothing, trauma, personal effects, trace evidence/foreign materials, atypical odors, and so on. Once the ME is satisfied with the overview of the body as received, the body is reevaluated when cleaned up and nude. The ME might proceed to an internal exam (see the right side of the circle in Figure 13.3) with a detailed examination of the internal organs of the torso and the brain. Three systems are most important in the acute sense of maintaining life: the heart, lungs, and brain (also referred to as the central nervous system, or CNS). All have in common the delivery and use of oxygen as the fuel that sustains life, with the respiratory system as the gas tank, the heart as the pump, and the brain as the engine driving the system. Most sudden deaths involve the failure

FIGURE 13.3
The broadest circle: the autopsy.

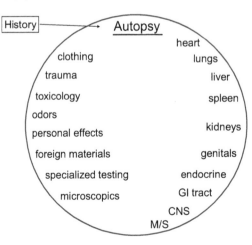

of one or more of these processes, the heart being the most common single cause of sudden unexpected death.

The gross examination of the body is far from the final step in the process. Evidence obtained from the examination will be analyzed and may provide pertinent data for the ME. For example, the blood and tissue samples collected at the autopsy may be sent for toxicology testing. Other tests (e.g., genetic testing in pediatric deaths) may also be requested. If the victim was treated in the field or in the hospital, those records should be made available to the ME. Admission blood and other samples should be retrieved as soon as possible because these more accurately reflect the level of drugs in the victim at the time of injury than they would subsequently. Similarly, if surgery removed possible evidence (e.g., a bullet in a gunshot wound case or a portion of skull in a head trauma case), it is prudent to attempt to recover such items as soon as possible. On occasion, a portion of a skull fracture may retain pattern evidence leading investigators back to a specific weapon. Hospitals and labs have specific policies regarding how long samples are held, and they often discard what they regard as "unnecessary" materials within a matter of days. A good operating premise for the MDI and the CSI is that it is better to have it and not need it than to need it and not have it.

Next, the MDI will come back to the history in order to obtain more specific information (see Figure 13.4). In many instances, this takes the form of generic open-ended questions followed by targeted

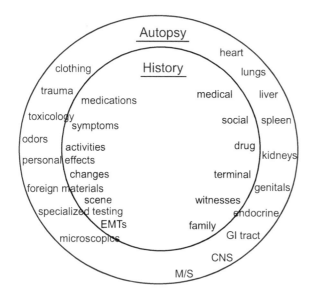

FIGURE 13.4
The circle gets narrower: history.

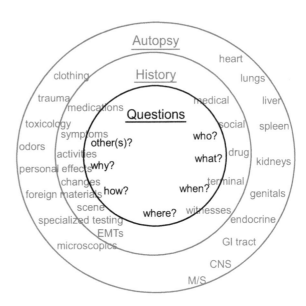

FIGURE 13.5
The circle gets narrower still: questions are asked about history to provide context.

queries intended to winnow out the specific circumstances associated with an individual death (see Figure 13.5).

These may take the form of interviews with associates, family, friends, emergency medical technicians/first responders, private physicians, and so on (basically anyone who might have history that is considered potentially enlightening based on investigative leads). The questioner may be particularly interested in issues such as changes demonstrated (in activities, behavior, or otherwise) at or near the time of death or immediately prior to terminal events, recent or past symptoms or signs, or medications (new, old, and altered). Each area explored may help in explaining gross observations at autopsy by helping place findings into a proper clinical context. For example, in a case of presumed drowning, an elicited past history of "butterflies in the chest" with exercise or episodic shortness of breath, not initially reported, may warrant a follow-up genetic test and medical investigation for cardiac anomalies such as long Q-T syndrome, which might explain why the subject succumbed. Once again, the context can provide the right answers.

Once sufficient additional history and testing have been conducted, the ME can narrow the focus to ascertain the fundamental answers as to why this person experienced these symptoms at this time.

Finally, when all the data are considered, one arrives at the correct diagnosis of the **cause of death (COD)**. Note that this approach starts with a very broad overview and, through a systematic analysis of all

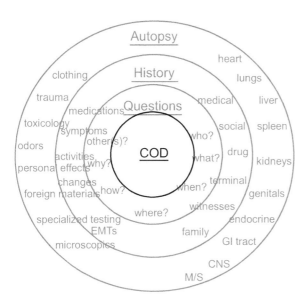

FIGURE 13.6
The circle zeros in on cause of death (COD).

available data, gradually focuses in on relevant (positive or negative) data, considering all possible diagnoses to eventually arrive at the most probable COD (see Figure 13.6).

The Report

Not all examinations are performed in every case. The basic internal medicolegal autopsy (see Figure 13.7) should include the examination of the skin and subcutaneous tissues of the torso, the chest wall, all the torso contents, the tissues of the scalp, the top and floor of the skull, and the brain and cranial contents. Some MEs may individually remove each organ for dissection (complete autopsy), whereas others target only specific tissues (limited autopsy) to determine the COD.

Specialized dissections may also be performed depending on the needs of a specific exam. For example, if there is a question of neck trauma, the ME may perform a posterior neck dissection to better evaluate the vertebrae and spinal cord. Finding a pulmonary thromboembolism (blood clot in the vessels of the lung) may necessitate turning the body over and dissecting the veins of the back

FIGURE 13.7
Opening the "Y" incision made by the medical examiner during the autopsy. *Tennessee State Medical Examiner's Office.*

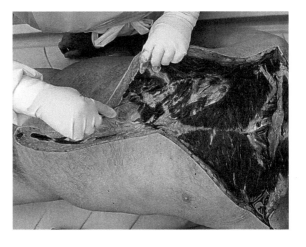

of the legs in order to find the point of origin of the clot. Similarly, if there is a possibility of pneumothorax (free air in the chest cavity), the chest may be opened under water to demonstrate the air. Inmates and victims of child abuse cases often have the body essentially flayed (the entire skin with subjacent soft tissues is dissected off) to expose the deeper tissues underneath, allowing the ME to confirm or refute inflicted trauma to inconspicuous areas. There are many additional examples, but the basic principle remains the same: the ME should perform a detailed exam to the extent necessary to document the physical state of the body and determine the COD.

Death Certification

One of the primary functions of the ME/C is to complete the death certificate (DC). The DC includes sections for demographic data, COD, other significant condition(s), manner of death, how injury occurred, certifier, and disposition of the body. The purpose of the DC is basically administrative: it allows proof that the individual designated is actually deceased, and it categorizes causes of death within a population for vital statistics/public health department use. To the extent that they are medical diagnoses, the statements of cause and manner of death are opinions and should be based on the best available data. The cause is usually derived from the triad of physical exam/autopsy, history/record review, and clinical testing. The manner is usually reliant on investigative circumstances.

Cause of Death

The COD is the initial event setting in motion the unbroken chain of events ultimately ending in death. Most times, the COD is determined by the ME/C based on the autopsy examination. Most cases coming to the ME/C's attention do not involve foul play. Atraumatic causes of death may include coronary artery disease, cancer, emphysema/chronic obstructive pulmonary disease (COPD), cirrhosis from hepatitis, diabetes mellitus, and so on. Traumatic causes of death might include gunshot wounds, stab wounds, multiple blunt force injuries, and the like. No way of stating the COD is unequivocally more right than others, but there might be better ways to state a cause depending on the specific case. For example, in a car crash, it would not be advisable to call the COD a motor vehicle *accident*, as this predetermines that the fatality was the result of an accident; a better term would be motor vehicle *crash* or *collision* (MVC). A better choice for the COD would be *blunt force injury* (BFI), although some might call the same case *multiple blunt force injuries* (MBFIs). Technically, even if the body is extensively traumatized in a car wreck, the causative kinetic energy resulting in death was applied only once.

This distinction allows a clearer distinction between a single MVC (BFI) and a decedent repeatedly beaten (MBFI). In addition, for the purposes of death certification, the death certificate includes a section for the ME/C to indicate "how injury occurred" to indicate a shorthand of the context. If an MVC were associated with the cause, it would properly be included in that section.

COD is a neutral objective summation of what happened to the decedent that ultimately ended in death. Often the deceased will have multiple diseases or conditions associated with death. The death certificate recognizes this possibility by including a separate section for listing "other significant conditions" (also known as "contributory cause of death") that are associated with the fatality but are not listed in the main section. An example might be coronary artery disease as the COD, with COPD as a contributory COD.

On occasion, a death may be so complex as to defy easy description. In such circumstances, it may be prudent to adopt an all-inclusive COD statement. For example, if an individual under the influence of crack cocaine overdose experiences an excited delirium state and becomes a danger to the public at large, the police might attempt to eliminate the threat. If, during attempts to subdue the individual, the officers utilize pepper spray and batons without the apparent desired effect and the subject becomes more agitated and grabs one of the officer's handguns, the escalation of the force continuum has reached the level at which lethal force is accepted. While wrestling over the weapon, an officer strangles the subject (hands being the only available weapon at that point in time) into unconsciousness. The subject is then placed in a prone position and handcuffed into a fetal position. On examination, the suspect is found to have no vital signs, and resuscitative efforts are unsuccessful. If the autopsy and investigation confirm all the foregoing events and exclude any additional pertinent findings, how would the COD be certified? It would be appropriate to condense the statement to a multifactorial description of what happened, such as "excited delirium (acute cocaine use) with multiple blunt force injuries (baton blows), pepper spray use, manual strangulation, and prone restraint"—or even more briefly as "excited delirium with subdual process." Because the death has so many overlapping and concurrent events, neither description is wrong, as long as the words used attempt to describe as best as possible the perimortem situation culminating in death.

The ME/C is concerned with the proximate COD, which may have occurred at a temporally distinct point from the physical death. Conceptually, the duration of such an interval would be irrelevant to the ME/C. For example, a patient with an HIV infection may have survived for years but eventually succumbed as a result of a suppressed immune system by way of an opportunistic infection. In some jurisdictions, there is a "year and a day" rule as a holdover from English common law. Such concerns are actually more appropriate for legal consideration in the medicolegal equation. A district attorney may decide that a delayed death may not be prosecutable due to the lack of a clear and unquestioned relational timeline between the initiating event and the death. Such justice system issues have no place in the medical decision-making process.

Manner of Death

The **manner of death (MOD)** is a description of the circumstances surrounding the COD. The MOD is usually, although not exclusively, determined by investigation. By convention, most areas limit the possible MOD to one of five choices: natural, homicide, suicide, accident, and undetermined. A few areas include "therapeutic misadventure" to describe those cases in which death occurred inadvertently in association with medical therapeutic endeavors.

Natural deaths are self-evident: those fatalities without any associated foul play. Although it would seem a very clear-cut category, there are many exceptions. For example, pneumonia is usually considered a natural death, but such is not necessarily the case.

Homicides (*homo* 5 man; *cide* 5 to kill) are likewise easily defined: the death of one person at the hands of another. It can become more difficult in the application, though, because some people mistakenly insert the legal construct of intent into the medical description of a death. ME/Cs should specifically ignore the intent behind the act; intent is the purview of the members of the jury, who make a determination among various legal gradations of culpability. Some homicides (e.g., deaths occurring as the result of an act of war, capital executions by the state, deaths committed by a persons in self-defense) are socially acceptable, yet they remain homicides.

Suicide (*sui* 5 self; *cide* 5 to kill) also seems deceptively simple: the death of a person by his or her own hand. Again, one need not invoke real or perceived intent as long as a lethal outcome is reasonably foreseen and reasonably foreseeable, and the deceased abrogates his or her volitional control preventing that outcome. For instance, if an individual were to take a bottle full of prescription medications in a suicidal gesture with the intent not of dying but of calling for help and being rescued, his or her plan may prove partially successful. If the person goes to the hospital and has his or her stomach pumped but develops fatal pneumonia as a consequence of the hospitalization, the death is still properly certified as suicide.

Accidental deaths would be those in which the lethal outcome is not reasonably foreseen or foreseeable and about which there is no volitional control. In the preceding example, although uncommon, hospital-acquired pneumonia is an accepted fact, and despite best therapeutic efforts cannot always be avoided. As such, a rare bad outcome is still an accepted risk. MVCs are most often accidents because it is not reasonable to foresee that at any given time a drunk driver will cross the center line and kill the occupants of the other vehicle. The ME/C calls such cases "accidents" by convention, but the courts would call the exact same circumstances "vehicular homicide." It is important to bear in mind that even though they overlap in the medicolegal arena, medical and legal terminologies may use the same words but attach different meanings.

Undetermined is a special category typically reserved for those cases not easily fitting into the other four designations. This class is typically reserved for approximately 2–5 percent of all MDI cases. If the investigation does not provide a clear indication of the circumstances, or if the ME/C finds that the investigation cannot be clearly delineated, then the death is called "undetermined." An obvious case in this category would be skeletal remains when there is no specific finding of any type, so both cause and manner may be unspecified. Another type of undetermined case involves suspicious deaths in which there is insufficient proof to establish exactly what happened to the decedent and the COD is designated undetermined. Because the cause is undetermined, reasonably there is little way to specify the circumstances surrounding the death. Many jurisdictions call all drug-associated deaths "undetermined" because they hold that the investigation cannot typically determine all of the variables associated with the death. Other ME/Cs classify all drug deaths as accidents unless they have clear evidence to the contrary. Again, neither approach is necessarily wrong, as they are based on local custom and practice that have proven effective and reproducible in that area over the years. The importance of context in reaching conclusions should be reiterated especially in these equivocal cases. When skeletonized remains bear minimal physical stigmata of trauma, the investigative circumstances may make a compelling case that the death occurred by nonnatural means, and in some cases, the determination of the COD as "unspecified violence" may be appropriate.

With an overview of all the manners of death, one can see that the same COD may have different manners of death. Pneumonia may seem at first to be natural, but it could actually fit all five manners depending on circumstances. The common community-acquired respiratory infection is natural; a delayed death from a car crash with rib fractures and related hospital- or home-acquired pneumonia is accidental; the overdose, cry-for-help, delayed death is suicidal; a gunshot wound causing paralysis with subsequent related pneumonia is homicidal; and the case with unclear circumstances is undetermined.

An acute alcohol overdose would typically be an accident. However, a chronic alcoholic's death, also due directly to the effects of ethanol, would by convention be a natural death because it is an accepted natural disease and a fatal outcome is common; there is no invocation of foul play. If an unnatural element occurs in the causation of death, then that unnatural element takes precedence over the natural, and the more unnatural over the less unnatural. Therefore, homicide would be the ultimate nonnatural manner, suicide would take precedence over accident, and so on. This determination makes no moral judgment or statement of intent; rather it is a shorthand descriptor of circumstances.

Time may be important to the legal aspect of a case but should be unimportant to the ME/C. The important factor in determining COD and MOD is linkage, not time. If one were trying to prove an association in court, it is far easier to do so the closer the proximate event is to the terminal event. A lay jury needs to be able to connect both points. With a lengthy gap of weeks, months, or years, they may fail to make the connection between the beginning and end. However, the circumstances associated with a death are what they are. If a paraplegic dies from associated pneumonia, and it is shown that said paraplegia was the result of a spinal cord injury from a gunshot wound at some significant period (e.g., 20 years) earlier, and that injury occurred during a robbery attempt in which the shooter pointed the weapon in the air with the bullet going through the roof to strike the victim in the room above, then the ultimate death is a homicide, regardless of the interval and regardless of the shooter's intent. In the medicolegal context, the result is what is important.

Postmortem Interval

One of the most misunderstood elements in all of medicolegal death investigation is the establishment of the **postmortem interval (PMI)**, that is, the estimated time since death. The only certain way to establish the PMI is to discover a witness with a watch. Short of that, the investigator is left with estimates based on observation and experience. An established progression of changes provides the data from which PMI estimates are derived. The important caution is that there is no single consistently reliable indicator. An example of significant potential error would be attempting to determine time since death based on gastric emptying. Because the content of the meal and other factors (such as alcohol consumption) are known to markedly impact the emptying rate, such indices should be considered as "soft" signs and used as supportive evidence rather than as definitive scientifically precise data points. Other estimates may be calculated based on vitreous humor (eye fluid), salt (specifically potassium) content, or other validated indices of degradation rate. A newer area of inquiry involves decompositional odor analysis. While promising, over-reliance on any one parameter and false confidence in precision can prove a recipe for disaster. In the end, the investigation of the scene typically proves most helpful with things such as receipts, phone records, mail, computer activity, and so on, giving significant potential clues.

Three general categories of postmortem changes occur: early, late, and tissue. Death involves obvious acute changes: loss of vital signs (pulse, respiration) in addition to short-interval changes. Longer intervals lead to delayed changes of decomposition. Temperature can have a significant impact. In general, heat accelerates the postmortem reaction, and cold delays it. Another confounding variable is the physical location of the body. A crude estimate is that one day on land is equivalent to one week in the water or one month buried, but all could be affected by the state of the body, including premortem and postmortem wounds, exposure (clothing, wrapping, etc.), temperature (extremes), and a host of other factors. Biological systems have myriad internal variables that combine with the variety of external conditions. This is where the experience of the medicolegal investigator is critical. It is important to understand how variables may be important in explaining the conditions observed at autopsy. If relevant information is not adequately documented, it could significantly impact the subsequent opinions formed. The net effect could lead the ME to a perfectly logical but completely erroneous cause and MOD determination.

The early changes of death are readily appreciable even to the novice: cessation of respiration, cessation of circulation, skin pallor, muscle relaxation, eye changes (both the cornea and retina), and blood coagulation/fluidity. Later changes include the classic indices of death: rigor mortis, livor mortis, and algor mortis.

Algor mortis, or the cooling of the body following death, can be crudely estimated as 1–1.5°F per hour or by the following formula:

$$98.6°F - [\text{measured rectal temperature } °F]/1.5 = \text{estimated hours since death}$$

Such a calculation assumes a normal precise starting temperature, however, which is seldom the case. In addition, temperature changes are affected by the decedent's health (e.g., an infection such as pneumonia may change a subject's baseline body temperature—up or down). Perimortem circumstances are also important: for example, an extreme struggle or exercise might produce a fever while prolonged shock could lead to an abnormally low temperature. Environmental temperature is an important consideration. The body temperature may also rise after death due to residual tissue metabolism and normal bacterial activity and may remain elevated for several hours. An investigator should never insert a probe or thermometer into a body cavity, orifice, or wound or create a defect in order to measure temperature unless explicitly so instructed. If a temperature reading is desired, an adhesive thermometer aquarium strip can be placed on the forehead, or an infrared device can be used to document the temperature in a noninvasive manner.

Livor mortis (lividity) is a physical process by which the color of the skin darkens due to time-dependent gravitational settling of the blood within the capillaries. Although the process starts immediately with death (or, rarely, could start before death if there is markedly low blood pressure), it is generally not visible in the first 30 minutes. Most observers should be able to appreciate livor mortis within 2–4 hours of death. Gravitationally dependent dark areas surround the area of the body in contact with the resting surface. The latter appears pale or blanched because the small vessels are compressed, precluding blood from settling there (see Figure 13.8). Likewise, tight clothing or body parts may restrict the settling, leading to a corresponding pattern on the body. In some cases (especially where the body was undressed, redressed, or moved), this provides vital information about the state the body was in after death. Lividity continues to form for up to 8–12 hours after death, at which time it will be maximal. If the body is cooled, this process can be slowed at a temperature-variable rate, and thus it may take 24–36 hours in a cool environment or perhaps even longer in a morgue refrigerator. Up to approximately 24 hours postmortem, the examiner can push in on the affected area, and the pressure of the fingertip will drive blood out of the affected capillaries. During this period, the lividity is described as "blanchable." If the body is moved during the period of blanchable lividity, the body may exhibit multiple patterns reflecting different gravitationally dependent positions. After the first day, the livor mortis will become

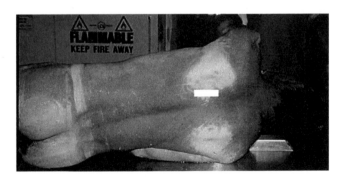

FIGURE 13.8
The lack of lividity on the shoulder blades and buttocks of the victim indicate that the body was lying against a hard surface prior to discovery. *Tennessee State Medical Examiner's Office.*

fixed and will no longer blanch with pressure. Livor mortis remains as formed once it becomes fixed; however, it will become obscured by other postmortem changes involving discoloration of the body. One special consideration in lividity is the formation of Tardieu spots, dark circular areas that are similar in appearance to petechial hemorrhages. These spots result from gravitationally dependent capillary ruptures and so are most common in the lowest areas of the body and are increased by a more anatomically vertical position.

Rigor mortis (rigidity), the postmortem stiffening of the body muscles, is also a time-dependent physical process. The process occurs immediately and at a uniform rate in all muscles simultaneously, although it is often first appreciated in the smaller muscles like the fingers and jaw. Experienced observers may detect rigor mortis within the first half-hour, and most should detect rigor by 1–6 hours postmortem. With increased time, the chemical reaction continues, reaching a maximum at somewhere between 6 and 24 hours. A shorter interval would be expected in hot environments and a longer one in cool environments. A unique category of instantaneous rigor mortis, termed *cadaveric spasm*, may be seen in deaths in which the subject had a high immediate premortem metabolic state with increased lactic acid and/or temperature—seizures/convulsions, exercise (swimming/running), violent struggle (physical assault), systemic infection (pneumonia/sepsis), and so on. This may be important in an investigation because the victim may grasp items at the point of death (*in extremis*) and such evidence may later prove significant. Various degrees of rigor may be designated as none (0); early, developing, partial (11/21); moderate (31); or full (41). If the muscles are forcibly moved, the cellular bonds are disrupted and the rigor mortis is described as "broken."

During the period in which rigor mortis is still forming, if sufficient cellular chemicals remain, it may reform after it has been broken. This principle is sometimes exploited to assist with estimating the PMI: rigor mortis can be broken in one extremity at the scene (test) with the opposite left as is (control). The areas are then reevaluated in the morgue to determine the extent to which rigor mortis has changed in the defined interval between body recovery and postmortem examination. Once the involved elements are depleted, the reaction reverses and it disappears or passes. This is very much temperature dependent: in hot environments, rigor mortis may pass within 24 hours (earlier if there was cadaveric spasm to start), whereas in colder climates and/or refrigerated bodies, rigor mortis may persist for up to a week or possibly longer. Freezing the body stops the chemical reaction, but the postmortem changes are accelerated after thawing due to microstructural damage associated with ice crystals. The specialized descriptor of *cutis anserina* refers to goose

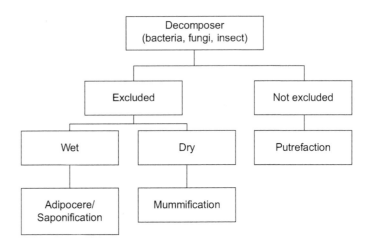

FIGURE 13.9
Patterns of decomposition.

bumps seen in a deceased body. These are the result of rigor mortis affecting the small muscles attached to individual hair follicles.

Tissue changes occur later, usually at 24 or more hours after death, and are time, temperature, climate, and environmentally driven. While classically individually described, all these changes occur at variable and overlapping rates and may be visible simultaneously in any one body. The major tissue degradation processes are decomposition, mummification, adipocere, and skeletonization (see Figure 13.9).

The first noticeable change is clouding of the corneas of the eyes, which occurs at approximately 24 hours. *Tache noire* (literally, "black touch") refers to the dark discoloration of the cornea when the eyelid is partially opened and results from the normally repeatedly moistened area being exposed and allowed to dry.

Decomposition involves two simultaneous processes: *autolysis* (self-digestion by released cellular enzymes) and *putrefaction* (microbial destruction). Factors influential in decomposition include the environment, clothing, temperature, humidity, light, covering, location, and so on.

Typically, significant decomposition is visible after approximately 24–36 hours, first as a green abdomen—usually the right lower quadrant. With increased time, the color becomes more prominent and darker. The next visible stage, at approximately 60–72 hours, is marbling (see Figure 13.10). The cutaneous blood vessels become visibly green-black to eventually dark purple-black due to intravascular hydrogen sulfide gas production. The pattern is reminiscent of a spider web on the skin. Beginning at about 36–48 hours, and maximal by about three days, the body enters the bloated stage of decomposition wherein the tissues swell due to the postmortem production of tissue gas. This is

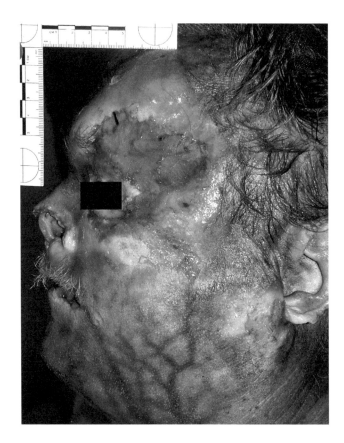

FIGURE 13.10
An example of marbling.

especially evident in the loose areas of the skin like the periorbital tissues and the external genitalia, especially the scrotum. The abdomen also becomes taut and tympanic due to bowel gas. The skin and tissues feel crackly (*crepitant*). Also during this stage, there is associated leakage of bloody fluid (*purge*) from the various bodily orifices, soiling the surroundings. The inexperienced investigator might mistake this for actual trauma or dismiss injury-associated blood as purge fluid.

The next stage is that of *skin slippage*, which is seen at about four to seven days postmortem. The superficial epithelial layer of the skin separates, or slips, from the subjacent tissue. The separation is indicated by large serosanguineous blisters on the skin surface. At this stage, the scalp hair and fingernails/toenails would tend to come off with variable minimal effort. The skin of the hands and feet is particularly known for this skin slip process, and it can be exploited in casework. The affected areas can have the epithelium removed as a "glove and stocking," which can then be used for identification purposes by means of fingerprints and/or footprints (see Figure 13.11).

FIGURE 13.11
Victim's hand is covered by the epithelial glove (top layers of the skin).

In addition, because the skin pigment resides in this outer skin layer, obscured tattoos can be revealed by wiping off or otherwise removing the superficial darker layers. The area surrounding the tattoo would appear white since the melanin skin pigment would be absent.

Mummification (or mummifaction) refers to drying of the body and organs due to dehydration. This occurs in environments with low humidity and high heat but can occur more slowly in cold. The net effect is a shriveling of the body with resultant desiccated leathery skin and organs. The change makes the body less attractive as a ready food source, so viscera tend to have fewer depredations. Saponification (*sapon* 5 soap; *ficare* 5 to make) is the hydrolysis of fat tissues forming a waxy, soap-like material termed **adipocere**. A very specific combination of conditions is required: a moist, cool environment; anaerobic conditions; specific bacteria (*Clostridium*); and an extended PMI of at least three months. This type of environment is common in buried bodies, leading adipocere to be given the common name of "grave wax." Adipocere also tends to discourage postmortem animal activity. In addition, the chemical nature of the material tends to preserve tissues to a certain extent, although degradation still continues.

Ultimately, tissue decomposition ends in **skeletonization**, at which point there is a bare skeleton. Depending on the area, a completely exposed body could be reduced to skeletal components in a week and a half. Again, this is highly variable. Local expertise is best for reaching sound conclusions with regard to PMI. A forensic anthropologist may be able to determine not only perimortem or older skeletal trauma but might also assist in identification via interpretation of specific skeletal anomalies and through general identification by determining estimated

FIGURE 13.12
Insect activity and maggot infestation on victim's body.

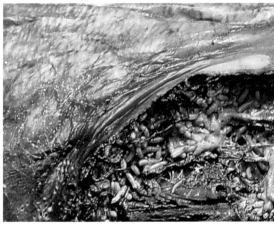

age, race, sex, occupation (via job-associated repetitive skeletal changes), and other data preserved within the remains. If the body is significantly decomposed, the remains may be reduced to the skeletal components by defleshing. Because the soft tissues are lost in this process, the pathologist should conduct a complete examination prior to calling in the anthropologist. Another specialized area that may be of assistance is forensic entomology, or the study of insect activity on the body as it relates to time since death (see Figure 13.12 and Chapter 14).

PATTERN RECOGNITION

The goal of the MDI is to determine what happened to an individual. The experienced investigator will recognize that certain circumstances are common. Recognition of the possible likely scenarios would allow a skilled investigator to ensure that the proper steps of evidence documentation and collection are followed. While developing case theories and working through case scenarios, the investigator should keep an open mind and remember that deduction comes from both knowledge and observation. It is important that the investigator not be so deeply invested in a working hypothesis as to develop tunnel vision.

Natural Deaths

Most cases investigated in a medicolegal system result from natural disease. Although the scope of natural diseases is far beyond the scope of this book, it is important to remember that people with natural disease can still die an unnatural death. If a case is written off as natural from the start without any consideration of possible foul play, then the subtle homicide could fall through the cracks and a killer could get away with murder. The basic investigation should be the same as for any other category of death: document scene specifics (such as body position, medical triage, surrounding materials, etc.), consult with treating medical professionals (the decedent's physician should be familiar with a patient's health status, especially a terminal patient, and be able to honestly determine if this death was expected), and review medical history (with emergency room staff and/or other treating doctors and the local MDI personnel).

If there is a reasonable question regarding the true circumstances of the case, then it is advisable to err on the side of caution. This is not to say that a full autopsy should be conducted in every natural death to specifically determine the precise cause or mechanism of death. The ME/C has statutory authority to investigate cases under his or her jurisdiction to the extent allowed. To include cases only marginally under the code would not serve the public interest. One has a duty to balance the responsibility of the office with the needs of those served.

If a case is designated as not falling within the jurisdiction of the ME/C, the case can be released. This might include cases with natural disease or trauma cases in which the investigation has determined that there is no superseding medicolegal interest. Examples of the latter might include a motor vehicle collision without pending criminal charges or an in-hospital death where the lethal condition and/or trauma has been well documented (e.g., a fall at work where the victim has multiple rib fractures and dies a week later from complications).

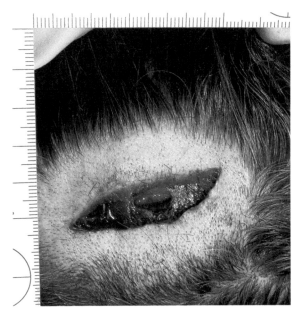

FIGURE 13.13
Blunt force trauma injury to scalp.

If survivors or investigators are insistent on an exam in such cases, they can try to persuade the ME/C or contract with the hospital pathologist or another private pathologist (neither of whom may have any forensic expertise) to perform an autopsy. Such exams, as well as postmortems on hospitalized patients dying natural deaths, are termed *hospital autopsies* and are markedly different from the ME/C autopsy. The authority for such exams is granted by the legal next of kin and may be limited to allow the autopsist to examine only very specific structures. The limitations in such an arrangement may bias the conclusion by limiting the available data and/or context. Another issue is that unless the health care providers perform the exam as a service (as required on a certain number of fatalities for accreditation), the survivors must pay for the service.

Trauma

A broad overview of common categories of trauma includes those due to physical, chemical, and environmental factors. Physical trauma includes (but is not limited to) blunt force, sharp force, firearms injuries, thermoelectric injuries, and asphyxiations. Chemical-associated fatalities include medicines, illicit drugs, and poisons. Environmental cases include exposure to temperature extremes and other adverse environments such as drowning and some asphyxial deaths related to the ambient air (the latter and fire-associated carbon monoxide are included in the description of physical asphyxial death for the sake of continuity).

Physical Trauma
Blunt Force

Blunt force refers to an impact on the body with a surface either from the object striking the body or the body striking the object, or both (see Figure 13.13). If the involved object leaves a recognizable mark on the body in the form of a wound, such injury is described as a patterned wound—for example, a shoeprint mark on someone who was kicked in the head. If there is the potential for a patterned injury, then the investigator may find it highly advisable to transfer suspect materials to the ME for comparison to the body (see Figure 13.14). Ideally

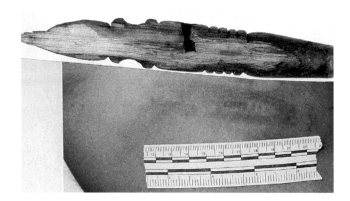

FIGURE 13.14
A broken chair leg used to beat a victim was compared to a similar impression on the victim's body with a high degree of correlation, indicating that this object, or one having similar physical characteristics, was the offending weapon.

and if practicable, this can be done during the course of the autopsy, or it can be done by means of photographs at some later date. Photographic comparisons do not allow manipulation of the object relative to the wound and thus potentially limit the amount of information that may be gleaned. Depending on the degree of force involved (fast or slow blow and mass of the object), the area struck (exposed skin or covered with clothing or hair), and the nature of the blow (straight on or glancing blow), a blunt force injury (BFI) may take the form of a contusion, an abrasion, or a laceration (see Figure 13.15).

A *contusion*, or bruise, results from the rupture of blood vessels under the skin surface and occurs while a victim is alive and has blood pressure to pump blood into an injury. For several hours after death, it may be possible to have blood ooze into the tissues around an injury and create a visually similar finding, which is technically not a bruise but a postmortem artifact. Such findings are known to occur when the arms, for example, are forcefully manipulated in moving the deceased body, resulting in "fingertip bruises" after death. Distinguishing the real from the artificial based solely on visual exam may be difficult if not impossible. A patterned bruise might result from being struck with a broom handle or other cylindrical object. The nature of such wounds is to compress the central injury and force the associated blood to the edges, outlining the area where the object hit. The resultant wound takes on the appearance of two parallel linear bands of bruising with a central linear

FIGURE 13.15
Impressions of vehicle tires are apparent on this victim.
K. Johnson, Georgetown County, SC.

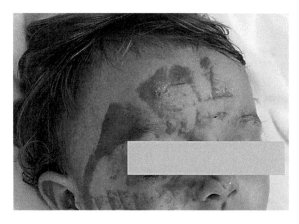

clearing, termed a *tram-track* bruise. The width area of the clearing can provide an estimate of the minimum diameter of the item in question. A more forceful blow would cause the weapon to pass deeper into the surrounding skin surface, providing a more accurate representation of the true cross-sectional diameter of the weapon.

A common question in interpreting bruises is attempting to date or age them related to when they first occurred. Such efforts, classically based on color, are notoriously unreliable. The general color timeline is red at 0–2 days, purple/blue at 2–5 days, green at 5–7 days, yellow at 7–10 days, brown at 10–14 days, and resolved (gone) by 2–4 weeks. These color changes are considered informational only and do not represent absolutes. Extent of injury is directly related to the depth of the inciting trauma, and deeper bruises require more time to become externally visible. Research has shown that the only truly reproducible change in color is that yellow begins to appear at greater than 18 hours; however, an important consideration in such research is the test subject involved. Human bruising parameters may differ from other animals. Bruises in multiple stages of healing are common—for instance, in chronic alcoholics due to repeated binge-associated falls and in battered children due to the repeated nature of the physical trauma.

An *abrasion* is a scraping away of the superficial layers of the skin due to a blow. This mechanism, which may be associated with contusions, is typically a rubbing or scraping motion, pushing the denuded epithelium in front of the leading edge, with the latter serving as an indicator of directionality. Postmortem abrasions, as caused by insect activity, are typically yellow or orange. The impact of an object, even through or by clothing, may also cause an abrasion. On occasion, an abrasion will be patterned, replicating the nature of the offending object to a greater or lesser extent. Similarly, the weave of overlying clothing may be imparted to the skin surface as part of the impact of the offending weapon. A pathologist may attempt microscopic aging of abrasions, as they do follow a general timeline but gross attempts at aging based on the physical appearance alone may be prone to error, such as drying artifact.

Lacerations are physical tears through the skin thickness. The hallmark is the bridging of the more elastic blood vessels and nerves at the depth of the wound so that they span the edges. Contusions are usually associated. The edges often have a marginal abrasion associated with the striking object. In the case of a fall, the laceration tends to be small and the abrasion/contusion large, and the wound is commonly located in a protuberant area such as the hat-band distribution around the head or the extremities. With a blow, the laceration tends to be large and the abrasion/contusion small. In the case of an object swung into the head, the leading edge is pushed forward, creating a cavitary space called *undermining*, which helps in assessing directionality. Trace evidence may be trapped within this space. Solid organs can also be lacerated, most typically the liver with a blow to the abdomen (as in a child abuse case), crushing it against the spine. The spleen is also commonly lacerated in MVCs. Fractures are examples of lacerations to bone. Unique features of such injuries may help to determine the causative mechanism (rotational, traction, angulation, penetrating, crush, or focal trauma).

A special type of blunt force pattern affecting the brain may be helpful in determining a simple fall as opposed to an inflicted head wound. When the head is struck by an object, the blow produces an injury (*coup* injury) to the immediately underlying brain. A smaller injury occasionally also forms on the opposite side of the brain. With a blow to the head, the coup injury is larger. In the case of a fall, the side of the brain opposite the impact (*contre coup* injury) sustains the more prominent wound.

Defensive wounds are a special category of trauma. They are typical on upper or lower extremities and are basically inflicted injuries of lesser severity than those elsewhere (due to location and motion) and occur as the victim is attempting to ward off an attack. Note that the victim may actually be attempting to terminate an assault by actively grabbing the assailant's weapon or otherwise physically reaching out to the attacker. Although technically *offensive* in that the victim initiated the force, any injuries sustained while so doing would still be defensive.

FIGURE 13.16
Multiple stab wounds.

Sharp Force

Sharp force injuries are the result of an edged weapon. The two basic forms are stabs and incisions. Stabs penetrate deeper into the body than coursing on the skin surface (see Figure 13.16), whereas incisions are longer than they are deep. If the blade penetrates to its maximal depth, it may leave a surrounding marginal wound (abrasion and/or contusion), termed a *hilt mark*. A blade may have one or two sharp edges. One or both may be replicated in the wound, depending on how the knife enters. If one end of the wound is not sharp, this is referred to as the *blunt edge* and would be the single best approximator of the thickness of the blade. In addition, because the knife can penetrate to various depths and enter at various angles, apparent blade length and width may differ significantly from that suggested by analysis of the wounds (see Figures 13.17 and 13.18). In fact, the same blade may produce multiple wounds of variable size (depth and length) despite the one fixed blade. Only

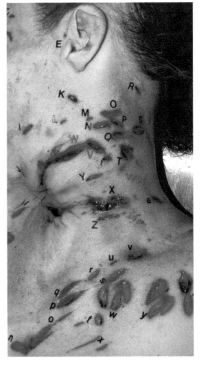

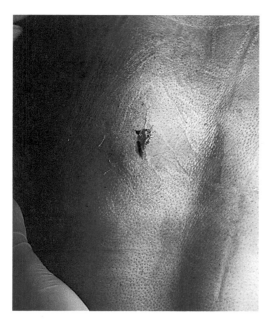

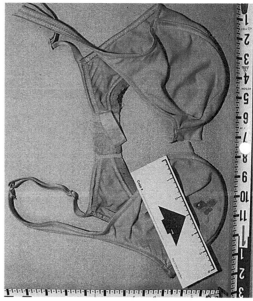

FIGURE 13.17
Photographic documentation of a knife wound to a victim's back.

FIGURE 13.18
A stabbing victim's bra, indicating the location of a stab wound.

the blade thickness remains constant. Many knives have a small portion of the blank form adjacent to the handle (technically, knives do not have hilts), termed the *ricasso*. The blade is typically dull on both sides at this area. There is no way to accurately determine the specifics of the inflicting blade based solely on the skin and soft tissue examination. Stab wounds to bone and cartilage provide better data and may accurately suggest a certain blade type. In addition, toolmarks from the blade's manufacturing process may be imparted on bone and/or cartilage and can be directly linked to a specific blade.

Chop wounds are a specialized subtype of sharp force injury resulting from a dull edge. The tissues are crushed as they are cut. Weapons inflicting these wounds include machetes, axes, and cleavers. The actual appearance of the specific wound would be directly related to how sharp the blade actually was. Propellers also cause chop wounds but due to the rotation of multiple blades, they tend to produce multiple roughly parallel repeating chop injuries.

Firearms

Firearms include handguns, rifles, and shotguns. All produce basically the same type of wound, with differences in the number of individual defects (significantly more with shotgun pellets), tissue damage (significantly more with shotgun rounds and high-velocity hunting rifles), trace evidence, and range of fire. The estimated range of firing is reproducible and is best determined by a qualified firearms examiner in the laboratory using the same weapon, ideally with the same ammunition. The scene investigator should have a basic understanding of range approximations to be able to assess whether certain scenarios are possible and if possible evidence should be sought at the scene.

When a firearm discharges, the projectile (bullet, pellets, wadding, etc.) is expelled and is driven out by the explosive force of the powder charge behind the projectile. In addition, *gun smoke* or *gunshot residue* (GSR), composed of partially burned and unburned gunpowder, soot, and trace material, is also expelled. The soot causes *fouling*, a light surface haze of smoke on the skin surface that can be wiped off with variable difficulty. The partially burned and unburned powder particles may abrade and/ or embed in the skin surface, termed powder *stippling* (abrasion) or *tattooing* (embedding). If the muzzle is sufficiently close to the target, the materials impact and stick on the target surface. In most cases, that initial target surface would be clothing (the outermost garment). During resuscitative efforts, EMTs often remove clothing to triage the patient. A decedent's clothing should always be sought and ideally transferred with the body for examination to maximize the recovery of trace evidence, such as GSR, and to allow matching of concordance of body wounds with clothing defects. Additionally, in some circumstances, the clothing may impart very specific injuries to the body.

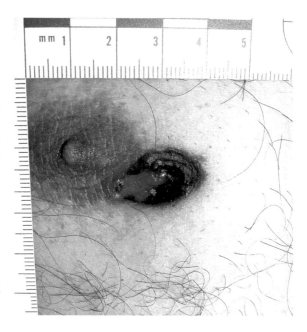

FIGURE 13.19
Contact gunshot wound to chest area.

The various ranges of fire are as follows (see also Figures 13.19–13.21):

- **Contact (hard contact)**—The muzzle is pressed into the skin/ clothing with all the GSR driven into the defect.
- **Loose contact**—Searing is seen at the wound edges, and there is marginal wound fouling but no stippling.
- **Close**—The range is less than about 6–8 inches, depending on the weapon and the load; stippling and fouling are seen surrounding the entry point.
- **Intermediate**—The range is variable, between about 6 and 30 inches; there is stippling without fouling the surrounding entry; the more widely dispersed the stipple grouping, the farther removed the muzzle is from the target distance.

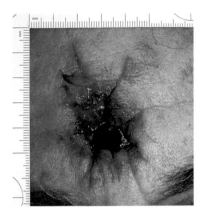

FIGURE 13.20
Contact gunshot wound to forehead.

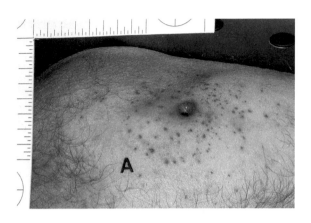

FIGURE 13.21
Gunshot residue stippling from a close-range gunshot.

- **Distant**—Neither fouling nor stippling is seen surrounding the entry point.
- **Indeterminate**—The specific range of fire cannot be estimated because the wound lacks associated indicators such as soot and powder; note that these may also occur in other instances where range cannot be assessed, such as when the primary target (clothing) is not made available for examination at autopsy.

Range estimates with shotgun wounds are heavily influenced by barrel length, choke, and shell. *Wad marks*, the paper or plastic material used to separate the shotgun pellets from the powder charge, have very poor aerodynamic properties and rapidly separate from the overall pellet grouping, striking the skin surface in as little as two feet with less powerful weapons.

Entry gunshot wounds are characteristically round to oval and have a variable circumferential *marginal abrasion border* where the projectile rubs against the edges of the skin defect as it passes through. This mark will typically be wider on the side from which the bullet started (more rub) and less prominent on the side toward which it travels. This type of mark may be useful in terms of understanding how a victim was positioned at the scene and in determining what areas need to be x-rayed to locate any projectiles potentially retained within the body.

Compared to entry gunshot wounds, exit wounds are generally larger, more linear, have irregular lacerations, and usually lack an abrasion border. Size is not the defining property of entry versus exit wounds. Contact entry wounds, especially over bone, can be significantly larger than exit wounds. In addition, when a projectile exits an area where the skin is pressed against a hard surface such as a wall or even tight clothing (termed *shored exit*), the skin may be driven against that surface and leave an irregular but typically larger marginal abrasion border. Similar irregular features can be seen with *re-entry wounds*. Even if a shot appears to exit, the involved area of the body should be x-rayed to determine if the bullet fragmented and/or the lead core separated from the copper jacket. It is important to confirm the presence or absence of retained projectiles. Many highly specialized rounds exist, and they are best considered on a case-by-case basis. One important special round is the hunting, or *high-velocity*, round, which travels at a significantly higher velocity than others. The characteristic finding is a radiographic *lead snowstorm*, as the round extensively fragments within the body. Moreover, due to the accompanying greater kinetic energy (ke 5 mass times velocity squared), the temporary cavity created by these rounds tends to be much more extensive than with conventional ammunition.

Thermoelectric Injuries

Inflicted thermal burns are most common in child abuse cases. In daily experience, house fires and other accidents would be routine. It is unusual for a burn to be immediately lethal because burns kill by fluid loss (immediate period) or by infection (delayed period). Children have a tremendous systemic reserve and can survive burns that would prove lethal in adults. Questions often revolve around bathing temperatures. Although water heaters are preset at the factory, they can be readjusted in the residence and lead to injury. Another consideration in burn injuries is location; in general, accidental burns in children are more common on areas above the waist while inflicted burns are more common below. As with everything in MDI, generalities are of little value in an isolated case; in a case in which the unusual occurred, the incidence is 100 percent.

Fire deaths kill most often by the combined effects of smoke inhalation (usually carbon monoxide but also other asphyxiants such as cyanide from burning plastics) and thermal injury (by means of creating physiologic systemic stress). Occasionally, a fireball consumes all the oxygen in a limited area, and the victim dies from oxygen deprivation before breathing in significant combustion products. A sure marker that an individual was alive during a fire is soot within the internal airway (tracheobronchial tree). The absence of soot does not prove that a person was dead but should create concern until sufficiently explained (e.g., a localized conflagration described earlier). Similarly, someone with advanced disease, such as emphysema or coronary artery disease, might succumb at a much lower carbon monoxide concentration than would an otherwise healthy individual. The positive, but nonspecific findings associated with fire deaths include bright red blood and tissues (from bound carbon monoxide), brain swelling, and acute pulmonary edema. If a person were to be consumed in a conflagration at the point of origin, one might also expect to find a thermally damaged airway.

Many fire-related artifacts can occur. In addition to premortem cutaneous thermal burns, the body may burn after death. Burning of the skin involves multiple stages or degrees of burns:

- **First-degree**—Superficial (redness; "sunburn")
- **Second-degree**—Partial thickness (blisters)
- **Third-degree**—Full thickness (dead tissue)
- **Fourth-degree**—Full thickness to subcutaneous tissue

Classically, partial burns have a margin of hyperemic or red skin that may be confused with a vital reaction, indicating that the victim was alive when burned. It is only possible to tell if a burn occurred before or after death based on microscopic (early) or gross (later) evidence of healing. Fourth-degree postmortem burns with exposure of the torso soft tissues and contents and organ charring are commonly seen, and thermal postmortem amputations are common.

It is extraordinarily difficult to completely burn a body. In fact, crematoriums have to resort to physical mechanisms after exposure to high heat over extended times to reduce the body to the cremains. Burning a wounded body creates certain artifacts, indicating the points and types of premortem trauma. Other common thermal artifacts at autopsy include parboiling or cooking of the various body tissues. The scalp is often not only charred to bone, but the skull itself becomes *calcined*—friable (crumbly) and white. The skull cap will be extensively fractured, and a chocolate-brown collection of artifactual blood may accumulate outside the dura mater within the skull (thermal epidural hemorrhage). The body also classically assumes a *pugilistic attitude*, with the arms flexed at the shoulders, elbows, and wrists. Similar but less marked flexion changes occur throughout the entire body. This does not demonstrate an effort by the decedent to fight back the fire immediately prior to death. Rather, it is a simple physiochemical change. When the muscles cook, the fibers shorten and the muscles contract. Within the body, flexor muscles (tending to pull things anatomically forward) are usually stronger than extensors (tending to pull things anatomically rearward); thus, the arms rise into a combative stance long after the victim has died.

Electrocutions can occur with alternating or direct current but are more common with the former. There are two major types of electrocution deaths: low voltage (less than 600 volts) and high voltage (more than 600 volts; see Figure 13.22). Low voltage typically causes cardiac death by means of ventricular fibrillation, whereas high voltage causes central nervous system derangement with respiratory paralysis. The human body is especially susceptible to currents at the

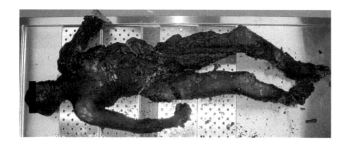

FIGURE 13.22
Charred body as the result of a high-voltage electrocution.

60-Hz range (household current range). Amperage, not voltage, is the most important factor in electrocutions.

How an electric exposure acts on the body is directly related to the resistance to electrical flow. Moist skin is a better conductor than dry skin. Likewise, salt is an excellent conductor, so sweat would greatly enhance electrical flow, thus minimizing burns by tending to allow current to flow on the body surface rather than through it. If there is an electrocution at low voltage, half of cases will have a specific point burn and half will have no change. Essentially, all high-voltage electrocutions have marked cutaneous burns, with secondary burns often associated with clothing catching on fire. If possible, it is prudent not only to autopsy the body but also to examine the scene and equipment. Any involved equipment can be sent to a competent, independent electrician for function testing and analysis.

Lightning strikes are an uncommon form of electrocution. Almost all victims have cutaneous burn injuries. A peculiar skin change involves tree-like marks extending across the skin surface. These marks begin to form almost immediately but may fade over the first day. In addition, more than three-fourths of lightning strike victims rupture their tympanic membranes (inner ear). Another clue would be magnetizing metal objects on the victim's person (such as coins, belt buckles, etc.).

FIGURE 13.23
Asphyxiation categories.

Asphyxiation

Asphyxiation is the exclusion of sufficient oxygen to maintain life (see Figure 13.23). Following a systematic approach, using the delivery of air to the cells of the body and proceeding from external to internal, asphyxiations may be suffocation/choking/mechanical (air content or airway blockage), strangulation/hanging (vascular compromise), or cellular (chemical inhibitors).

- Suffocation—air/airway
- Vessels—strangulation
- Cells—(bio)chemical

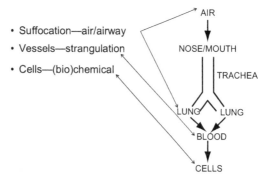

Suffocating gases are inert and displace necessary oxygen from the ambient air. The human body is designed to function in a 21 percent ambient oxygen environment. A decrease to 16 percent ambient oxygen can prove fatal; 11 percent can be rapidly lethal. Specific environmental testing can be conducted, often in consultation with fire departments or occupational testing consultants, on an as-needed basis. An example of a suffocating gas would be carbon dioxide (CO_2), which is slightly heavier than other ambient air gases and tends to pool near the ground. CO_2 displaces the normal oxygen, albeit temporarily, from that specific location. If someone were exposed for a sufficient period (minutes) to a high enough local concentration, there could be inadequate local oxygen and death might ensue. Other environmental concerns would include a confined space with rusting or oxidation of metal objects in the presence of water. Because the oxide is oxygen, the environmental oxygen is removed, leaving a possibly inadequate amount to sustain life.

Physical suffocation is a simple mechanical blockage of the external air entering the mouth. This may happen by means of a covering hand or a plastic bag over the head. The latter might also involve at least some component of localized oxygen consumption and depletion. *Choking* involves a physical blockage of the internal airway, most commonly by means of an aspirated foreign body but could also occur from any physical structure sufficiently impinging on the airway (e.g., aspirated fluid like blood or vomit, or a growth such as a benign or malignant tumor). *Mechanical suffocation* is the external compression of the thorax, physically preventing inhalation, causing no gas exchange to occur. This type of asphyxia is seen when a victim is pinned underneath a heavy load and cannot physically use the bellows action of the lung. Another common setting is in *overlay*, in which an adult inadvertently rolls over on top of the child while sleeping and suffocates the child. In adults, the same process is sometimes called *Burking*, after the British resurrectionists Burke and Hare, who murdered prostitutes by these means rather than exert the effort to dig up cadavers (http://definitions.uslegal.com/b/burking)/). *Positional asphyxia* or *postural asphyxia* is putting the body in a physical position wherein the bellows action of breathing is impaired. Most commonly, this is associated with an inverted position; the effort to breathe in this position taxes the respiratory muscles of the diaphragm and chest wall to exhaustion.

Vascular compromise in the neck kills by preventing oxygenated blood from reaching the brain, ending in brain hypoxia and death within minutes. Unconsciousness occurs in about 10–15 seconds if blood flow to the brain is terminated. Surprisingly little physical force is required (only about five or six pounds of pressure blocks the jugular veins). If blood cannot flow out of the brain via the veins, eventually the system backs up and blood will no longer flow in. The airway is seldom physically compromised because its closure requires many times more force than occlusion of the vessels. Mechanisms by which the blood vessels of the neck are blocked include *hanging* (see Figure 13.24) and *strangulation* (both *manual* and *ligature*). Because hanging causes vascular compromise, the neck need not be broken and in fact seldom is, except in judicial executions, which are specifically intended to fracture the neck to cause instantaneous death. The elongate neck evident in many hanging cases is not from a broken neck but rather the result of tissues being stretched while supporting the entire body weight (see Figure 13.25). Both manual and ligature strangulations act by blocking blood flow to the brain, but these tend to have more damage to neck structures and hemorrhage due to the victim struggling against the attacker. The net effect can be one of the classic markers of both types of strangulation: pinpoint or *petechial hemorrhages* in the mucous membranes of the eye, the mouth, and possibly the facial skin. These are not necessarily present in all cases, and their presence is no assurance that an individual case is in fact a strangulation death.

As noted previously, asphyxia is the relative lack of oxygen delivery and use at the cellular level. *Asphyxiating chemicals* block the cells' ability to breathe the delivered oxygen. Certain gases (such as carbon

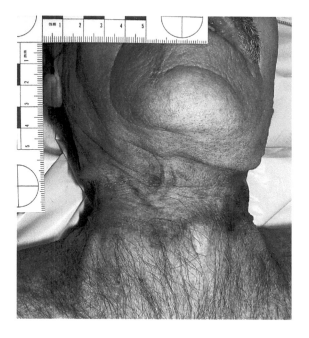

FIGURE 13.24

Scene of a hanging victim. Note the steps used to climb upon.

FIGURE 13.25

Victim from Figure 13.24, showing an unusual contusion made from the rope.

monoxide) can prevent oxygen delivery to the cell by binding to the oxygen-transporting molecule hemoglobin with such affinity that oxygen cannot bind in order to be carried to the cell. Other chemicals, such as cyanide and hydrogen sulfide, block the cellular process of respiration. Other means of asphyxia would be suffocating gases, which basically exclude oxygen from the environment. Last, the environment itself may be depleted of oxygen if the environmental replacement consumption fails to keep pace with consumption.

Chemical Trauma

A drug can be considered to be any chemical with actions(s) assisting the patient and a poison as any chemical with detrimental action(s). In fact, any agent can be a medicine or a poison, depending on the dose and the effect on the individual. Some illicit drugs, like cocaine, might have a therapeutic effect in some circumstances. Other drugs, such as LSD and mescaline, have no legitimate recognized therapeutic action. Scene investigators may encounter a great number of drugs at death scenes and should be generally aware of the significance of what they find. Medications can be categorized in several different ways. For the investigator, the general action of the drug is probably the easiest system. Medications can be sorted into chemotherapeutic (fighting cancer and infection), pharmacodynamic (direct impact of the drug on the body), and other (local anesthetics, narcotics, etc.) types.

Most would consider the dangers of drug overdose as the primary concern of the scene investigator. It is critical to remember that no definitive conclusions can be drawn simply from the discovery of an empty drug vial. Some individuals may redistribute their medications to a pill organizer, leaving numerous empty prescription bottles. If a month's worth of tablets were reallocated, it might appear at first glance that excessive drug use is a factor in a death, whereas the reverse might actually be the case. Similarly, an individual might have his or her drugs allocated by another (e.g., a nurse in a nursing home, a trusted associate). All circumstances should be considered and documented affirmatively and/or negatively. Of course, an actual empty container could have real significance. In a patient with chronic seizures, an empty phenytoin (Dilantin®) bottle might be the only positive clue in an otherwise completely negative seizure-related death.

The scene investigator should recognize and collect as evidence all medications and packages (empty or otherwise) on or around the decedent at the scene and additionally any other medications prescribed for the victim. These should be inventoried with pertinent prescription information (if available), such as count remaining and originally prescribed, date prescribed, physician, and number. Prescription medications should not be discarded or returned to individuals at the scene because they are intended only for the use of the person for whom they were ordered.

Patterns suggesting that a death might involve drugs include the presence of drug paraphernalia. For example, a crumpled soda can may just be refuse or may have been used as a crack cocaine pipe. A broken-off portion of radio antenna might be used for the same purpose. Other illicit drug-associated items are more obvious, for example, syringes and tourniquets. The presence of medications and/or containers at the scene is also significant. Transdermal agents may indicate a specific prior disease (e.g., an opioid patch for chronic pain relief). These clues may provide important information in explaining what happened to the decedent. Ideally, all such items should be documented if discovered at the death scene. If located on the body, they should be left in place for the pathologist to collect at the postmortem examination. Devices located at a scene may also have been involved in a death. In some situations, their involvement is obvious (e.g., the automobile involved in a motor vehicle crash).

Environmental Factors

Extremes of heat and cold are generally not well tolerated. The normal body temperature is reported as 98.6°F but may actually vary plus or minus 1.0°F in an individual and may further vary by a similar amount throughout the course of a day. The autopsy proper may reveal no specific anatomic findings in heat or cold deaths, and the results may hinge exclusively on the investigation and documentation of pertinent negatives. Age extremes, people with diseases, and those on certain medications may be more prone to both heat and cold injury. Chronic exposure may lead to surreptitious temperature regulation issues or electrolyte abnormalities.

Fever is defined as temperatures above 100°F oral for an adult or 100.4°F in a child. Heat injury takes the form of a spectrum, with failure of the body to sufficiently shed excess heat. Heat exhaustion, the lesser injury, can be marked by cool, moist, pale skin; excessive sweating; cramps; nausea/vomiting; and dark urine. If allowed to progress, the victim may undergo the medical emergency of heat stroke, marked by a body temperature above 105.1°F. Signs include confusion, lack of sweating, collapse, and shock. Temperature and humidity can combine in deadly heat indexes whereby the apparent ambient temperature is markedly higher than the actual temperature. This situation is most dangerous with the first heat wave of the season because the populace has not had an opportunity to acclimatize to the heat. Strenuous exercise under these conditions can be lethal, and appropriate precautions such as water breaks and rest periods should be employed. The autopsy might document an increased core temperature or specific end-organ destruction in a nonspecific pattern. The diagnosis rests largely on the context and documentation of the perimortem circumstances, especially the environmental conditions. Certain diseases and medications can put an individual at increased risk when environmental conditions are adverse.

Most people tolerate cold with body temperatures at levels between 95°F and 89.6°F fairly well. Cold can kill, especially when combined with water, with a damp body showing increased conductive and convective heat loss. Hypothermia is diagnosed when the temperature falls 3.6°F below baseline. Cold illness is considered severe when the body temperature falls below 95°F and a medical emergency at 90.0°F when the heat-generating shivering process stops. The mechanism involves slowing of the body's metabolic processes with decreases in the vital signs, including pulse, respirations, and blood pressure. When severe, the brain undergoes central nervous system depression, and the heart commences dysrhythmias (potentially fatal irregular heartbeats).

In cases of hypothermia, gradual rewarming may allow the patient to be salvaged. Cold water immersion takes place when a body is suddenly placed in extremely cold water, which literally takes the breath away and incapacitates the person. If this initial event is survived, then the accelerated direct heat loss to the significantly cooler water can cause hypothermia in short order. Ambient cold alone can also cause death. Certain diseases, such as dementia and stroke, and drugs, such as alcohol, put an individual at increased risk for hypothermia by altering central thermoregulation in the brain (the former) or by vasodilation (the latter). The only anatomic finding may be hemorrhaging erosions on the mucosal surface of the stomach wall. In some cases, victims may show *paradoxical undressing*, in which they remove their clothing because in their debilitated state they perceive the extreme cold as heat. This can confuse matters by creating investigative concern for a possible sexual component to the death.

ROLE OF THE CSI AT AUTOPSY

Physical evidence from a deceased body should be collected at the morgue. Minimize the possibility of losing transient or trace evidence by wrapping the body in a clean sheet or blanket prior to transport to the morgue. In cases where warranted or suspected, before releasing the decedent's body to be transported from the crime scene to the morgue, place paper bags over the hands of the victim and secure them in place with string, tape, etc. Examine the body for hair and fibers that may be lost during transit. Document and collect hairs and fibers with adhesive tape; then prepare the body for transport to the medical facility. Remember that the scene is not the place to conduct an autopsy and that the ME will have a facility specifically designed to facilitate evidence collection. Avoid transfer or cross-contamination of items by individually bagging each item in clean paper (never plastic; see Figure 13.26). Ensure the integrity of the evidence on the body by affixing a seal to the body bag prior to releasing it for removal from the crime scene. If possible, an officer or CSI should accompany the body to the morgue, and then a receipt for the body should be issued that is placed in the case file. The seal on the body bag should be broken only by the medical examiner's staff when preparing the body for autopsy.

Many things occur prior to the actual autopsy of a victim's body. Your case documentation from the crime scene should continue with the removal of the evidence seal on the body bag used to transport the victim to the morgue. Include the name and official position of those present for the autopsy as well as the names of the medical examiners or pathologists who perform the examination. Remember to utilize proper PPE, including protective outer clothing, shoe covers, hair cover, and face shield, during the autopsy.

FIGURE 13.26
Collect all clothing from victims and wrap each item individually in paper to prevent loss of trace evidence.

Before the physical autopsy begins, where indicated, a morgue technician may take x-rays and/or CT scans or other imaging studies of the victim's body. The films are displayed on the light box or monitor in the autopsy suite for reference during the examination. If bullets or other foreign objects are present in the body, the x-rays will assist the ME in the location of the evidence as the autopsy progresses. Imaging can also reveal fresh or healed fractures and other alterations to the skeletal system, such as arthritis and artificial joints, as well as the presence of pacemakers and other medical appliances. This information may be helpful in establishing the identity of an unidentified victim.

An external examination of the victim will then be conducted, starting with the clothing. Jurisdictional differences dictate precise roles for the various people present at the autopsy, most notably when it comes to the actual collection of potential evidence. In many areas, the ME and staff will thoroughly process and document the decedent's body, including the clothing. Regardless of with whom the ultimate responsibility lies, participants should coordinate efforts to ensure that a thorough examination is conducted and that important information (positive and negative) is not missed. Photographs and/or diagrams will be completed to document any damage, such as tears, missing buttons, or other defects. Damage to the clothing should be documented in relation to the location of any wound on the body. Prior to disrobing the body, the examiner may use a forensic light source to locate any potential biological or trace evidence not visible to the naked eye. Gunshot residue, paint chips, glass fragments, or other trace evidence not readily observable at the crime scene may be present on the clothing. If evidence is discovered, it should be photographed (if possible) in place before being collected and packaged.

All clothing items are potential evidence, even if they do not seem important to the investigation at the time. Wet items, especially those soiled with blood or biological fluids, should be air-dried to avoid the loss of physical evidence. Fingernail clippings or scrapings may yield skin cells of the assailant in certain cases and should be collected where indicated. Process each hand separately and properly label and seal the envelope to prevent the loss of DNA evidence. Where indicated, retain the paper bags because they may contain transfer evidence from the victim's hands. Document any injuries to the hands and then obtain inked impressions of each finger and the palm prints of the victim. Remember to label the fingerprint cards before placing the ink on the fingers to avoid misidentification at a later time. In homicide cases, a control sample of blood for potential DNA analysis and a control sample of the victim's hair are advisable.

Conduct a visual search for hair and fibers on clothing, and collect this evidence using adhesive tape and standard secure packaging techniques. Each item of clothing should be removed and individually wrapped in paper packaging, taped closed, and appropriately labeled. If the clothing is wet or contains blood or other biological fluids, be sure to attach a "Biohazard" label and make the proper notations that the item must be removed from the package to be air-dried as soon as possible prior to submission to the crime laboratory. Also collect the sheet that was used to wrap the body for transport to the morgue. Transient evidence may be found on the sheet when it is examined in the crime laboratory.

A preautopsy review provides an opportunity for the CSI to share case notes, information, and photographs of the scene with the medical examiner's office prior to the initiation of an autopsy. At such meetings, copies of sketches, photographs, and videotapes made at the scene should be available to the ME who will be conducting the autopsy. This review is important because it provides the ME with critical context and allows the case to be properly triaged with an eye toward collecting potentially useful evidence that might otherwise go unrecognized.

Decomposition is an ongoing process, and many times the appearance of a body will change dramatically from the time it is recovered and sent to the morgue until the time the body bag is opened by the ME. Accurate notes and photos taken at the scene can assist with the proper identification of antemortem (before death) and postmortem (after death) injuries. An accurate depiction of the scene includes body position and location, temperature, transient variables (lighting, wind, etc.), and the like.

The investigator's case notes should include observations of rigor mortis, liver mortis, algor mortis, and all injuries noted before CPR was administered. Like observations will be included in the final autopsy report. The temperature of the location where the body was found is also important because it may assist with the determination of the time of death. Both the temperature of the air and how the body is clothed will impact the rate of cooling of the body.

It is essential to maintain the chain of custody of all evidence, including the body, throughout the investigation. As the autopsy progresses, the CSI can answer many questions that may arise as injuries and abnormalities are discovered throughout the examination. Depending on local custom and laboratory procedures, items of evidentiary value that are recovered during the autopsy can immediately be taken into the custody of the CSI. This establishes the chain of custody and ensures that proper collection and preservation techniques are followed. In other areas, the materials are directly transferred from the ME to the lab, providing a much simpler chain of custody.

In certain cases, it is important to keep the crime scene under police control until after the completion of the autopsy. The ME may determine the need for the CSI to conduct further searches at the scene. This simple step will ensure the admissibility of any additional evidence that may be recovered at the scene after the autopsy is finalized. Delaying the release of the scene to the family also eliminates the need to acquire a search warrant to reenter the scene. A small dose of preventative caution can go a long way. If there is ever a question about a need for a search warrant, it is always advisable to play it safe.

Documentation is critically important to the death scene investigation and any subsequent prosecution. A comprehensive case file may include diagrams, overlays (tracings of pattern wounds), and photographs taken by the CSI and the ME or morgue technician. The first photograph in the file should contain case-identifying information and may include an 18 percent gray card (as a way to produce consistent image exposure and/or color in photography). Digital photography provides far more detailed electronic data regarding image information, including date and time stamp, exposure settings, etc. Multiple pictures are essential; injuries and wounds must be documented with scales included in the photographs. Additionally, photos without a scale (ruler) may be useful in some instances. As for all laboratory metrics, the scales utilized in the photographs should be traceable to an accepted standard to ensure their admissibility in future court proceedings. Certain decedents warrant special attention: the young, the old, the weak, the infirm, and the healthy. Several criteria merit increased scrutiny, including the sudden and unexpected death of individuals who are 1–30 years of age; are greater than 70 years of age; have no diagnosed illnesses; or have no observable injuries.

The compilation of information from the CSI, including the case reports, photographs, and video made of the crime scene, assist the ME or coroner in the final determination of the cause and MOD. It is critical to be ever aware that these opinions are reached, to a large part, by the circumstances surrounding the death. The better the documentation, the more confidence in the result. Although the autopsy is not a black box, spitting out all the answers in a case after a physical examination, it can provide important information that helps in the resolution of a case. Physical evidence is collected. Injuries and potential effects are enumerated. Victim actions and reactions can be understood. The autopsy also can reveal evidence of sexual assault that may have previously gone undetected or unsuspected, the location of any foreign objects in the body, and whether the deceased was under the influence of alcohol or other drugs. The final report can substantiate or refute claims of a struggle and provide definitive expertise that allows the prosecutor to either move forward with criminal proceedings or close the investigation.

During an autopsy, samples of the blood, urine, vitreous fluid, and bile may be collected and placed in nonreactive glass or other containers to preserve the integrity of the samples. Additional toxicological samples can be removed from gastric and other organs, muscles, hair, nails, and the blood surrounding the brain (subdural).

In all deaths, especially suspicious and child fatalities, the CSI may assist an ME's investigation by following these suggestions:

- Take copious photos (high-quality digital photos are preferred) of the scene and bring them to the autopsy.
- Collect suspect weapons and allow the ME to examine and compare them to wounds.
- Collect all (unused, open, or empty) containers of prescription and over-the-counter medications administered or prescribed for the decedent.
- Collect a water sample if pertinent (drowning).
- Check for/document potential environmental issues (possibility of electrocution, heat/cold, gases, etc.).
- Obtain a history from the last person to see the decedent alive.

- Obtain a history from the first person to find the person dead.
- Obtain the 911 recording if available (digital copy preferred).
- Obtain emergency medical services records, emergency department records, and hospital records (or document none exists).
- Obtain past medical records (birth to death in a child case).
- Check social services and other agency history (or document none exists).
- Collect the decedent's clothing (leave on body, if possible).

Following are other considerations, especially in child cases:

- Collect other objects of potential significance in the victim's immediate environment (in child deaths, this includes bedding, pillows, parents' clothing, etc.).
- Collect food and drink samples (bottles, cups, foods, and other items to which the child was recently exposed).
- In cases of alleged falls, measure thicknesses of fabrics, bedding, and so forth.
- In cases of alleged bathtub burns, measure heights, water temperatures, time required to fill bathtub, and so forth.
- In cases of thermal burns from water, check/photograph water heater, including documenting if any action (such as flushing a toilet) makes the water hot/cold.
- Reconstruct events. (In child deaths, ask the individuals who found the body and/or last saw the child alive to use a doll or stuffed animal to show exactly what they saw or did and photograph it. This may involve the use of bedding and so forth to show how the child was positioned.)

Identifying Remains

One of the primary roles of the ME/C in death investigations is to identify the remains. Facial identification of deceased victims is not scientific and not always possible. It is important to make a definitive confirmation of the identification of the deceased because probate actions and insurance claims cannot be processed without the issuance of a death certificate. Moreover, family members need to experience closure, and positive identification of victims allows this process to begin. One final need for affirmation of the identification of the remains is to eliminate the possibility that a perpetrator has faked his or her own death for insurance purposes or to escape prosecution for other crimes.

Most decedent identification (ID) is made by nonscientific means—visual comparison with a driver's license or facial recognition by someone familiar with the individual. Circumstances are often employed as corroboration but are also unscientific. Science involves comparative testing. The single most accurate means of specific scientific identification of remains is DNA analysis, utilizing nuclear DNA, which is unique to each individual with the lone exception of identical twins. Mitochondrial DNA (mDNA) is more resistant to decomposition but is also much less specific to the individual, being shared by all blood relatives passed along on the mother's side. Regardless whether nuclear or mitochondrial, DNA ID is expensive and time consuming. The most rapid, cost-effective means of identification is dental comparison, which can be effected within minutes. Many other means of potential ID exist but all share the requirement of knowing a potential ID for the remains in question. Even in the recently deceased, there must be a comparison point in order to perform that comparison. Too often, as with illegal immigrants, transients, body "dumps," homicide victims, etc., that known reference is lacking, thus prohibiting identification, which hinders case resolution. Recently, officials have recognized a "silent epidemic" of unidentified dead bodies all across the United States. In the not-too-distant past, information sharing regarding the unidentified dead was not uniform—even in physically adjacent jurisdictions. The effort to identify the unknown has been greatly facilitated by the National Missing and Unidentified Persons System (NamUs; www.namus.gov/), allowing investigators, ME/C, and families to combine efforts for the purposes of putting names to the faces of the unidentified dead.

The identification of decomposed or skeletonized human remains often requires a multidisciplinary approach that may utilize scientific and nonscientific means, employing the skills of a forensic anthropologist, odontologist, DNA analyst, personal physician, and other professionals, including a forensic artist, genealogist, botanist, or even a tailor, dry cleaner, or local jeweler. Combining the personal knowledge of these individuals with dental and medical records can assist the investigator in a positive tentative identification of the victim. However, when there are no family members or local ties linked to the unidentified remains, the skills of the various disciplines will be integrated in an attempt to properly identify the remains.

If soft tissue is still present, the ME will conduct an examination of the remains to determine the presence of unique physical features such as scars, birthmarks, or tattoos that may be compared to the missing-person reports on file (see Figure 13.27). Medical appliances and other implants, including joint replacements and pacemakers, may contain serial numbers that can be traced to the originating medical facility. Dentures and other orthodontic appliances may bear names and/or identifying numbers that can lead to the identification of the victim.

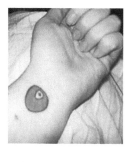

FIGURE 13.27
Unique tattoos often can provide investigative leads to identify victims.

In many cases, it may not be possible to obtain inked fingerprint impressions from the victim. The ME may have to disarticulate (cut off) the hands and submit them to a crime laboratory for processing.

In extreme cases, a forensic anthropologist can study the skeletal remains to identify any abnormalities such as joint wear or arthritis, and may also be able to determine the sex, race, and age range of the victim. Sometimes, a forensic artist can work with the skull of the victim to reconstruct the physical features of the deceased. These recreations can then be photographed and distributed in an attempt to glean information that will lead to the identification of unidentified remains.

Another expert who will be interested in the skull is the forensic odontologist. Teeth can reveal quite a lot of information about the victim, including range of age, probable lifestyle (condition of teeth), the presence or lack of dental work, and the original position of teeth that had been removed from the jawbones. The forensic odontologist will chart each tooth and compare it to dental records provided by the personal dentists of missing persons.

The following observations should be made at the crime scene and included in documentation when trying to establish the identity of a victim:

1. Clothing found on or near the body should be examined for laundry marks, logos, and whether the sizes of the clothing are consistent with the physical size of the victim.
2. Wallets, backpacks, and purses may contain jewelry, keys, and eyeglasses. Also check for papers containing handwriting; receipts from stores, restaurants, or ATM transactions; and cards issued by stores that can be linked to the owner. If the Social Security card or number is found, the first three digits of the number indicate the state of birth. This data is available on the Social Security Administration's website.

The identification of the remains and determining the COD are both part of a team effort with the CSI and medical personnel. It is essential for the CSI to develop a good working relationship with the staff at the morgue where autopsies are conducted. Every death investigation is unique and presents new challenges to both the ME and law enforcement investigators. Both groups are working on behalf of the victim and society, and maintaining an ongoing dialog as well as establishing and following a systematic process are effective means of ensuring quality control and the credibility of the evidence in pursuit of truth.

Discussion Questions

1. In the medical sense, what is considered to be death? What is considered to be death in the legal sense? Discuss each vital function.
2. Explain how the MDI uses history along with the autopsy to focus in on the COD.
3. What are the five categories of MOD? Give examples of each.
4. Discuss the changes a body goes through after death. How can these changes assist investigators in establishing a time and location of death?

REFERENCES

ANSI/ASB. (2021). *Organizational and Foundational Standard for Medicolegal Death Investigation* (Standard No.125). Retrieved from https://www.aafs.org/asb-standard/organizational-and-foundational-standard-medicolegal-death-investigation

Centers for Disease Control and Prevention (n.d.). *Summary of Medical Examiner and Coroner System in the United States*. Retrieved from http://www.cdc.gov/EPO/dphsi/mecisp/summaries.htm

Hirsch, C. S., & Adams, V. I. (1993). Sudden and Unexpected Death from Natural Causes in Adults. In W. U. Spitz (Ed.), *Medicolegal investigation of death* (pp. 137–174). Springfield, IL: Charles C. Thomas.

http://definitions.uslegal.com/b/burking/

CHAPTER 14

Forensic Anthropology, Odontology, and Entomology

Alveolar region	Forensic entomology	NamUs
Entomology	Humerus	Occipital bone
Femur	Mandible	Odontology
Forensic anthropology	Mastoid process	Sternum
	Maxilla	Supraorbital ridges

What You Will Learn

Bones, teeth, and other skeletal remains are the framework of the human body. World-famous forensic anthropologist Dr. William Bass has taught thousands of police officers and anthropologists how to locate and excavate buried human remains. The first part of this chapter presents the highlights of those lessons, providing decades of real-world experience with academic training focused on crime scene investigation. The second part of this chapter will introduce you to the field of forensic entomology, and how insects can be used to help investigators determine the time since death.

MURDER IN THE NEW YEAR

Forensic Anthropology, Odontology, and Entomology

Detective Mavis Fletcher's ringtone on her cellphone was the sound of a police siren. After several nods of the head and okays, the detective ended her conversation with a "thank you."

She closed the cellphone and placed it on her desk.

CSI Smith dropped the Honey Bun wrapper in the trash can and drained the last of his Starbucks coffee. "What's the word, Detective?"

DOI: 10.4324/9780429261657-14

"Doctor Pierce, a dentist who specializes in Forensic Odontology, faxed the CME his report. You want to guess what his findings were?"

Tom smiled mischievously. "The wound on Mr. Morton's neck was a love bite, compliments of Mrs. Morton—a passion-fueled response from a troubled marriage looking forward to better days."

"Exactly. Photographs taken of the neck injury were compared to a dental stone cast made from Margie Morton's teeth. The pattern area injury was a perfect match to Margie's teeth."

Mavis Fletcher threw a breath mint to Tom. "And the winner is CSI Smith."

Tom caught the breath mint and slipped it into his mouth. "Time to call the DA."

INTRODUCTION

When a dead body is discovered, forensic anthropologists and forensic entomologists are often called upon to help identify the victim and determine the time since death. While the forensic anthropologist will evaluate the bones to determine the victim's age at death, race, sex, and stature, the forensic entomologist will evaluate the insects that are found on and around the corpse to determine the time since death. Although the forensic anthropologist is usually asked to assist the death investigator when a body has decayed to such an extent that only bones remain, the forensic entomologist may be asked to assist the investigator at any stage of the decomposition process. However, the death investigator will find that forensic entomologists are most helpful during the early stages of decomposition when their time since death estimates are the most accurate. Because forensic anthropologists provide the most help when a body is found in the last stage of decomposition, and forensic entomologists provide the most help during the earliest stages of decomposition, the two professionals rarely encounter one another at a crime scene. However, when both fields of expertise are requested to assist the death investigator, the entomological evidence should be collected before the remains are removed from the crime scene and subsequently evaluated by a forensic anthropologist. The CSI should develop working relationships with forensic anthropologists and forensic entomologists because your paths will cross when you are called to the scene where unidentified remains have been located.

ANTHROPOLOGY

T. Dale Stewart in *Essentials of Forensic Anthropology* (1979) provides the definition of **forensic anthropology** as anthropological studies dealing with skeletal remains that appear to be human in origin. Beyond the elimination of nonhuman elements, the identification process is undertaken to provide opinions regarding sex, age, race, stature, and other characteristics of each individual involved that may lead to his or her identification.

Stewart's definition takes into account certain practices in the forensic field that have grown out of the fact that identity depends primarily on the soft parts and only secondarily on the skeletal parts. Coroners and/or medical examiners (today usually forensic pathologists), whose duty it is in the first instance to investigate unexplained civilian deaths, are trained primarily to deal with fleshed remains. When confronted with remains, the flesh covering of which no longer yields identification clues, these investigators realize that the only possibility of getting the desired information is through study of the skeleton. At this point, they may call on forensic anthropologists for help because of their greater osteological expertise. Professional forensic anthropologists are certified by the American Board of Forensic Anthropology.

The forensic anthropologist is usually the last person in the chain in identifying human remains. Most often bodies can be identified by morphological features or fingerprints, but occasionally bodies burned or decomposed beyond recognition require the expertise of a trained osteologist. Anthropology is that field of science that studies humankind from its earliest beginnings on the earth (about 5 million years ago) to the present. Thus, the scientific study of the skeleton (both human and animal) is found in anthropology. The application of these skills to modern forensic cases is forensic anthropology.

Three areas of forensic anthropology will be discussed in this chapter: (1) determining a skeleton's age at death, (2) determining the sex of the skeleton, and (3) determining race and calculating stature from the skeleton. While CSIs will never establish the identity of skeletal remains (this is left to the experts), this chapter will provide useful reference information that may provide general assistance to case detectives working to establish investigative leads. As a CSI, you should be familiar with the types of forensic examiners who may be able to provide expertise in the identification of unidentified skeletal remains. In an ideal situation, these scientists would be able to visit the location where the remains were discovered. In reality, the CSI usually collects the evidence; completes detailed written documentation, photographs, and sketches; and takes the remains to the local or regional medical examiner's office.

Caution should always be observed when determining the sex of a skeleton on the basis of associated clothing or personal items. The literature is full of examples in which attempts at true identity have been confused by substitution of clothing of the opposite sex.

THE DETERMINATION OF A SKELETON'S AGE AT DEATH

When medical examiners, law enforcement officers, or lawyers encounter a skeleton, one of the first questions asked is "How old is it?" In actuality, two questions relating to age are involved: (1) How old was the individual when he or she died? (2) How long has the individual been dead (which is a much more complicated and difficult question)?

Present research is being conducted at the University of Tennessee on decay rates of human cadavers both above ground and buried. Research on insect activity and its relationship to the decay rates of human cadavers found above ground has been reported on by Rodriguez and Bass (1983). This research has provided an additional reliable method for determining the time interval since death of a decaying corpse.

A basic knowledge of human biology, growth and development, and the aging process is needed to identify the gradual changes that occur in the skeleton from birth to old age. Aging can be divided into two major categories: maturation and degeneration. What follows is a short summary that can be used as a general guide. Experience is one of the best teachers. For in-depth coverage of every bone in the human skeleton, refer to Bass's *Human Osteology: A Laboratory and Field Manual* (2005).

Maturation
Dentition
The human is a mammal and has two sets of teeth: deciduous (baby or milk teeth) and adult. The deciduous teeth begin to appear at approximately six months of age when the lower central incisors erupt. By approximately 24 months of age, all 20 deciduous teeth have usually erupted. The second deciduous molars are the last to appear. Deciduous teeth have a thinner enamel covering over the dentin, and they appear to be more yellow in color than adult teeth. Human beings retain their deciduous teeth from approximately two to six years of age. As the skeleton grows, spaces develop between the teeth. Once they have erupted, teeth do not get larger, but the bone does grow.

The adult teeth are larger in size and whiter in color than deciduous teeth. At approximately six years of age, the first adult tooth, the six-year molar, appears behind the 20 deciduous teeth. Beginning at approximately 6.5 years and proceeding to 11.5 years of age, there is a period of mixed dentition during which the deciduous teeth are replaced by adult teeth. Usually, all deciduous teeth have been lost by age 12, and the second molars erupt. When people are about 18 years old, the third molars (wisdom teeth) may begin to erupt. Genetically, the species is losing the third molars, and in many people, they are impacted or never erupt. Any number (from one to four) of the third molars may be missing.

Epiphyses

The epiphysis is the end of a long bone, such as a leg (femur), that is covered in cartilage. Over time, the cartilage ossifies and the parts of the bone become fused. This process allows the forensic anthropologist to make an accurate estimation of the age of the victim. During the growth process of the human being, there are 806 centers of ossification that unite to form the 206 bones in the adult skeleton. By age 13 in girls and 15 in boys, the epiphyses begin to unite to the diaphyses (or shaft). The most active period of epiphyseal union occurs between the ages of 13 and 17. This is the period of the circumpubertal spurt in growth, with the major growth of the body terminating with the closure of the epiphyses. The sternal end of the clavicle is the last epiphysis to unite, and this occurs at about age 25. During the growth process, age can be determined by measuring the length of any long bones and comparing them with published standards (see Figure 14.1).

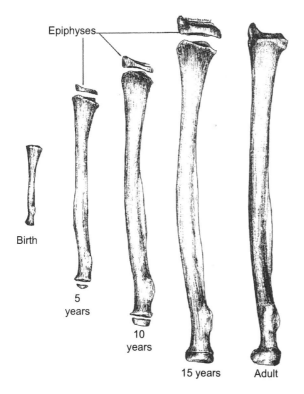

FIGURE 14.1
Growth of the left radius showing epiphyses.

Degeneration

Following the end of the growth period, which is signaled by closure of most of the epiphyses, the skeleton begins a slow process of wearing out. These degenerative changes appear in the early 20s and are present in ever-increasing degrees until death. In human identification, the three best ways to estimate age at death of an adult are to look for changes in the pubic symphysis, conduct osteon counting, and examine for osteoarthritic lipping.

CHANGES IN THE PUBIC SYMPHYSIS

Standards for the pubic symphyses of males were first published in the 1920s by T. Wingate Todd, an anatomist at Western Reserve University. Because cadaver populations contain mainly older individuals, little data existed on young males until 1957, when Tom McKern and T. Dale Stewart published data obtained on young American males killed during the Korean War. It was not until 1973 that data on changes in female pubic symphyses were published by Gilbert and McKern.

Standards for comparison of pubic symphyseal changes are available in the forensic anthropological literature. Essentially what happens is that as one grows older, the face of the pubic symphysis changes from one that is rough, with an appearance of mountains and valleys, to one that becomes smoother, with the mountains wearing off and the valleys filling up.

To determine age at death, a forensic anthropologist compares the measurements of the unknown specimen with the published standards that now exist for both males and females. One caution, however, is that in late life, changes of the pubic symphysis become more obscure, and it is difficult to determine age at death within a five-year range for those in their 60s and 70s. Care and experience are needed to make an accurate age estimation. Current research is continuing, and more accurate methods are anticipated.

Osteon Counting

A method developed by Ellis R. Kerley (1965) can be used to determine age at death from the microscopic structure of bone. The method, which has proved to be quite accurate, requires sectioning a long bone (usually the **femur**, which is the largest and strongest bone in the body, extending from the pelvis to the knee) at its midshaft; cutting, grinding, and polishing a thin section (80 microns) of it; and viewing this section through polarized light. Standards for the amount of lamellar bone, osteons, osteon fragments, Haversian, and non-Haversian canals have been published and are available to local forensic anthropologists as a basis for comparison. These osteolog-ical structures are found in the long bones of mammals, reptiles, birds, and amphibians, and provide a wealth of information regard-ing the age of the bone. Combined with other data, the results of the analysis conducted by a forensic anthropologist can provide a very accurate estimate of the age of the bone.

Osteoarthritic Lipping

Lipping is an additional bone growth around the edges of vertebrae (see Figure 14.2), a degenerative process that can be utilized in the collection of various data points to assist the forensic anthropologist in establishing the age of skeletal remains. Lipping most commonly occurs in older adults who have arthritis or osteoporosis, but it may also form at the site of bone trauma. It is known that as individuals age, their skeletons reflect the various stresses encountered through-out life. A gross quantification of these changes, especially in the vertebral column, has been published by Stewart (1979) and allows estimation of the age of older individuals by a forensic anthropolo-gist assisting a case detective on an investigation.

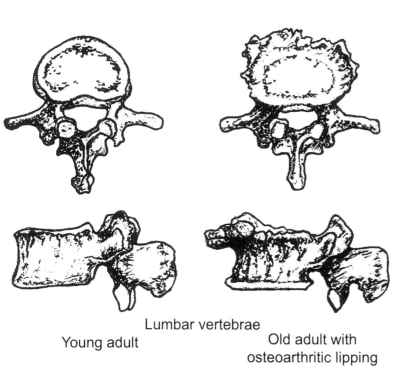

Lumbar vertebrae

Young adult   Old adult with
                                   osteoarthritic lipping

FIGURE 14.2
Osteoarthritic lipping occurring with old age in a lumbar vertebra.

Using all of the preceding methods, other indicators, and experience, a forensic anthropologist can fairly accurately determine age at death.

THE DETERMINATION OF A SKELETON'S SEX

As a CSI, you should know from the onset of this discussion that with the present state of knowledge, it is difficult, if not impossible, to determine the sex from the skeleton of subadult individuals. Skeletal sexual criteria manifest themselves at puberty, and are not clear in the skeleton below 12–15 years of age.

The best area to determine the sex of an adult skeleton is from the pelvis; second best, the skull; and, last, the rest of the skeleton (ANSI/ASB, 2019b).

The Pelvis

Women generally have broader hips than men. This width in the pelvis comes in three different areas:

- **Length of pubic bone**—When the innominate bone is held so that the pubic portion can be viewed from either the anterior or posterior aspect, you will see that the female has a long pubic portion and a much wider subpubic angle (see Figure 14.3). The innominate bone is more commonly referred to as the hip bone, but is actually the fusion of the ischium, ilium, and pubis bones in the pelvic region.
- **Width of the sciatic notch**—The notch is narrow in males and broad in females. If you insert your thumb into the sciatic notch, the notch should be relatively filled in a male, allowing for little lateral movement, whereas, in a female with a wider or broader notch, lateral movement of the thumb is possible. Considerable variability in this trait has been observed. Occasionally, males with "wide" notches are found, so it is best not to base your judgment of sex on this one criterion.
- **Bone buildup on the sacroiliac joint**—A wide pelvis is desirable in females for ease in childbirth. Starting in the unarticular area posterior to the sacroiliac articulation in a male skeleton, you can normally draw a pencil across the sacroiliac articulation of the ilium. This portion of the ilium, where it articulates (connects) with the sacrum (a triangular bone composed of five fused vertebrae, forming the posterior of the pelvis), is flat in males. There is a buildup of bone in this same area in a female so that beginning at the same area as above, the pencil encounters a ridge of bone in the sacroiliac articular area (see Figure 14.3).

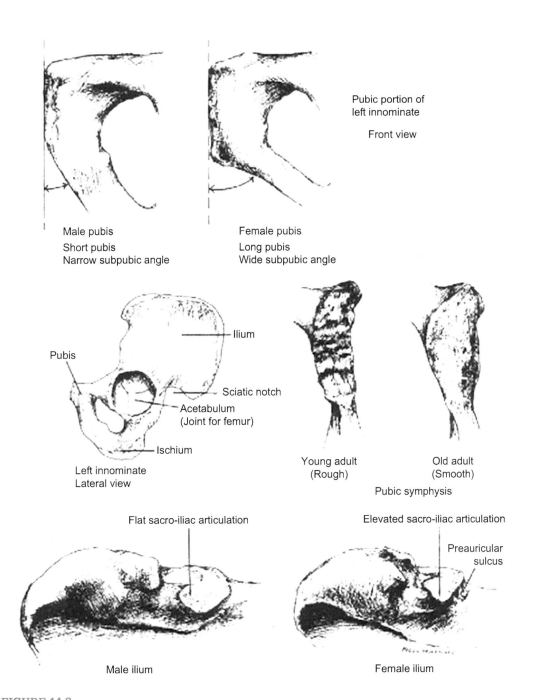

Pubic portion of
left innominate

Front view

Male pubis
Short pubis
Narrow subpubic angle

Female pubis
Long pubis
Wide subpubic angle

Pubis

Ilium

Sciatic notch

Acetabulum
(Joint for femur)

Ischium

Left innominate
Lateral view

Young adult
(Rough)

Old adult
(Smooth)

Pubic symphysis

Flat sacro-iliac articulation

Elevated sacro-iliac articulation

Preauricular
sulcus

Male ilium

Female ilium

FIGURE 14.3
The front view of the pubic portion of the left innominate.

The Skull

Sex differences in the skull are mainly due to sexual dimorphism: that is, the male skull is larger, more rugged, and muscle marked, and the female skull is smaller, more gracile, and smooth. Males have a larger **mastoid process** (which refers to the conical projection below the mastoid portion of the temporal bone, behind the ear at the base of the skull), well-marked **supraorbital ridges** (the curved upper border of the entrance to the eye socket), prominent muscle markings in the occipital region, and a larger mouth (measured metrically). Females usually have a smooth forehead with little or no supraorbital ridges, and because of less physical activity, have shallow muscle markings on the **occipital bone**, a compound bone that forms the posterior of the skull. The chin in a male is usually square; in females, it comes to a point (Giles & Elliot, 1963).

It is difficult to determine sex from anthropometric measurements of the teeth. However, anthropometric measurements of the skull have been used successfully by Giles (1964) to establish multivariate statistical procedures to determine the sex of unknown skulls. Giles also documented a discriminant function for sex discrimination of the **mandible**, which is the lower jawbone of a vertebrate.

The Rest of the Skeleton

If you do not have access to the pelvis or the skull, determining the sex of the skeleton is more difficult. Differences that can be observed are due mainly to sexual dimorphism, with males usually being larger in size because they normally reach puberty two years later than girls, which means they are growing for two years longer. Overall size is the main criterion, but specific areas you should look at are as follows:

- **Maximum diameter of the head of the femur**—Begin by measuring the maximum diameter of the articular surface. A measurement below 43 mm suggests a female; above 45 mm suggests a male. This is also true of the **humerus** (arm bone), with approximately the same measurements.
- **Width of the ala of the sacrum**—The width of the (articular) area of the sacrum for the fifth lumbar vertebra in a male will be greater than half the width of the entire sacrum. (A male's larger skeletal structure requires bigger articular areas.) The ala in females is less than half of the width of the sacrum.
- **Length of the sternum**—The **sternum**, also called the breastbone, is a long flat bone located in the chest that is connected to the ribs. The gender-predictive value of the length of the sternum has long been known, but an article by Stewart and McCormick in 1983 on measurements of sternal lengths on chest

plate x-rays for 617 autopsied adults from the United States provided valuable data for US forensic cases. Some researchers have
found indications that the length of the manubrium in males is
greater than one-half of the length of the gladiolus (blade). In
females, the length of the manubrium would be less than half
the length of the blade.

Septal Apertures of the Humerus

The presence of a supra condyloid foramen in the distal end of the
humerus (what Aleš Hrdlička in 1932 called "septal apertures") has
long been known to have a greater frequency in females.

THE DETERMINATION OF RACE (ANCESTRY) AND STATURE FROM THE SKELETON

Race (ancestry) is one of the most difficult determinations that the forensic anthropologist is required to establish. The most reliable area
of the skeleton for the determination of race is the skull—specifically
the face. Some research has been done on anterior-posterior femo-
ral curvature, but the results are not clear at this time. Craig (1994)
showed that the intercondylar shelf angle at the distal end of the
femur provides an 85 percent accuracy in determining race between
whites and blacks.

If your investigation at the crime scene has yielded a skull with the
face intact (i.e., there is little or no damage to the bone), the following criteria can be used to determine the race of the individual.

Anthropometric Measurements

In 1962, Eugene Giles and Orville Elliot published information on
the use of anthropometric measurements in a multivariate statistical analysis to determine the race of a skull. This procedure allows
for discrimination among Caucasoids (white/European), Negroids
(black/African), and Mongoloids (Asian/American Indian).

Prognathism (in Negroid Skulls)

Prognathism is the protrusion of the **alveolar region** (the section of
the jawbones containing the tooth sockets) of the mandible and the
maxilla (a pair of bones fused together that form the upper jawline).
It is common in Negroid (black) individuals, is seen slightly in Mongoloids (Asians), and only occasionally in Caucasoids (whites). A
quick test is to occlude (close) the lower jaw of the skull in its proper

dental occlusion and with a pencil or pen attempt to touch the base of the nasal aperture and chin at the same time. If this can be done, the skull is likely Caucasoid. Negroid individuals have a protrusion of the alveolar portion of the mandible and maxilla, so in the skulls of black people, the pencil usually will not touch the base of the nose and the chin at the same time.

Nasal Sill (in Caucasoid Skulls)

Observe carefully the base of the nasal aperture. With your pencil or pen resting against the bone of the maxilla just below the nasal opening, try to run the pencil or pen gently into the nasal opening. In Caucasoid skulls, there is usually a dam or nasal sill that will stop the instrument. In Negroid skulls, though, there is no dam or nasal sill, and the pen will glide easily into the nasal aperture.

Flat Face (in Mongoloid Skulls)

Hold the skull with the occipital region in one hand with the face up. Balance a pencil or pen across the nasal aperture. Now try to insert your finger between the instrument and the cheekbone under the lateral edge of the eye. If you can insert your finger without knocking off the pencil, the skull is probably Caucasoid. This is difficult, if not impossible, to do with Mongoloid skulls. Mongoloids (including American Indians) are the only race of humans that is cold adapted. They have flat, usually round, faces, whereas the nose and the faces of whites and others generally come to a point along the midline.

Edge-to-Edge Bite in Incisor Region (in Mongoloid Skulls)

When most Caucasoid and Negroid people occlude their teeth, they will have an overbite, a situation in which the upper or maxillary incisors are in front of the lower or mandibular incisors. Mongoloids, however (especially American Indians), generally have an edge-to-edge bite in the incisor region. If you are examining a skull with the incisor teeth present, look for wear on the occlusal (biting) surface of the incisor teeth. If wear is present (i.e., the enamel is worn off, exposing the dentin), you probably have an American Indian skull.

Stature: The Estimation of Stature from the Long Bones

A number of formulas exist that enable calculation of stature from long bones (ANSI/ASB, 2019a). In general, most calculations are based on the maximum length of the long bones. Probably the best formulas were developed by Trotter and Gleser in 1958 on the skeletons of Caucasians, Negroids, American Mongoloids, Mexican, and Puerto Rican males.

In 1994, Moore-Jansen et al. published *Data Collection Procedures for Forensic Skeletal Material*. Later, Jantz and Ousley (2005) combined anthropometric measurements for a number of populations around the world in FORDISC 3, a computer-generated method of determining race (ancestry). Forensic anthropologists from around the country submit demographic, metric, and nonmetric observations of their forensic cases to FORDISC 3, which currently contains skeletal data that has resulted in the development of new ancestry and sex discriminant functions.

ODONTOLOGY

Odontology, commonly referred to as dentistry, is the scientific study of teeth and their surrounding tissue. The forensic analysis of teeth is a separate field from anthropology, but every forensic anthropologist needs to know the basic knowledge of human dentition, such as the names of each tooth, how to identify an individual tooth, the age at which the tooth erupts (comes through the gum), whether teeth are deciduous or adult, when deciduous teeth are replaced by adult teeth, and the basic anatomy of a tooth.

Teeth, if available, are probably the best area of the human skeleton for determining a positive identification of an unidentified skull. Most people have been to a dentist at some point in their life, and an accurate record of any decay and damage or repair to the teeth has been compiled. X-rays of all the teeth should be contained in dentists' files, which the case detective should be able to obtain.

If you respond to a scene with a burned body found in an auto fire, you will be able to determine the owner of the car from the license plate and the VIN. If the owner is suspected of being the victim, you can locate the owner's dentist and submit the dental records for comparison with the dentition recovered from the excavation of the burned body. A forensic odontologist or dentist should be able to make a positive identification if there is a match with the dental records. If not, someone else was in the car when it was burned.

Dental evidence can survive temperatures of approximately 1,400°F and sometimes makes this type of evidence critical in an ongoing death investigation. According to the National Funeral Directors Association (NFDA), crematories operate at a temperature between 1,400 and 1,800°F, and even at these extreme temperatures, the cremation time is about two hours (nfda.org). The average vehicle fire does not burn at these temperature extremes, and there is not enough fuel for a two-hour fire. If no dental evidence is found at the scene of a vehicle fire, it stands to reason there was no human body in the fire.

This chapter's section on dentition (see the "Maturation" section earlier) covered the basic eruption sequence of both the deciduous and adult teeth. While students in forensic anthropology have difficulty determining whether a single tooth is deciduous (subadult) or adult, a dentist or forensic odontologist will be able to make that determination. Obtaining a working knowledge of dentition requires much study and practice, and that usually falls within the discipline of odontology (dentistry).

Dental evidence includes tooth enamel, dental fillings, and dental appliances that can withstand the human decomposition process. The CSI should exercise great care to retrieve every tooth when recovering a skeleton. Sometimes teeth may be scattered on the surface or buried. Frequently, a single tooth can be the main factor in a positive identification. Forensic odontologists will use dental evidence compared with dental records, charting, and x-rays to assist in death investigations.

Incidents involving mass disasters—for example, a jet crash, earthquake, or other situation where evidence such as fingerprints or DNA is not available from the decedents—will require the use of forensic odontologists to make positive identifications. Organized teams, such as the Disaster Mortuary Operational Response Team (DMORT), are trained to facilitate the identification of dental evidence at scenes. It is important to become familiar with what types of outside assistance are available to your agency before such an event occurs.

Human Dentition

There are 32 teeth in adults and 20 teeth in children. The study of teeth is very important to the anthropologist and paleontologist because teeth are constructed of dense and hard material, resist decay in the ground, and often outlast bone. There are four types of teeth in the human dental arch: incisors, canines, premolars, and molars (see Figure 14.4). This classification is based on both the morphology and function of the respective teeth. The following is the formula for adult dentition:

$$I\ \frac{2}{2}\ C\ \frac{1}{1}\ PM\ \frac{2}{2}\ M\ \frac{3}{3}\ = 16 \times 2 = 32$$

where

I=Incisor—teeth designed for cutting
C=Canine—teeth with pointed cusps for tearing and incising
PM=Premolars—teeth with broad occlusal surfaces with multiple cusps for grinding and reducing food material as an aid to digestion
M=Molars—same as premolars, but with broader occlusal surfaces

The dental formula expresses the number of teeth in the upper jaw (numbers above the line), but in only one-half of the mouth. The numbers recorded in the formula must be multiplied by two to determine the total number of teeth in the mouth. Often teeth will be referred to as M^1, M^2, and so on, indicating the first and second upper molars, and M_1, M_2, and so on, indicating the lower molars.

Humans develop two sets of teeth. Usually, no teeth are visible at birth, but at approximately six months of age, the first deciduous (baby) teeth—the lower central incisors—erupt. The deciduous set consists of 20 teeth and may be represented in a formula as follows:

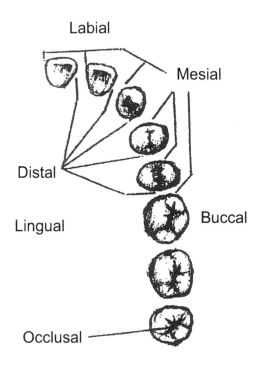

FIGURE 14.4
Tooth surfaces.

$$i \, \frac{2}{2} \, c \, \frac{1}{1} \, m \, \frac{2}{2} \, = 10 \times 2 = 20$$

The names of the teeth are abbreviated in the same way as the adult dental formula, but with lowercase letters. (Note that there are no premolars in the human deciduous formula.) The deciduous dentition consists of eight incisors, four canines, and eight molars. The deciduous incisors and canines are miniature replicas of the adult incisors and canines. The same criteria used to differentiate between adult incisors and canines may be employed for the corresponding deciduous teeth. The first deciduous molars are the precursors of the adult maxillary (upper) premolars. The deciduous second molars are replicas of the permanent first molars in the respective maxilla or mandible.

Sexual dimorphism is not marked enough in either the adult or the deciduous dentition to allow sex determinations to be made. However, as a general rule, males tend to have slightly larger teeth.

The Anatomy of a Tooth

Each tooth has three areas:

- **Crown**—That part of the tooth situated above the gum and covered with enamel.
- **Neck**—A slightly constricted portion just below the crown and the area known as the cemento-enamel junction.
- **Root**—That portion of the tooth below the crown and neck. It is enclosed in the tooth socket and covered with cementum.

Each tooth consists of

- **Enamel**—A white, compact, and very hard substance that covers and protects the dentin of the crown of the tooth.
- **Cementum**—A layer of bony tissue covering the root of a tooth.
- **Dentin**—The chief tissue of the tooth that surrounds the pulp cavity. It is covered by enamel on most of the exposed parts of the tooth and by cementum on the part implanted in the jaw. Dentin forms the main bulk of the tooth.
- **Pulp cavity**—The pulp chamber and canal within the tooth. It contains a soft tissue called pulp.

Each tooth has five surfaces (see Figure 14.4):

- **Labial (lips) or buccal (cheek)**—Labial, the side toward the lips, is used with incisors and canines; buccal, the side toward the cheek, is used with premolars and molars.
- **Lingual**—The side toward the tongue.

- **Occlusal**—The surface on the tooth that comes into contact with the teeth of the opposite jaw (the biting surface).
- **Mesial**—The surface of the tooth that lies against an adjoining tooth and faces toward the median line.
- **Distal**—The surface of the tooth that lies against an adjoining tooth and faces away from the median line.

Teeth vary in their morphology and thus can be good clues for a positive identification (see Figures 14.5a–14.5c). Many people smile while being photographed. As such, a photograph will often show the structure of teeth (crowned, crowded, or misaligned); any spacing, staining (from smoking or chewing tobacco), or chipping; carious lesions (cavities); peg-shaped lateral incisors; or postmortem loss. All of these unique characteristics can be used in arriving at a positive identification.

Dr. William M. Bass is a forensic anthropologist renowned for his research on human osteology and decomposition at the University of Tennessee's Forensic Anthropology Research Facility in Knoxville, popularly known as the "Body Farm." He was involved in an exhumation to determine the positive identification of an adult female who went missing in 1978. In the spring of 1979, a decomposed and mummified skeleton was found in an adjoining county. No positive identification of the skeletal remains was made by the medical examiner, but on circumstantial evidence, the skeleton was buried as the missing woman. For years the children of the missing woman have been worried about whether the body buried is really that of their mother. With the advent of DNA, they had obtained

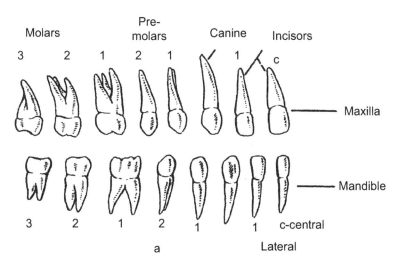

FIGURE 14.5A
Tooth types.

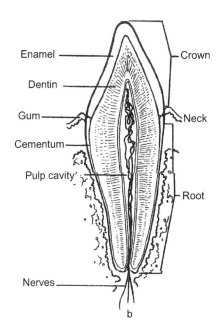

Enamel — Crown

Dentin —

Gum — Neck

Cementum —

Pulp cavity'

Root

Nerves —

b

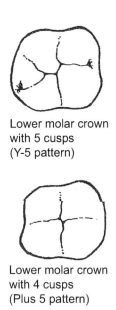

Lower molar crown
with 5 cusps
(Y-5 pattern)

Lower molar crown
with 4 cusps
(Plus 5 pattern)

c

FIGURE 14.5B
Anatomical terms for teeth.

FIGURE 14.5C
Cusp patterns.

legal approval to exhume the skeleton in hopes of making a positive identification from DNA analysis of a tooth or bone sample. In an attempt to save the family the considerable expense of a DNA analysis, Bass encouraged the family to locate a photograph of the woman in hopes of matching the dentition of the skull, but no photograph of the woman smiling was found.

Two DNA samples revealed that the skeleton thought to be that of their mother does not match the DNA of the two daughters. Instead of solving one unidentified person case from more than 25 years ago, there are now two unsolved identifications—that of the missing mother (for which no skeletal material or information exists), and that of the unidentified female whose skeletal remains were buried in the wrong grave.

The University of Tennessee's Anthropological Research Facility is the oldest of the five investigative projects in the world that use human cadavers to facilitate research (see Figure 14.6). The faculty and graduate students scientifically document postmortem change and provide training opportunities to law enforcement, medico-legal death investigators, and the Federal Bureau of Investigation (http:// fac.utk.edu/facilities.html). The newest research facility is also located in Tennessee, and will focus on the environmental/ecological effects of animal and human flesh decomposition.

FIGURE 14.6
Wood and wire cages prevent predator damage to cadavers at outdoor anthropological research facilities. Arthur Bohanan, thebodyfarm.org.

NAMUS

NamUs, the National Missing and Unidentified Persons System, is a clearinghouse for missing persons and unidentified decedent records. There are approximately 40,000 unidentified human remains records in the United States, with about 4,400 new cases each year. After one year, approximately 1,000 of those new cases will remain unnamed. NamUs is a free online system that medical examiners, coroners, law enforcement officials, and the general public can search to solve these cases. This system was created through the National Institute of Justice and the National Association of Medical Examiners as they seek to support investigators working to identify cases involving unidentified remains or missing persons (www.namus.gov).

The Unidentified Persons Database contains information entered by medical examiners and coroners. Unidentified persons are people who have died and whose bodies have not been identified. Anyone can search this database using characteristics such as sex, race, distinct body features, and even dental information.

The Missing Persons Database contains information about missing persons that anyone can enter; before it appears as a case on NamUs, the information is verified. NamUs provides the ability to print missing persons posters and even map out possible travel routes in a search for a missing person. A short video explaining how family members or others searching for lost loved ones can use NamUs is available at www.findthemissing.org/homes/how_it_works_video. Other resources include links to state clearinghouses, medical examiner and coroner offices, law enforcement agencies, victim assistance groups, and pertinent legislation.

When a new missing person or unidentified decedent case is entered into NamUs, the system automatically performs cross-matching comparisons between the databases, searching for matches or similarities between cases. NamUs provides free DNA testing and other forensic services, such as anthropology and odontology assistance. There is also an Unclaimed Persons page on the NamUs website that allows a search of deceased persons who have been identified by name, but for whom no family member or next of kin has been located. Through this database, the remains of deceased individuals can link families so the body can be claimed for burial or other disposition (https://claimus.org).

ENTOMOLOGY

Entomology is that branch of science dealing with the study of insects. This section is provided as an introduction for the CSI into a subarea of entomology known as "forensic entomology." **Forensic entomology** is the field in which arthropod science and the judicial system interact. The area of forensic entomology has developed over the years to become an increasingly important aspect of the "forensic sciences" in North America. Death investigators from every field have observed that in recent deaths—especially outdoors where flies and beetles have easy access—maggots and corpses go together.

The information provided here is a procedural guide for the CSI on what to look for and how best to collect the entomological evidence. For more information on the value of entomology in estimating the length of time since death, you should review the following three publications: Byrd and Tomberlin's *Forensic Entomology: The Utility of Arthropods in Legal Investigation* (2020), Catts and Haskell's *Entomology and Death: A Procedural Guide* (1990), and Goff's *A Fly for the Prosecution* (2000). The authors of these books have extensive education, research, and experience working with law enforcement to determine the time since death. Professional forensic entomologists are certified by the American Board of Forensic Entomology.

THE DETERMINATION OF TIME SINCE DEATH

While forensic anthropologists determine the age at death, the main focus of forensic entomology is to establish scientifically the time since death: the **postmortem interval (PMI)**. This requires careful observation of the location of the remains (whether in sunlight or shade), clothing or no clothing, indoors or outdoors, rural or urban setting, and especially the temperature where the corpse is lying. Decomposition is driven by many factors, but the major ones are temperature and bacterial and insect action. Because of these main factors, a dead body will decay much faster in the summer than in the winter or in warmer climates than in colder climates. Therefore, insects can help the investigator determine the PMI in two ways. First, blow flies are the earliest insects to arrive to the dead body, and in combination with the climatic conditions at the crime scene, their development from egg to adult follows a predictable pattern. Therefore, blow fly developmental rates can be used to estimate how long the insects have been feeding on the body, which will provide an indication of how long the victim has been dead. Second, the order in which different insect species arrive to, and leave from, the dead body can help investigators estimate the PMI. However, of the two methods identified above, insect succession is the most difficult way to estimate the PMI because it is greatly affected by season, habitat, and the geographical region. In general, a dead body undergoes four stages of decomposition where different insects will colonize the remains in a predictable sequence. However, the sequence can vary depending on the geographic location. Although a well-trained professional will be able to identify the stage of decomposition and all of the insects associated with the dead body, if the succession of insect species for a particular geographic region is unknown, then an accurate estimation of the PMI is unlikely. Currently, several insect succession databases have been created for a variety of regions across North America, and additional databases are being developed. Below is a general overview of the four stages of decomposition and the insects that are typically associated with each stage. See Byrd and Castner (2010) for a more detailed discussion of insect colonization of a corpse.

STAGES OF DECOMPOSITION

Fresh Stage

The first stage of decomposition is the fresh stage. During the fresh stage, blood and oxygen flow stops and the body begins cooling (algor mortis), the cells and tissues begin breaking down, the muscular tissue becomes rigid (rigor mortis), and the process of microbial proliferation (putrefaction) begins (Damann & Carter, 2013). In general, the first insects to be attracted to the decaying body are the blow flies (family Calliphoridae), muscid flies (family Muscidae), and the flesh flies (family Sarcophagidae). Female blow flies and muscid flies lay eggs in the moist orifices of the body (eye, ears, nose, mouth, or any wound in the body). Flesh flies do not lay eggs on the corpse, but deposit live maggots directly on the natural body openings or wounds.

Bloated Stage

The early decomposition or "bloat" stage is where anaerobic metabolism takes place, leading to the accumulation of gases that give the body a bloated appearance. During this stage, the skin will become discolored and some blistering, skin slippage, and hair loss will occur (Damann & Carter, 2013). In addition to increased levels of blow fly, muscid fly, and flesh fly activity, the first beetle species appear. More specifically, carrion beetles (family Silphidae), rove beetles (family Staphylinidae), and clown beetles (family Histeridae) arrive to feed on the large number of maggots that are consuming the dead body. Because these beetle species feed on fly larvae, they will remain present throughout the decomposition process.

Decay Stage

During the decay stage, the overall body mass is decreased due to the loss of internal organs and the draining of decomposition fluids to the surrounding environment. The abdominal cavity will cave in, and depending on the environment, the outer tissue may begin to mummify (Rivers & Dahlem, 2014). In the early part of this stage, the blow flies, muscid flies, and flesh flies will continue to be active, but as the decomposing body transitions into the later stages of decay, these flies will disappear. In their place, other flies such as black scavenger flies (family Sepsidae) and soldier flies (family Stratiomyidae) will become more prevalent. The latter part of this stage will also be characterized by the arrival of checkered beetles (family Cleridae), hide beetles (family Trogidae), scarab beetles (family Scarabaeidae), and sap beetles (family Nitidulidae).

Dry Stage

In the final stage of decomposition, referred to as the dry or post decay stage, all that remains is dry skin, cartilage, and bones (Damann & Carter, 2013). The insects that colonize the body during the post decay stage will be feeding on the remaining dry tissue, hair, fungus found on the corpse, and the other insect species that remain. Some of these insects include checkered beetles, hide beetles, scarab beetles, sap beetles, and the late arriving dermestid beetles (family Dermestidae). The scavenger and soldier flies will increase in number, and skipper flies (family Piophilidae) will also be present.

If a body is in the fresh or bloated stage of decomposition, then blow fly developmental rates are used to determine the PMI. In general (with variations depending on the area, conditions, season, blow fly species, etc.), the common blow fly life cycle is 10 to 20 days. Eggs are deposited at about one to two days; maggots appear shortly after the eggs have been laid and proceed through three stages over a total of about two more days. The third stage forms a pupa about five days later, and the adult fly forms from the pupa at approximately another six days. If, however, the remains are in the advanced decay or dry stage, then estimating age from insect succession data may be used.

It is also important to keep in mind that not all parts of a body decay at the same speed. Because the skull has many openings, it will decay faster than other parts of the body, such as the legs and arms, which have no natural openings. The CSI should be especially careful of deferential decay. For example, a decomposing body may be located whose right hand has decayed down to the bone, but you could still get fingerprints from the left hand. This suggests that at or near the time of death, the deceased may have been attacked and saw the blow or knife coming. The victim may have put up the right hand as protection, and thus the right hand is cut. Remember that flies are looking for blood or a fresh cut so they will be attracted to the freshly injured hand. In cases like this, the CSI should carefully examine the bones of the right hand for cuts or bludgeon damage, and compare them with those of the left hand. Always be aware of decay in areas where you would not expect it—especially when making left and right comparisons.

COLLECTION AND HANDLING OF INSECTS AT THE CRIME SCENE

As a crime scene investigator, you will be responsible for the collection, preservation, documentation, and shipment of entomological evidence to the forensic entomologist. Therefore, the proper handling and preservation of the collected insects is extremely important. If the insects are not collected and preserved properly, then a species level identification may not be attained. Additionally, without thorough documentation of the crime scene and the collection of supplemental data (e.g., temperature), the interpretation of the entomological evidence will be limited. Moreover, the courts require that the proper collection, preservation, and chain-of-custody procedures are followed and documented throughout the process. Below is a brief overview of the procedures that should be followed when collecting insects at a crime scene. For a more in-depth discussion of the recommended procedures for collecting insect specimens at a crime scene, see Byrd and Castner's *Forensic Entomology: The Utility of Arthropods in Legal Investigation* (2010).

Assessment of the Crime Scene

Dead bodies are found in a variety of environments. Therefore, when you first arrive to the crime scene, you should note the body's location and condition. For example, is the body inside or outside of a building? Is it located in a rural or urban area? Is the body in a forest, field, buried, hanging from a tree, in the trunk of a car, burned, or submerged in water? You should also note the stage of decomposition (e.g., fresh, bloat, early decay, advanced decay, dry/skeleton) and if there are any potential insect barriers such as clothing, concealment, submerged in water, and any scavengers. After your initial assessment, it is important to make sure that the body remains undisturbed until the entomological evidence has been collected. Limiting the number of people, and the amount of activity, around the corpse is important because too much activity can impact the presence of insects that are on and around the body. Thus, when you first arrive to the crime scene, you should consult with the ranking investigator to determine who and how many individuals have been near the body, what physical evidence has been recovered, and what should not be disturbed. Following your initial assessment of the crime scene, you should slowly approach the body and begin collecting insects. The collection of insects should be done before and after the body has been removed.

Collecting and Preserving Adult Insects

Adult insects should be collected from the body and the surrounding area using an insect net and feather-weight forceps. The insect net is used to collect flying insects, whereas the forceps are used to collect ground crawling insects. Collected specimens should be placed in a container that contains ethyl acetate. These containers, also referred to as kill jars, are inexpensive and can be purchased online. After a few seconds of being in the kill jar, the dead insects can be transferred to a labeled shipping container. In addition to the case and specimen number, each label should contain information on the date and time the specimen was collected, the location it was collected from, and the CSI who collected it. Additional information about each specimen will be reported on the entomological sample log sheet (see Figure 14.7).

Collecting and Preserving Immature Insects

Immature insects (e.g., egg, larvae, pupae) should also be collected from the body and the surrounding environment. Feather-weight forceps and vials should be used to collect and transport the specimens. Egg masses will often be found in, or close to, wounds and natural openings. Eggs should be collected from each mass found on and around the body. Each egg mass should be divided into two. One half should be placed in a vial containing 70–75 percent alcohol

(ETOH), and the other half should be kept alive by placing them in a vial that contains a piece of damp paper towel to prevent desiccation. Larvae should be collected from each site of maggot activity, and half of each sample should be killed and preserved in a vial containing 70–75 percent alcohol (ETOH), and the other half should be kept alive in a vial with a piece of damp paper towel. Pupae are generally collected from the soil under and around the body. However, the clothing and hair should also be searched. All pupae should be placed in a dry vial with a piece of damp paper towel. Each container and vial should be labeled and contain the same information as the labels used for the adult insects. For a more thorough discussion of how to collect and preserve immature insects, see Anderson and Cervenka's *Insects Associated with the Body: Their Use and Analysis* (2001).

Collecting Climatic Data

Temperature is essential in order to estimate the postmortem interval. Therefore, several temperature readings should be taken at the crime scene. The ambient air temperature should be recorded at 1 ft and 4 ft heights near the body. Additional readings should include the ground surface temperature, body surface temperature, under-body surface temperature, soil temperatures at 10 cm and 20 cm, maggot mass temperatures taken by inserting the thermometer into the center of the maggot mass, and the water and indoor temperature if appropriate. Weather data such as the body's exposure to the sun and if there has been any recent rain or snow should also be recorded, along with the maximum and minimum daily temperature and precipitation for a period of two weeks before the victim's disappearance and five days after the body was discovered. This information can be obtained from the nearest national weather service office.

Remember that you get only one chance to investigate a crime scene. Photograph everything before anything is moved. As a crime scene is investigated, it is dismantled, so detailed documentation and photographs are essential. Goff states, "As a rule the more time elapses between death and the discovery of the body, the less accurate is the estimation of the postmortem interval based on entomological evidence" (Goff, 2000, p. 67). Although this is true, temperature and the proper identification of the collected insects are the two most important factors in the field of forensic entomology. Without a correct species identification, the estimated PMI will be invalid. Therefore, insect identifications should only be made by professional entomologists. For aid in the identification of the entomological evidence, contact a professional entomologist at your nearest college or university. Even an entomologist who is not interested in forensic evidence should be able to direct you to someone in your geographic area who can provide assistance.

Death Scene Collection Notes

Prepared By: _____ Case No: _____ Date _____ Time _____

SCENE NOTES

Temperature: Ambient _____ Body surface _____ Ground surface _____ Under-body interface _____ Soil (10 cm depth) _____ Soil (20 cm depth) _____ Maggot mass _____ Water (if aquatic) _____ Enclosed structure _____

Weather Conditions _____
_____
_____

DEATH SCENE HABITAT

Rural: Forest ____ Field ____ Pasture ____ Roadside ____ Closed bldg. ____ Open bldg. ____ Other _____

Urban/Suburban: Closed bldg. ____ Open bldg. ____ Dumpster ____ Parking lot ____ Other _____

Aquatic: Lake ____ Pond ____ River (sm) ____ River (lg) ____ Creek ____ Canal ____ Other _____

BODY NOTES

Sex _____ Height (estimate) _____ Weight (estimate) _____

Body Exposure: Open air _____ Burial _____ Other _____

Enclosed: Entire ____ Partial ____ Nude ____ Portion of body clothed _____

Stage of Decomposition: Fresh ____ Bloat ____ Active Decay ____ Advanced Decay ____ Dry ____ Remains ____

Evidence of Scavengers: Y/N Description: _____

Defects Present: Y/N Defect Description: _____

Trauma Contribution to Insect Activity: _____

INSECT NOTES

Present Stages: Eggs _____ Larvae ____ Nymph ____ Puparium ____ Adult ____ Maggot Mass ____

Number of Samples Obtained: Preserved _____ Live _____

Identified Specimens: _____ Location: _____

FIGURE 14.7
Death scene collection notes.

Discussion Questions

1. List what a forensic anthropologist may be able to identify on skeletonized remains of a human. Briefly discuss each.
2. What are some of the ways bones and teeth can help in the positive identification of an unidentified body?
3. What web-based tool can law enforcement and members of the general public use to search for lost or missing people? How can CSIs use this information?
4. What is the main purpose of forensic entomology? Does the environment contribute to the decay of a body? If so, why?
5. Which insects are typically first to be found postmortem? Do all parts of the body decay evenly? Why or why not?

REFERENCES

Anderson, G. S., & Cervenka, V. J. (2001). Insects associated with the body: Their use and analysis. In W. D. Haglund and M. H. Sorg (Eds.), *Advances in forensic taphonomy: Method, theory, and archaeological perspectives* (pp. 173200). Boca Raton, FL: CRC Press.

ANSI/ASB. (2019a). *Standard for Stature Estimation in Forensic Anthropology* (Standard No. 45). Retrieved from https://www.aafs.org/asb-standard/standard-stature-estimation-forensic-anthropology

ANSI/ASB. (2019b). *Standard for Sex Estimation in Forensic Anthropology* (Standard No. 90). Retrieved from https://www.aafs.org/asb-standard/standard-sex-estimation-forensic-anthropology

Bass, W. M. (2005). *Human osteology: A laboratory and field manual* (5th Edition). Columbia, MO: Missouri Archaeological Society.

Byrd, J. H., & Tomberlin, J. K. (2020). *Forensic entomology: The utility of arthropods in legal investigations* (3rd Edition). Boca Raton, FL: CRC Press.

Catts, E. P., & Haskell, N. H. (1990). *Entomology and death: A procedural guide.* Clemson, SC: Joyce's Print Shop.

Craig, E. (1994). Bones of the knee joint and individual features that can be used for forensic identification. Ph.D. Dissertation, The University of Tennessee.

Damann, F. E., & Carter, D. O. (2013). Human decomposition ecology and postmortem microbiology. In J. T. Pokines and S. A. Symes (Eds.), *Manual of forensic taphonomy* (pp.175192). Boca Raton, FL: CRC Press.

Gilbert, M. B., & McKern, T. W. (1973). A method for aging the female os pubis. *American Journal of Physical Anthropology, 38*, 31–38.

Giles, E. (1964). Sex determination by discriminant function analysis of the mandible. *American Journal of Physical Anthropology, 22*, 129–135.

Giles, E., & Elliot, O. (1962). Race identification from cranial measurements. *Journal of Forensic Sciences, 7*, 147–157.

Giles, E., & Elliot, O. (1963). Sex determination by discriminant function analysis of crania. *American Journal of Physical Anthropology, 21*, 53–68.

Goff, L. M. (2000). *A fly for the prosecution: How insect evidence helps solve crimes.* Cambridge, MA: Harvard University Press.

Hrdlička, A. (1932). The principle dimensions, absolute and relative, of the humerus in the white race. *American Journal of Physical Anthropology, 16*, 431–450.

Jantz, R. L., & Ousley, S. D. (2005). *FORDISC 3: Computer forensic discriminant function*. Knoxville, TN: University of Tennessee. (Version 3.0) (Computer software).

Kerley, E. R. (1965). The microscopic determination of age in human bone. *American Journal of Physical Anthropology, 23*, 149–164.

McKern, T. W., & Stewart, D. (1957). *Skeletal age changes in young American males, analyzed from standpoint of identification*. Natick, MA: Headquarters Quartermaster Research and Development Command. (Technical Report EP-45).

Moore-Jansen, P. M., Ousley, S. D., & Jantz, R. L. (1994). *Data collection procedures for forensic skeletal material*. Knoxville, TN: University of Tennessee. (Report of Investigation No. 48, Department of Anthropology).

Rivers, D. B., & Dahlem, G. A. (2014). *The science of forensic entomology*. Hoboken, NJ: Wiley Blackwell.

Rodriguez, W. C., & Bass, W. M. (1983). Insect activity and its relationship to decay rates of human cadavers in East Tennessee. *Journal of Forensic Sciences, 28*, 423–432.

Stewart, T. D. (1979). Essentials of forensic anthropology. Springfield, IL: Charles C. Thomas.

Stewart, J. H., & McCormick, W. F. (1983). The gender predictive value of sternal length. *American Journal of Forensic Medicine and Pathology, 4*, 217–220.

Todd, W. T. (1920). Age changes in the pubic bone I: The male white pubic. *American Journal of Physical Anthropology, 3*, 285–334.

Trotter, M., & Gleser, G. C. (1958). A re-evaluation of stature based on measurements taken during life and of long bones after death. *American Journal of Physical Anthropology, 16*, 79–123.

CHAPTER 15

Documenting the Actions of the CSI and Presenting Facts in Court

What You Will Learn

The final chapter presents the CSI with the realities of bringing all the documentation together for completion of the case file. Working with the prosecutor's office in preparation for court testimony is an essential part of the CSI's responsibility. Protocols must be explained in laymen's terms to the court (including the jury), and it is important that the laboratory analyst is included with the investigative efforts.

MURDER IN THE NEW YEAR

Documenting the Actions of the CSI

It was a clear, cold day. Tom Smith smiled at Detective Mavis Fletcher and patted his stomach. "You can't beat the 'country boy breakfast' at Mel's."

"The omelet wasn't the best, but hey, you're paying, so all I have to spring for is an extra-strength roll of Tums," Mavis said with a laugh.

Tom looked up at the sky. "You know, I can take cold weather a lot better with the sun shining."

"True enough," Mavis replied, "but for Dean Michael Sellers, the sun isn't shining so brightly. In fact, it's beginning to set."

DOI: 10.4324/9780429261657-15

"I thought six hours with the DA on our last case was a long sit-down, but this one took the cake—eight hours and change," Tom replied, sticking a toothpick in the corner of his mouth.

Mavis Fletcher put on her gloves. "The dean is pretty well connected, and the college figures prominently in our good town. Politics and public relations as well as law and order are always part of the DA's job description."

Tom grinned at Mavis. "And future political aspirations?"

The detective put her gloved hands into her coat pocket as the two of them walked toward her car. "Perhaps, but whatever his agenda, we always have to carefully follow crime scene protocols and evidence submission and meet with the prosecutor's office when we are immersed in a complex case."

"Yep," Tom replied, positioning his baseball cap on his head. "'Course, we never found the gun."

Mavis shrugged.

> We haven't found it yet. The digital forensics and computer evidence give us a strong, if not foolproof, hand to play as well as the strong circumstantial evidence. There's enough there for a jury that's paying attention to the evidence identification, preservation, and chain of custody.

Tom Smith opened Detective Fletcher's car door for her. "At least, ol' Sellers finally wised up and got himself a lawyer."

"And none too soon," Mavis replied as she slid into the driver's seat.

She nodded to Tom as she closed the door. "Until next time, CSI Smith."

Tom tipped his hat. "Adios, Detective."

INTRODUCTION

Crime scene reconstruction is the systematic process of piecing together information and evidence in an investigation to gain a better understanding of the actions that took place between the victim and the offender during the commission of a crime. The crime scene reconstructionist uses forensic evidence and information to infer what occurred during the interaction between the offender and the victim. CSI personnel are responsible for accurate preparation and prompt submission of all crime scene documentation. The written reports establish the scene at the time the responding officer arrived and verify the actions of the CSI at the crime scene. All paperwork must be thorough and properly prepared, including copies of all evidence and photography logs. Legible, comprehensive reports must be submitted in a timely manner so that detectives and crime laboratory personnel have access to the information and are up-to-date on all aspects of the investigation. The case file is the foundation of all investigations and is usually the basis for prosecutorial actions. If it is not included in the case file, it did not happen! According to the FBI, forensic evidence cannot be overdocumented; take time to review the case file and check for consistency and accuracy.

CASE FILES

The **case file** is the compilation of all case documents pertaining to an investigation, including evidence and photography logs, photographs, sketches, case narrative, chain of custody forms, laboratory requests and reports, and other records. The written reports contained in the case file will form the basis for your testimony when criminal charges or civil actions result in judicial proceedings. It is essential that all pertinent facts, as well as all actions you took, are included in the records to substantiate the validity of the forensic evidence identified, collected, and preserved at the crime scene. Your written documentation will be used by all entities within and many outside the criminal justice system, including lawyers (prosecutors and defense attorneys), judges, jurors, government officials, insurance investigators, citizens, defendants, media representatives, crime lab analysts, and other investigating agencies. The entire case file and court transcripts become a permanent part of the public record.

The **case narrative** is a running description of the entire crime scene investigation and should be presented in the same systematic, methodical, and logical manner in which you conducted your activities at the scene. Document all actions, including discoveries that were made during the course of the investigation. If additional resources were required, identify when these resources were notified and their arrival on the scene. Any reports prepared by these additional personnel should also be integrated into your case file. All narrative reports must address the questions of who, what, where, when, how, and why. Do not include irrelevant information; remain concise and state only factual information.

The written narrative is your first introduction to the court and should reflect positively on your knowledge, skills, and ability to fulfill the responsibilities of a CSI. In addition to good job performance regarding the crime scene, you must develop the ability to relate your actions truthfully and correctly in the written narrative so that others are presented with objective and unbiased case information. All activities should be documented in chronological order, which is important in demonstrating to the court that the crime scene processing was conducted in a systematic manner.

The CSI's primary responsibilities are to locate, identify, document, collect, and preserve the physical evidence at a crime scene. You are not there to prove or disprove any theories but to collect the data and physical evidence that will be considered by the decision makers in the proper forum. Let the evidence speak for itself. Remain unbiased in your crime scene processing and documentation of those efforts. The case may not be resolved for many years, and your case notes and documentation must stand the test of time. With the advancement of DNA analysis and other technologies, decades-old cold cases are being reopened, and the validity of the evidence collected 10, 20, or even 30 years or more ago is being subjected to intense new scrutiny. Convicted inmates now have the right to case review where there is the potential for exoneration based on the analysis of physical evidence for the presence or lack of biological fluids. Wrongful conviction cases based on present-day DNA analysis techniques are now showing up on court dockets in growing numbers. This should remind you that even though a case may have been adjudicated, the American judicial system is designed for redress of previous errors, so the importance of credible case documentation cannot be underestimated.

The narrative portion of your report must provide a detailed description of the crime scene that can be clarified with photographs and videos taken at the scene. Consider the reader's perspective as you write to ensure that the words and phrases you use are clearly understandable. State your observations upon arrival at the scene, including the scene's precise location, and describe the specific actions you took in your capacity as the CSI. If GPS coordinates are available, include them in the reports. This technology has become readily acceptable in court proceedings and is a reliable way to establish exact locations. Many digital cameras can also record GPS coordinates to document the precise spot where photographs were taken. This information can be used to substantiate the testimony, logs, sketches, and reports. Remember to report all actions in sequential order. Stick to the facts and do not offer analyses or conclusions. The actions you took to secure the scene should have effectively frozen in time the conditions of the crime scene.

Itemize all evidence and cross-reference these entries with photographs. List the steps you took to document, identify, collect, and preserve the evidence. Report the disposition of each item. For example, the evidence could have been submitted to a local or state crime lab for additional analysis. However, it is certainly possible that forensic evidence could still be secured in the agency's property unit, having been processed at the local level. These reports should always be written in the first person and in present tense. Refer to other persons involved in the investigation by the appropriate role (e.g., victim, witness) or by name. Do not use police slang, radio signals, or jargon in your reports because these words may be interpreted differently at another agency or by those of another discipline. If the language in your reports is clear and accurate, this eliminates possible confusion during the investigation and any subsequent court proceedings.

Include copies of search warrants or signed consent-to-search forms in the case file. When appropriate, it is also important to document requests for family members and others present at the crime scene to provide known standards of inked fingerprint impressions and DNA samples. Entries should be made into the case file about when and under what conditions these known samples were gathered. When it is necessary for the case detective to obtain a search warrant in order for these samples to be collected, copies of these warrants should be kept in the case file to validate the legality of the sample collection process and clearly establish the chain of custody.

Remember to continue the written narrative for every action that you take on the case. No detail is too insignificant to note. If something catches someone's attention, include that information in your notes. Minor details can turn into major leads, which may provide associative evidence or linkages in the investigation. Cross-check the written narrative with both the evidence and photograph logs to ensure accuracy and completeness of the case documentation. The narrative report is utilized to convey only the facts and should not leave anything open to question. Clarity, good grammar, and accuracy contribute to the narrative report becoming a useful tool for subsequent legal proceedings. Although many forms can now be completed online, some forms must still be completed manually, so be sure to write legibly in ink and sign your name clearly.

CRIME SCENE PROTOCOLS

Every crime scene investigation is unique and requires an individual approach. The features of different cases must be carefully examined by the CSI, and a thorough assessment of the scene must be completed prior to beginning to process the scene. A report of this preliminary survey or walkthrough should be contained in the narrative report because it establishes the groundwork for the strategic plan that was devised to ensure thoroughness and accuracy of the investigation.

Written protocols and **standard operating procedures (SOPs)** are adopted by law enforcement agencies in cooperation with regional, state, and federal crime laboratories to ensure that all CSI personnel follow accepted scientific practices. The use of SOPs and standard forms provides a routine method for quickly identifying and processing physical evidence. This creates more time for the CSI to deal with the unique aspects of each particular crime scene. Agency-specific documentation must be completed and placed into the case file. Be sure to continue double-checking every entry into the case file to maintain the consistency and credibility of the investigation process.

Regardless of the varying formats and procedures in place at different agencies, the fundamental principles of investigating and documenting a crime scene must be followed in every situation, every time. The size of the agency, resource availability, and jurisdictional concerns may all impact the amount of time that a CSI can spend processing the scene; however, the adage "the job's not finished until the paperwork is done" is most appropriate to conducting a thorough and precisely documented crime scene investigation.

While it is true that the only consistent factors among crime scenes are the inconsistencies, following established protocols provides a frame of reference for all components of the criminal justice system. A standard format with which prosecutors are familiar facilitates access to information, allows them to obtain necessary warrants and check for any missing information or discrepancies, and helps prepare cases for court presentation.

Because procedures cannot be written to cover all eventualities, CSIs will need to deal with unforeseen situations and circumstances. Advanced training and experience will allow you to implement procedures that will stand up to courtroom scrutiny to deal with situations that are not covered in the SOP manual. Adherence to standards of operation and performance will ensure the credibility of the CSI and the integrity of the physical evidence and the crime scenes processed. Many accrediting organizations require that protocols and SOPs be created and followed for the agency to remain in compliance with mandatory standards.

Certain protocols are universally accepted and relate specifically to evidence-labeling practices. Using the standardized abbreviation of "Q" for questioned or evidentiary items to precede the item number clearly denotes the origin of the item and incorporates terminology such as "unknown," "latent," and "evidence" into a uniform category. For example, if you collect four latent fingerprints at a scene, the items would be labeled Q1, Q2, Q3, and Q4, which eliminates any confusion as to the status of those items of evidence.

Comparison samples are composed of physical evidence from the crime scene that can be compared with samples from suspects, victims, and known standards. The evidence analysts at the crime laboratory perform a comparison of the unknown "Q" items to known "K" samples that are submitted by the CSI. The analyst will seek to determine whether the Q and the K items originated from the same source. If you develop a suspect and submit an inked fingerprint card as K1, it will be compared to Q1, Q2, Q3, and Q4 to determine if the suspect created the latent fingerprints found at the scene. This simple but universal labeling scheme makes it possible for a CSI in any part of the nation to submit evidence to the FBI Laboratory and request comparison of the knowns and unknowns without confusion or misinterpretation of the requested examinations.

Known samples are materials from an identified or known source that are provided to the crime laboratory for comparison to unknown or **questioned samples** (which are samples whose source is unconfirmed). There are two types of known samples: standards and exemplars. Standards are submitted by the CSI for comparison against the Q, or unknown, samples. An example of a standard would be a tube of blood drawn by medical personnel from the suspect (K1) to be compared against Q1, blood samples taken from a bloody jacket found at the scene of the crime. Exemplars are taken from the known samples by the evidence analyst for comparison purposes. The exemplar will be extracted using established protocols, and this extraction process allows untainted amounts of the known sample to be preserved for future testing (if necessary) by a third party retained by the defense.

Consider a CSI who is processing an arson scene in which an accelerant was used to ignite the fire. The CSI would collect samples of carpet where the presence of accelerant is suspected as well as samples of the carpet where there is no indication that accelerant was present. The forensic analyst would then compare those two samples to a known exemplar (provided by the carpet manufacturer) to (1) confirm that both samples submitted by the CSI are from the same location and indicate the presence or absence of the accelerant and (2) confirm the manufacturer and that no traces of accelerant should be found in a normal sample of the product.

Reference standards are specimens that have been collected and maintained in a standardized database and are used for comparative analysis when attempting to identify the source of an unknown sample. An example of a reference database is the auto manufacturers' paint sample database maintained by the FBI.

RELEASING THE SCENE

You have only one chance to conduct a proper and thorough crime scene search. Once you release the scene, it will be necessary to obtain a search warrant to reenter unless an authorized person agrees to sign a consent-to-search form. Even then, there may be an issue that prevents additional evidence from being accepted in court because the law enforcement agency has not maintained control of the scene, and it will become necessary to prove the integrity of any additional evidence.

A good rule of thumb is to review your actions with one foot in the courtroom. Prepare your documentation to accurately reflect the crime scene, the conditions on your arrival, and the actions you took to process the scene.

Prior to releasing the crime scene, you must complete several steps to ensure that you have fulfilled your responsibility to identify, document, collect, and preserve all physical evidence. Ensuring that all steps have been completed requires the same systematic and methodical steps you completed on arrival at the scene.

Consult with the case detective and review the crime scene processing plan that was developed during the preliminary survey (crime scene assessment). Check to see that all objectives that were defined have been met and that all personnel have completed all assignments. Be sure to discuss any initial false assumptions that may have been made and determine how these preliminary observations have been handled.

When forensic specialists such as entomologists or anthropologists have been summoned to the scene, ensure that they have completed their investigative efforts and are prepared to release their assigned work area. Make sure any forensic evidence located by these specialists as well as their exit from the crime scene is accurately documented on the entry-exit logs. Cross-check the evidence logs and written documentation against the packaged evidence inventory. Verify that all gloves and other disposable PPE that was utilized while the scene was being processed have been collected (see Figure 15.1). Confirm that everything is properly bagged, labeled, and removed from the scene. This practice is part of the normal protocols for the closing stages of crime scene processing; however, another final check will eliminate the loss of any evidence, soiled PPE, and equipment.

FIGURE 15.1
Ensure proper disposal of personal protective equipment by utilizing a biohazard bag outside the perimeter of the crime scene.

Take a final set of photographs that depict the physical condition of the scene upon completion of the crime scene search. Gather all equipment and recheck it against your equipment and inventory logs. This inventory will also become a part of the case file to demonstrate the continuous integrity of the investigative process. Remember to store and transport separately any equipment and supplies that must be decontaminated. This will ensure that all items will be cleaned prior to being utilized at another crime scene and reduce the potential for cross-contamination between crime scenes.

Before releasing the scene, complete a final survey and make sure the case detective has contacted any outside officials who may need to visit the scene (e.g., the prosecutor or the death investigator for the medical examiner's office). Discuss any new investigative leads that were developed as a result of the crime scene search to determine if any additional steps need to be taken before the scene is released.

It is important to report and address the presence of any dangerous materials or conditions to the proper authorities prior to the scene's being released. In some instances, the instability of the structure or the presence of hazardous materials will require custody of the scene to be passed on to the fire department, Hazmat team, or codes enforcement officer. This information should also be entered into the narrative portion of the case documentation.

Document not only the final conditions at the scene but to whom the scene was released. If possible, obtain this person's signature. Be sure to leave a receipt for all property taken (if applicable) as physical evidence. Enter the date and time that the scene was released as well as the acceptor's name into your written documentation. These steps not only validate you have followed the SOPs but also can prevent allegations of theft or damage that may arise afterward.

CROSS-CONTAMINATION

At the crime scene, it is essential that every effort be taken to avoid cross-contamination of physical evidence between items, locations, and personnel who are working within the secure perimeter. Cross-contamination refers to the unwanted transfer of material between two or more sources of physical evidence. Every item must be identified, collected, and preserved individually. It is always necessary to wear two sets of latex or nitrile gloves and change the outer pair frequently to provide protection for yourself as well as to prevent the possibility of the evidence being subject to contamination. Never smoke, eat, drink, or chew gum while processing a crime scene, and do not allow these activities to occur within the secure perimeter of the crime scene. The accidental exchange of DNA between the investigators in the crime scene may create reasonable doubt as to the integrity of the evidence.

Never use a telephone or cellphone while processing a scene. The potential for contamination is huge, and you do not want to lose your cellphone through exposure to hazardous substances.

If you cannot use disposable tools to collect evidence, metal ones are acceptable, but you must remember to clean them between every individual use. A bleach mixture (ten percent) is sufficient for cleaning the tools. Be sure to dry them on sterile cloth prior to using them on the next item. Bodily fluids are biological hazards and must be handled carefully and labeled appropriately to protect both the CSI and the laboratory personnel who will examine the evidence. Affix

"Biohazard" labels to the outside of every package that contains physical evidence that might include biological fluids.

All forensic evidence and accompanying paperwork must be logged in and accepted by the investigating agency's property/evidence custodian. The chain of custody from the scene to secure storage creates the first opportunity for the evidence to move from the control of the CSI to storage. Larger agencies may process much of the forensic evidence internally, while smaller agencies must store packages until they can be transported to a regional or state crime lab for processing.

A secure, temperature-controlled environment ensures the integrity of the evidence. Properly labeled evidence and documentation are essential to prevent the deterioration of possible biological matter (i.e., items containing bodily fluids must be dried in an evidence dryer or other measures taken to prevent contamination or loss of DNA). Agency SOPs dictate the exact protocols, and CSIs must be familiar with the process.

CSIs who are trained to process physical evidence must continue to protect the chain of custody and integrity of the forensic evidence. This includes maintaining a clean work area, being ever conscious of the possibility of cross-contamination. Evidence must be checked out from the property/ evidence unit showing secure storage until the CSI is prepared to process. For example, packages containing items to be processed for latent fingerprints should be open and processed individually. Photograph, process, photograph, and then lift any identifiable ridge impressions. Be sure the photographs are taken without and with a scale and that the item is properly labeled. Each step must be fully documented. The evidence will not be admitted into court if it has been collected and preserved correctly but subjected to cross-contamination in the laboratory. Ensure that the safeguards and protocols you followed at the crime scene are also adhered to inside the office and the evidence-processing areas. Impressions that are lifted from the item become a separate piece of evidence linked to the original evidence number. This practice simplifies yet documents the latents for entry into AFIS and subsequent examiner confirmation. Written documentation of this process is also placed into the case file. When processing is complete, repackage the item, seal it, and return it to the property/evidence unit with the appropriate signatures to preserve the chain of custody documentation.

THE FBI CRIME LABORATORY

The FBI operates one of the largest and most comprehensive crime laboratories in the world. A new state-of-the-art facility opened in 2003 in Quantico, Virginia, that can accommodate more than 650

forensic scientists and evidence examiners (see Figure 15.2). State and local
crime laboratories may send scientists to
the FBI for training and to gain experience in all aspects of forensic evidence
examination.

There is no charge to any governmental
entity submitting evidence to the FBI
Laboratory for analysis; however, only
physical evidence relating to crimes of
violence will be accepted from state and
local agencies. The FBI will also provide
expert testimony by the scientist completing the analysis when subpoenaed
by the court. The FBI will not process evidence that has already been
examined by a state or regional crime laboratory. Be sure to check
the FBI's evidence-processing guidelines (www.fbi.gov/about-us/
lab/handbook-of-forensic-services-pdf) for the latest regulations and
procedures governing submission regulations.

FIGURE 15.2
The FBI Laboratory in
Quantico, Virginia.

All evidence must be submitted to the appropriate crime laboratory
with written requests on agency letterhead. A list of all evidence and
the examinations requested should also accompany the cover letter.

COMMUNICATING WITH A CRIME LAB

After you arrive at a crime scene is not the proper time to make your
first contact with crime laboratory personnel. Every CSI should
schedule a visit to the local, regional, or state crime laboratory where
evidence is submitted. Touring the facilities and developing an understanding of the scientific methodologies and protocols followed
by the laboratory will create a better understanding of the overall
processes involved in forensic evidence analysis.

Forensic scientists are interested in meeting the personnel who identify, collect, preserve, and submit physical evidence to the laboratories. Establishing a good working relationship with the scientists
who perform the analyses on the forensic evidence you submit is
beneficial to the operation of a successful crime scene investigation
unit. Once you have met the forensic scientists, it will be much easier
for you to contact them to ask for recommendations when you encounter situations that are atypical and require additional expertise
in the collection and preservation of evidence.

It has become an acceptable practice for a CSI to contact a laboratory
analyst when unusual circumstances are discovered during the crime

scene search. The use of wireless technology has enhanced the ability of the CSI to transmit digital photographs or video to the analyst at the crime laboratory so that all parties have a clear understanding of the situation. The laboratory analyst will usually have instant access to multitudes of databases that can provide additional information to the CSI in the field regarding the correct procedure to follow under unusual or potentially hazardous conditions.

Although you should never use a cellphone inside the secure perimeter of a crime scene, it is certainly acceptable to contact the crime laboratory from your vehicle or outside the crime scene to discuss unique situations or request advice on specific evidence collection techniques. Forensic evidence examiners have access to computer databases and can provide expertise in collection and preservation techniques that should prevent compromise of the integrity of the evidentiary sample.

Evidence Submittal to a Crime Lab

Discuss the capabilities of the crime laboratory with the forensic scientists prior to submitting physical evidence to them. Include this information in the request for examination and provide contact information that can be used if additional questions arise when the examiner is conducting the analyses of the evidence.

Many times, the property/evidence unit will be responsible for packaging the evidence for shipment to the lab. If it is your duty to perform this task, contact the pertinent unit to determine if specific handling or packaging conditions are required. Depending on the physical properties of the evidence, special transportation requirements may be necessary. Make arrangements for this in advance so the package can be transported to the crime laboratory in a timely manner.

Include a copy of the examination request in the package and be sure to affix appropriate labels (evidence, biohazard, etc.) on the outside of the packaging. Attach or send any requested photographs as well. Place all evidence packages in a clean, sturdy container and use shock-absorbent packaging to ensure that the packages will not be subjected to unnecessary movement. Do not use Styrofoam peanuts for packing materials because they generate static electricity, which may damage the physical condition of the forensic evidence. Secure the outer container with tamper-resistant tape and initial the tape when the package is sealed. Be sure to provide instructions advising the laboratory about return of the evidence to your agency after the analyses have been completed. Standard practices include the return of forensic evidence to the property/evidence unit for secure storage until court proceedings move forward or end.

Make arrangements for the evidence to be shipped to the crime laboratory unless you or another CSI will personally deliver the package. Document the shipper and the date and time of shipment, and keep a copy of the tracking information in your case file for future reference.

For specific information on examinations the FBI Crime Laboratory can conduct, you should visit their website and download the *Handbook of Forensic Services*. This publication is provided as a reference manual to assist you and your local laboratory in determining if any needed examinations should be conducted by the FBI.

CASE FILE PREPARATION

Make sure that your case file contains copies of all documents relating to the crime scene investigation, including the crime laboratory reports that were completed after analysis of the physical evidence. A duplicate set of photographs stored on a CD or other electronic media is useful as you prepare to meet with the prosecutor's office prior to the beginning of the court proceedings. The original documents should remain in the case file, and copies should be utilized as working documents to avoid loss or damage to the originals.

WORKING WITH THE PROSECUTOR'S OFFICE

The CSI must be familiar with federal and state rules of evidence to be able to process a crime scene properly and successfully introduce the physical evidence into the courtroom. *Daubert v. Merrell Dow Pharmaceuticals, Inc.* (1993), gave the trial judge the responsibility for determining the admissibility of scientific evidence. *Daubert* standards were established to eliminate the introduction of testimony regarding procedures that have not met scientifically proven methodologies or have not been accepted in the scientific community. The *Daubert* rules also ensure the analyses used on the physical evidence are valid, reliable, and can be duplicated resulting in the same outcomes.

It is the responsibility of the CSI to identify and document evidence at the crime scene. This evidence may establish probable cause. The prosecutor will determine which evidence is necessary in building a case that establishes proof beyond a reasonable doubt, and a jury or judge will weigh the evidence and the testimony to determine the guilt or innocence of the alleged perpetrator. Always remember your role as an unbiased and objective CSI when you work with the prosecutor's office to develop the presentation of the crime scene investigation.

Not all cases will be concluded in a courtroom. These decisions are made by the prosecutor's office or by a guilty plea being entered by the defendant. The CSI must follow the investigative strategy established by the detectives; the probability of success or failure of the proceedings in the courtroom will be carefully evaluated by the prosecutor's office. If there was any break in the chain of custody, there was any chance for cross-contamination to occur, there is a lack of witnesses, or the ability to substantiate important factors is not present, the case may not be taken to trial. The end of a prosecution track is not a failure on the part of the CSI, but the CSI's office should regularly examine contributing circumstances to determine any weak areas of SOPs that resulted in a lack of prosecution.

Pretrial Preparation

The prosecuting attorney will usually schedule a pretrial conference with the witnesses who are expected to testify in a proceeding. During this meeting, you must be prepared to discuss the actions you took at the crime scene and the prosecution's strategy for presenting the case to the court. If your credentials are going to be presented to qualify you as an expert witness, be sure to provide a complete and accurate résumé and a list of specialized training courses for the prosecutor to review. To ensure your credibility on the witness stand, be sure to clarify the boundaries of your area of expertise so that your qualifications are not misrepresented.

It is advisable to review your testimony with the prosecutor who will be presenting the case to the court so that everyone is familiar with the procedures you will present and the evidentiary items that will be offered to the court for admission. If you plan to use PowerPoint or other presentation technologies, these should also be reviewed for accuracy and consistency during the pretrial meeting. One more reminder: if a series of CSIs and laboratory analysts will be testifying, each one should attend the pretrial conference to ensure there are no discrepancies in the prosecutor's trial strategy.

PROFESSIONAL CREDENTIALS

CSIs must become adept in relating the facts of the crime scene investigation to a courtroom that may include a jury whose education on forensics originates from watching popular crime scene television shows. To maintain your proficiency, you must persevere in learning about new advances in crime scene processing and attending training seminars designed to provide continuous professional development. The International Association of Identification (IAI) is the world's largest organization of individuals who work in the field of forensic identification. More than 6,500 members from 77 countries work together to maintain rigorous training and certification processes (www.theiai.org). By gaining membership in a local or state association or attending the IAI annual conference, CSIs can acquire timely training while learning new technologies and procedures. The organization also publishes the bimonthly *Journal of Forensic Identification*, a scientific journal that publishes articles to share dispositions of *Daubert* hearings, case studies, and research outcomes (www.theiai.org/publications). Many other specialty organizations also are recognized by courts for ongoing professional education opportunities.

State agencies and some universities also offer annual training sessions designed to enhance your knowledge and skills as a CSI. Criminal justice programs housed at community colleges and private and state universities also offer certified training opportunities with the completion of higher education degrees.

When you are testifying, additional credentials you have earned should be entered into the court records to enhance your credibility as a specialist in your profession. Obtaining supplemental knowledge will demonstrate that you are committed to continuing to gain experience and will enhance the integrity of your work as you perform the many tasks of a well-trained CSI.

As you continue to prepare for an upcoming trial, review all the documentation in the case file. Be diligent in your effort to present well-organized testimony; it is permissible for you to take documents to the witness stand for reference purposes.

COURTROOM TESTIMONY

It is customary to exclude witnesses from the courtroom until it is time for each to testify. Pay attention to your appearance; many agencies have specific requirements as to proper courtroom attire. Do not wear anything that will distract the judge or jury from listening to what you have to say. Take time to respond to each question. Do not add information that was not part of the question. If you do not fully understand the question, then ask for clarification.

Present your testimony accurately and in terminology that is understandable to a nontechnical decision maker. It is important to develop skills that allow you to effectively communicate the actions you took to the participants in a courtroom. Remain calm and objective. Remember that forensic evidence is unbiased and you performed your assignment in a fair and impartial manner.

It is the defense attorney's job to attempt to discredit you or the actions you took, and it is your job to rise above all attempts made to create reasonable doubt. This is not personal, but be prepared for your work and the evidence to be challenged. Your confidence in your knowledge, skills, and abilities, as well as the credibility you establish through your credentials and your demeanor, are key to having the physical evidence and crime scene processing procedures accepted by the courtroom participants.

The manner in which you convey your information to the court is just as important as the forensic evidence you will be presenting during the proceedings. When you are asked to explain your training and experience to the court, it is perfectly acceptable for you to refer to a résumé to make certain all your professional credentials are available for the court's consideration. Attendance at specialized schools and annual proficiency testing is especially important in establishing credibility. Continuing professional development and certifications should also be introduced during this introduction to the jury. Do not attempt to qualify yourself as an expert; it is up to the court to weigh the value of your credentials, and you are permitted only to express your opinions if the court rules that your training, education, and experience have met the test of an expert witness. Never presume that the court is familiar with the boundaries of your knowledge and expertise, and never testify to anything that exceeds your level of proven knowledge.

Following the SOPs each and every time will leave little room for the defense team to attack your work. The purpose of the trial is not to defend the SOPs; you are testifying only to your specific actions and the forensic evidence you documented at the scene. It is the prosecutor's responsibility to object when questions are directed away from your role. The courtroom is not a forum for personal statements, although this is quite often a strategy defense teams will attempt to use to divert focus from your actions at the scene as they try to establish reasonable doubt in the mind of the jury or judge.

Your testimony and the introduction of physical evidence that accompanies your statements will be presented in a logical sequence. Professional demeanor is critical. It is important that you do not appear overzealous or create the impression that you are being evasive or less than truthful about your actions at the crime scene. The purpose of your testimony is to present an objective and unbiased recitation of the crime scene and the physical evidence to be considered by the court. As a witness, you are testifying to facts, not opinions or beliefs. Always tell the truth. Do not allow defense attorneys to lead you to anger, and remain neutral during the time you are in or around the courtroom.

Demonstrative Exhibits

Today's courtrooms are often electronically equipped so that the CSI can display 3D crime scenes, utilize video and audio recordings, and even employ reconstruction software to present accurate depictions of the crime scene. Prior to preparing your presentation for court, you should visit the facility to determine what equipment is available in the courtroom as well as the operational status of the equipment. It does not benefit the case if your electronic presentations cannot be introduced for consideration because of an equipment malfunction. Most smaller and more rural courtrooms do not have LCD projectors or other electronic devices, so you must gear your presentation materials with the thought that you may be passing photographs to the prosecutor rather than projecting a PowerPoint presentation on a viewing screen.

The Importance of Physical Evidence

Physical evidence provides the court and the jury with something tangible to establish linkages among the victim, the suspect, and the crime scene. Even if only a single hair or a partial latent fingerprint has been identified as physical evidence, its existence demonstrates to the judge or jury that law enforcement conducted a thorough investigation of the crime scene to establish that a crime was committed and to identify the perpetrator. Physical evidence can be subjected to scientific analysis and may be used to corroborate or rebut statements from the suspect, victim, or witnesses.

Various scientific disciplines may be introduced during courtroom proceedings, depending on the types of physical evidence and the technologies available for scientific analysis. Juries today expect physical evidence and may often comment on the absence of physical evidence during their deliberations. Known as the **CSI effect**, the real-world expectations of crime victims and jury members, which are often based on unrealistic television and film portrayals, pressure prosecutors to deliver more forensic evidence in court or explain why there is little or no physical evidence presented for the court to consider.

When forensic scientists perform comparative analyses, they are comparing an unknown sample (Q) to a known sample (K), and the examination will yield one of these findings:

- The questioned or unknown sample (Q) matches the known sample (K).
- The questioned sample (Q) has some similarities to the known sample (K).
- The questioned sample (Q) bears no similarity to the known sample (K).

Ethical Considerations

Every time you respond to a crime scene as a CSI, the potential for presenting your actions in a courtroom exists. As a CSI, you stake your reputation on the veracity of your work. Never assume anything and question everything. You are responsible for the identification, collection, preservation, and presentation of physical evidence to the court. Your actions, or lack thereof, are the voice of the victim. While justice may be blind, you must present objective and unbiased testimony that clearly and accurately recreates the crime scene for the judge and jury. It will be up to these triers of fact to arrive at a verdict, and the actions and demeanor of the CSI should not detract from the credibility of the physical evidence, scientific analysis, and subsequent case investigation.

Every witness who offers testimony in the courtroom is subject to the penalty of perjury (testifying untruthfully). As a CSI and a representative of the victim, your statements will be truthful. Others, who swear or affirm to tell the truth, may not maintain the same high ethical standards; that means some statements may directly contradict your testimony. It will be the prosecutor's responsibility to discredit those statements. Again, remain confident and do not show outward emotion when other statements create discrepancies. If you detect misinformation that could be detrimental, write a note for the prosecutor and discuss the concern outside the courtroom.

EMERGING TRENDS

Advances in technology and improvements in the capacity to analyze and interpret forensic evidence will continue to boost the probability that justice will be served in the courtroom. These enhancements will place an even greater responsibility on the CSI to ensure the proper identification, documentation, preservation, and collection of physical evidence so there is no margin for error. The significance of every element of physical evidence is increased with the acceptance of modern analytical technologies in the courtroom.

The National Institute of Justice (NIJ), the research agency of the US Department of Justice, supports and funds research, evaluation, and development of technology. It maintains the world's largest repository of criminal justice information and also supports dual-use technologies developed for national defense and law enforcement agencies. Through the NIJ, five regional sections of the National Law Enforcement and Corrections Technology Centers (NLECTCs) actively sponsor and test new technologies focused on improving the criminal justice system. Examples of new technologies being developed and implemented under the research capabilities of the NIJ include correctional technologies; criminal justice electronic crime technologies; forensics technology; informational and geospatial technologies; sensor, surveillance, and biometric technologies; and weapons and protective systems. The NLECTC Centers of Excellence maintain ongoing training and an extensive website to assist you in following the advancements in forensic science technology (www.justnet.org).

Staying abreast of new analytical processes that may impact your profession as well as recent court rulings regarding the admissibility of advancing technologies is essential to your effectiveness and credibility. The NLECTC also distributes an electronic newsletter for interested practitioners and maintains a virtual library of resources that can lead you to additional information regarding specific technologies. NLECTC also provides abstracts of articles, equipment specifications, and grant information to local agencies. CSIs must be knowledgeable about scientifically based outcomes that are available through the analysis of forensic evidence. Technology transition workshops are offered by NLECTC on a regional basis to share new knowledge and standardize procedures required for the adoption of new processes.

There are also several organizations that offer low- or no-cost online training. The National Institute of Justice funds the Forensic Technology Center of Excellence (FTCoE), according to www.forensiccoe.org. The project is managed by RTI International, which offers expertise, knowledge, and training. Both live and on-demand training for forensic professionals is available at www.forensiced.org. Topics from forensic chemistry to medicolegal death investigation, crime scene investigation, and sexual assault are part of the more than 24 modules available at no charge. The courses are targeted to forensic science professionals; however, they are also beneficial to students, professors, and criminal justice professionals.

The National Forensic Science Technology Center (NFSTC) supports justice and defense communities through innovation programs, technology evaluation, training consulting, and laboratory support at www.nfstc.org (the website is subtitled "Science Serving Justice"). Free online training is available from NFSTC at http://projects.nfstc.org.

Discussion Questions

1. What are the primary responsibilities of the CSI? What is the importance of written documentation? Who ultimately must be convinced by this documentation?

2. Who determines the admissibility of evidence during a trial? What court case set the standard?
3. Other than becoming a proficient investigator, what other characteristics must the CSI possess to be successful in presenting actions taken at the crime scene?
4. Discuss the ethical considerations for the CSI. Identify others who are not held to the same ethical standards as law enforcement and prosecutorial representatives.

REFERENCE

Daubert v. Merrell Dow Pharmaceuticals, Inc. (1993) *509 U.S. 579.*

Crime Scene Supply Checklist

Documentation equipment:
    Laser measuring device
    Tape measure (100') and (25')
    ABFO scales
    Other sticky-sided measuring device
    Clipboard and graph paper, notebook
    Ruler or other straight-edge instrument
    Protractor
    Compass
Camera equipment:
    Digital single-lens reflex camera (35 mm)
    Flash unit
    Extra memory cards
    Network transmitter
    Additional lenses of varying focal length
    Digital video camera
    Extra batteries and charger with power cord
    Crime scene tape to establish perimeter
Evidence collection equipment:
    Flashlight
    Magnifying glass
    Small glass vials
    Small cardboard boxes
    Paper envelopes
    Zip-lock evidence bags
    Disposable scalpels
    Plastic tweezers
    Knife or handgun cardboard boxes
    Evidence tape
    Heat sealer with bags
        Labels
        Brown wrapping paper
        Medium and large paper bags
    Alternate light source
    Fingerprint kit: tapes, cards, fingerprint powder, brushes

Dental casting kits
Nitrile gloves in various sizes and thickness
Tyvek coveralls or disposable lab coats
Shoe covers
Face shields
Goggles or other eye protection
Biohazard bag for disposal of used Tyvek, gloves, and other trash
Boots
Shovel, sifting screens
String kit (blood spatter analysis)
Presumptive testing kits
Luminol or similar reaction agent
Emergency lighting with access to generator
Canopy tent

Glossary

A

ABFO scale A photographic scale designed by the American Board of Forensic Od-ontology that is used to ensure accurate depiction of injuries and other items of physical evidence.

Adipocere A grayish-white waxy or soapy-like substance that forms in the fatty tissues of the body and is usually formed when a body is placed in a damp environment such as water, a cave, or in a grave.

Algor mortis The cooling of the body after death occurs.

Alternate light source (ALS) A forensic light source created when a high-intensity light is focused through a fiber-optic cable using various filters.

Alveolar region The section of the jawbone containing the tooth sockets.

American Society for Testing and Materials (ASTM) The recognized organization that establishes protocols and standards for testing and examination, including for the forensic sciences.

Arches The fingerprint class characterized by ridge lines entering the print from one side and flowing or tending to flow out the other side. There are two types of arches: plain and tented. The friction ridges forming a plain arch form a wave pattern. The tented arch has a sharp upthrust or spike in the center that gives the impression of a tent.

Area of origin In arson investigations, the location where the heat ignited the first fuel; it is also the area with the most visible damage in the fire scene.

ASA/ISO A standard (American and international) nomenclature for depicting a film's ability to record light in terms of speed. The higher the ASA/ISO number, the less light it takes to record an image on film.

Autopsy A medical procedure involving the internal and external examination of a dead body conducted by a pathologist or medical examiner to determine the cause and manner of a person's death and to evaluate any disease or injury that may be found.

B

Ballistics The study of a projectile in motion.

Baseline measures A line of reference from which measurements are taken, usually a wall using 90-degree angles.

Biohazard bags Containers for materials that have been exposed to blood or other bi-ological fluids. Gloves and other personal protective equipment worn at the crime scene by personnel should be collected in a biohazard bag that is then removed and disposed of properly by the agency conducting the investigation.

Biological fluids Any fluids encountered that are thought to be of human or animal origin. The most common fluids are blood, saliva, semen, urine, or sweat. Any evidence suspected of containing biological fluids should have a biohazard label affixed to the package used to collect the evidence.

423

Bloodborne pathogens Infectious disease-causing microorganisms that may be found or transported in biological fluids.

Bloodstain pattern analysis (BPA) The examination of the shapes, locations, and distribution patterns of bloodstains, in order to provide an interpretation of the physical events that occurred at the crime scene.

Burn patterns Visible effects from a fire, such as charring, smoke, and soot deposits; changes in the character of materials; and the consumption of consumables that may indicate the ignition source of a fire.

C

Cadaveric spasm The rapid stiffening of the hand and sometimes the forearms that sometimes occurs at the time of death.

Case file A compilation of all case documents pertaining to an investigation, including evidence and photography logs, photographs, sketches, case narrative, laboratory requests and reports, and other records.

Case narrative A running description of the entire crime scene investigation that should be presented in the same systematic, methodical, and logical manner in which the activities were conducted at the scene.

Cast-off patterns Bloodstain patterns created when blood is released or thrown from a blood-bearing object in motion, such as a baseball bat or a pipe.

Cause of death (COD) The reason a person ceased to live, whether by injury or disease; must be determined by the medical examiner during the autopsy.

CBC (cyanoacrylate blowing contraption) A fuming device developed by Arthur M. Bohanon of the Knoxville (Tennessee) Police Department in the early 1990s. It is specifically designed to detect latent fingerprints on dead human bodies.

CBRNE A common acronym used when discussing weapons of mass destruction; the letters represent chemical, biological, radiological, nuclear, or explosive agents.

Chain of custody The proper documentation showing each change in possession and/or storage of an item of evidence from its seizure to trial presentation.

Chop shop A structure or location used for receiving, dismantling, destroying, or concealing passenger motor vehicles or parts that were illegally obtained.

CODIS (Combined DNA Index System) A database maintained by the FBI as a central repository for DNA profiles. CODIS allows law enforcement agencies and state crime labs to exchange and match DNA profiles electronically. It contains a Forensic Index of profiles from crime scene evidence and an Offender Index composed of profiles of subjects convicted of violent crimes and sex offenses.

Comparison samples Physical evidence from the crime scene that can be compared with samples from suspects, victims, and known standards.

Compression toolmarks Toolmark impressions that are created when a tool is pressed into a softer material, usually showing the outline of the tool used to create the impression.

Computer crime A term describing a myriad group of offenses defined by state and federal statutes and including activities such as unauthorized access, software piracy, alteration or theft of electronically stored information, transmission of destructive viruses or commands, and child pornography and predatory activities.

Concentric fractures A glass fracture pattern consisting of a series of circular cracks that surround the impact site and move away from the site, with each circular fracture increasing as it propagates outward.

Confirmatory test A separate test that is conducted in the laboratory on a sample to confirm the identity of a substance or (in the case of body fluids) an individual.

Contact stains In bloodstain pattern analysis, stains created when a bloody object comes into direct contact with a surface, for example, bloody fingerprints found on a countertop.

Control or blank sample Material from a verifiable source that is uncontaminated; a good example is a segment of unaffected carpet which is removed from the scene of a suspected arson that does not appear to have been affected with an accelerant.

Coroner An elected or appointed official whose duty it is to investigate deaths that occur within jurisdictional limits. Responsibilities of coroners vary depending on the statutory requirements of the individual county or state.

Corpus delicti The determination of the essential facts that demonstrate that a crime has occurred.

Crime scene investigator Specially trained personnel assigned to process locations where crimes have been committed. CSIs may be sworn police officers or civilian personnel.

Crime scene reconstruction The systematic process of piecing together information and evidence in an investigation to gain a better understanding of what occurred between the victim and the offender during the commission of a crime. The crime scene reconstructionist uses physical evidence and information to infer what occurred during the interaction between the offender and the victim.

Crime scene staging In cybercrime investigations, when the perpetrator attempts to plant or fabricate digital evidence that will implicate another individual.

Cross-contamination The transfer of material between two or more sources of physical evidence.

Cross-sectional plans Two-dimensional drawings most easily described as cutaways of the exteriors of elevations; they reveal the interior, floors, and subterranean levels of buildings or structures.

CSI effect The recent phenomenon that takes place when the real-world expectations of crime victims and jury members, which are based on unrealistic television and film portrayals, pressure prosecutors to deliver more forensic evidence than usual in court or explain why they cannot do so.

Cutting toolmarks Marks created by tools such as bolt cutters or tin snips and usually found on chains and hasp locks that have been cut through.

Cyberbullying The use of the Internet to send or post text or images intended to hurt or embarrass another person.

Cybercrime Technology-assisted crimes that generally involve the use of the Internet.

Cyberstalking The pursuit and harassment of victims through use of the Internet.

Cybertailing The actions of tracking a cybercrime perpetrator through various computer networks to identify a suspect.

D

Daubert rulings Court rulings which established that human friction ridges are unique and permanent. The *Daubert* rulings clarified the scientific acceptance of the uniqueness of friction ridges in court proceedings.

Defensive wounds Wounds that occur as the victim is attempting to ward off an attack; typically on upper or lower extremities and are of lesser severity than those elsewhere.

Dental stone A casting medium composed of calcium sulfate (plaster of Paris) with potassium sulfate added for greater hardness. It is generally preferred over plaster of Paris because it is harder and less brittle.

DFO (1,8-diazafluoren-9-one) A chemical that reacts to amino acids and is effective in visualizing latent fingerprints on porous materials.

Digital evidence Data stored or transmitted using a computer that is probative in nature and can be used to generate investigative leads.

Digital forensics The extraction and analysis of digital evidence from computers.

Directionality The directionality of a bloodstain or pattern that indicates the direction the blood was traveling when it impacted a surface. The geometric shape of a bloodstain can usually establish the directionality of a flight of a blood drop.

Domain Name System (DNS) A hierarchical naming system for computers, services, or any resource connected to the Internet or a private network, which associates various information with domain names assigned to each of the participants.

Driver's point of view The view of the driver of a vehicle through all windows at the time a vehicle was being operated. This is a useful documentation point that may be used to identify or eliminate obstructions or causative factors of a motor vehicle crash.

E

EDTA (ethylenediaminetetraacetic acid) An anticoagulant and preservative added to test tubes used for the collection of liquid blood samples. EDTA tubes are usually equipped with lavender-colored rubber tops for easy identification.

Electronic signature A symbol, sound, or process attached to or logically associated with a record, and executed or adopted by a person with the intent to sign the record.

Electrostatic dust print lifter A device that utilizes an electrical charge applied to a metallized lifting mat that will attract positively charged dust particles; this results in a mirror image of impressions made by footwear or tires.

Elevation plans Two-dimensional, side-view representations of the walls, sides of furniture, cabinetry, and fixtures of an interior scene.

Elimination samples Samples taken from individuals who have had legal access to a crime scene that will be used as a comparison with evidence collected from the scene.

Encryption The process of converting readable digital objects (plain text) into unreadable digital objects (ciphertext) using a mathematical function.

Entomology The branch of science that deals with the study of insects.

ESDA (electrostatic detection apparatus) A device that examines paper for indentations and other latent impressions.

Evidence dynamics Influences that may change, relocate, obscure, or obliterate evidence, regardless of whether intent existed, between the time evidence is transferred from the crime scene and the time the case is resolved. If these changes occur, it becomes more difficult for the prosecution to prove the authenticity and reliability of the evidence.

Exemplars In handwriting analysis, standards of known handwriting used for comparison purposes.

F

Femur The largest and strongest bone in the body, which extends from the pelvis to the knee.

Fire triangle The three components necessary for a fire to burn: heat, fuel, and oxygen. If any one of these components is removed, the fire will be extinguished, and the fire triangle has been dismantled.

Floor plans Two-dimensional, bird's-eye views of a room or a series of rooms that make up a floor of a structure or building.

Forensic anthropologist A practitioner in the branch of physical anthropology that deals with the identification of skeletonized human remains.

Forensic biology The study of life, including both cellular and molecular biology. This is essential to the scientific analyses required in crime laboratories.

Forensic entomology The field in which arthropod science and the judicial system interact.

Forensic linguistics The field of forensic science that uses phrases, word usage, punctuation, letter forms, and number forms to determine the personality and/or type of the writer of a document.

Forensic nurse A medical professional who has received training in the medicolegal aspects that encompass treatment and physical evidence identification in treatment facilities.

Forensic scientist An individual trained as a biologist or chemist and skilled in the protocols of scientific analysis in the laboratory setting.

G

Gas chromatography An instrument in the crime laboratory that is used to analyze and identify suspect samples. The samples are separated during the analysis, and often the gas chromatograph is linked to the mass spectrometer, which provides positive identification.

Gentian violet A staining solution that is used to process adhesive tape for latent fingerprints.

Global adjustments In photography, gross adjustments that affect the entire world within the image, equally affecting the entire photograph (e.g., orientation, brightness, contrast).

GPS (global positioning system) Based on 24 satellites that circle the earth providing accurate longitude, latitude, and altitude positions to GPS receivers on earth.

Graphology The field of psychology that attempts to profile the personality of an individual based on his or her handwriting characteristics.

Grid search A crime scene search pattern in which a strip search is made in one direction and then repeated over the same area in a right angle; also known as the double-strip search method.

Gunshot residue (GSR) A substance expended from the barrel of a weapon when it is discharged; composed of gunpowder residue and soot.

H

Hackers Internet crime perpetrators who attempt to break into networks in order to gain access to secure information or use to commit other offenses.

Handwriting complexity Generally, the number of complex moves necessary to create a signature or handwriting consisting of curves, loops, and embellishments.

High explosives Substances that explode at a detonation velocity faster than the speed of sound through that material (above 3,300 feet per second). High explosives do not need to be confined to function.

Humerus The long bone of the arm, which extends from the shoulder to the elbow.

I

Identity theft Crime that occurs when a perpetrator pretends to be another person for the purpose of committing fraud.

IEDs Improvised explosive devices.

Impact spatter Bloodstains that are smaller than a freely forming drop.

Impression evidence Marks or imprints that are created when one object comes into contact with a second item, resulting in characteristics of the first object being left on the surface of the second. A good example is a shoeprint left in a muddy driveway.

IND (1,2-Indanedione) Used in conjunction with an alternate light source to visualize latent fingerprints on nonporous surfaces.

Initial walkthrough/preliminary assessment The initial review of the crime scene by the CSI and lead detective to determine the strategy and define the scope of the crime scene investigation.

Inked impressions Fingerprints that are generated when ink is applied to the friction ridges and the fingers are rolled side to side in an orderly manner on a 10-print card.

Integrated Automated Fingerprint Identification System (IAFIS) The digitized computer database of fingerprints maintained by the FBI.

Internet A global computer network of interconnected smaller computer networks that are linked and enable information sharing via common communication protocols

Internet protocol (IP) A dynamic numeric locator assigned to a computer by an Internet service provider. The IP address consists of four sets of numbers, and each set contains digits ranging from 0 to 255. Example: 112.32.4422.6500.

Internet service providers (ISPs) Commercial companies (such as AOL, Earthlink, and Verizon) that make the Internet accessible to the public by maintaining thousands of servers.

K

Known samples Materials from an identified or known source that are provided to the crime laboratory for comparison to unknown or questioned samples.

L

Lands and grooves Ridges ground inside the barrel of a gun in order to make a bullet travel straight. The original surfaces of the barrel are referred to as lands (or hills) and the newly created ridges are called grooves (or valleys), and they twist down the length of a gun to improve accuracy.

Laser protractor kit A specially designed zero-based laser protractor that is used for determining trajectories.

Legend A note on a map or crime scene sketch that explains specific information of interest; may also contain the definition of symbols used on the sketch or map.

Line quality The level of skill, including the complexity, of handwriting.

Link search A crime scene search technique that uses logical associations among the victim, suspect, and physical evidence to locate physical evidence.

Livor mortis Lividity that appears when blood stops circulating and sinks to the lowest portions of the body.

Locard's theory of exchange A theory that maintains that transfer of evidence will occur between a suspect and victim and a location whenever contact occurs; also known as Locard's exchange principle.

Loops The fingerprint class characterized by ridge lines that enter from one side of the pattern and curve around to exit from the same side of the pattern. All loops have one delta, and the center of the pattern area is the core. If the loop opens toward the little finger, it is an ulnar loop (the ulna bone is the small bone on the outside of the forearm). If the loop opens toward the thumb, it is called a radial loop (the radial bone is the larger, inner bone of the forearm).

Low explosives Explosives in which components burn rather than explode; they are propellants that travel at speeds of less than 3,300 feet per second. Black powder is the most common type of low explosive, and it is used to make safety fuses. Smokeless powder is another type of low explosive and is found in small arms ammunition.

Luminol A chemical process used to detect the presence of blood in conjunction with an alternate light source.

M

Mandible The lower jawbone of a vertebrate.

Manner of death (MOD) The circumstances that caused a death to occur; may be natural, suicide, homicide, accidental, or undetermined.

Mass spectrometry The action of vaporizing material and then measuring the molecular mass of the sample, resulting in the destruction of the evidence. The mass spectrometer is often used in conjunction with the gas chromatograph in the analysis of unknown substances.

Mastoid process The conical projection below the mastoid portion of the temporal bone, behind the ear at the base of the skull.

Maxilla A pair of bones fused together that form the upper jawline.

Medical examiner (ME) The individual responsible for investigating all sudden, unexplained, unnatural, or suspicious deaths in a jurisdiction. The medical examiner is a public official and is generally a licensed physician who has completed training in the investigation of injuries and diseases that cause the death of humans.

Medicolegal death investigation (MDI) The statutory responsibility to examine cases of sudden, unnatural, unexpected death; these statutory duties are delineated in myriad ways in various jurisdictions.

Minutiae Characteristics that occur at the end of a ridge or at a bifurcation on a fingerprint.

Mitochondrial DNA (mtDNA) DNA that is transmitted only through the maternal line. Results can be determined from hair samples. Comparison samples can be obtained from any maternal relative for submission to the lab.

Modus operandi (MO) A criminal's "signature" or preferred method of operation. Criminals tend to repeat their behavior, and a certain behavior becomes their MO— for example, car thieves gain access to vehicles using the same techniques, arsonists use the same methods/accelerants to start fires.

Mummification The dehydration or desiccation of a body that occurs during the decomposition process.

N

NamUs (The National Missing and Unidentified Persons System) A clearinghouse for missing persons and unidentified decedent records.

National Fire Protection Association (NFPA) An international nonprofit association that provides codes and standards, research, training, and education on fire prevention.

National Insurance Crime Bureau (NICB) An agency that collects information regarding stolen vehicles and maintains a website for investigators and the public regarding auto theft statistics.

O

Occipital bone A compound bone that forms the posterior of the skull.

Odontology The study of the teeth and the tissue that surrounds the teeth.

P

"Painting with light" A time exposure on a camera by which an external flash is fired multiple times from different locations in order to illuminate the scene in the photograph.

Passive stains Stains created by drips, flows, pools, and saturation.

Pathologist A licensed physician who specializes in the study of diseases and injuries as related to human deaths.

Personal protective equipment (PPE) Articles, such as disposable gloves, masks, and eye protection, that are utilized to keep biological or chemical hazards from contacting the skin, eyes, and mucous membranes and to avoid contamination of the crime scene. Public safety agencies are required to provide PPE for all first responders.

Perspective grid A measurement system involving photographing a known scale within a scene and using that scale to measure items in the photograph; also known as photogrammetry.

Phishing An Internet fraud scheme that utilizes fake websites that appear to be legitimate bank or credit card sites.

Physical evidence Any and all objects that can establish that a crime has been committed or can provide a link between a crime and its victim or a crime and its perpetrator, and are used in the discovery of the facts.

Pixilated image In digital photography, an image that is enlarged to the point that the individual pixels making up the image are seen.

Plain impressions Inked fingerprints that are obtained by simultaneously pressing all four digits of the hand into the ink and then onto a fingerprint card.

Point of convergence The common point or area on a two-dimensional surface over which the directionality of several blood drops can be determined by using strings to re-create the flight of blood (or another substance).

Point of impact (POI) In motor vehicle investigations, the specific point where the automobile was impacted.

Point of origin or impact In bloodstain analysis, the common point or area in three-dimensional space resulting from the retracing of the trajectories of several blood drops; also the location where two objects collided.

Polar coordinates A measurement system using a transit or compass to measure angles taken from a known point to two fixed points. Similar to triangulation but it covers larger areas.

Postmortem interval (PMI) The time between the last time a person was reported alive and when the body was found. It is only an estimate unless there is a witness to the death of the individual.

Postprocessing What a photographer does to a photo after it has been taken in order to correct errors in exposure or to enhance the quality of the photo.

Presumptive test A test conducted initially to eliminate compounds from consideration; used at the crime scene to quickly identify the potential presence of blood or drugs.

Prostate-specific antigen (PSA) A protein produced by the cells of the prostate gland. Prostate-specific antigen is released into the blood of men, and a positive acid phosphatase test indicates the presence of semen.

PROTECT Act of 2003 Federal legislation that defines child pornography as contraband. PROTECT stands for Prosecutorial Remedies and Other Tools to end the Exploitation of Children Today.

Putrefaction The process that begins when death occurs and the body decomposes as degenerative processes caused by bacteria create internal gases.

Q

Questioned samples Materials or evidentiary samples the source of which is unconfirmed and that are collected at the crime scene and submitted to the crime laboratory for comparison to known samples.

R

Radial fractures A glass fracture compound consisting of cracks that begin at the center of the impact site and propagate outward like an asterisk symbol and occur on the exit side of the glass due to the tension breaks.

Rigor mortis Stiffening of the joints that occurs after death.

S

Script kiddie An inexperienced hacker who uses commonly available tools to search for vulnerable computers on a network. The goal of the script kiddie is to "own" the system and delete files.

Serial fires Two or more incendiary fires displaying trends of geographic clustering, temporal frequency, and materials and methods.

Serology The analysis of the properties and effects of serums (e.g., blood, semen, saliva, sweat, fecal matter).

Sexual assault nurse examiner (SANE) A specially trained nurse skilled in the collection of physical evidence that can be entered into a chain of custody and submitted for scientific analysis by the crime laboratory.

Simulated signature An attempt to duplicate a known signature; commonly associated with forgery.

Site plans Two-dimensional, overhead views of exterior locations.

Skeletonization Complete decomposition of the nonbony tissues of a corpse, leading to a bare skeleton.

Skid marks Marks on the roadway that are created when the brakes on a motor vehicle are applied quickly in order to slow down or stop a vehicle's motion. Skid marks can be useful in identifying the point of impact between two objects.

Sliding toolmarks Impressions that are created when a tool is slid along a softer surface, leaving parallel striations on the object.

Small particle reagent (SPR) A chemical used to process wet or greasy items for latent fingerprints.

Sodium fluoride A preservative added to test tubes that are used to collect liquid blood samples primarily for blood alcohol analysis. These tubes are usually topped with gray rubber caps for quick identification.

Spiral search An inward or contracting crime scene search pattern.

Spoliation The destruction or alteration of evidence, or the failure to preserve property as evidence in pending or potential litigation (whether civil or criminal).

Spyware Malicious software embedded in other software that monitors activity on personal computers and provides this information to third parties.

Standard operating procedures (SOPs) Written guidelines issued by agencies to establish protocols and activities that follow accepted scientific practices.

Standard or reference sample Material from a verifiable source that is gathered for comparison against unknown items of evidence.

Statement analysis An examination of stress as indicated by the written word; sometimes used to determine the truthfulness of a writer.

Sternum A long flat bone located in the chest, which is connected to the ribs; also called the breastbone.

Striations In firearms analysis, unique longitudinal marks created (by the lands and grooves on the inside of a gun barrel) on the sides of bullets as they travel through the barrel. Striations are also found in toolmark impressions and can be matched to specific tools.

Strip search A crime scene search pattern using overlapping strips, much like mowing a yard.

Supraorbital ridges The curved upper border of the entrance to the eye socket.

T

Tattooing A physical defect in skin caused by the penetration of the skin by gunpowder particles.

Thin-layer chromatography (TLC) A destructive test for ink pigment identification.

Touch DNA Trace evidence left when people touch items. DNA analysis techniques have become so sophisticated that they can identify amino acids and skin cells found in latent fingerprints.

Toxicology The study and analysis of toxins (poisons) and their effects on the human body.

Trace evidence Evidence found at the crime scene. From Locard's theory that traces of the victim and the scene will be carried away by the perpetrator; traces of the perpetrator will remain on the victim; the victim may leave traces of himself or herself on the perpetrator; and traces of the perpetrator will be left at the scene.

Trailers or streamers Fire patterns that are created when ignitable substances—which may be solid, liquid, or gaseous—are deliberately "trailed" from one area to another in an incendiary fire.

Trajectory The path a bullet takes when a weapon is discharged.

Transfer stain A stain that occurs from wipes, swipes, or transfers when a bloody objec comes into contact with a secondary surface.

Transient evidence Physical evidence that is fragile or subject to be destroyed, dam aged, or lost if not collected and preserved as soon as possible.

Trash marks Foreign carbon deposits on xerographic copies made from scratches or the glass platen or defects and dirt on the copy machine that reproduces itself or a copy.

Triangulation A measurement system that involves measuring from two fixed points to the item of interest.

U

URL (uniform resource locator) A website address.

V

VIN Vehicle identification number, a number used to uniquely identify a motor vehicle This is sometimes referred to as the Public VIN (PVIN) because it is displayed on the left dashboard of every vehicle. Portions of the VIN are stamped on variou other locations of a vehicle, and car manufacturers can provide these hidden loca tions to case detectives.

W

Wheel search A crime scene search pattern in which searchers start at a center and move outward along straight lines or rays; also known as a ray or pie search pattern.

Whorls The fingerprint class characterized by ridge patterns that are generally rounded or circular in shape and have two deltas. There are four distinct types of whorls plain, central pocket loop, double loop, and accidental.

Wipe patterns Patterns created on a surface when blood is wiped with a cloth or othe porous material.

Z

Zone search A crime scene search pattern in which a square or rectangular area i marked off and searched for evidence. A zone can be a room or, in outdoor scenes a zoned-off area.

Index

Note: **Bold** page numbers refer to tables and *italic* page numbers refer to figures.

ABFO scale 113
abrasion 352
accelerant-detection K-9 (ACD) 222–223
additional evidence technicians/ equipment 50
adipocere 348
admissibility of evidence and testimony 21–22
aerial search team 48
algor mortis 343
alternate light source (ALS) 99, *99*, 116, *148*, 154
Alzheimer's disease 286–287
American Academy of Forensic Sciences (AAFS) 8; specialty sections of 9
American Board of Medicolegal Death Investigators (ABMDI) 328–329
American Society of Crime Laboratory Directors (ASCLD) 27
American Society of Trace Evidence Examiners 135
America's criminal justice system 2
amido black 106, 127
Analyze, Compare, and Evaluate (ACE) method 270
Anti-Car Theft Act of 1992 310–311
arches 86–87
area of origin 213
Arson and Explosives Incident System (AEXIS) 230
arson evidence: accelerant-detection K-9 (ACD)

222–223; area of origin 213; burn patterns 214–215; case example 209–210; code violations 219; collection and preservation of 221–226; covering up another crime 217–218; crime scene processing 212–216; electronic detectors and instruments 223–226; identification of victims at a fire scene 229–230; impact of fire suppression on the crime scene 215–216; motives of arsonist 217; precautions against contamination 210–211; preservation of 226–228; product reliability 218–219; recovery of burned bodies 228–230; safety equipment during investigation 210
asphyxiating chemicals 356
Association for Crime Scene Reconstruction 135
Association of Firearm and Toolmark Examiners (AFTE) 205
associative evidence 17

ballistics 178
bank fraud 244
baseline measures 78
Bass, William M. 389–390
Bill of Rights 19
biological evidence 1–3, 15

biological fluids 39
biometric signature 279
bitemark impressions 129–131; examination of 131
Black Dahlia case 268
blanchable lividity 344–345
blood analysis 145–147, *146*
bloodborne pathogens 40
blood spatter evidence: case example 161
bloodstain pattern analysis 162; detecting invisible bloodstains 171; documentation 169–171; impact spatter 164–166; interpreting evidence 172–173; measuring techniques 170; nature of 163–169; photographing of 171–172; point of origin or impact 173; size of blood splatters 164–165; three-dimensional projections 164; transfer stain 167; wipe patterns 168
bloodstain pattern analyst (BPA) 162, 169
bloodstain patterns 77
BLUESTARforensic® 157
blunt force 350–353
board-certified forensic pathologist (BCFP) 328
Body Farm 389
body fluid evidence: blood 145–147; case example 137; locating, collecting, and preserving 151–159;

collection of clothing 153–154; collection of DNA samples 154; at the crime scene 151–152; steps to protect evidence 155; from a victim or a suspect 152–158; saliva 149; semen 147–149; urine 149–150; vaginal secretions 150
body positions 77
Bombing Arson Tracking System (BATS) databases 230
bomb scene investigations 230–234; locating and collecting evidence of explosive devices 232; post-blast investigation techniques 232–234
boundaries 37
brain writing 282
bubble rings 168
bullets 179–181; characteristics of 182; effect on glass 193; possible conclusions concerning suspect weapon 184
bullycide 247
burking 360
burn patterns 214–215

cadaver/bomb/drug-sniffing dogs 50
camcorder for crime scene investigations 65–66
cameras for crime scene photography 63–65; single-lens reflex (SLR) camera 65; digital 65; TIFF and RAW settings 65; video 65–66
case file 403–405
case file preparation 413
cast-off patterns 166
catridge casings 179–181, 179, 180, 183; anatomy of 180; characteristics of 182
CBC (cyanoacrylate blowing contraption) 107
CBRNE crime scenes 222
certifications 8
Certified Hazardous Material Technician 35

chain of custody 23–24, 24
chemical spills 44
chemical warfare agent (CWA) 43
chemiluminescence 155
child pornography 246
children, internet crimes against 245–247; cyberbullying 248; cyberstalking 247–250; pornography 246; predators 246–247; sexting 249–250
choking 360
chop shop 310–311
chop wounds 354
circumstantial evidence 18–19
clandestine methamphetamine labs 44
class evidence 17
clothing 77
Code 921: A Guide to Fire and Explosion Investigation 228
CODIS (Combined DNA Index System) database 142
collar abrasion 191–192
collection and preservation of evidence 54
color filter 67
computer-aided drafting and design (CADD) software 81
computer crime 240
concentric fractures 192
condom trace evidence 158–159
confirmatory test 139
contact stains 168
control or blank samples 114
contusion 351–352
Coomassie blue 106
coroner 8, 326
courtroom testimony 415–417
credit card fraud 244
crime laboratories 410–411; communication with 411–413; evidence submittal 412–413
crime lab personnel 2
crime scene: determining the scope of 37–47; boundaries 37–38; CSI personal safety concerns 38–46; multiple scenes 38; DNA testing and investigation of 142–145;

documentation of 24–26; first response to a crime scene, case example 31; forensic evidence and 15–19; initial walkthrough/ preliminary assessment of 48–49; in adverse weather conditions 49; identification of transient evidence 48; photographic and video plans 48; legal issues and 19–26; objectives of investigation 61; outside scene searches 49; scientific analyses of 27–28; quality control practices 27; standards 27; searches 53–57; patterns 55–56; vehicle 56–57; supply checklist 421; team effort in investigating 49–52; potential team members 50; written protocols and standard operating procedures (SOPs) 405–407
crime scene investigator (CSI) 2–5; admissibility of evidence 3–4; admissibility of evidence and testimony 21; alternate light source (ALS) units 99; continuing education opportunities for 7–8; differences between individual: and class characteristics of physical evidence 17–18; ethics and professionalism 12–13; items processed as evidence 5; jobs and descriptions 4–7; notes 47; personal safety concerns 38–46; biological threat agents (BTAs) 42–44; from bloodborne pathogens 40; face protection 41; gloves 39–41; from light sources 42; personal protective equipment (PPE) 39; protective clothing 41–42; protective goggles 100; safety measures 39; toxic

industrial chemicals (TICs) 42–44; preparation for courtroom testimony 11; primary responsibilities 403–404; professional credentials 414–415; professional development and certifications 7–10; role at autopsy 364–371; role in forensic science 3–15; as sworn police officers or civilian personnel 5; technical skills of 5; technology as aid for 239; training in Hazmat and Hazwopper courses 6; varying titles of 4

crime scene reconstruction 402

crime scene search, goals of 3

crime scene staging 259

cross-contamination of physical evidence 39

cross-sectional plans 75–77

Crowle's double stain 106

cyberbullying 249

cybercrime 240–243; packaging of evidence in 241; physical evidence in 241; prevalence of 243; professional organizations focusing on 253

cyberharassment 249

cyberstalking 247–250

dactyloscopy 86

Daubert v. Merrell Dow Pharmaceuticals, Inc. 23, 413; rulings 89

death investigation case example 323; decedent identification (ID) 369–371; medical examiner (ME), authorization of 330–332; medical examiner systems, United States 327; medicolegal 326–332; ME's investigation 368–369; pattern recognition 349–364; abrasion 352; asphyxiation 359–362; contusion 351–352; electrocutions 358–359;

entry gunshot wounds 356; fingertip bruises 351–352; firearm injuries 354–357; fourth-degree burns 358; hilt mark 353–354; lacerations 352–353; lightning strikes burns 359; natural deaths 349–350; patterned bruise 351–352; re-entry wounds 356–357; sharp force injuries 353–354; thermoelectric injuries 357–359; tram-track bruise 351–352; trauma 350–364; wad marks 356; processing a death scene 332–348; accidental deaths 340–341; acute alcohol overdose, death from 342; autopsy 334–337, 334, 335, 336; cause of death (COD), diagnosis of 336–340; death certification 338; homicides 340; manner of death (MOD), diagnosis of 330–342; natural deaths 340; pneumonia, death from 341–342; postmortem interval (PMI) 342–348; preparation 332–333; report 337–338; specialized dissections 337–338; suicide 340; undetermined deaths 341; protocols 324; role of CSI at autopsy 364–371; structure and bias 329–330

defense attorney 26

defense technique 12

defensive wounds 353

dementia 286

dental stone 133–134

detectives, communication among 49, 54

detonation of explosives 232

3-D EyeWitness software 76

DFO (1,8-diazafluoren-9-one) 102

diaminobenzidine (DAB) 106

digital cryptographic signature 279

digital evidence 239

digital evidence examiners 241

digital forensics 239

digital single-lens reflex (SLR) camera 65; lenses and filters 66–67

Dilantin® 362

direct evidence 18

directionality 164

discharged cartridge case 187

dithiooxamide 190

dive/underwater search teams 50

DNA probative value 143

DNA profiles 106, 114–115, 129–130, 140; computer generated 141; to identify victims 159

DNA testing/analysis 17; advantages of 144; collection of DNA evidence 142–143; crime scene investigation 142–145; saliva 149; semen 148; of a tooth or bone sample 390; in toxicology 144–145

documentary evidence: case example 265; court acceptance of 281–282; distinguishing between genuine and simulated handwriting 282; scientific validity and reliability 281–282; handwriting identification 275–281; investigative techniques for examination 270–273; for chemical erasures 271; infrared (IR) light, use of 271; methods for developing latent impressions 272–273; nondestructive lighting techniques 272; ultraviolet (UV) light, use of 271; machine produced documents 274–275; procedures for handling and recording 268–270; questioned document, case study 293–295; recovered in crime scene investigations 267–268 documentation of crime scene 23–26; actions of CSI: case example 401; case file preparation 413; case files 403–405; case narrative 403; comparison samples 406; courtroom testimony 415–418; cross-contamination of physical evidence 409–410; demonstrative exhibits 417; emerging trends 418–419; ethical considerations 418; GPS coordinates 404; known samples 407; pretrial preparation 414; releasing the crime scene 408; unknown or questioned samples 407; use of SOPs and standard; forms 405–407; working with the prosecutor's office 413–414; bloodstain pattern analysis 169–171; bloodstain patterns 77; body positions 77; case sample 59; clothing 77; glass 121; identity of a victim 371; post-processing of evidence photographs 67–70; tools for 61; camcorder 65–65; cameras for crime scene photography 63–65; external flashes 66; lenses and filters 66–67; video cameras 65–66; use of digital technology 25–26; wound diagrams/sketches 77

domain name system (DNS) server 242
double-glove technique 40
double-swab technique 150–151
dusty footprint *125*

ear prints 88–89
EDTA (ethylenediaminetetraacetic acid) 153
electronic crime scene case example 237; biometric system 262; cellphones 260–261; color-coded labels 253–254; crime scene analysis 262; cybercrime 240–243; fax and digital answering machines and caller-ID devices 262; hackers 250–252; hardware as evidence 257–259; identity theft 243–244; individual computers 257–258; Internet crimes against children 245–247; multiple-scene seizure 255; network computers 258; peripheral equipment 259; processing 253–257, *254-256*; scams 252–253; scraps of paper and printouts 256; single-scene seizure 255; spyware 245; tablets, smartphones, and other mobile devices 261; virtual evidence 259–260

electronic signature 279–280
electrostatic dust print lifter 133–134
elevation plans 73–74
elimination prints 91, *91, 92*
elimination samples 114
emergency departments (EDs) 7
Entomology and Death: A Procedural Guide 392
epithelial cells 144
ESDA (electrostatic detection apparatus) 273
evidence-based medicine (EBM) 326
exemplars 276
expert witness 10–12, *11*, 52; decision on status of 11; testimony of 10
explosives: case example 209; possibility of secondary devices and unexploded residues 212
external flashes 66

fabric imprints 124
Faraday bag 241
FBI: crime laboratories 410–411, *411*; 12-step process 36
federal multijurisdictional task forces 50

Federal Rules of Evidence 22
fingerprint powder: DFO (1,8-diazafluoren-9-one) 102; fluorescent powders 101; gray powders 100–101; IND (1,2-indanedione) 102; iodine fuming 97; magnetic-sensitive powder 101; ninhydrin 97, 101–102, *101*; silver nitrate 97
fingerprints: case example 85; of deceased 92–94, *93, 94*; elimination prints 91, *91, 92*; of fingertips with badly distorted ridges 93–94; Henry 10-print fingerprint card 89–90, *90*; inking pad 94; latent 95; pattern types 87; as physical evidence 89; plain impressions 91; postmortem finger extenders 93; postmortem "spoon" with card inserted 93; principles 87–89, *88*; records as a means of identification 94; residue, composition of 88; suspect prints 92; tools 89; types of 89
fingertip bruises 351–352
firearms evidence: agency protocol 186; ballistic damage evidence 191; ballistic trajectory information 195, 198–199, *198*; bullets and catridge casings 179–181, *179-181*; case example 175; class *vs* individual characteristics 182–184, *183-184*; clothing 188; discharged cartridge case patterns (ejection patterns), in identifying shooter 190–191; distance determination 199–202, *199-201*; firearm recovered from under water 188–189; firearm transportation from the crime scene 186; glass fracture patterns 192, *194*; locating and collecting

evidence 184–189, *185–188*; marking the cylinder 183, 184, *185*; radial-fracture line-termination points 194–195; revolver, pistol, and ammunition characteristics *181*; sealing the packages 187; trajectories and measurements 190–199, *191, 193, 194*; use of comparison microscopes 177; *see also* bullets; catridge casings

firearms examiner 178

fire-related deaths 211

fire scenes, investigation of 216–219, *216, 218, 219*; motives of arsonist 217; motor vehicle fire investigation 219–221, *220*; primary reasons 217; *see also* arson evidence

fire tetrahedron 213

fire triangle 213

first response to a crime scene assessment of physical conditions of location 34; case example 31; FBI's 12-step process 36; problem of "swoop and scoop" 34

flame ionization detector (FID) 224

floor plans 72; examples *72, 73*

fluorescein *157*, 158

A Fly for the Prosecution 392

fly spot patterns 168

footwear impressions 127–128, *128*

forensic anthropologist 6–7, 50, 159, 348, 374

forensic anthropology 374; ala of sacrum 382; anthropometric measurements 383–384; areas of 375; bone buildup on the sacroiliac joint 380; degenerative changes 378–379; dentition 376–377; edge-to-edge bite in incisor region 384; epiphysis 377, *377*;

flat face 384; head of femur 382; length of pubic bone 380, *381*; mandible 382; maturation 376–377; nasal sill 384; osteoarthritic lipping 378; osteological structures 379; pelvis 380, *381*; prognathism 383–384; pubic portion of the left innominate *381*; pubic symphyses, changes in 378; race, determination of a 383–384; skeleton's age at death, determination of a 376–382; skeleton's sex, determination of a 380–383, *381*; skull, sex differences in 382; stature 384–385; sternum, length of 382–383; width of the sciatic notch 380

forensic archeologist 8

forensic biology 139

forensic botanist 8

forensic document examiners 281

forensic entomologist 8

forensic entomology 392; focus of 392

Forensic Entomology: The Utility of Arthropods in Legal Investigation 392

forensic evidence 1–2, 24; crime scene and 15–19, *16*; DNA, value of 6; factors determining value of 4; gunshots and knife wounds, marks of 6–7

forensic evidence and crime scene 15–19, *16*

Forensic Index 142

forensic laboratories 187

forensic light source/alternate light source (FLS/ALS) devices 226

forensic linguistics 291

forensic odontologist 8, 131

Forensic Odontology 385–392; anatomy of tooth 388–391, *389–391*; human dentition 386–388, *387*

forensic pathologist 8

forensic podiatrist 126

forensic science, challenges to 13–15

forensic serology 139

Forensic Specialties Accreditation Board (FSAB) 10

Forensic Technology Center of Excellence (FTCoE) 419

forensic toxicology 139

Fourier transform infrared spectroscopy (FTIR) 224–225, *225*

Fourth Amendment 19–20

freehand simulation 278

fruit of the poisonous tree 21

Frye v. United States 22

gas chromatography/mass spectrometry (GC/MS) test 139, *139*, 225, 226

gentian violet 105–106

geographic information systems (GIS) software and databases 82

glass fragment examination 119–122

global positioning system (GPS) 81–82, 239–240, 306, 314

gloves 39

government documents, fraudulently obtaining 244

grid search 55

gunshot residue (GSR) testing 122–123, *201*, 203–204

hackers 250–252; criminal 252; ethical 252; inside 252; motives for 251; outside 251; profit-driven 251

hair morphology *115*

handwriting analysis: age 283–284; behavioral profiling and 287–290, *289, 289,* **290**; danger signs in handwriting 289–290, **290**; forensic psychology and 282–283; gender 284–285, **284**; graphic indices of expression **289**; handedness 285; handwriting signs of dishonesty 292–293, **292**; literacy and occupation 285–286; physical and mental health 286–287, 287; physical profiling and 283–287, **284**, 287

handwriting complexity 278

handwriting identification 275–281, *275–277*, **278–279**, *279–280*; elements **278**

hanging 359, 361

hazard communication (HazCom) 44–46, *45*, *46*

Hazardous Materials Identification System (HMIS) 45

Hazardous Material Technicians 35

Hazmat Response Team 43, 48

Heirens, William George 268, *268*

Henry 10-print fingerprint card 89–90, *90*

hepatitis 40

high explosives 232

high-velocity impact spatter (MVIS) 166

hilt mark 353–354

hull identification number (HIN) 313

human dentition 386–388, *387*

human immunodeficiency virus (HIV/AIDS) 40

Human Osteology: A Laboratory and Field Manual 376

hydrogen cyanide 44

hydrogen sulfide 43

hypodermic syringes, handling of 42

identity theft 243–244

Identity Theft and Assumption Deterrence Act of 1998 244

ignitable substance residues (ISRs) 222

impact spatter 164–166

impression evidence 124–135, *125–126*, *128–130*, *132–135*; bitemark impressions 129–131, *130*; case example 111; casting and lifting techniques for 133–134, *133*, *134*; from crime scene involving motor vehicles 310; footwear impressions 127–128, *128*; forensic podiatry 126–127; inked impressions 132–133, *132*; "known" standards 125; photography of 131; shoe and footprints 127; in snow 134–135; tire impressions 128–129; using dental stone 133–134

improvised explosive devices (IEDs) 233

IND (1,2-indanedione) 102

individual characteristics 17

industrial scenes 43

infrared filter 67

initial walkthrough/preliminary assessment of 61; in adverse weather conditions 48–49; in case of death of a person 51; dealing with family members 51–52; identification of transient evidence 48; multidisciplinary approach to 51; photographic and video plans 48

initial walkthrough/preliminary assessment of crime scene 48–49

inked impressions 88–92, *90–92*, 132–133, *132*

Integrated Automated Fingerprint Identification System (IAFIS) 90

interaction with detectives 47

International Association for Identification (IAI) 8

International Mobile Equipment Identity (IMEI) 261

Internet crimes against children 245–247; cyberbullying 248; cyberstalking 247–249, *248*; pornography 246; predators 246–247; sexting 249–250

Internet Crimes against Children (ICAC) 256

Internet predators 246

Internet protocol (IP) 241–242

Internet service providers (ISPs) 241–242

iodine fuming 97, *98*

jacketed bullets 180–181

Jeffreys, Sir Alec 141

jobs and descriptions: crime scene investigator (CSI) 4–7, *5*; forensic anthropologist 6–7; forensic nurse 7; forensic scientist 6

Journal of Forensic Science 9

Kerley, Ellis R. 378

laboratory instrumentation services (LIS) 224, *224*

lacerations 352–353

laser protractor kit 196

laser trajectory rod kit 197–199, *198*

latent fingerprints 95; case example 85; chemicals used for enhancing 97, *98*; in children 95–97; developed with fluorescent powder *96*; developed with magnetic fingerprint powder *96*; "fixing" the prints 103; fuming wands 103; gelatin or rubber lifters 104–105; gel lifters 104–105; gentian violet 105–106; Integrated Automated Fingerprint Identification System (IAFIS) and 109–110; lifting 103–109, *104–105*, *108*; locating and documenting 99–100, *99*; locating latent prints on adhesive tape 105; method of processing an item 97–110; methods and techniques of developing and collecting 100–103, *101*, *102*; from motor vehicles 316; processing wet or bloody fingerprints 106–107; putty-like casting material 105; from skin 107–109,

108; standard operating procedures (SOPs) 103; superglue (cyanoacrylate) 102–103; tape lift 104; use of fingerprint powder 100–103

Latent prints 89

legal issues and crime scene 19–26, *20, 24–26*

legend 71, 77–78

lenses and filters 66–67

leucocrystal violet (LCV) 106, 127

leucomalachite green 145

line quality 278

link search 55–56

lip prints 88–89

livor mortis (lividity) 344–345, *344*

loans, fraudulently obtaining 244

Locard's exchange principle 39, 112

loops 86–87

low explosives 231

low-velocity impact spatter (LVIS) 165

luminol (3-aminophthal-hydrazide) 106, 127, 145, 155, 171, 315

MacPhail's reagent 145

man-made fibers 116

manufacturer's certificate of origin (MCO) 313

McKern, Tom 378

measurements 78–83, *78, 80–83*; baseline measures 79; perspective grid method 79; photogrammetry 79; polar coordinates 79; technological advancement in 80, *81–83, 82, 83*; triangulation measures 78

mechanical suffocation 360

medical examiner (ME) 326

medical examiner/coroner's medicolegal death investigators 50

medicolegal death investigation (MDI) 326–332

medium-velocity impact spatter (MVIS) 166

metal oxide transistor 223

Mikrosil™ 126

Mincey v. Arizona 21

MiniRAE 2000 224

minutiae 87, 97–99

Missing Persons Database 391–392

mitochondrial DNA analysis (mtDNA) 115, 141–142

medical examiner 8

motor vehicle fire investigation 219–221; contraband search 319; direction-of-impact examinations 317; documenting injuries 320–321, *320–321*; fiber evidence 317; homicide 321; motor vehicles as vehicles 319–321, *320–321*; processing exterior surfaces of vehicles 314; stolen property 318–319; trace evidence 316–318, *317*

motor vehicles as crime scenes: car parts ripped from a vehicle 308; case example 301; chop shop 310–311, *311*; collection techniques 309–310; driver's point of view 302; electronic vehicle tracking and recovery 313; glass fragments 308; hit-and-run cases 305–306, *305*; imprint evidence 310; latent fingerprints 316; odometer tampering 314; paint 307; photography of 302–305, *303, 304*, 315; physical evidences 307–309, *308, 309*; point of impact (POI) 302–303; position of all light switches, documentation of 303–304; processing exterior surfaces of vehicles 308–313; rip area 311; salvaged vehicles 311; seatbelt and shoulder harness 305; skid marks 302–303; soil sample 309;

stolen vehicles 310–314; trace evidence 307; VIN locations 311–313, *312*

multiple scenes 38

multiple-scene seizure 255

Mylar® 132, 190

National Academy of Sciences (NAS) 13; recommendations of 14; "Strengthening Forensic Science in the United States: A Path Forward" 13

National Association of Medical Examiners (NAME) 328–329

National Automotive Paint File 307–308

National Crime Information Center (NCIC) 310

National Crime Prevention Council 248

National Fire Protection Association (NFPA) 221–222

National Forensic Science Technology Center (NFSTC) 141, 419

National Highway Traffic Safety Administration 312

National Institute of Justice (NIJ) 15

National Insurance Crime Bureau (NICB) 310

National Integrated Ballistics Information Network (NIBIN) 202–203, *202*

National Missing and Unidentified Persons System (NamUs) 391–392

natural fibers 116

Ninhydrin 97, 101–102

normal variations 19

notes 61

Occupational Safety and Health Administration (OSHA) 39; hazard communication (HazCom) 44–46, *45, 46*

odometer tampering 314

offensive bitemarks 130

O.J. effect 12

Omegle 249
On-Board Diagnostics (OBD) 312
o-tolidine 145
outside scene searches 49, 54

"painting with light" technique 63, *63, 64*
palmprints, principles 87, 88, 89
paradoxical undressing 364
passive bloodstains 163
passive stains 166
patterned bruise 351–352
personal protective equipment (PPE) 35, 39, 140
perspective grid method 79
petechial hemorrhages 361
Pettus v. United States 281
phenolphthalein 145
phishing 252
photogrammetry 79
photography 61–70, *64, 70*; bitemarks 130; of bloodstain patterns 171–172; of blood treated with luminol and latent fingerprints 63–65, *64*; cameras for crime scene 63–65, *64*; impression evidence 131; motor vehicles as crime scenes 302–305; stolen vehicles 315
photoionization detectors (PIDs) 223–224, *224*
photoshop infrared filter 69–70, *70*
physical evidence 1–3, 15, 58, 61; differences between individual and class characteristics of 17–18; fingerprints as 89; importance of 417
physical evidence recovery kits (PERKs) 152–153, *152*
physical suffocation 360
plain impressions 91
plastic prints 89
podiatric medicine 126
point of convergence 164
polar coordinates 79
polarizing filter 67
polyester fibers 17
pornography 246

positional asphyxia 360
postmortem interval (PMI) 342–348; algor mortis 343; blanchable lividity 344–345; categories of postmortem changes 343; confounding variables 343; decomposition 346–347; livor mortis (lividity) 344–345; mummification (or mummifaction) 348; rigor mortis (rigidity) 345; skin slippage 347–348; "soft" signs 342–343; temperature changes 343–344; tissue changes 346
post-processing of crime scene photographs 67–70; common form of 68; global adjustments 68; need for 68; rules 68–69
postural asphyxia 360
presumptive test 139
product identification number (PIN) 313
professional organization: offering certifications 9–10; of practitioners 8
projected spatter stains 166
prosecutorial/legal resources 50
prostate-specific antigen (PSA) 147–148
PROTECT Act of 2003 246
purple-top Vacutainer tube 153, *153*

QR reader application 250, *249*
quality control/quality assurance (QA/QC) program 223
questioned document 267

rabies 40
radial fractures 192
rape kits 152–153
recollections of the incident 1–2
reconstruction of a crime scene 1–2, 57–58, *57*
red filter 67
restricting access to crime scene 46–47, *46*; egress 46; ingress 46; unauthorized personnel 47
ricasso 354

rigor mortis (rigidity) 345
rip area 311

saliva evidence 149
salvage switching 311
saponification 348
scan station laser scanner unit 82–83, *83*
scene security 2
scientific validity of the process 21
Scientific Working Group for Forensic Document Examination (SWGDOC) 271
script kiddie 251
searching the scene 53–56; patterns 55–56; security of 56; vehicle 56–57, *57*
search warrants 19–21, *20*
seizing of evidence 21
self-contained breathing apparatus (SCBA) 43
semen evidence 147–149, *148*; identification of non-motile spermatozoa or spermatozoa heads 148
serial number restoration 204–205, *204*
serology 139
sexting 249–250, *249*
sexual assault nurse examiner (SANE) 153
sexual assault response team (SART) 153
sexual assault victims, investigation of 150–151
sexually transmitted diseases (STDs) 40
sharp force injuries 353–354
shoe covers 39
silver nitrate 97
Simpson, O.J., 12
simulated signature 277
single-scene seizure 255
site plans 74, 75, *76*; examples 76
skeletonization 348
skeletonized stains 168
sketches 61, 70–77, *72–76*; of death scene 71; floor plans 72–73, *72–73*; types of rough field diagrams 71
skin slippage 347
small particle reagent (SPR) 106

Snow Print Wax® 134–135
sodium rhodizonate test 190
soil evidence 122
spiral search 56
spoliation 226
standard operating procedure (SOP) 65
standard or reference sample 114
statement analysis 291
State of South Carolina's Department of Revenue databases 243
Stewart, T. Dale 378
strangulation 361
striations 182
strip search 55
Sudan black 107
suffocating gases 360
Superglue (cyanoacrylate) 102–103
Superglue fuming 107
suspect prints 92
suspects at the scene 52

technology-assisted crimes *see* cybercrime
Tennessee Bureau of Investigation (TBI) 12
tertiary explosives 232
test bullet recovery water tank *183*
testimony of an expert witness 10
Tetramethylbenzidine (TMB) 106, 145
thin-layer chromatography (TLC) 273
tire impressions 128–129
title block 77–78
Todd, T. Wingate 378
toolmark evidence 205–206; case example 175; testing and comparison techniques 206–207; use of comparison microscopes 177
tooth, anatomy of 388–391; cementum 388; crown 388;

dentin 388; distal 389; enamel 388; labial (lips) or buccal (cheek) 388; lingual 388 mesial 389; neck 388; occlusal 389; pulp cavity 388; root 388
total station surveying system (TSSS) units 80
touch DNA 144–145
toxicology 140–141; DNA techniques and impact of technological advances 141–142; urine and blood samples, analyses of 140
trace evidence 112; condom 158–159; glass 119–122; gunshot residue 122–123; hairs and fibers 114–119: animal hairs 116, *117*; arm and leg hairs 116; body hairs 116; cross-transference of fibers 116; druggist fold **120**; important factors in an investigation 115; preserving fiber evidence 119, **120**; involving motor vehicles 307; from motor vehicles 316–318; soil 122; summary 123–124
trailers or streamers 214–215
tram-track bruise 352
transfer stain 167–168
transient evidence 21; identification of 48
trash marks 274
trauma death 350–364; chemical trauma 362–363; environmental factors 363–364; physical trauma 350–362
triage system 143
triangulation measures 78–79
Tyvek™ suits 39

unauthorized personnel 47
United States v. Paul 281

United States v. Starzecpyzel 281
University of Tennessee's Forensic Anthropology Research Facility 389–391
unquestioned document 267
unsolicited e-mail 252
urine evidence 150
URL (uniform resource locator) 252
U.S. Secret Service 243
utilities fraud 244

vaginal secretions 150
Vehicle Identification Number (VIN) 220
vehicle searches 56–57
Victimology 247
victims of crimes 7
video cameras 65–66
videography 61
virtual evidence 259–260; biometric system 262; cellphones 260–261; fax and digital answering machines and caller-ID devices 262; tablets, smartphones, and other mobile devices 261
visible prints 89
void patterns 168

warning labels 46
wet prints 89
wheel search 56
whorls 86–87
"who-what-when-where-why" questions 24
wipe patterns 168
workplace and pre-employment drug screenings 140
wound diagrams/sketches 77

zero-base protractor 196
Ziploc-type bag 322
Zodiac serial killer 268, 289
zone search 56